Zimbabwe: Mired in Transition

Zimbabwe: Mired in Transition

edited by
Eldred V. Masunungure & Jabusile M. Shumba

WEAVER
W
PRESS

IDA**Z M**
Institute for a Democratic
Alternative for Zimbabwe

Published by
Weaver Press, Box A1922,
Avondale, Harare, Zimbabwe
with
IDAZIM
329 Samora Machel Ave,
Harare, Zimbabwe

© The Institute for a Democratic Alternative (IDAZIM),
Harare, Zimbabwe, 2012

Typeset by forzalibro designs
Cover: Danes Designs, Harare
Printed by Sable Press, Harare

IDAZIM also notes that any opinions and views expressed
in this publication are the responsibility of the individual authors
and that IDAZIM does not necessarily subscribe to these
opinions and views of the contributors.

ISBN: 978-1-77922-202-2

Contents

Acknowledgments

Many individuals contributed towards the preparation and production of this book, and to all we are extremely grateful. Foremost we extend our profound gratitude to the authors, who painstakingly persevered throughout the iterative journey of this publication; we appreciate their patience. Special thanks to the meticulous work of the editorial team. Frances Marks, who joined the team mid-stream but soon assumed the steering wheel, earning herself the reputation of being a 'tough, no-nonsense' editor, deserves special mention. Thanks also to Murray McCartney and Irene Staunton at Weaver Press for accepting our work in their tight publishing schedule.

The team at the Institute for a Democratic Alternative for Zimbabwe also lent their full support to the project. Anyway Ndapwaza-Chingwete and Obert Hodzi worked tirelessly with the Institute support team, and Antonetta Guveya and Viola Chideme provided the logistical and administrative support. Davie Malungisa, the Executive Director, and Joy Mabenge, the Programmes Director, facilitated the project and ensured that we remained on course.

Last but not least, we thank our partners who generously supported the project. To them we are most grateful.

None but ourselves bear the responsibility for any deficiencies.

Foreword

Zimbabwe's democratization debate has occupied much discourse on whether the conflict-ridden country is in transition or not. This is in a context where there is doubt about the nature of the state itself: on one hand, is it a fragile state, and on the other, is it a strong and unco-operative regime? Our conceptualization is that a transition is an interval of intense contestation and uncertain outcomes between political regimes. Zimbabwe entered such a period with the signing of the GPA, but the transition is nascent, fragile and far from complete.

The pre-2009 state had, by many measures, deteriorated into a fragile one. Electoral controversy resulted in international isolation. By the end of 2002, the European Union had imposed a non-comprehensive set of sanctions and restrictive measures, while the United States of America enacted the Zimbabwe Democracy and Economic Recovery Act. The 11 March 2007 violence against pro-democracy actors invited regional attention, forcing the SADC bloc to appoint South Africa's President Thabo Mbeki as an inter-party dialogue facilitator. The tortuous and rather secretive negotiations culminated in the signing of the Global Political Agreement (GPA) in September 2008.

Thus, the deteriorating socio-economic and political situation was, in part, reversed. The Inclusive Government (IG) brought into the picture a new trajectory in the country's democratization. Political and economic reforms were agreed, and helped in halting the slide towards an economic implosion. To its credit, the IG introduced, *inter alia,* the Government Work Programme (2009); the Short-Term Emergency Recovery Program, STERP I (2009) and the three-year Macro-Economic and Budget Framework, STERP II (2010); the Medium Term Plan (2011); the National Trade Policy (2012); the Industrial Policy (2012) and the Accelerated Arrears Clearance, Debt and Development Strategy (2012). However, the terms of international re-engagement are yet to be defined, and a shift towards a neo-liberal order cannot be ruled out.

On the political front, the IG has introduced key political reforms. These include the constitutional reform process, guided by the Constitutional Parliamentary Committee. Key parliamentary commissions such as the Human Rights Commission, the Anti-Corruption Commission and the Media Commission are in place, and are enjoying mixed success. However, the absence of a paradigm shift in the exercise of political authority is evident. Distrust among the political parties has actually increased, the security services sector still wields overbearing political power and electoral reforms are limping along.

Is Zimbabwe moving backward or forward? Faced with such a question, the search for a rigorous analysis has always been crucial. Both state and non-state actors are paralyzed when it comes to finding a way out of the seemingly complex transition. As an Institute specializing in democratic governance, our mandate is to step back and contribute to the analytical debate; this book was conceived as an attempt to fulfill that mandate. The chapters in *Zimbabwe: Mired in Transition* seek to explore the dynamics working for and against a successful democratic outcome. The search for a democratic alternative – where citizens are at the centre of democratic governance – remains IDAZIM's value proposition.

Davie Malungisa
IDAZIM Executive Director
Harare
May 2012

Introduction

Eldred V. Masunungure & Jabusile M. Shumba

From its inception as a modern state in 1890 through to the present, Zimbabwe has never been a full-fledged democracy, despite having regular (if flawed) elections. During the 90 years of settler colonialism, which ended in 1980 with the achievement of majority rule, it was characterised as an 'intra-White democracy'[1] that systematically disenfranchised and oppressed more than 90 per cent of the indigenous population. After independence, Zimbabwe metamorphosed into a 'semi-democracy'[2] but one which, by the late 1980s, was becoming ever less democratic. And by the first decade of the new millennium even this quasi-democracy had broken down. By the time of the inter-party political pact of September 2008, Zimbabwe had transformed into a full-fledged authoritarian state with regular but violence-ridden elections as its only claim to any semblance of democratic practices.

This book is about the possibilities and challenges of Zimbabwe's transformation from an unstable, non-democratic regime towards a stable, democratic political order. This transformation takes place in the context of a comprehensive, decade-old crisis. Thus, a common characterisation today is that Zimbabwe is in transition, but a difficult, tortuous and protracted one. As attested in the chapters in this volume, the country's transition is also multi-dimensional. It is equally important to stress that the country is in the initial stages of the democratic transition and thus faces enormous and powerful centres of resistance.

Political transition in a 'fragile situation'

The transition paradigm

Democratic transition as an analytical paradigm arose from the need to make sense of what Thomas Carothers (2002: 5) described as 'a dominant characteristic' of the last quarter of the twentieth-century, i.e., the simultaneous movement in many parts of the world away from dictatorial rule toward more liberal and often more democratic governance. This global phenomenon started in the mid-1970s in southern Europe and was given impetus with the collapse of one-party and dominant-party regimes in eastern Europe following the fall of the Soviet Union. Samuel Huntington (1991) called this tide of political change the 'third wave' of democracy, a model previously triggered by the seminal work of Guillermo O'Donnell and Phillippe Schmitter (1986) in relation to understanding the phenomenon.

In his paper, Carothers arrives at the conclusion that 'it is time to recognise that the transition paradigm has outlived its usefulness and to look for a better lens' (2002: 6).[3] Critiquing the transition paradigm, he starts by interrogating what he identifies as 'five core assumptions' that define the paradigm, namely:

1. That any country moving *away* from dictatorial rule can be considered a country in transition *toward* democracy.

2. That democratization tends to unfold in a set sequence of three stages from *opening*, then regime *breakdown* to *consolidation*.

3. The belief in the determinative importance of elections, that is, the notion that achieving regular, genuine elections, will both confer democratic legitimacy on new governments and continuously deepen political participation and democratic accountability.

4. That the underlying structural conditions in transition countries – for example, political history/legacies, the economic level, sociocultural traditions, ethnic make up – will not be major variables in either the onset or the outcome of the transition process.

5. That the democratic transitions making up the third wave are being built on coherent, functioning states.

Carothers debunks these five assumptions by juxtaposing them against the record of experience. He concludes that, taken together, 'the political trajectories of most third-wave countries call into serious doubt the transition paradigm' (2002: 14), and thus that 'it is time for the democracy-promotion community to discard the transition paradigm' (Ibid.: 17). Put plainly, '[t]he transition paradigm was a product of a certain time – the heady days of the third wave – and that time has now passed' and that it is now necessary for democracy activists 'to move on to new frameworks' (Ibid.: 20).

However, until 'a better lens' is discovered, it makes sense to make do with the one that is available.

A transition – any transition – by definition entails motion from one point to another. This may be a linear or curvilinear process and may involve way stations on the journey to the intended destination. The transitions under consideration here are *political regime transitions*, i.e., change from one political regime type to another. Two prominent writers on political transition offer what can be regarded as a standard definition of regime transitions:

> the interval between one political regime and another .... Transitions are delimited, on the one side, by the launching of the process of dissolution of an authoritarian regime and, on the other side, by the installation of some form of democracy, the return to some form of authoritarian rule, or the emergence of a revolutionary alternative. It is characteristic of the transition that during it the rules of the political game are not defined. (O'Donnell and Schmitter 1986: 6)

This perspective is later echoed by Michael Bratton and Nicholas van de Walle, who point out that a transition to democracy is only one of several possible outcomes following the breakdown of an authoritarian regime:

> an interval of intense political uncertainty during which the shape of the new institutional dispensation is up for grabs by incumbent and opposition contenders. For this reason, a regime transition can be depicted as a struggle by competing political forces over the rules of the political game and for the resources with which the game is played. (1997: 10)

A transition is preceded by system disequilibrium. On this, Kurt Lewin's 'force-field theory' of change becomes relevant for the understanding of transitions in the sense that it posits the existence of two sets of forces that stand in opposition to each other. It seeks to explain the dynamic involved, namely that the opposing forces consist, on one hand, of forces for change and, on the other, those that seek to maintain the status quo. In Cole's paraphrasing of Lewin:

> Change can be achieved either by exerting stronger pressure on the forces for change in order to overcome the resistance and thus push through change, or by weakening the forces for the status quo, thus permitting change to flood gently in. (1995: 264)

Zimbabwe's political transition, like all transitions, embodies disequilibrium, but the key point – which also motivates this volume – is that the transition is in search of a new equilibrium. Disequilibrium is inherently dynamic, meaning that the forces for change may be more powerful today but weaker tomorrow than the force of status quo (and vice versa), depending on the specific configuration of forces internally *and* externally. There is general consensus in the case of Zimbabwe that in 2008 and up to around mid-2010, the forces for resistance were much weaker than the forces for change. Since then, and coinciding with the onset of the constitution-making process, anti-change forces began to reassert their 'hard power', largely based on the newly found, diamond-generated, revenue bonanza on the part of one of the Inclusive Government (IG) partners. This became a decisive game-changer, resulting in a stalemate that the World Bank (2009) has described as 'contested equilibrium', suggesting that the balance of forces is inherently unstable.

Zimbabwe's transition appears to be a perfect illustration of the relevance of force-field theory. Two sets of opposing forces are locked in a bitter and protracted contest for supremacy. These are the old regime forces (which have historically held power) personified by incumbent President Robert Mugabe and his Zimbabwe African National Union Patriotic Front (ZANU-PF) party on one hand, and, on the other hand, the two formations of the Movement for Democratic Change (MDC), which, until the Inclusive Government (IG), have historically been out of power. Until 2008, the former had ruled Zimbabwe as a dominant and de facto one-party regime, resisting any changes that threatened its continued prolongation in power and the perquisites that power brings. The two MDC factions have been fighting for change for over a decade, with Morgan Tsvangirai (leader of the main faction, MDC-T) personifying their epic struggle.

This characterisation tends to simplify a more complex and nuanced picture, given that each party has its own hard-liners and moderates. The World Bank (2009) makes a further distinction here, arguing that there are ideological and opportunistic actors within each of the two sets of forces. Thus:

> On the anti-change side, ideological hard-liners are deeply committed to the *status quo ante*, likely to resist a political transition to the bitter end, and positioned to constantly threaten a reactionary backlash. By contrast, opportunistic hard-liners – who are driven principally by a desire for self-preservation – may be induced by the right set of incentives to buy into a transitional compromise. (World Bank, 2009: 6)

Though hard-liners of both types exist in ZANU-PF and in the main formation of the MDC, they preponderate in the former. What is the situation in the other set of forces? Here, the World Banks says that:

> On the pro-change side, ideological moderates display value commitments to democratic procedures and can be expected to be reliable allies of reform. But they usually constitute a minority, since others in the pro-change camp have opportunistic motivations, being willing to support political and economic reform only so long as these measures serve their own instrumental goals. (Ibid.)

On the pro-change side, as in the anti-change side, both ideological and opportunistic moderates inhabit both parties. However, they now tend to preponderate in the MDC, at least in the public domain, as it is unfashionable for those within ZANU-PF to be publicly labelled as a moderate.

A further and necessary nuance needs to be made. In the post-IG era, the configuration of forces is such that the anti-change elements are in command and deploy *hard power* while the pro-change forces hold *soft power*. The former are consequently depicted as hard-liners who brook little compromise and are fixated on holding on to power by any means, while the latter are portrayed as moderates or 'soft liners' who are given to the political game of compromise and moderation. The practical effect of this distinction is that 'hard' power-wielders can, with few exceptions, define their agenda and get it done, despite the resistance of the 'soft' power-holders.

The uncertainty of transitions

A transition also connotes uncertainty, of both process and outcome. In terms of process, O'Donnell and Schmitter observe that 'It is characteristic of the transition that during it the rules of the political game are not defined' (1986: 6).

The Zimbabwe case is a classic illustration of the uncertainty of transitions in both senses. Zimbabwe is a difficult and complex case of a country in transition to something that presently looks quite uncertain. There is a general consensus among political actors, citizens and observers that the current situation is very fluid and could take any direction.

This is clearly so with flagship agenda items outlined in the GPA, for example, constitution-making, institutional/legislative reforms, media reforms and elections. In fact, the irony is that the tripartite pact is commonly referred to as 'a roadmap', yet in practice travellers are compelled to constantly ask passers-by for directions. At the time of writing, no one can say with any semblance of certainty when the next elections will be held, or if they will be held under the old or the envisaged new constitution. It is not even clear whether there will be a referendum on the draft constitution. Perhaps this is in the nature of fragile situations, a point which is discussed below.

Fragile situations

Though it was popular and common in the third decade of Zimbabwe's independence to refer to the country as a failed state, our view is that it was premature to make such a declaration.[4] Indeed, it may be argued that Zimbabwe was and still is a 'strong but reluctant state', not only in the sense of possessing residual state strength but also in that when state elites do decide on a course of action, they are able to marshal the resources and capacities to achieve it. For instance, when the policy elites decided to embark on Operation Murambatsvina in 2005, the agencies of the state were able to swiftly, albeit viciously and inhumanely, implement it. Similarly, when the regime was defeated in the March 2008 elections and decided to turn this loss into a victory in the run-off election, ZANU-PF mobilised all the resources of violence to murder, torture, intimidate and carry out other human rights violations on such a scale that Morgan Tsvangirai was forced to withdraw from the presidential race, giving the incumbent Mugabe a pyrrhic victory in the June 2008 election. Few failed states have achieved such feats.

The trajectory and pace of the multidimensional crisis suggests that had it not been for the GPA and its coalition government, the country would have – and probably within two years – ended up a failed state in the sense of the concept used by Derick Brinkerhoff. According to the latter, states fail when they lose all of the three attributes of statehood: i) a monopoly on the legitimate use of force, ii) the capacity to provide basic public services, and iii) recognition of state sovereignty abroad (Brinkerhoff, 2007: 2). Zimbabwe was failing in terms of the second attribute but passed the test in relation to the first and third; though not yet a failed state, it was clearly a fragile one.

The notion of fragility avoids difficulties attendant on using the failed state terminology. For Alina Menocal and Timothy Othieno, state fragility involves:

> the presence of weak institutions and governance systems and a fundamental lack of ... state capacity and/or political will to fulfil essential state functions, especially in terms of providing basic services to the poor .... At its core, fragility is a deeply political phenomenon, even if this is something that donors are sometimes reluctant to acknowledge explicitly. (2008: 1-2)

There is a general consensus that a fragile state is one where the government displays inability or unwillingness to deliver the core functions to the majority of its population. Because fragility in the context of a syndrome of multilayered crises afflicts institutions well beyond the state (i.e., to include non-state institutions), the notion of 'fragile situation' rather than 'fragile state' is increasingly being preferred. For the World Bank, in a fragile situation there are i) weak governance; ii) weak policies; and iii) weak institutions, with the World Bank ranking such countries below 3 in its Country Policy and Institutional Assessment (CPIA) index.[5] Zimbabwe witnessed a precipitous fall in its CPIA ranking from 3.3 in 1999 to 1.76 in 2007 and to 1.67 in 2008 before slowly recovering to 1.80 in 2009, 1.91 in 2010 and 2.14 in 2011. In other words, the country is still to recover from its fragile situation, despite having registered significant gains in the last three years.

A survey of Zimbabwe's state and non-state institutions suggests that they too are fragile. This is clearly evident from the eleven contributions that follow. Without explicitly using the framework of fragile situations, the evidence presented and the attendant discussion in each chapter points to fragility of the areas under the spotlight.

An overview of the book

The book opens with a chapter by Eldred V. Masunungure and Anyway Ndapwadza-Chingwete on Zimbabwe's public mood. It presents the country's political and socio-economic transition from the perspective of the citizens themselves, offering key findings from various public opinion surveys and focus group discussions (FGD) largely conducted after the installation of the Inclusive Government (IG). These empirical studies covered a wide range of issues: peoples' perceptions on the state of the economy and how they have fared in it, constitution-making, transitional justice, and the performance and role of the coalition government in all these areas.

While the quantitative and qualitative studies show that Zimbabweans are generally more buoyant and optimistic than they were before the tripartite government they also indicate that there are many areas of public concern. For instance, the economic conditions at both macro- and micro-level are seen to have vastly improved, but close to half the adult population is still unhappy with the state of the economy. Unemployment still looms as the greatest economic problem, and with all the associated social and political difficulties, including the erosion of public optimism. Zimbabweans also displayed reservations about the constitution-making process, which seems still to be sunk in partisan controversy. The chapter also puts on full display the ambivalence of Zimbabweans in respect of elections: 'they prefer a government they choose themselves in free and fair elections but are realistic enough to fear them, given the history of electoral violence and intimidation'.

A worrying finding is the public perception that civil and political rights and liberties have been further eroded since the formation of the IG, with every dimension of these rights registering a decline, especially regarding freedom of expression. Lastly, the chapter broaches the highly controversial and emotionally charged issue of transitional justice (TJ). Both survey and FGD evidence point to public support for some form of accountability rather than amnesty for perpetrators of politically motivated violence. Further, opinion on TJ tends to be split along regional and ethnic lines, especially in respect of the time period that should be covered by the TJ investigations. For instance, while large minorities in the Gukurahundi belt (Matabeleland provinces) would prefer inquiries into politically motivated violence to begin in 1980, the majorities in the Mashonaland provinces favour investigations to start from 2000.

The chapter closes with the conclusion that current public opinion 'reflects a quest for change from the militarised, electoral authoritarianism' to a more democratic political order. It also states the case for the more robust use by the present and future governments of public opinion as a barometer of peoples' views on various socio-economic and political issues. It is only then that public policy can be sensitive to the heartbeat of the nation.

In Chapter 2, Lyndon Nkomo writes on political speech and access to public broadcast media by political parties. This contribution offers a strong defence of political speech, which the author regards as a necessary condition for a healthy plural society. Nkomo proceeds from the theoretical premise that public broadcasters carry the heavy burden of ensuring that citizens are provided with comprehensive information and a platform for the exchange of ideas. Discharging such a function ensures that the government is open, responsive and accountable.

The author notes the fact that the GPA demanded public media reform, a recognition that this sector was not playing its proper role and that it was being monopolised and abused by the erstwhile hegemonic ZANU-PF. This, he argues, was in violation of the legal framework governing public broadcasting in the country that provides for fair, unbiased and objective reporting and programming. He attributes this unhealthy media situation to government control of the media and to a weak regulatory system. He also argues that to the extent that the Zimbabwe Broadcasting Corporation (ZBC) uses national resources such as radio frequencies and public funds, all citizens have basic rights to claim access to its broadcast media.

Nkomo also raises some fundamental constitutional issues that merit attention by the framers of the new constitution. One of these is that the present constitution lacks 'founding values' that act as 'a shining beacon that guides a nation in the interpretation and application of its Constitution'. To him, this weakness partly explains the Constitution's failure to guarantee the establishment of an independent broadcasting regulator in place of the structurally weak Broadcasting Authority of Zimbabwe (BAZ), which is also controlled by the minister in charge of ZBC.

The chapter also discusses a number of challenges facing the country during its transitional period. Most are about depoliticising the public media that is presently overwhelmingly controlled by ZANU-PF at both strategic and operational levels, particularly 'the Janus-like powers of the Minister'. The writer calls for urgent legal reforms to remedy these flaws, including overhauling the selection process for members of the ZBC and BAZ to make it transparent and independent of government. Nkomo also makes the crucial point that effective changes must go beyond the legal domain to include attitudinal changes on the part of both politicians and citizens, i.e., changes in political culture.

Nkomo's analysis of the legal framework that governs election broadcasts and political advertisements reveals numerous loopholes that militate against the fair and equal treatment of political parties and candidates. His chapter concludes by emphasising that media reform 'is an immediate imperative in this transitional phase' and outlines a raft of specific reforms that need to be instituted to protect free political speech by all and avoid abuse by those in government.

Reinforcing the importance of constitutions is Greg Linington's chapter, which reflects on the significance of constitutions as political institutions and constitutionalism as a practice. It demonstrates, in Zimbabwe's polity, the supremacy of the constitution vis-à-vis other potentially competing political institutions, notably parliament. Linington notes that the supremacy of the constitution must, however, be undergirded by its reverence at the empirical level, i.e. there must be constitutionalism. He argues persuasively that to achieve this requires an independent judiciary that can impartially adjudge the constitutionality or otherwise of enacted legislation and attendant actions taken by political practitioners.

From his diagnosis and discussion of a selected number of contentious constitutional issues, the author asserts that 'Many of the problems that beset Zimbabwe today have their origins in the breakdown of constitutionalism and the rule of law.' Thus, in Linington's view, constitutionalism has been the missing link in Zimbabwe's post-independence constitutional history, and he draws attention to some of the significant issues that ought to be addressed in the context of the country's highly contested constitution-making process.

For example, he argues that a good constitution must ensure that its provisions are enforceable. This means making them justiciable. But that, by itself, is not enough. Unless the *locus standi* threshold – the circumstances under which a person will have standing to initiate constitutional litigation – is set at a relatively low level, effective judicial protection of the Constitution will be impossible. People need to know that easy access to the courts is a reality in constitutional matters. Zimbabwe's experience since independence shows that naked power is a very dangerous thing, particularly when it is concentrated in the hands of one person or a small clique. Linington believes that executive power has to be limited and controlled effectively. The President – and all other office bearers and government departments – must be subordinate to the Constitution. This is what constitutional supremacy entails. He concludes by saying that a new Constitution must stipulate that the President can only exercise those powers conferred upon him by the Constitution, in the manner specified by the Constitution, and for the purposes set out in the Constitution.

From issues of the intrinsic and extrinsic value of the supreme law, Chapter 4 engages one of the most troublesome problems in Zimbabwe since colonialism, namely gender discrimination, and more specifically sexual and gender-based violence (SGBV). Annie Barbara Chikwana identifies a plethora of interlocking barriers that victims of SGBV face in post-conflict societies that range from those that are culturally rooted to legal and systemic hurdles. Given the weight and history of these barriers, it will be no easy task to overcome the problem in the foreseeable future, not least because of the lack of political will.

The writer takes a critical look at the continuities and discontinuities in the role and place of women during and after the protracted struggle for independence. While women played a salutary role during the war and were celebrated for it, independence in 1980 seemed to mark a rupture, whereby they were urged to revert to 'their' traditional roles. The chapter is thus in part a lamentation of the manner in which women have been used over time for instrumental purposes, especially during political struggles, only to be forgotten or neglected when it comes to the 'eating' of the fruits after the struggle. Chikwana zeroes in on the post-liberation security sector as a special case. She is also sceptical about the efficacy of the current emphasis on reconciliation and healing as ways of delivering post-conflict justice. She exposes and dissects the intricate web of institutionalised violence and discrimination against women, especially during electoral cycles.

Chikwana recommends a battery of interventions to begin to remedy the deep, historically and culturally anchored problem but is emphatic that the reforms must put humans, and not the state, at the centre of security provision. Further, the reforms 'must be all-embracing, addressing policies, legislation, structural and behavioural patterns to ensure that they uphold the rule of law and respect human rights'.

In Chapter 5, Eldred Masunungure and Jabusile Shumba venture to decipher the 'spectre of electoral authoritarianism' in the country's multi-faceted and multi-directional political transition, describing it as 'a cunning and perfidious type of governance'. They then wonder how the resilient authoritarianism that has hardened over time can be exorcised. The authors locate transparent, free, fair, and credible elections at the centre of their inquiry and boldly assert that 'unless the ghost of electoral authoritarianism is exorcised, elections in the country will be a mere replay of previous ones, that is, elections without a choice, which are a mere institutional facade of democracy'.

The chapter views the GPA as a tripartite pact and governance roadmap for changing the architecture of the country's politics in a democratic and open direction. It focuses on the two-sided challenge of reforming electoral institutions and dismantling the infrastructure of state-led violence. It then proceeds to describe the present flawed institutional framework governing elections and discusses proposals to remedy the defects, including overhauling and cleansing the widely condemned voters register that lies at the centre of the menu of electoral manipulation. An associated recommendation is the reform and professionalization of the Zimbabwe Electoral Commission (ZEC), particularly at its operational levels.

Masunungure and Shumba also identify the security sector as a fly in the electoral ointment that has been associated with the post-2000 election-related violence. On this, they posit that 'the most significant issue during the transition should be reorienting the security sector, reducing the potential for abuse, and institutionalising a system of checks and balances'. The authors commend SADC for playing a salutary role in trying to unblock and exorcise the spectre by, among other things, taming ZANU-PF's penchant for political risk-taking and uni-lateralist behaviour on issues of grave national importance.

Chapters 6 and 7 tackle the country's economic problems more directly. Chapter 6, by Jabusile Shumba and Mohammed Jahed, dis-cusses one of Zimbabwe's most obstinate and enduring problems, i.e., the complex issue of expanding fiscal space so as to stimulate eco-nomic growth and development. Their chapter adopts neo-Keynesian Endogenous Growth models which emphasise the positive impact of government expenditure in driving economic growth as their analyti-cal framework. Shumba and Jahed document Zimbabwe's fiscal space challenges since 2000 and proceed to highlight the burdens of eco-nomic recovery that have been placed on the shoulders of the country's constrained fiscal space, notably the energy, transport, health and edu-cation sectors.

The chapter also highlights key reforms by the IG to stabilise the macro-economy, including cash budgeting, multi-currency frame-work, and public finance management. Revenue collections have improved but they have yet to reach levels seen prior to the decade of economic decline, while the current levels of investment in produc-tive sectors continue to fall far short of the levels necessary to realise spin-off effects and stimulate economic growth. The authors argue for extensive public expenditure reforms and explore some policy options for increasing fiscal space for what they call 'growth-enabling pri-orities'. They propose policy options that include public expenditure reform, especially cutting down the public sector wage bill and cutting down safety and security sector spending; parastatal reforms; creating public-private partnerships; extensive tax reform, for example, sim-plifying the tax regime, broadening the tax base while reducing tax rates and abolishing tax incentives; and creating an enabling business environment, especially with an eye on reforming the property rights system. They conclude by noting that 'the country has no option but to reform its budget and financial management and move away from political grandstanding, instilling strong fiscal controls and proce-dures instead'. Further, political consensus and commitment will be the 'foundational imperatives for the economic recovery agenda'.

Chapter 7, by Daniel Makina, discusses migration and development, wherein he observes that the chief tendency in international migration is that migrants move from a country with a higher Human Development Index (HDI) than their own and that the Zimbabwe experience confirms this pattern. Unsurprisingly then, South Africa is the favourite destination for the three to four million Zimbabweans living abroad. Makina notes that the major push factor for Zimbabweans in the post-2000 'lost' decade was economic collapse, and that this had had a particularly devastating impact on training institutions. Such out-migration has continued almost unabated, despite the establishment of the transitional government in February 2009. A refreshing finding though is that most diasporan Zimbabweans –skilled and unskilled – expect to trek back home and contribute to national economic and political development once the country regains normalcy.

Contrary to most conventional thinking, migration is a mutually beneficial phenomenon; it benefits both the origin and the destination country, Makina asserts. The impact of remittances is particularly critical as they represent 'the most visible and tangible link between migration and development', and this is especially so if the remittances 'are invested and saved in financial institutions'. However, the full development impact of remittances is seldom felt in poor, developing countries like Zimbabwe because of lack of access to formal financing by both migrants and recipients of remittances. Among Zimbabwe-ans, for instance, one survey study found that only two per cent of migrants reported using official banking channels, with the vast majority preferring to send remittances through informal channels such as bus drivers, friends and relatives visiting home. This suggests that the country is not fully benefiting from the developmental potential inherent in large volumes of remittances arising from international migration.

Makina ends his chapter by offering several policy recommendations. These include the need for a national labour migration policy; leveraging remittances for development by, for instance, mainstreaming labour migration issues in national policies and development plans; allowing dual citizenship to nationals living abroad; establishing a recognition system for skills gained from abroad; promoting the productive use of migrant workers' remittances and widening remittance channels and providing return and reintegration services; and setting up a comprehensive labour migration information and data system.

To effectively perform its core functions, a state needs an effective and competent bureaucracy. This is the issue that Myo Naing discusses in Chapter 8. He adopts Max Weber's 'ideal type' bureaucracy as his analytical framework in order to examine Zimbabwe's public sector reform and identify the missing elements and how these can be addressed. Naing argues from the premise that bureaucracy plays 'a significant and indispensable role' in the development of a nation. To him, the key is not quantity but quality, especially the appropriate skills mix, accountability mechanisms, and insulation of the bureaucracy from day-to-day political interference. He agrees with the observation that the poor development performance of most African countries is largely attributable to their pathological bureaucracies.

His chapter traces the development of Zimbabwe's post-colonial public service. He notes the initial and laudable attempts to create a performance-oriented sector through a number of interventions, including training, but that by the end of the 1980s bureaucratic pathologies had set in, necessitating a public service review commission to diagnose the problems. Naing discusses the deterioration of the bureaucracy despite the public service reform programme and the introduction of a performance management system. He identifies and discusses what he calls the missing 'essential ingredients': the introduction of meaningful meritocracy; the provision of competitive salaries and incentives; the creation and implementation of full-grown anti-corruption strategies; fully insulating the bureaucracy from political intervention; and a monitoring and evaluation system and total quality management.

As the political and economic crisis deepened after 2000, it took a heavy toll on the bureaucracy, notably through severe brain drain and massive corruption. Naing argues that political reform is necessary but is not in itself adequate; there must also be developed a committed, competent and efficient bureaucracy that can successfully implement planned programmes and projects. To him, five important problems must be addressed: leadership failure, lack of political will as well as lack of rule of law; slothfulness and lack of civil service neutrality; poor conditions of service such as low salaries and allowances; the need for adequate financial resources to kick-start bureaucratic reforms; and the 'liberator syndrome' or the 'freedom-fighter curse'.

To restore the quality of Zimbabwe's bureaucracy, Naing recommends a number of interventions. These include institutional and attitudinal changes; generating public acceptance of the change management reforms to be implemented; providing continuous training to public servants; institutionalising performance management in the public service; strengthening anti-corruption mechanisms; institutionalising a merit-based system; and improving conditions of service, notably by paying competitive salaries.

In Chapter 9, on the role of local authorities in democratic transition, Norbert Musekiwa explores the role that these sub-national institutions can play in facilitating (or retarding) the country's democratic transition. He starts from the contestable premise that local-level institutions 'are currently governed by representatives that were democratically elected by the people' and therefore that 'constitutional and democratic transition is already taking place at that level', before proceeding to outline and analyse the structure, functions, strengths and limitations of the country's local government system. For instance, he notes that the local government sector comprises elected, appointed, and traditional leadership structures and that there are four types of local authorities: urban councils, rural district councils, provincial councils, and traditional leaders, each of which is established under different pieces of legislation.

Musekiwa also discusses the chequered history of traditional authorities from during the colonial era and notes that they have tended to be exploited as instruments in struggles for power and popular legitimacy, especially when an incumbent regime is undergoing a legitimacy crisis, as happened under settler colonialism (especially under Ian Smith's Rhodesia Front regime in the 60s and 70s) and in the ZANU-PF regime after 1990. The author devotes considerable attention to the pervasive and intrusive ministerial interventions in the affairs of local authorities, and concludes that despite the travails of local authorities in Zimbabwe, they are 'effective agents of democratic transition'.

In the book's penultimate chapter, Mary Ndlovu examines the knottiest problems that is likely to haunt the country for generations to come, i.e., that of the youth and their predicament. She traces their ordeal from the idyllic days of independence through to the present, and focuses on three key issues: the need for an appropriate education; the need for access to employment or some form of income-generation; and the need for socialisation by adults into a moral order. Her verdict is that 'there have been failures in all three areas' and attributes this to policy flaws since independence.

As she sees it, education was not adequately calibrated to economic development nor did the policies plan for the social consequences resulting from the massive expansion of the post-independence education sector. Ndlovu discusses some of the major imperatives that drove education policies, especially during the first decade of independence, for example, socialism and the policy of equal and free education for all in order to produce the idealised classless society. She laments the sad fact that 'Politics had been at the root of the post-independence restructuring of education, and politics would prevent government from backtracking.'

She observes, as others have done before, that although the education sector churned out thousands of school-leavers, only a minute proportion could be absorbed into the economy, which was itself later decimated by the ill-fated structural adjustment programme of the 1990s and the politically-motivated and often violently executed land reform programme from 2000 onwards. The latter spawned its multiplier negative consequences beyond the economy.

Ndlovu further argues that those institutions – family, church, school, etc. – that would have acted as agents of socialisation to the youth were themselves badly fractured by the multidimensional crisis. Some of these social institutions have since lost much of their innocence and are now not only failing to instil the appropriate values in the youth but have also become instruments in the hands of predatory political gladiators.

Despite this depressing picture, Ndlovu sees glimmers of hope, all the while acknowledging that 'the way back will be long and tortuous'. Further, the solution lies largely in the realm of politics, 'when a stable, legitimate and dedicated government is in place to guide a determined recovery'. To her, the recovery should encompass a complete overhaul of the education system, positive growth of both the economy's formal and informal sectors, the cessation of state-sponsored violence and a return to public and private morality and the rule of law.

The last chapter, by Vupenyu Dzingirai, Emmanuel Manzungu and Owen Nyamwanza, tackles the thorny and politically and emotionally contentious issue of the impact of the post-2000 fast track land reform programme (FTLRP) on the environment and agriculture. The authors use the framework of transactional populism as the lens through which to examine the consequences of the FTLRP in the last decade, as well as the interests of the powerful in land and the state of social service delivery on new farms. They note the generally accepted position that the FTLRP was motivated by fear of a loss of political power after the formation of the Movement for Democratic Change that posed a serious threat to the ZANU-PF regime's continued hold on power. The execution of this politically motivated programme, they argue, required a suspension of the official rules and well-established property rights to landowning and use. New rules of the game were created in the image of the ruling party and beneficiaries were selected on partisan grounds to benefit not only the pro-ZANU-PF villagers but also the allies of the ruling elite.

The authors discuss and lament the environmental costs of the programme. These include the destruction of commercial and indigenous forests to pave the way for more land for crop production, the reinforcing of claims of rights over land, the establishment of new settlements and the need to satisfy a huge demand for fuel wood, and the deleterious impact on wildlife through eradication of habitat and poaching. The writers also draw attention to the various ways in which commercial agriculture became a casualty of the FTLRP and the contagious effect this had on the rest of the agro-based economy. The widely acknowledged so-called 'breadbasket' of the continent soon degenerated into Africa's 'basket case', having to rely on international charity to feed half of its population. The destruction of agriculture was accompanied by the collapse of social amenities on farms, with diseases of all kinds becoming widespread as a result of poor infrastructure and healthcare.

As part of the solution to the destruction wrought by the populist-driven FTLRP, the authors propose a 'rationalisation of the reform process in such a way that it is more equitable, efficient and beneficial to the environment'. To them, this requires 'revising the issue of multiple [land] ownership, resolving the issue of beneficiary selection, wise use of the environment and improving social amenities'.

References

Bowman, Larry. 1973. *Politics in Rhodesia: White Power in an African State*. Cambridge, Mass.: Harvard University Press.

Bratton Michael and Nicholas van de Walle. 1997. *Democratic Experiments in Africa: Regime Transitions in Comparative Perspective*. Cambridge: Cambridge University Press.

Brinkerhoff, Derick (ed.). 2006. *Governance in Post-Conflict Societies: Rebuilding Fragile States*. London: Routledge.

Carothers, Thomas. 2002. 'The End of the Transition Paradigm', *Journal of Democracy*, 13, 1, (January), 5-21.

Cole, G.A. 1995. *Organisational Behaviour: Theory and Practice*. London: DP Publishers.

Diamond, Larry. 1996. 'Is the Third Wave Over?', *Journal of Democracy*, 7 (July), 20-37.

Diamond, Larry, Juan J. Linz, and Seymour Martin Lipset. 1996. *Politics in Developing Countries: Comparing Experiences with Democracy*. Boulder and London: Lynne Rienner Publishers.

Kaufmann, Daniel, Aart Kraay, and Massimo Mastruzzi. 1996. Governance Matters 111, Policy Research Working Paper No. 3106. Washington DC: World Bank. Available at www.info.worldbank.org/governance/wgi/pdf/govmatters3.pdf

Menocal, Alina Rocha and Timothy Othieno. 2008. 'The World Bank in Fragile Situations: An Issues Paper'. Paper prepared for a conference on 'An Eye on the Future: The World Bank Group in a Changing World', Amsterdam, 12-13 July.

O'Donnell, Guillermo and Phillippe C. Schmitter. 1986. *Transitions from Authoritarian Rule: Tentative Conclusions About Uncertain Democracies*. Baltimore: Johns Hopkins University Press.

Huntington, Samuel. 1991. *The Third Wave: Democratization in the Late Twentieth Century*. Norman: University of Oklahoma Press.

Sithole, Masipula. 1990. 'Zimbabwe: In Search of a Stable Democracy', in Larry Diamond et al. (1996) *Politics in Developing Countries: Comparing Experiences with Democracy*. Boulder and London: Lynne Rienner Publishers: 449-90.

World Bank. 2009. *The Political Economy and Governance Context of Transition and Recovery in Zimbabwe*. Harare: Multi-Donor Trust Fund.

Notes

1 This term is associated with the late Professor Masipula Sithole (1990: 452) and was an elaboration of Larry W. Bowman's thesis that white Rhodesian settler political conflict took place 'within a "democratic" political process'.

2 According to Larry Diamond et al. (1996: 7-8), a semi-democracy is one in which 'the effective power of elected officials is so limited, or political party competition so restricted, or the freedom and fairness of elections so compromised, that electoral outcomes, while competitive, still deviate significantly from popular preferences; or where civil and political liberties are so limited that some political orientations and interests are unable to organize and express themselves'.

3 Five years earlier, Larry Diamond had also wondered if the third wave was over (1996).

4 The Fund for Peace (www.fundforpeace.org) annually publishes the list of 'failed states' called the Failed States Index (FSI) published by *Foreign Policy*. The FSI is a ranking of what the Fund determines to be the world's most dysfunctional states. According to its criteria, Zimbabwe has consistently been in its top ten: it was 3rd in 2008, 2nd in 2009, 4th in 2010; its 'best' performance was 6th in 2011.

5 The World Bank's list of low-income countries under stress (LICUS) is based on a range of indicators of the Bank's CPIA. In terms of interpretation, a country with a LICUS score of 3.0 or less is seen as a fragile. These are further classified as 'core' LICUS if the CPIA is 2.6-3.0 and 'severe' if the CPIA is 2.5 or less. Zimbabwe is now in the 'core' LICUS group, having languished in the 'severe' LICUS group for a number of years.

1

The Public Mood on Zimbabwe's Political Transition

Eldred V. Masunungure & Anyway Ndapwadza-Chingwete

Introduction

Following a political impasse resulting from the flawed 2008 elections, three major political parties (the long-ruling Zimbabwe African National Union – Patriotic Front (ZANU-PF) and the two Movement for Democratic Change (MDC) parties[1]), under the auspices of former South African President Thabo Mbeki's mediation process, agreed in September 2008 to form a coalition government. Six months later, the Global Political Agreement (GPA) gave birth to the self-styled Inclusive Government (IG) in February 2009. The power-sharing deal sought to resolve the syndrome of national crises that had paralysed the country for more than a decade. The three parties declared and agreed 'to work together to create a genuine, viable, permanent, sustainable and nationally acceptable solution to the Zimbabwe situation'.[2]

The signing of the GPA formally launched a political and socioeconomic transition in the country. Great strides were made in resurrecting the near-comatose economy, with basic commodities once again available in the formal markets and inflation tamed with the introduction of the multi-currency system. However, the political side of the equation remained problematic and resistant to change.

This chapter presents and analyses public perceptions of Zimbabwe's transition along several dimensions. Without presenting the voice of the people as captured in public opinion studies, the story of the country's transition would be grossly incomplete.

The importance of public opinion

Today, the role of public opinion is more salient than when James Bryce asserted more than a century ago that:

> Opinion has really been the chief and ultimate power in nearly all times .... Governments have always rested and, special cases apart, must rest, if not on the affection, then on the silent acquiescence, of the numerical majority.[3]

In non-democratic governments, the people acquiesce or give passive consent to authority, either out of respect, habitual obedience or fear of repression. By contrast, the distinguishing feature of democracy is that governmental authority is built, controlled and conditioned by the force of active public opinion. Seeking public opinion should be a necessary though obviously insufficient feature of modern governance. This is the most direct way governments can take the pulse of the nation, for example, by knowing what social services people want and what they say about the performance of government in various areas of governance. Knowing the public mood is even more critical in a polity in transition, as is Zimbabwe.

Public opinion therefore plays a critical role in policy planning, formulation and implementation. Regrettably, the use of public opinion remains underappreciated in Zimbabwe and is often suppressed or restrained, especially if the findings are inconsistent with the wishes and political messages of the ruling regime.

Methodology

This section outlines the methods used to tap public opinion. The research used data from both quantitative (national surveys and snap surveys) and qualitative studies (focus group discussions) carried out between September 2009 and February 2011. All national surveys involved face-to-face interviews in one of three national languages (English, Shona or Ndebele), with a nationally representative probability sample size of 1,200 adult Zimbabweans selected from all ten provinces. The sampling method applied the stratified, multistage, random probability proportionate to population size (PPPS) method.

The 1,200 sample size yields a margin of error of +/-3 per cent at the 95 per cent confidence level. In the first stage of sampling, a total of 100 enumeration areas (EAs) for all national surveys – except for the Afrobarometer surveys which involve 150 EAs – were randomly selected from a frame of EAs stratified by urban–rural differences. The probability of selection was proportionate to population size, based on the population projections of the 2002 census population, projected for the relevant year of the survey. This ensured that every eligible adult Zimbabwean aged 18 years and above had an equal and known chance of being randomly selected. In the second stage of sampling, 12 households were randomly selected within each EA. In the third and final stage, one adult Zimbabwean was randomly selected from each household. With 12 respondents from each of the 100 EAs, a total sample size of 1,200 was achieved. Additionally, interviews were alternated between males and females to achieve an equal gender quota.

The AB surveys employed the same sampling methods and passed through the same sampling stages as explained above, except that more EAs (150 instead of 100) were selected. As a result, fewer inter-views were carried out in each EA (eight interviews instead of 12), but nonetheless giving a total sample size of 1,200.

The February 2011 urban-based survey was different as it targeted only urban centres in the ten administrative provinces. The initial plan was to cover all the provinces, but interviews in Mashonaland Central's urban centres were aborted to ensure safety of the field researchers after incidents of their harassment in Manicaland. The planned sample size was 1,008 but fewer interviews (922) were conducted. Nonetheless, the reduced sample size maintained the margin of error of +/-3 per cent at the 95 per cent confidence interval. For all these surveys, the implementing agencies recruited a team of qualified research assistants to carry out the interviews using prescribed sampling methods. Field supervisors provided leadership and quality control during the data collection exercise. As a quality control measure, all field researchers underwent intensive training sessions in data collection and interview techniques before carrying out the interviews. The implementing agencies also dispatched a team of research officers to monitor the process to further enhance quality of the research exercise.

Focus group discussions (FGDs) were conducted in ten provinces,

Province	Gender	Age	Ethnicity	Area	Level of education
Harare	Male	18-30	Shona	Urban	Secondary (complete)
	Female	31-45	Shona	Urban	Tertiary+ (some)
Mash. East	Male	31-45	Shona	Rural	Primary & secondary (O-level)
	Female	46+	Shona	Rural	Secondary (some)
Mash. Central	Male	18-30	Shona	Rural	Secondary (complete)
	Female	31-45	Shona	Rural	Tertiary+ (some)
Mash. West	Male	31-45	Shona	Rural	Secondary (complete)
	Female	18-30	Shona	Rural	Primary & secondary (O-level)
Masvingo	Male	18-30	Shona	Rural	Secondary (complete)
	Female	31-45	Shona	Rural	Tertiary+ (some)
Midlands	Male	31-45	Shona	Rural	Primary & secondary (O-level)
	Female	46+	Shona	Rural	Secondary (some)
Manicaland	Male	31-45	Shona	Rural	Secondary (complete)
	Female	18-30	Shona	Rural	Primary & secondary (O-level)
Bulawayo	Male	31-45	Ndebele	Urban	Primary & secondary (O-level)
	Female	46+	Ndebele	Urban	Secondary (some)
Mat. South	Male	31-45	Ndebele	Rural	Secondary (complete)
	Female	46+	Ndebele	Rural	Primary & secondary (O-level)
Mat. North	Male	18-30	Ndebele	Rural	Secondary (complete)
	Female	31-45	Ndebele	Rural	Tertiary+ (some)

Table 1: Demographic matrix for FGD participants

with two focus group sessions per province (one female and one male group). Further, the two groups within each province had homogenous demographic characteristics in terms of age, gender, place of residence and level of education (Table 1). The FGDs were conducted by trained facilitators. Whilst each group targeted ten participants, group representation ranged from seven to ten, which is the normal sample size for meaningful group discussions.

Findings on the public mood on Zimbabwe's transition

The various quantitative and qualitative studies mentioned above interrogated a number of dimensions of the country's transition, including those pertaining to the economy, service delivery, the constitution, and electoral issues.

An economy in transition
Green shoots of hope?
The most significant and visible performance of the IG since its inception has been in the economic arena, specifically the resuscitation of an ailing economy that had been on its deathbed for a decade. The multi-currency system[4] introduced in early 2009 revived the country's formal market, with basic commodities finally finding their way back to formal market shelves. The scarcity of commodities had been exacerbated by the ill-advised and poorly executed 'Operation Reduce Prices' of mid-2007, where all retailers had been compelled to cut prices by 50 per cent and where the implementation of the directive by security agencies was anything but professional.

The 'dollarisation' of the economy immediately turned things around. In terms of public opinion, the dominant feeling was one of hope, especially given that basic commodities were once again available in shops. It is best captured by one male focus group participant from Mashonaland West:

> Things have gotten better as compared to the past years. At least now our children can have buttered bread, transport is now available and we can now afford to visit our relatives.

By contrast, in October 2005, an Afrobarometer survey[5] showed that only seven per cent of respondents reported that their 'present' economic conditions were good. After the IG, this figure jumped to 38 per cent (May 2009) and further rose to 50 per cent (November-December 2010)[6]. This latter survey also saw nearly half (46 per cent) applauding the coalition government for its overall performance, with only a fifth condemning it as a failure. Further, in November 2010, pluralities (31 per cent) from the IDAZIM survey believed that the economic stabilisation policy was the IG's biggest achievement, although 14 per cent disagreed and felt the policy was the IG's greatest failure. Obviously, after a decade of a ruinous economy and a life of scavenging, people's expectations were high, being perhaps a case where 'much is not enough' (Shumba and Chingwete, 2011).

Hoping in despair
Zimbabweans bemoan economic regression
While the first 18 months of the transition witnessed an economic upturn, the period since then has registered evidence of a slow-motion relapse. Prime Minister Morgan Tsvangirai acknowledged this at the launch of the country's 2011 Medium-Term Plan when he blamed the acrimony, bickering and discord within the IG for the serious impediments to the normal functioning of the economy:

> The President and I yesterday agreed that if you look at the Inclusive Government, the first one and half years of this Inclusive Government was progressive such that we were able to deliver, but for the last six months what has come out in the public is discord ... we ask ourselves why don't we go back to the situation where there was political and policy stability?[7]

Indeed, surveys conducted during the first year of the IG's operation reveal signs of optimism but later surveys showed a downward trend. In May 2009, nearly four in ten (38 per cent) said that their personal living conditions were 'good', this being a huge jump from only 7 per cent who had volunteered this response during the October 2005 survey. Further, between November-December 2010, half of the surveyed adult Zimbabweans reported that their living conditions were good, a big achievement towards economic stabilisation. However, the latest MPOI survey on political transition in Zimbabwe recorded a reversal of gains achieved in the previous years. In February 2011, only 36 per cent of Zimbabweans were happy about their economic condition and 44 per cent complained about deteriorating living standards.

This downward trend was also captured in qualitative studies. For instance, in FGDs conducted in November 2010, one male participant from Mashonaland West Province compared the early IG to the later period:

> In my area the situation had improved after the formation of the Inclusive Government, and indeed it was better than it is this year [2010]. It appears as if the situation is returning to the crisis levels. Employment is now a challenge to secure these days, while money is now scarce. The situation is now bad.

The IG's performance in respect of unemployment has been singularly unimpressive, according to public opinion. Supported by official data for the period 2006 to 2009, unemployment levels remained high, at levels well above 80 per cent.[8] A report from the UN Office for the Co-ordination of Humanitarian Affairs (OCHA) revealed that at the end of 2008, only six per cent of the population was formally employed, down from 30 per cent in 2003. In other words, of the country's 12 million people, only 480,000 had formal jobs at this time, a staggering drop from the 3.6 million of 2003. In 2010, unemployment was estimated at 94 per cent[9], which is extremely high, both in absolute terms and in comparison to other sub-Saharan African countries. For example, South Africa's level of unemployment is estimated at 24 per cent, whilst Botswana's is pegged at just 7.5 per cent.[10]

The series of Afrobarometer surveys conducted since have consistently revealed unemployment as the second most serious national problem after management of the economy. In 1999, Zimbabweans ranked unemployment the second most serious problem, with 14 per cent of the surveyed respondents mentioning this as the number one problem facing the country. The corresponding statistics for 2004, 2005, and 2009 were 18 per cent, 14 per cent, and 12 per cent respectively. By October 2010, the figure had climbed to 16 per cent. However, caution should be exercised in interpreting these figures and their ranking in the policy agenda because 'economic management' was also consistently at the apex of the list of the 'most serious' problems. Unemployment is essentially an integral part of the economic management problem and not entirely separate from it. In November 2010, job creation was ranked third among the IG's greatest failures with 13 per cent giving this verdict, after economic instability (15 per cent) and political instability (14 per cent).

Thus, the IG has not been able to forge a sustainable developmental

Services	Survey periods and satisfaction levels		
	October 2005	May 2009	November 2010
Health	33	64	47
Education	45	51	47
Water and sanitation	31	52	44
Electricity supply	*	42	14
Road maintenance	*	24	27
	N=1200	N=1200	N=1200

*Figures represent proportions of surveyed respondents who were satisfied with service delivery. *Indicates where opinions about performance in service delivery were not sought.*

Table 2: Public perceptions on the state of service delivery in Zimbabwe

agenda and, if this grave problem persists, public trust and confidence in the government will soon be eroded.

The quest for improved service delivery

One of the biggest casualties of the decade-long multidimensional crisis was service delivery, which almost completely collapsed. Urban residents had to endure a life of rationed water (when available) and massive electricity load-shedding. In some high-density suburbs residents received water only once in six months but were still required to pay unreasonable rates bills. The near-collapse of such services had had devastating ripple effects on major social and economic sectors – health, education, manufacturing and the agricultural sectors. Local authorities failed to respond to the crisis as fiscal transfers from the central government dried up and their capacities to repair equipment, improve infrastructure and provide basic services were severely eroded. However, with the inception of the IG raised citizens' hopes that the broken service delivery systems would be repaired.

Verdicts on the success of the IG in this regard were varied. A study on local governance in transition conducted by IDAZIM in collaboration with the Research Triangle International (RTI) in June 2009 (five months into the IG) revealed that the majority were upbeat and had perceptions of positive changes in local service delivery. Close to six in ten (58 per cent) local officials interviewed reported that the situation had improved, although a third stated that they had not seen any difference, and only a minute three per cent felt that service delivery had further deteriorated. Public opinion surveys also affirmed such positive assessments. For instance, in May 2009, 64 per cent of the polled respondents in an Afrobarometer Round 4 survey reported an improved health service delivery, doubling the statistics for October 2005 (33 per cent); 51 per cent reported improved education services in May 2009 (compared to 45 per cent recorded in October 2005); 52 per cent said water and sanitation services had improved (against 31 per cent for 2005). Improvements were also registered in electricity supply (42 per cent) and road maintenance (24 per cent) (Table 2).

Despite such positive developments in the early life of the IG, it appears that these improvements were not sustained over time. By November 2010, public opinion had become depressed with respect to improvements in health services (there was a 17 percentage-point gap in positive assessment, for example). As Table 2 clearly shows, people's evaluations had declined in four of the five service areas. The largest performance gap was in respect of electricity supply, with a whopping 28 percentage-point gap between May 2009 and November 2010. The sense of despair had returned, though not to the same levels as in the pre-IG era.

The November 2010 IDAZIM survey asked the respondents how they rated service delivery. Across the spectrum, the majority felt it was poor. They were particularly distressed by the poor supply of electricity and the state of physical infrastructure, with more than three quarters (78 per cent) condemning performance in these areas. Areas of 'best' performance were health services, where 40 per cent rated it as either fair or good, education (41 per cent) and clean water supply (44 per cent). Empirical evidence therefore points to eroding optimism within the existing lifespan of the coalition government.

Zimbabweans were also unhappy with the disparity between the quality of service delivery and utility charges. An overwhelming majority complained about high education fees (74 per cent), 68 per cent bemoaned high health service costs, while 59 per cent and 41 per cent decried electricity costs and water service charges respectively. These high service charges are in the context of perceived poor and deteriorating delivery.

In a political economy where the government is expected to be the main provider of goods and services, perceived poor delivery can be politically very costly. And, given that the life of the coalition government will end with elections, those contenders for power who, in the public's eye, are adjudged to be responsible for poor performance may pay a high price. It is therefore in the best interests of all IG partners to enhance their performance in preparation for the people's verdict at the ballot.

Reforming the Constitution

Under Article 6 of the GPA, the three political parties who signed the GPA agreed to spearhead a constitutional reform process. The GPA explicitly defines the framework for a new constitution and the time-lines to be observed, with the end result being a new constitution in place within 18 months, i.e. by October 2010. However, virtually all deadlines were missed, often by wide margins. Indeed, at the time of writing (April 2012), the drafting had yet to be completed, the whole progress having been hamstrung by complex inter-party contestations. Even then, it continued to be a stop–go process.

The most critical stage of the process, an outreach programme to solicit people's views on their constitutional preferences, finally took off in June and ended in November 2010. Many observers – including ZZZICOMP[11] and media agencies – reported that the public consultations were marred by political violence, intimidation, manipulation, lack of transparency and prior coaching of participants (especially in the rural areas) to favour certain political parties. This motivated nationally representative public opinion studies on the matter, with questions ranging from 'Was the constitutional outreach process conducted fairly and to the people's satisfaction?' and 'What do people want in terms of the process and content of the constitution?' to 'Do people believe their views will be reflected in the final document?' Some of the findings of these surveys, which were conducted between September 2009 and February 2011, are given in the sections that follow.

The process of Constitution-making

The first survey to engage the public on the constitutional reform process was carried out in September 2009. The findings revealed a huge knowledge gap among respondents. Only 40 per cent had ever heard of the Constitution of Zimbabwe; the survey thereafter excluded the 60 per cent who lacked this knowledge from any further questioning on the process of the reform. Of those who claimed to have heard of the existing constitution, an overwhelming 88 per cent wished for some sort of constitutional change, although they were split on whether to go the *amendment* or *replacement* route (39 versus 49 per cent). The survey revealed that people evidently preferred a participatory mode of constitution-making, a point noted in the survey report:

> when asked how they wanted to express their own views on constitutional reform, a plurality of respondents opted for voting in a referendum (41 per cent). They preferred this form of participation to expressing their views in a community meeting (26 per cent), to an independent commission (17 per cent), or to a parliamentary committee (13 per cent).[12]

An equally overwhelming majority (91 per cent) agreed that 'all peoples, Zimbabweans included, have a right to establish the constitutional rules under which they are governed'. This position was affirmed in the November 2010 survey, where 79 per cent said 'it is the duty of the Inclusive Government to ensure enough public participation in making the Constitution'.[13]

Also noteworthy from the September 2009 survey was that more than one third (36 per cent) feared that the citizens' views collected during the outreach process would not be reflected in the new constitution. Only 42 per cent trusted the government to do so. This suspicion was warranted given the surreptitious amendment of the 2000 draft constitution before the February 2000 referendum. Further, the constitutional process was not fully publicised, especially to the rural communities, nor was the public sufficiently mobilised. Unsurprisingly, the survey conducted in December 2010 showed that only one third of all adult Zimbabweans attended the COPAC outreach meetings. Further analysis revealed that more rural residents (39 per cent) than their urban colleagues (20 per cent) attended the meetings. Participation also rose with age: attendance was highest among those older than 51 (40 per cent); 35 per cent among the middle-aged (31-50 years); and 26 per cent among the youth (18-30 years). This was substantiated by the November 2010 ZZZICOMP report on the outreach process which noted that of the 716,340 total participants recorded by the close of the outreach programme, the youth constituted only 21 per cent. This is despite the fact that Zimbabwe's youth constitutes more than one third of the total population of Zimbabwe. The future leaders of the country seemed not too keen to actively participate in crafting a constitution under which they would govern or be governed.

The outreach process was marked by serious problems, principally persistent financial constraints, the dearth of information about the programme in most rural communities and political violence instigated by political gladiators and their parties, not to mention a host of other disruptive challenges. For instance, on several occasions, outreach teams arrived at designated venues only to find that communities – even in urban settings – were unaware of the meetings' specific dates and venues. In some instances, the scheduled times and venues of outreach meetings were different to those advertised by COPAC, in other cases venues were deliberately changed by some mischievous local political leadership. In some communities, war veterans were also seen roaming around, instilling fear amongst the general public. In short, the constitutional reform process left much to be desired in terms of garnering popular legitimacy.

The content of the Constitution

Issues of constitutional process and those of constitutional content are different but are equally important. Often, people may reject the content out of hand because the process leading to it is flawed; this is the stance of the National Constitutional Assembly which is agitating for the rejection of whatever draft comes out of a process that they regard as not being 'people-driven'. The content issues posed in the surveys were informed by the widely accepted weaknesses of the extant constitution and some of the 'Talking Points' used by COPAC in soliciting public views.

One pertinent and persistent concern among Zimbabweans (and beyond) is the issue of presidential term limits. Zimbabwe has had only one political chief executive since independence and many rightly or unjustly attribute the governance crisis in the country to this fact. The survey asked citizens to speak on this. In September 2009, more than three quarters (78 per cent) preferred limiting the president's tenure to two terms, with 77 per cent expressing the same preference in December 2010. It is notable that partisanship has since entered the equation, with 80 per cent of MDC-T people endorsing the two-term option against 60 per cent from ZANU-PF supporters. The significant finding, however, is still that there is substantial support for a two-term limit, even from the beneficiaries of the no-term limits provision in the current constitution. Table 3 summarises public opinion on some of the major content issues and what people would like in the supreme law of the country.

A closely related and critical matter was in respect of the form of government. Three options were presented to respondents in September 2009: a) a presidential system in which an executive holds most power: b) a parliamentary system in which a prime minister holds most power; and c) a mixed system in which a president and prime minister share power. Though none of the three options attracted majority support, nearly half (48 per cent) said they would prefer a mixed system, presumably one resembling the current power-sharing government. The next preferred is where the prime minister holds most power, an option supported by 27 per cent, with the least popular (20 per cent) being the presidential system,[14] the very form of government that Zimbabwe had had since 1987 until the IG was established.

But what do Zimbabweans think about the structure of the legislature, i.e. whether unicameral or bicameral? Opinions have been consistently divided on this. In September 2009, opinion was evenly split between those for a two-chamber parliament (42 per cent) and those against (43 per cent); the corresponding figures in the December 2010 survey were 40 per cent and 42 per cent.

Zimbabweans also overwhelmingly support a fully elected legislature rather than a system where the president may appoint some members of parliament. There is consistent endorsement on this dimension, with citizens insisting on the vertical accountability borne out of elections. In September 2009, an overwhelming 85 per cent of respondents wanted the legislature to be composed only of elected MPs, a preference confirmed in December 2010 when 80 per cent expressed this position.

Nor are Zimbabweans keen to perpetuate the decades-old practice of appointing chiefs into national legislative chambers. In September

Issue	Option 1		Option 2	
President's term be limited to two, or unlimited	Limit to two terms		Unlimited terms	
	2009	2010	2009	2010
	78	77	14	16
One or two houses for parliament	Abolish senate		Keep both houses	
	2009	2010	2009	2010
	43	42	42	40
Appointment versus election of MPs	President has power to appoint MPs		All MPs elected	
	2009	2010	2009	2010
	11	13	84	80
Role of traditional leaders facilitated or limited	Reserve position for chiefs		Limit role to local government	
	2009	2010	2009	2010
	26	23	65	70
Courts to be independent or politically loyal	Establish independent courts		Judges must be politically loyal	
	2009	2010	2009	2010
	78	87	12	7
Election run by independent or government body	Election run by government agency		Election run by independent commission	
	2009	2010	2009	2010
	20	16	73	77

Note: Percentages in this table represent the joint percentage on the respective items for 'agree with' and 'agree very strongly with'.

Table 3: Constitutional preferences over two surveys (Source: Adapted from Freedom House, 'Changing Perceptions in Zimbabwe – Nationwide Survey of the Political Climate in Zimbabwe', November 2010-January 2011.)

2009, two-thirds said they wanted traditional leaders restricted to local government and not awarded ex officio status in the legislature, as is presently the case. By December 2010 this proportion had increased to 70 per cent, indicating that citizens think the ongoing practice is a vitiation of core democratic principles.

Shifting from vertical to horizontal accountability, we found that Zimbabweans also favour independent countervailing agencies of restraint. Two illustrations will suffice. Zimbabweans clearly value the independence of the courts, with 80 per cent in September 2009 agreeing that 'the Constitution should establish independent courts'; this preference increased to 87 per cent in December 2010. Citizens also cherish an independent election commission; a preference favoured by 73 per cent in September 2009 and affirmed by a larger proportion (77 per cent) in December 2010.

Finally, in relation to constitutional content issues, adult citizens have consistently expressed a yearning for political and civil liberties. Two Freedom House surveys provide irrefutable evidence of this. In September 2009, three quarters (76 per cent) of the respondents agreed that 'the Constitution should protect every individual's right to freely express political views', a preference affirmed in 2010 when 80 per cent expressed this same stance.

The people's mood regarding elections

This chapter echoes Masunungure's (2009) observation that elections in the contemporary world remain the best known and most effective device for connecting citizens to policy-makers. They have the potential to confer legitimacy, moderate dissent, engender compliance and heighten citizen efficacy (Moehler 2005). Elections are a necessary but insufficient ingredient for democracy. And yet the history of elections in Zimbabwe is a history of gross irregularities in the form of electoral fraud, violence and intimidation. In fact, apart from constitutional reform, elections in present-day Zimbabwe are the most hotly contested issue and their timing has been a bone of contention within and outside the IG, including at the SADC level. The lone but powerful voice for early elections – even before the new supreme law is in place – comes from the former ruling party, especially the hardliners within

How free and fair do you expect the next general elections to be? *(All figures represent percentages)*			
Not free & fair at all	*Hardly free & fair, with major problems*	*Free & fair with minor problems*	*Completely free & fair*
10	25	30	16
Compared with March 2008, the next round of elections will be ...			
More free & fair		*Less free & fair*	*No difference*
43		15	24
Compared with June 2008, the next round of elections will be ...			
More free & fair		*Less free & fair*	*No difference*
46		17	19

Note: Table does not report on 'don't know' or 'refuse' responses.

Table 4: Zimbabweans' expectations of 'free and fair elections' for the next round (December 2010)

it. The two MDC formations, with the support of the regional guarantors (SADC and the African Union), insist on elections after a new constitution has been enacted and a favourable political and security environment created. Other commentators actually warn of regression to the violence-ridden period of the 2008 presidential runoff. Bratton (2010:1), for example, apprehensively observed that:

> With a public outreach program on constitutional reform marred by violence, with security forces and ZANU-PF militias redeployed around the country, and with both sides calling for fresh elections, the country risked relapse into another dangerous period of political instability.

Crucial and timely questions emerge as one assesses the ripeness of the environment for democratic polls in the country. Do Zimbabweans want early elections? Are the conditions right? Are the oversight bodies (e.g., the media) and the electoral management body (the Zimbabwe Electoral Commission) ready for free, fair and credible elections? In the next section we present the public mood on this critical subject.

The political mood in Zimbabwe: A public opinion perspective

Zimbabweans today are ambivalent about elections: they prefer a government they choose themselves in free and fair elections but are realistic enough to fear them, given the history of electoral violence and intimidation. The Freedom House report on the December 2010 findings comments that 'The contradictions of contemporary Zimbabwe are nowhere more evident than in Zimbabweans' expectations and experiences of elections'.[15] Thus, in the Afrobarometer survey of October 2010, an overwhelming 86 per cent agreed that 'we should choose our leaders in this country through regular, open, and honest elections', a figure higher than the 80 per cent recorded in May 2009. This is solid confirmation that the electorate yearns for free, fair and credible elections that produce an uncontested outcome.

Nevertheless, Zimbabweans are realistic enough to realise that they may not get what they yearn for. Even in the euphoric mood of September 2009, only a slim majority (52 per cent) was optimistic that the next cycle of elections would be free and fair, dropping to 46 per cent by December 2010. In the latter poll, 35 per cent were still sceptical about the fairness and freeness of the next elections. Table 4 breaks down the findings in more detail.

More worrying is that some would-be voters expect the next elections to be as horrendous as the bloody June 2008 run-off elections (19 per cent) or even envisage that they will be 'less free and fair' (17 per cent). Less than half the electorate (46 per cent) expect them to be freer and fairer than the June 2008 elections. This is a matter that merits urgent and decisive attention by the domestic power-wielders and by SADC if a semblance of transparent, free and fair polls is to be attained. To date, there is no evidence that the fears[16] of the electorate are without merit.

Zimbabweans are also clear-minded on the fact that their civil and political rights and liberties have been further eroded since the formation of the IG. Indeed, every dimension of political liberties has registered a steep decline, with people feeling the sharpest decline (minus 17 percentage points) in respect of freedom of speech, prompting Bratton to comment that 'confidence in democratic liberties is being gradually replaced by a resurgence of political fear'.[17] This sense

Questions: For the September 2009 and December 2010 surveys, the wording was: 'In your opinion, when should the next presidential and parliamentary elections be held?' For the October 2010 survey, the wording was: 'Do you think that Zimbabwe should hold elections next year, that is, in 2011?'

Survey	2011	Later/other	Don't know
September 2009	56	37	7
October 2010	70	23	7
December 2010	57	29	15

Table 5: Desired timing for the next elections

of being gagged was confirmed in a December 2010 survey, where a staggering 86 per cent said they felt they had to be careful about what they said politically. Unsurprisingly, the IDAZIM survey of November 2010 had also shown more than half (52 per cent) of the respondents reporting that the political environment was not conducive for a credible election, although a large minority (41 per cent) disagreed with this assessment and expressed satisfaction with the prevailing conditions. In fact, survey after survey has confirmed the unevenness and skewness of the political and electoral playing ground.

The timing of the next electoral contest

The evidence presented would make most rational voters balk at any suggestion of an early election for the simple reason that the political and security situation is far from ripe. Yet, despite the deep fear of violence and intimidation, the paradox is that Zimbabweans in 2010 repeatedly expressed their desire or at least willingness to exercise their sovereign right to vote. In the 2010 surveys, the majority preferred elections 'immediately' or 'next year' (meaning 2011).

The key message coming out of the three surveys conducted in 2010 (September, October and December) (Table 5) is that the majority indicated that adult Zimbabweans are keen to elect leaders of their choice despite the huge impediments they faced. This is surely a striking finding, if not a 'testament to the impressive depth of Zimbabweans' commitment to political rights'.[18]

This baffling preference for elections in 2011 must be put in context. First, the preference is not unconditional. This comes out from the December 2010 survey in which respondents clearly expressed a sequential order in which the new constitutional referendum is conducted and a new constitution enacted *before* the next elections. Nearly three-quarters (73 per cent) demanded that the constitution be finalised before elections were held, with only 17 per cent reckoning that 'elections [could] be brought forward, whether the new constitution is finalised or not'. Second, most Zimbabweans (political partisanship notwithstanding) are fed up with the unending quarrelling within the IG and the accompanying immobility and policy gridlock and would rather have a legitimate government composed of one party. The preference for elections is therefore not an irrational quest, but is informed by the reality of practical politics as the public witnesses it.

It must be noted that survey and FGD findings at the end of 2010 do not seem to converge. Though opinion was also divided, most FGD participants seem to be against early elections, saying the country is not ready for them:

> People no longer look forward to elections here in Zimbabwe because they bring a lot of pain, suffering and death as people are burnt alive in their own homes. (Matabeleland South male)

> In Zimbabwe, there was never a free and fair election so I don't see the need for elections because with this environment, nothing is going to change. (Bulawayo female)

> We no longer have a free and fair election in this country, the last free and fair election that was ever held in this country was the one held in 1980. (Manicaland male)

> They (elections) should be postponed for five or so years or even a decade because if you look at what was happening during the outreach programme, it's an indication that we are not politically mature to handle an election. (Mashonaland East male)

FGD participants did lay down some conditions that in their opinion need to be met before the country embarks on a new cycle of elections:

> As long as there is no new constitution which protects us, we will not be ready for elections. (Mashonaland West male)

> Let's give a chance to the economy, so that the economy can recover. (Mashonaland Central female)

> We prefer having international observers from around the world who have nothing to do with any of us and not from Africa per se to come and monitor our elections. (Manicaland males)

When all is said and done, Zimbabweans are passionate about elections as the only legitimate mechanism for choosing their leaders.

They are knowledgeable about the difficult electoral environment and are apprehensive about it, but nonetheless are keenly anxious to pass their verdict as soon as practicable, especially after a new supreme law is in place. This captures the complexity of the country's multifaceted problems, which are not only institutional but also operate at the psychosocial level. This takes us to the next fundamental, long-running and equally contestable problem – that of transitional justice in the country.

Transitional justice

As defined by the Zimbabwe Human Rights (ZHR) NGO Forum, transitional justice is the pursuit of comprehensive justice during times of political transition, i.e., the development, analysis and practical application of a wide variety of strategies for confronting the legacy of past human rights abuses in order to create a more just and democratic future.[19] The concept was adopted as a means to deal with past human rights abuses, which in the case of Zimbabwe date back prior to independence. Since then, violations of human rights have taken centre stage in Zimbabwe, with Gukurahundi,[20] Operation Murambatsvina and the pre- and post-election violence that has marked nearly every poll in Zimbabwe. The country's obligations to enhance justice and peace and ensure security of persons are enshrined in Articles 7 and 18 of the GPA, where parties agreed to promote equality, national healing, cohesion and unity for its citizens, whilst ensuring security of persons. This broad and huge task is shouldered by the Organ on National Healing, Reconciliation and Integration, a body that is neither widely known nor effective. The debate in Zimbabwe has for long centred on whether Zimbabweans prefer *accountability* to *amnesty*, and if the former, which measures should be undertaken to heal victims of past human rights abuses. In other words, what form should the healing process take and who should be involved? Other critical questions inquired into the kind of measures to be put in place to ensure peace prevails in the country.

Justice versus amnesty

In September 2009, a slim majority (55 per cent) agreed that 'revealing the truth about what happened in the past is necessary for Zimbabwe to move ahead', whilst a significant minority (43 per cent) considered that 'in order for our country to make progress, it would be best to forget what happened in the past'. Thus, most Zimbabweans prefer truth-telling about human rights abuses to forgetting. Commenting on holding perpetrators to account versus granting them amnesty, a clear majority (62 per cent) opted for prosecution rather than immunity, which was preferred by nearly a third (31 per cent). Indeed, while more than half of all Zimbabweans interviewed thought that the provision of amnesty would be 'fair' to perpetrators (55 per cent), more than four-fifths (84 per cent) thought it would be 'unfair' (65 per cent 'very unfair', 19 per cent 'unfair') to victims.

More than a year later, the November 2010 survey fully supported accountability for political crimes, with close to six in ten (57 per cent) being in agreement with the statement that 'there must be a means to punish persons responsible for political crimes'. A disaggregated analysis revealed that of the 57 per cent that called for accountability, the breakdown was 22 per cent advocating for justice, 19 per cent pre-ferring reparation, 15 per cent desiring criminal prosecution, and only one per cent favouring institutional reform and memorialisation as the basis for national healing and reconciliation in Zimbabwe. A total of 34 per cent believed truth-telling and forgiveness would provide the panacea for national healing and reconciliation.

The need for compensation also came out clearly during the ZHR NGO forum outreach research.[21] The effect of Gukurahundi was prominent across Matabeleland, with most participants calling on the government to confess to political crimes committed against civilians and compensate the people for losses encountered. For example, one participant from Umguza said that 'There is no need to trust the gov-ernment if it does not take responsibility for past abuses and repent. Accountability must start with the government itself.' Equally sup-portive of the need for compensation, one female participant from Buhera Central (Manicaland Province) stated that 'Arresting offenders is not enough; they must pay back what they looted and repair what they damaged.'

Similarly, most participants from MPOI's FGDs held in Novem-ber-December 2010 rallied behind accountability for political crimes as a means to ensure justice. Many lamented the level of crimes that were committed and most believed forgiveness would promote political crimes in the future. The scars that remain, most participants explained, can only be managed through an 'eye for an eye'. Some were quick to point to the need to apply the law as a rightful means for ensuring justice:

> No, we can't just forgive like that! Forgiving just like that? Although we are religious people, it is very difficult. There are certain things that are pardonable while others are not. The situation requires the victim to say out his mind to the perpetrator and the victim can make a decision to forgive the culprit or not. We must not just start by forgiving these culprits because they committed very serious crimes. The painful experiences are unforgettable. (Midlands male)

> We now want to institute punitive measures that tally with the crimes. We should have punishments that are commensurate with the crime. (Harare male)

> You know that if you forgive a perpetrator, the following day the perpetrator will repeat the same crime. If you leave a rotten peach fruit in a basket with fresh peaches, the rotten peach fruit will spoil all the fresh fruits. So people should be accountable for their crimes, so as to deter those with intentions to commit similar crimes. And how will our laws work if we just forgive these people? We do not have laws that say a person should be forgiven for any wrongdoing. Forgiving each other applies in churches for the evangelists only. (Harare female)

Evidently, most Mashonaland participants believe that holding people to account for their actions would bring justice and healing to their victims. However, a few participants who called for forgiveness premised their argument on the nature and magnitude of the crime and that the Organ on National Healing should determine the magnitude of punishment equivalent to the level of the crime(s) committed. A few female participants from Mashonaland West Province denounced the state of lawlessness in Zimbabwe, given that it promotes the perpetration of political violence and other political crimes in the country:

> I think they can be pardoned depending on the magnitude of the crime, for instance, it will be difficult to forgive murderers, and those who burned people's homes. (Mashonaland East female)

> I would want to say there are different crimes that are committed like murder and chopping off people's hands. These are different crimes with different penalties so the law should be invoked to take its course. Some of these criminals should receive a life sentence. What we hate is a situation whereby a perpetrator is arrested and immediately released. These people will continue committing the same offenses. Those who kill others should

Question: With regard to the process of reconciliation, what period should it cover?

Province	UDI to present (per cent)	1980–2010 (per cent)	2000–2010 (per cent)	Don't know (per cent)
Harare	10	22	56	9
Bulawayo	18	25	32	14
Midlands	15	33	38	11
Masvingo	4	18	76	3
Manicaland	7	17	63	8
Mash. East	7	18	65	8
Mash. West	4	13	77	6
Mash. Central	2	18	71	8
Mat. North	21	47	15	17
Mat. South	17	42	19	18

Table 6: Public views on preferred timeframe for reconciliation process, November 2010

be penalised according to the relevant laws. (Mashonaland East male)

I think the punishment is dependent on the crime committed. I think the people leading the national healing and reconciliation process should decide on the best way to deal with the criminals. (Mashonaland West female)

On the national healing and reconciliation process

If there is to be a national healing and reconciliation process, someone should lead it; it will not just happen. In respect of whom Zimbabweans think should lead the process, the November 2010 IDAZIM survey revealed that a large minority (44 per cent) would prefer the government to do so. Churches also attracted reasonable trust, with close to two in ten (18 per cent) supporting it. Civil society ranked third, with 12 per cent support. Political parties and traditional leaders attracted eight per cent and six per cent support respectively. The other leaders/institutions (e.g., President, Prime Minister) did not emerge as popular candidates for this task.

When next asked what period the inquiry into such political crimes should cover (Table 6), Zimbabweans were more focused on the recent past. In September 2009, a small majority (53 per cent) preferred that investigations concentrate on the period since 2000, a finding that was confirmed by the IDAZIM survey, where 55 per cent preferred the same period. However, all surveys revealed significant minorities that favoured going back 30 years, to Independence in 1980 (21 per cent in September 2009 and 23 per cent in November 2010), or even as far back as the Unilateral Declaration of Independence (UDI) in 1965 (seven per cent in September 2009 and nine per cent in November 2010). In November 2010, only three per cent stated that there should be no reconciliation process in Zimbabwe, while nine per cent offered no response.

Further analysis revealed differences along ethnic (Shona and Ndebele) and regional lines, most likely due to the experiential factor. The Ndebele in western Zimbabwe were legitimately concerned about and focused on the murderous Gukurahundi period, where nothing to date has been done to redress political crimes; not even a full, official apology has been forthcoming. Large majorities in Mashonaland would prefer the investigations to be delimited to more recent times, i.e., post-2000, which is when these areas fell victim to politically motivated violence, including Operation *Mavhotera Papi*.[22]

Significantly, all four provinces in the 'Gukurahundi belt' (the three Matabeleland provinces plus the Midlands) registered the highest number of 'don't know' responses, with Matabeleland South topping the list with 18 per cent, followed closely by Matabeleland North (17 per cent), Bulawayo (14 per cent) and Midlands (11 per cent). The remaining six provinces came in at less than nine per cent each, with Masvingo having the lowest (three per cent). We speculate that the legacy of fear still grips the Gukurahundi provinces to the point of being reticent to share their preferences with strangers, even on deeply emotional topics. The sharp regionalisation of opinon on this subject suggests that any intervention/s must be sensitive to the different perspectives based on differential experiences. A 'one-size-fits-all' approach may be the most inappropriate one of all.

The overarching message is that Zimbabweans *do* want something to be done about putting their past(s) to rest, even if they are not fully agreed on the methodology, something that needs greater and more open public debate.

Conclusion

This chapter presents Zimbabwe's political and socioeconomic transition from the perspective of the citizens themselves. The public perceptions focused on the key dimensions that are part of the ongoing or expected macro-processes, viz. the constitution-making process and the subsequent referendum and the next set of general elections. Overall, Zimbabweans value both processes and clearly see the link between them and prefer a sequencing whereby the new supreme law is enacted before elections take place. This is the clear and unambiguous message to those in power.

Given the country's tortuous history, issues of transitional justice and national reconciliation are also close to the hearts of citizens. The first, transitional justice, tends to present itself in binary terms: *prosecution* of perpetrators of serious human rights abuses versus offering them some kind of *amnesty*. A difficult choice will need to be made as to the best route to take, and when. The other priority issue is which crimes will be regarded as meriting some transitional justice and which ones could be amnestied. Not all crimes could benefit from the latter, if only because this would be in violation of the applicable international law which, for instance, disallows blanket amnesty in the case of war crimes, crimes against humanity and genocide. It would appear that this sensitive issue needs a government with uncontested popular legitimacy to tackle it effectively and decisively, something that appears to be beyond the handling capacity of the current shared and fragile government.

Finally, our evidence suggests that although public opinion in Zimbabwe is itself evolving with time and circumstances, overall, it reflects a quest for change from the militarised, electoral authoritarianism discussed in chapter 5. It is important that any future policies on the many contentious issues facing the nation be informed by the pulse of public opinion. It is only then that the government can do the right thing in the right way.

Notes

1   The two MDC parties were the mainstream one led by Morgan Tsvangirai

(MDC-T) and the smaller formation then led by Arthur Mutambara (MDC-M). The latter split in early 2011 and its main faction is now led by Welshman Ncube (MDC-N).

2 The agreement between ZANU-PF and the two MDC formations on resolving the challenges facing Zimbabwe, 15 September 2008.

3 James Bryce, *The American Commonwealth*, Vol. 2 (1888), Chapter 77.

4 The currencies adopted were the US dollar, the South African rand, Botswana pula, the British pound, and the Euro. The first two are the most widely used and circulated and the reforms are generally referred to as 'dollarisation'.

5 afrobarometer survey conducted by the Mass Public Opinion Institute (MPOI), October 2005.

6 The May 2009 and November/December 2010 surveys were conducted by MPOI for Afrobarometer and Freedom House respectively.

7 'PM wary of GNU fallout', *Daily News*, 8 July 2011.

8 The Central Intelligence Agency (CIA), *World Factbook*, March 2011.

9 Ibid.

10 Ibid.

11 ZZZICOMP is an collective acronym for the Zimbabwe Election Support Network (ZESN), Zimbabwe Lawyers for Human Rights (ZLHR), the Zimbabwe Peace Project (ZPP) and the Independent Constitution Monitoring Project.

12 Freedom House, 'Report on the Public Attitudes to Constitutional Reform and Transitional Justice in Zimbabwe', Report prepared for Freedom House, September 2009, p. 4.

13 The interviewees also highlighted that the constitutional reform process had not been sufficiently informative and consultative.

14 This is in line with the consistent finding across all Afrobarometer surveys that reject one-man rule: this was rejected by 78 per cent in 1999, 80 per cent in 2004, 90 per cent in 2005, and 85 per cent in 2009.

15 Freedom House, 'Changing Perceptions in Zimbabwe – Nationwide Survey of the Political Climate in Zimbabwe November 2010-January 2011', Freedom House, 4 March 2011, p. 7.

16 In the December 2010 survey, nearly half (46 per cent) disagreed with the statement that 'This time around, elections will be different, there will be nothing to fear'. Only 26 per cent agreed with it. In the same survey, a majority (albeit tiny) of 52 per cent subscribed to the idea that 'Political parties in Zimbabwe use violence to ensure victory in elections and nothing is going to change', against 22 per cent who disagreed.

17 Bratton (2010:3).

18 Ibid., 6.

19 ZHRF Outreach Report, *Taking Transitional Justice to the People*, Vol. 1, 2009.

20 Gukurahundi was a state-orchestrated military campaign that ran soon after independence when a small group of disgruntled former ZIPRA war veterans (so-called 'dissidents') took up arms and terrorised tourists and local villagers. The state reacted viciously to quell the insurgency and killed over 20,000 people between 1982 and 1987. It was a dreadful and fearful era for most residents in the affected region and the quest for justice remains a burning issue.

21 Ibid., Vol. 2, 2010.

22 77 per cent of respondents in Mashonaland West preferred this recent era, followed by 76 per cent in Masvingo, 71 per cent in Mashonaland Central Mashonaland East (65 per cent) and Manicaland (63 per cent).

References

Bland, G. 2009. 'Zimbabwe in Transition: What About the Local Level?' RTI Press Publication No. OP-0003-1009. Research Triangle Park, NC: RTI Press. Available at www.rti.org/rtipress. Accessed 21 April 2012.

Bratton, M. 2010. 'Zimbabwe: The Evolving Public Mood', Afrobarometer Briefing Paper No. 97.

Bryce, J. 1888. *The American Commonwealth*, Vol. 2, Chap 77. Available at www.oll.libertyfund.org. Accessed 23 September 2011.

Central Intelligence Agency. 2011. World Factbook, March.

Chingwete A.N E. and E. Muchena. 2009. 'The Quest for Change: Public Opinion and the Harmonized March Elections', in E.V. Masunungure (ed.). 2009. *Defying the Winds of Change, Zimbabwe's 2008 Elections*. Harare: Weaver Press.

Civil Society Monitoring Mechanism. CISOMM. 2010. Periodic Report: January–March 2010. Harare, CISOMM.

Daily News. 2011. 'PM wary of GNU fallout', 8 July.

Freedom House. 2009. 'Report on the Public Attitudes to Constitutional Reform and Transitional Justice in Zimbabwe'. Report prepared for Freedom House, September.

—. 2011. 'Changing Perceptions in Zimbabwe – Nationwide Survey of the Political Climate in Zimbabwe'. Report compiled by Susan Booysen, Johannesburg, March.

Logan, C. 2011. 'The use of the Afrobarometer in Policy Planning, Program Design and Evaluation'. Afrobarometer Briefing Paper No. 98, January.

Masunungure, E.V. 2009. 'Voting for Change: The 29 March Harmonized Elections', in E.V. Masunungure (ed.). *Defying the Winds of*

Change, Zimbabwe's 2008 Elections. Harare: Weaver Press.

Moehler, S.C. 2005. 'Free, fair or fraudulent and forged: Elections and legitimacy in Africa'. Afrobarometer Working Paper No. 55.

Oko, O. 2009. 'Dissecting the Anatomy of Fraudulent Elections in Africa: Proposals for Reforming the Nigeria's Electoral Process'. Available at www.works.bepress.com/okechukwu_oko/4.

Research and Advocacy Unit (RAU). 2009. 'Transitional Justice in Zimbabwe: A Pilot survey of the views of activists and victims'. Harare: RAU.

Shumba, J. and A. Chingwete. 2011. 'Public Opinion: What people say about the GPA'. Available at www.kubatana.net/docs/demgg/osisa_gpa_public_opin_110630.pdf.

Zimbabwe Election Support Network. ZESN. 2009. 'Report on the Zimbabwe 29 March 2008 Harmonized Elections and 27 June Presidential Runoff.' Harare: ZESN.

Zimbabwe Human Rights NGO Forum. 2010. 'Taking Transitional Justice to the People'. Outreach Report, Vol. 2. Harare: ZHR NGO Forum.

2

Political Speech & Access to Public Broadcast Media by Political Parties in Zimbabwe

Lyndon Tuyani Nkomo

SECTION I

The theoretical framework

Free political discourse is an essential tenet of any functioning democracy. Citizens and organised societies must be able to fully engage themselves in unhindered political debates and as such must have equal access to the media that enables them to express their views in a fair and balanced manner. When this is possible, the philosophy is that 'competing views, opinions and policies are publicly debated and exposed to public scrutiny [and] then the good will, over time, drive out the bad and the truth will prevail over the false'.[1] Where this is the case, the public will be able to make their own political choices in the course of the democratic process, wherein it is a given right to be able to choose political leaders.[2] In this regard, public broadcasters carry the critical statutory responsibility of ensuring that citizens are provided with both comprehensive information and a platform for the exchange of ideas. As they discharge this duty, they become important agents in ensuring that the government is open, responsive and accountable.[3]

Broadcasters are ordinarily subject to diverse political and economic forces which, if left alone, will tilt the landscape in favour of the political opinions of well-funded forces. Lord Bingham of Cornhill argues *in obiter dictum* that 'the risk is that objects which are essentially political may come to be accepted by the public not because they are shown in public debates to be right but because, by dint of constant repetition, the public has been conditioned to accept them',[4] hence the need for statutory regulation of party election broadcasts or political advertisements. Such regulation is not uncommon and is not necessarily unconstitutional in a fully democratic state.

Plural democracy and the role of broadcast media

Plural democracy in a political context suggests the existence of heterogeneous political philosophies represented by different political groupings existing in a particular society seeking to convince the majority of the people to elect them into offices of governance of the state.[5] Thus the basic tenet of plural democracy is that such political formations must freely and equally be given opportunities to debate and engage each other in various political contests in order to win the votes of the electorate. According to Justice Brandeis in *Whitney v California*:[6]

> public discussion is a political duty … it is hazardous to discourage thought, hope, imagination; that fear breeds repression; that repression breeds hate; that hate menaces stable government; that the path of safety lies in the opportunity to discuss freely supposed grievances and proposed remedies.

This formulation of free speech is what forms the basis of a healthy plural democracy.

The role of the broadcasting media

Broadcast media plays a crucial role in ensuring that citizens are able to not only make responsible political decisions but also participate effectively in public life. This is a duty that is recognised in South Africa, as observed by the South African Constitutional Court.[7] This duty is not foreign to Zimbabwe; one of the key objectives of broadcast media as provided in Section 2A of the Broadcasting Services Act, Chapter 12:06, is to ensure 'public debate on political, social and economic issues of public interests'. This provision thus recognises the political duty that Justice Brandeis spoke about in *Whitney v California* (supra). However, the greatest challenge in Zimbabwe's transitional phase is how to ensure that this duty is fulfilled, for if the powers enacting the laws have a tendency to ignore them in order to suit their political agenda, the statute books risk becoming irrelevant.

The importance of the freedom of speech within the context of the Broadcasting Services Act, Chapter 12:06

Section 2A of the Broadcasting Services Act (Chapter 12:06) outlines the key objectives of the regulation of broadcasting in Zimbabwe, which, *inter alia*, provides in Section 2A (d) (ii):

> that the broadcasting services in Zimbabwe, taken as a whole ... must ensure public debate on political, social and economic issues of public interest ... so as to foster and maintain a healthy plural democracy.

It is therefore the duty of all licensed broadcasters to foster a healthy plural democracy through political debates. This duty, which also rests upon the electronic media, is recognised in many jurisdictions that embrace democratic pluralism. If free speech is shackled, then the objectives of Section 2A of the Broadcasting Services Act will not be achieved. Judge Learned Hand observed that free speech 'presupposes that right conclusions are more likely to be gathered out of a multitude of tongues than through any kind of authoritative selection'.[8] The essence of political debate is to bring about political change that is desired by the people.[9] Only governments that fear change will shackle the voices of the people and kill the spirit of democratic pluralism. The gravity of muting the voices of the people by denying them the means to be heard is an unforgivable sin in modern democratic constitutionalism.

SECTION II

The case of Zimbabwe

The political landscape in Zimbabwe has to a very large extent been influenced by the manner in which political discourse has been disseminated via the government-owned Zimbabwe Broadcasting Corporation

(ZBC), which runs the country's only television station and a number of radio stations. Political parties, especially the Movement for Democratic Change (MDC) groupings, and some political commentators, have complained of lack of access to state media, accusing ZANU-PF of monopolising the electronic broadcasting media.[10] This allegation was largely proven by failed efforts made by MDC-Tsvangirai (MDC-T) to broadcast their political advertisements on e-TV, a South African television station, during the 2008[11] harmonised elections as well as their attempted use of internet sites such as YouTube with files linked from websites like www.newszimbabwe.com in order to reach out to some parts of the electorate because they allege that they were not granted access to electronic broadcast media.

The signing of the Global Political Agreement (GPA) between these political rivals, one which culminated in the formation of a Government of National Unity comprising MDC-T, ZANU-PF and MDC-Mutambara (MDC-M) in 2008, ushered in a new political dispensation that, among other things, demanded a number of media reforms emanating from ZANU-PF's alleged monopolisation of the state media. In particular, Article 19.1 (d) and (e) of the GPA tasked the Inclusive Government to:

> (d)... ensure that the public media provides balanced and fair coverage to all political parties for their legitimate political activities.
>
> (e) ensure that the public and private media shall refrain from using abusive language that may incite hostility, political intolerance and ethnic hatred or that unfairly undermines political parties and other organisations.

These objectives point to the existence of a polarised media in Zimbabwe at the time this agreement was consummated. Paragraph (d) cited above may be construed as making reference to the ZBC being the only public broadcaster in Zimbabwe providing radio and television services. This objective again suggests that there may have not been fair and balanced reporting and coverage of the activities of all political parties and that some political parties may have had little or no access to broadcasting media, which are perceived to have more immediate and powerful impact than print media,[12] particularly in a country where the availability of printed media in rural areas is rather limited.

Elections in Zimbabwe and access to the media

The main political groupings in Zimbabwe agreeing to address the issue of equal access to the broadcasting media by all citizens and political formations suggests that the existing broadcaster was continuing to fail to discharge its public mandate. The orgy of violence that preceded the 2002, 2005 and 2008[13] elections fulfilled the prophetic opinion of Justice Brandeis[14] that the suppression of speech would breed hatred, repression and violence. In all these elections, only one voice was dominant on both radio and television stations.

For example, a report from the Media Monitoring Project Zimbabwe (MMPZ) showed that the ZBC allocated ZANU-PF 755 minutes of campaign airtime outside their news bulletins (including paid-for advertisements) as against 310 minutes for the MDC-T faction, 155 minutes for MDC-M faction and 217 minutes for independent candidate Simba Makoni in the period preceding the 2008 elections.[15] These numbers indicate biased programming by the public broadcaster, quite possibly the dual result of government control over this media and a weak media regulatory system that left decisions pertaining to political party election broadcasts in the hands of the state-owned public broadcaster rather than an independent regulatory authority with the power to impose penalties for the public broadcaster failing to fulfil its mandate. The Seventh Schedule to the Broadcasting Service Act (Chapter 12:06) provides that:

> The broadcasting services operated by the public broadcaster shall; ... (d) provide news and public affairs programming which meets the highest standards of journalism, and which is fair and unbiased and independent from government, commercial or other interests.

This objective is consistent with the provisions of Section 2A (1) (f) of the Broadcasting Services Act (Chapter 12:06), which provides that one of the key purposes of broadcasting in Zimbabwe is 'to ensure the independence, impartiality and viability of public broadcasting services'.

The issues of equitable access to the electronic media by different political parties and the independence of the media are not only critical but also inseparable. This is the basis upon which the right of reply is founded to ensure that those whose positions are challenged have an opportunity to respond to their critics. This, in turn, ensures that 'reason' is let free in the minds of the people to judge for themselves concerning the subject matter of the discourse. Regrettably, when news and public affairs issues are manipulated to make the Zimbabwean public hear only what is acceptable political content to those in the newsrooms as well as the government of the day, the public broadcaster is seriously transgressing both the law and the terms of its broadcast licence, thus unleashing 'media terror'.[16]

Thus, in this transitional phase another major challenge is establishing an independent media whose structures are not suffused with individuals with overwhelming political allegiance to a particular political party. It must have its operational roots in the Constitution, which must provide for the establishment of an independent media regulator. The MMPZ report alleges that the manner in which ZBC managed coverage of the MDC-T faction epitomised political prejudice against that party, in particular the programme that was hosted by Mr Happison Muchechetere on 2 June 2008, as well as the participation by what the report termed as 'ZANU-PF apologists' such as Claude Mararike and Vimbai Chivaura.[17] While caution must be exercised in respect of the report prepared by MMPZ because it contains highly emotional overtones, if these allegations are true, then the ZBC transgressed not only the law, its licence obligations and basic journalistic ethics, but also regional instruments such as the SADC 'Editors' Guidelines and Principles for Broadcast Coverage of Elections', and in particular Article 6 thereof, which provides that:

> Broadcasters will make sure that any impression of one-sidedness is avoided in all programming. They must act and be seen to be acting in a fair and independent manner and not be influenced by political or other interests.[18]

Hence, if ZBC broadcasters allowed personal sympathy with any political formation to colour their work they should have recused themselves from hosting or moderating programmes these views could affect. The fact that individuals with political inclinations or interests are found within the structures of most public broadcasters is not uncommon, particularly in the SADC regional bloc, and is a serious threat to equal access to the media by some political formations and individuals who hold different opinions from those of the governments of the day. In the recent judgment of the South Gauteng High

Court (Johannesburg) the South African Broadcasting Corporation's (SABC) former Director of News, Dr Snuki Zikalala, during the period 2005–2006 period was similarly accused of manipulating its news and current affairs as well as attempting to cover up this manipulation.[19] Of particular interest was the manner in which it covered the 2005 election in Zimbabwe. The extent of the manipulation included a ban on identified independent commentators such as Elinor Sisulu, Moeletsi Mbeki, Trevor Ncube and Archbishop Pius Ncube being interviewed by the SABC.[20] The court in this matter held that 'the conduct of Dr Zikalala amounts sadly, to a "tyranny of the mind of man" by disallowing views expressed contrary to his political opinion and that of the government of the day, and in that process, he "killed reason" instead of allowing reason to be "let free"'.[21] The Malawi Broadcasting Corporation (MBC) was also found to have transgressed the law when it denied opposition political parties in Malawi equitable access to the broadcast media by broadcasting only live political rallies of the then president, Bakili Muluzi.[22] The MBC's contention was that it was age-old practice in Malawi to broadcast live all presidential functions. However, the High Court of Malawi, emphasising the concept of equal treatment of all political parties, observed *in obiter dictum*, that:

> if campaign messages are broadcast live at a presidential function, then equal treatment means that campaign rallies of other political parties or at least the presidential candidates be broadcast live. That would give other political parties or at least campaign rallies of other candidates an opportunity to reply to matters raised.[23]

For Zimbabwe, then, the future demands that those who hold political power must choose the path of safety and give the nation's people the free and unhindered opportunity to engage in political discourse, making available both public and private resources for them to fulfil this 'political duty'[24] in order to foster a healthy democracy.

The institutionalisation of political philosophies in public broadcasting: the implications

Another major challenge for this transitional era is how to de-institutionalise the public broadcaster from political party ideologies and presumably remove from its ranks those that allow its political sympathies to spill over into the workplace. Once the public broadcaster becomes susceptible to such institutionalisation of a specific political philosophy and/or agenda it negates the ideals of democratic pluralism enshrined in the Broadcasting Services Act, ensuring the death of 'independence, impartiality and viability of public broadcasting'.[25] This breeds intolerance which leads to pre-broadcast censorship of different voices, because:

> The media tells us not what to think, but how to think, proposing categories which influence how we organize and interpret the information we acquire. Ultimately, the media influence the agendas we set.[26]

The worst transgression of political institutionalisation of broadcast media was the role that radio broadcasts played in fuelling the instability and genocide in Rwanda in 1994, especially those of Radio RTLM.[27] Disruption of state stability is an ever-present danger that societies face when those in charge of broadcast media elect to limit the diversity of voices by ignoring democratic pluralism and pursuing the agenda of political monopoly.

The fiduciary nature of the public broadcast mandate

When the law gives an office or an institution a public mandate, it elevates that institution or office into a position of trust. This position of trust imposes fiduciary duties or obligations on those that agree to run any such institution or office. Fiduciary duties require these individuals to act in good faith and in the best interest of the principal. Any violation of the terms of the mandate is a fundamental breach of trust. Public broadcasting assumes fiduciary responsibilities to the generality of the Zimbabweans in that it uses public funds as well as public resources such as radio frequencies.

Thus the fact that the public broadcaster in Zimbabwe has never been held to account for its alleged transgressions is an indicator of either a weak or partisan broadcast regulator which cannot continue to act as a faithful overseer of the implementation of the public mandate. Trivialising public mandate is a serious transgression and those who deliberately do so should not be deemed fit to hold public offices. The existence of a politically monogamous broadcast media is also evidence of lack of editorial independence, which is one of the hallmarks of freedom of expression in any democratic society. Editorial independence is the ability of the media to analyse, report and broadcast on any event of public interest without fear of or interference by government or other interests[28] in order to foster the growth of plural democracy. A public broadcaster that gives in to the massages of some political fingers can easily mutate into a propaganda tool, which is an affront to the key purposes of broadcasting regulation pertaining to ensuring 'the independence, impartiality and viability of public broadcasting services'.[29]

SECTION III

An analysis of the legal and regulatory framework

The question of equitable media access is ultimately a legal matter and as such it is imperative to examine the existing legislation in Zimbabwe to assess whether it supports equitable access to the public broadcast media by a diversity of voices, particularly from different political formations.

The Constitution of Zimbabwe

Section 20 of the Constitution of Zimbabwe is the basis upon which freedom of expression is protected in this country, and Section 20(1) provides that:

> Except with his own consent or by way of parental consent no person shall be hindered in the enjoyment of his freedom of expression, that is to say freedom to hold opinions and impart ideas and information without interference, and freedom from interference with his correspondence.

The starting point in any legal analysis that involves human rights issues is to make reference to the Constitution as the source of protection of fundamental rights. The provisions of Section 20 (1) referred to above protect all forms of speech, including political speech. The question that arises is whether the Constitution guarantees the 'means' for expression by the citizens. Political parties are barred by virtue of the provisions of Section 20 of the Broadcasting Services Act (Chapter 12:06) from holding or having control of any broadcasting licensee or signal carrier. It is now a settled principle of law that:

Section 20(1) of the Constitution enjoined not only that persons be free to express themselves but that they be not hindered in their means of doing so. The protection of the freedom of expression applied not only to the content of information but also to the means of transmission and reception of such information. A restriction imposed on the means of transmission or reception necessarily interfered with the right to receive and impart information.[30]

While individuals' rights to access the means of expression is guaranteed under the Constitution as per the decision of the Supreme Court in *Retrofit (Pvt) Limited v The Posts and Telecommunications Corporation* (supra), Section 20 (2) provides a limitation to this right, particularly in so far as it relates to the 'means' of expression so as to:

> regulate the technical administration, technical operation or general efficiency of telephony, telegraphy, posts, wireless broadcasting or television or to create or regulate any monopoly in these fields.

The reasoning behind this limitation is that some of the resources that are used in telecommunications and broadcasting are finite, particularly radio frequencies. While not everyone will be able to hold a licence to either provide a telecommunications or broadcasting service, as White J in *Red Lion Broadcasting Company Inc v Federal Communications Commission (No 2)* stated:

> the people as a whole retain their interest in free speech by radio and their collective right to have the medium function consistently with the ends and purposes of the First Amendment. It is the right of the viewers and listeners, not the right of the broadcasters, which is paramount.[31]

This decision was quoted with approval by Gubbay CJ in the case of *Retrofit (Private) Limited* (supra) and as such, even though only a few individuals may hold broadcasting licenses, citizens do retain a public interest in the 'means' that licensees use to broadcast in order for them to express themselves. The rationale for this can also be justified from the fact that as broadcasters are ordinarily allocated finite public resources in order for them to provide services to the public and that as society gives them the licence to broadcast, the public therefore has a right to use the means provided for by broadcasters to express themselves. This reasoning is based on the public utility principle set out in the American case of *Munn v Illinois* (1877), which established the principle that when someone devotes their property to use in which the public has interest, they in effect grant the public an interest in that use and must agree to be controlled by the public for the common good to the extent of the interest they have created.[32]

In any case, notwithstanding the public utility principle and the allocation and use of public resources like radio frequencies, the ZBC is a public institution which was set up using public funds. As such, no one can lay an exclusive ownership claim on the national broadcaster, or deny anyone access to use its media platform in order to express themselves. Furthermore, the ZBC remains partly publicly funded as it is empowered, by law, to collect licence fees from all persons who possess radio or television receivers in Zimbabwe. Furthermore, Section 38C of the Broadcasting Services Act provides that the 'Licence fees referred to in Section 49, less such amounts as may be payable for the services of the agents of the broadcasting company, shall be paid into the general funds of the company for the use of the company.' This is another legal basis upon which *all* Zimbabweans have basic rights to claim access to ZBC's broadcast media. The public broadcaster thus belongs to the people of Zimbabwe and thus no one political party should be able to monopolise access to it.

The decision of the Supreme Court in *Retrofit (Private) Limited* (supra) indicates that access to the means of communications is a fundamental right which must not be easily trammelled. Any attempt to prohibit or proscribe political voices that may be heard on radio or television would amount to discrimination on the basis of political opinion which is a transgression of Section 23 of the Constitution of Zimbabwe. Moreover, Section 23A of the Constitution provides for the:

> right for every citizen to free, fair and regular legislative, Presidential, local elections and referendums and for any adult citizen to stand for public office and if elected to hold office.

The elevation of the protection of political rights, which include the expression of political speech and the right of people to freely hold different political opinions, is a clear indication of the commitment of the people of Zimbabwe to plural democracy. The fundamental rights provided for in the current Constitution are interdependent to the extent that a denial of one may invariably lead to a violation of the other. This position can be summed up by the following words from the Vienna Declaration and Programme of Action which was unanimously adopted by all the participating 171 member states of the United Nations in 1993:

> All human rights are universal, indivisible and interdependent and interrelated. The international community must treat human rights globally in fair and equal manner, on the same footing, and with the same emphasis.[33]

Thus the nature of the commitment to plural democracy from the people of Zimbabwe is such that:

> debate on public issues should be uninhibited, robust, wide open and that it may well include vehement caustic and sometimes unpleasantly sharp attacks on government and public officials.[34]

Free and fair elections contemplated by the provisions of Section 23A of the Constitution of Zimbabwe will only be achieved when those desiring political office have equal access to the means that make them reach out to the electorate in order to market their political manifestoes. M.P. Mkandawire J, in *Dr Charles Kafumba and 2 Others v The Electoral Commission and the Malawi Broadcasting Corporation* (supra), noted that 'equal treatment of all competitors is a component of free and fair elections'. Those desiring political offices can only be known if they speak to the people and their manifestoes can only be known if they are freely disseminated to the people. Only when people engage each other in uninhibited political debate will the electorate be able to make free and sound judgment when they vote,[35] hence the importance of equal access to the media. The challenge, therefore, in the transitional phase is to make the public broadcaster accept that access to the media is not a privilege but a basic right of every Zimbabwean, regardless of their political views.

Under American law, the Federal Communications Commission imposed on the broadcasters a 'doctrine of fairness' which requires that public issues be presented by broadcasters and that each side of those issues be given 'fair coverage'.[36] In other words, broadcasting must be done in the public interest, particularly in a democratic society, especially where the public broadcaster uses public resources such as radio frequencies and is publicly funded. In this regard, the doctrine of fairness and the concept of public interest that appears is implied in the objectives of the Broadcasting Services Act, in particular Section 3(d),which demands that political speech be given platform for expression regardless of one's political background. This statutory duty must be exercised independently and impartially. Hence, the doctrines of 'fairness' and 'public interest' are the essential ingredients of a 'healthy plural democracy' that is envisaged by the Broadcasting Service Act.

Shortcomings of the Constitution of Zimbabwe

The first major weakness in the Constitution that directly impacts on how some of the fundamental freedoms and rights are protected is its lack of founding values. Founding constitutional values will always be a shining beacon that guides a nation in the interpretation and application of its Constitution. The South African Constitution, for example, is based on values such as human dignity, accountability, responsiveness and openness of their multi-party system of a democratic government.[37] These are the values that shape South Africa as a nation and guide it towards attaining its national vision. The people of Zimbabwe face a momentous task of formulating constitutional values that will bind and guide them as a nation into the future as a multi-party state that respects its citizens' fundamental rights.

The failure of the existing Constitution to guarantee the establishment of an independent broadcasting regulator may also be a contributing factor towards the allegedly discriminatory behaviour of the ZBC, because the Broadcasting Authority of Zimbabwe (BAZ) is structurally weak and cannot impose sanctions on the public broadcaster for any violation of the Broadcasting Services Act. Paragraph (d) of The Seventh Schedule of the Broadcasting Services Act requires, among other things, that the public broadcaster should:

> provide news and public affairs programming which meets the highest standards of journalism and which is fair and unbiased and independent from government, commercial or other interests.

The first major challenge is that both the ZBC and the BAZ are controlled by the same minister, and as such the BAZ may find it politically embarrassing to impose sanctions on another entity that is controlled by the same minister. Situations of this nature may be avoided if the BAZ's independence was guaranteed by the Constitution. Regulatory independence would certainly minimise the risk of ministerial interference in the regulation of the broadcasting sector. A similar provision to Section 192 of the South African Constitution would be useful.

It provides for the:

> establishment of an independent authority to regulate broadcasting in the public interest and to ensure fairness and diversity of views broadly representing the South African society.

Whilst the Independent Communications Authority of South Africa (ICASA) has its own weaknesses, particularly those embedded in the ICASA Act that tend to compromise its independence, it has, on a number of occasions, been able to successfully deal with cases involving state enterprises such as the SABC and Telkom SA, including fair allocation of political broadcast airtime during election periods in South Africa.

In practice, an independent regulator would be able to co-ordinate issues pertaining to equitable access to broadcasting services by political parties and their candidates, including the development of a suitable formula for allocating broadcasting airtime and advertising slots, as well as for determining election advertising fees in consultation with the stakeholders concerned – broadcasters, political parties and the independent electoral commission.[38] The regulator will ensure broadcasters adhere to the 'cooling off' period, i.e., a complete ban on election advertising and political party broadcasting to 'allow for electors to consider their stance on the issues without the influences of electronic media advertising' in the days before votes are cast.[39]

An independent regulator will also be able to impose and enforce appropriate sanctions against a delinquent broadcaster. Here, it must be noted that the process of managing election broadcasts, including political party election broadcasts, requires engagement of all stakeholders to ensure that a fair, transparent and equitable election broadcasting code of practice is developed. This cannot be done by a single entity, as is currently the case in Zimbabwe.

The Broadcasting Services Act Amendment (BSAA) No. 19/2007
Consistent with the constitutional guarantees in Section 20 (1) of the Constitution of Zimbabwe, Section 2A (1) (d) (ii) of the BSAA provides that:

> broadcasting services in Zimbabwe, taken as a whole provide, must ensure public debate on political, social and economic issues of public interest, so as to foster and maintain a healthy plural democracy.

The significance of this objective is that it recognises the 'political duty' of the citizens to engage into political discourse as well as what the US court in *Whitney v California* termed 'the path of safety', something which allows citizens to discuss freely supposed grievances and proposed solutions and that it is hazardous to discourage thought, hope and imagination.[40] This should be the basis on which the public broadcaster is to avail equal access to the different political parties and other independent voices during an election period.

In other words, this provision places on broadcasters a statutory mandate to ensure that unhindered political debates are conducted on both radio and television. The media in general must facilitate public participation in matters of national interests, as observed by Langa CJ in *South African Broadcasting Corporation Ltd v National Director of Public Prosecution and Others*,[41] where the court noted that a vibrant media encourages citizens to be actively involved in public affairs and to derive the benefits that flow from living in a democracy.[42] Implicit in this provision is the concept of equal access to the media, the doctrine of fairness and issues pertaining to right of reply. A conversation can only be considered debate if it involves opposing views expressed in free and unhindered discourse on a particular issue of interest. Hence the argument that both Section 20 (1) of the Constitution as read with Section 2 A (1) (d) (ii) implies access to the means of receiving and imparting information, ideas and opinions.[43]

As it is the right of the public and not of the broadcaster that is paramount,[44] it is imperative that the public broadcaster be fair in the manner in which it covers and reports on issues of public interest. The ultimate goal of the Broadcasting Services Act is the 'fostering of a healthy plural democracy', but if the public broadcaster muzzles voices that oppose the government of the day it suppresses the ideals of free expression as identified by the Supreme Court of Zimbabwe, namely:

- To help an individual to obtain self-fulfilment
- To assist in the discovery of truth
- To strengthen the capacity of an individual to participate in decision-making
- To provide a mechanism by which it would be possible to establish a reasonable balance between stability and social change.[45]

A further challenge for Zimbabwe during this transitional period is the control that the Minister of Information has over the public broadcaster that weakens its editorial independence and influences its political slant. In terms of the ZBC (Commercialisation) Act No. 26 of 2001, the minister is tasked with a number of responsibilities over the public broadcaster. Section 3 requires the minister to ensure the formation of two successor companies to the former parastatal. In terms of Section 5, he is empowered to nominate shareholders in the successor companies on behalf of the government. This effectively made the Minister of Information the shareholder representative by virtue of the initial shareholders being mere nominees who have no power to appoint or elect anybody to the board of directors of the new successor companies. Section 5 (2) provides that 'Any person so appointed to hold shares, shall do so nominally as an agent for the State', thus disempowering nominees from exercising what would ordinarily be shareholder powers by ensuring that such powers remain vested in the state as represented by the minister. As a result, the minister is able to appoint members of the board of directors of the two companies and continue to have influence over the activities of the public broadcaster.

Section 8 of this Act further empowers the minister to issue directions to the boards of the successor companies, including a very wide provision in Section 8 (c) providing for the:

> production of any report and the provision of any information concerning the conduct of the Corporation or the Board or anything done by or on behalf of the Corporation or the Board.

The tone of Section 8 cited above is peremptory, affording them no room to question the minster's directives. A later part of this Section 8 reads: 'the Board shall without delay comply with every such direction', which gives it no time to establish or question the rationale behind the minister's directives. Moreover, the minister's powers even extend to matters pertaining to contracts of employment or the determination of whom the ZBC is able to employ.

As a consequence, the powers that the minister exerts over the ZBC fall foul of the spirit of Section 2A 1 (d) and (f) of the BSAA referred to above. The minister being a political appointee with allegiance to a particular political party raises issues of conflict of his or her interests with those of the general public, particularly with regard to media freedom and the need for balanced, fair and impartial broadcasting that obliges the demands for diversity of views. This problem is exacerbated by the fact that the same minister is not only the policy-maker for the broadcasting sector[46] but also controls the BAZ, its regulatory authority. The minister is thus effectively the referee and a player. This 'double-faced' structure does not augur well for the independence and impartiality of the public broadcaster. The statistics from the 2008 MMPZ report support this argument, and as such the Janus-like powers of the minister are a potential hazard to plural democracy. As a negation of the spirit of Section 2A of the BSAA, they must be done away with.

Legal reforms are needed urgently. The selection process for members of the board of directors of the public broadcaster as well as the BAZ must be transparent and be carried out independently by a parliamentary committee set up for this purpose. The potential candidates should also be publicly interviewed. The appointment of the Board should then be done by the President of the Republic or the minister with the approval of the Parliamentary Committee. The board of the public broadcaster must report to a parliamentary committee on an annual basis in order to enhance its independence. The Constitution and the relevant sector legislation and regulations must guarantee editorial independence of the public broadcaster as well as the independence of the BAZ, the regulator.

With regard to the nature of this independence, William Melody explains that it:

> does not imply independence from government policy, or usurping the power to make policy, but rather independence to implement policy without undue interference from politicians and industry lobbyists. (Melody, 1997:195-9)

The suggested approach of appointing board members of both the public operator and the regulator would give the board members some sense of independence because they would have earned their appointments not by being known to the President or the minister but through a credible and rigorous public process that is transparent and based on merit as opposed to political affiliation. The assumption, therefore, is that a process of this nature would be an essential ingredient of media independence, which in turn would allow for equal access by a diversity of voices to the airwaves. This process is not uncommon. For instance, Section 13 of the Broadcasting Act No. 4 of 1999 of South Africa provides that the 12 non-executive members of the board of the SABC must be appointed by the President on the advice of the National Assembly. Section 13 (2) provides that the appointment of the non-executive members of the Board shall be done by way of public participation in the nomination process which must be transparent and open and that the shortlist must be gazetted for the public to see. Finally, the board of the SABC is also legally charged with the responsibility of protecting matters referred to in Section 6 (2) of the same Act, which provides that:

> In terms of this Charter, the Corporation will in pursuit of its objectives and in exercise of its powers, enjoy freedom of expression and journalistic, creative and programming independence.

This provision is a guarantee of the independence of the public broadcaster, and it also guarantees editorial independence, which is one of the essential conditions for healthy plural democracy.

Although legislation is critical as a basis for ensuring the independence of media, it may not be enough to guarantee independence in general or even that of the public broadcaster. M.E. Price and P. Krug have argued that 'For free media to work, the community in question must value the role that the media play.'[47] Therefore, unless there is a change of attitude in our politicians and the citizens alike, the goal of a free media able to give birth to equal access to the media by different political formations and voices may remain out of reach. Rob Atkinson also argues that 'creating a civil society by legal fiat is an impossible bootstrap operation, both practically and conceptually'.[48]

As argued before, this process will require the de-institutionalisation of the public broadcaster from certain political ideologies and practices and the new Constitution setting out the much-needed foundational values of a new Zimbabwe based on our previous experiences, and to which the nation will commit itself through a referendum.

The language used in Section 2 A (2) of the BSAA, which requires the BAZ, the minister and all other persons required or permitted to exercise functions under this law to 'pay regard' to the objectives of the Act as they exercise functions under the Act, is loose and potentially subject to abuse. The use of the term 'pay regard' on a matter of importance like media independence could undermine the good intentions of the key objectives given in this section, as to pay regard to something means to merely take cognizance or recognition of something but not to oblige compliance with the requirements of a particular situation. This phrase, among others, does not impose a mandatory duty on the persons entrusted with functions under the BSSA to comply with the provisions of Section 2 A (1).

The Regulatory Authority

The degree of independence that a sector regulator enjoys also has an impact on how that regulator deals with incumbent operators. The weaker the regulator, the more the incumbent operator may exercise liberties that exceed the law with impunity. Independence in this regard means independence from both the operator(s) and government interference to the extent that the regulator is captured by neither, making the former pliable or easily manipulated in decision-making.

This challenge does not end with legislative redress; it also depends on the regulatory design and how other institutions support the regulatory structure. As Irene Wu notes, 'the challenge of regulatory independence is to design a regulatory institution that is insulated from the vagaries of politics'.[49] Regrettably, most governments mistrust the concept of regulatory independence and as such there is always a desire to control the regulator and manipulate its functions. A case in point is that of *Altech Autopage Cellular (Pty) Ltd v The Chairperson of ICASA, Minister of Communications and Others*[50] in which the South African minister was accused of unduly influencing ICASA by issuing it with concrete directives on how it was to handle specific issues even though the latter's independence is specifically entrenched in the Constitution.[51]

The BAZ appears to exist only in name and has not been able to discharge its full regulatory mandate because of the powers the Minister of Information has over it. As neither the Constitution nor the enabling legislation guarantees the independence of the BAZ, the market is a *de facto* monopoly, one which is wholly controlled by government. This is a fertile seedbed for undue government influence that is to the detriment of freedom of speech and access to media by government critics and opposition political voices.

The weaknesses of BAZ are exacerbated by a number of issues, including the following:

1. *The nature of board appointments* – As already mentioned, the process by which members of the BAZ Board are appointed is not transparent. Section 4 (2) (a) provides that 'Subject to sub-Section (3) the Board shall consist of twelve (12) members, of whom:

> The following nine (9) members shall be appointed by the President after consultation with the Minister and the Committee on Standing Rules and Orders.

> Three (3) members shall be appointed by the President from a list of six (6) nominees submitted by the Committee on Standing Rules and Orders.

The questions that arise are; where do these prospective board members' names come from? Where and how are these people identified? Is it on the basis of political affiliation or competence? Although the Act sets out criteria as to who qualifies to be appointed to the board, the other questions raised above remain unanswered. There is no obligation on the part of the President or the minister to interview the candidates on their personal philosophies and views on freedom of expression even though they may be engaged to regulate a sector that must be driven by the ideals of free speech. The conclusion may be that such appointments are based on 'who knows who' and not necessarily on merit. Nor does the requirement to consult necessarily guarantee that the appointments will be based on merit. Thus there is no transparency in the selection and nomination process of the members of the board of the regulator.

2. *Powers to dismiss* – The fact that Section 1 (3) of the Third Schedule allows the minister to fix the terms and conditions of the Board is an ingredient for board manipulation and is potentially detrimental to free political speech. This is particularly so if Section 4 (1) (b) is taken into account, as this empowers the minister to require any member to vacate their office if they fail to comply with his or her terms and conditions. What is important to note here is that there are no guidelines set out to assist the minister in formulating the latter. This task is left entirely to the discretion of the minister and it is not unusual for discretionary powers to be abused, particularly in politics.

Nor are summary dismissals healthy for the independence and effective functioning of public bodies. If members know that they are subject to summary dismissals, then they are more likely to take decisions that will please their principals.

3. Regulatory and policy-making powers of the minister – There appears to be no separation between the policy-making powers of the minister and the regulatory powers of the board. By virtue of the provisions of Section 46 (6) of the BSAA, the minister has absolute control over broadcasting regulatory functions, and although the BSAA attempted to dilute these by bequeathing them to the board of the BAZ, Section 46 (6) restores the same powers to the minister by ensuring that no regulation, order or notice made under Section 46 (2) of the Act will have effect unless approved by the minister and published in *The Government Gazette*. As the minister will not approve any regulation, order or notice that he/she disagrees with, Section 46 (6) obliterates the functional divide between the minister as a policy-maker[52] and the regulatory functions of BAZ.[53] Effectively, then, the minister makes sector-specific policies and regulates the broadcasting sector, thereby making the BAZ structurally weak and all but irrelevant.

As Zimbabwe moves forward, there must clear and separate responsibilities between the minister and the regulator. The role of the minister must be limited to that of policy-maker if the regulator is to gain strength and implement policies fairly as it executes its statutory functions. The structural handicap that is embedded in the BSAA must therefore be removed. If the regulator remains and the minister has the power to control the public operator, there will always be room to manipulate the public media for political ends.

4. Election broadcasts – Section 2 (1) of the Fifth Schedule guarantees reasonable and equal opportunities for broadcasting election matters during an election period. The treatment of political parties in respect of both forms of broadcast transmissions must also be equal and fair. This, however, can only be achieved where there is an agreed formula for calculation and allocation of airtime and time slots to political parties during an election period. (And as long as a political party is willing to pay for election broadcasts, it must be given the opportunity to do so.) However, one of the BSAA's shortcomings is that it has no such formula in place.

Moreover, the allocation of election broadcast airtime is a process that requires wider engagement involving political parties, the BAZ, the Zimbabwe Electoral Commission and the broadcasters. Ideally, it should be the responsibility of an impartial regulatory body.

Under South African Law, this matter is left in the hands of ICASA, which, in terms of Section 57 (2), (3) and (4) of the Electronic Communications Act No. 36 of 2005, is required to determine the time to be made available to political parties, including the duration and scheduling of party election broadcasts in consultation with the parties concerned. In the UK, Ofcom, the communications sector regulator overseeing telecommunications and broadcasting, is empowered to regulate election broadcasts in terms of Section 333 of the Communications Act, 2003. It appears that the major reason for putting this responsibility on the shoulders of the sector regulators is that they are empowered by law to impose sanctions on any delinquent operator under their jurisdiction.

The Zimbabwean situation, however, is more intricate. Statutory Instrument 33 of 2008 gives the ZEC very wide and undefined powers and the BAZ has jurisdiction over the public broadcaster. In addition, there are practical and conceptual problems between general regulations and sector-specific regulations emanating from concurrent jurisdiction. The duplication of procedures creates delays, higher transaction costs and increased legal uncertainty for the operators, and 'from a public policy perspective overlapping authority is costly in that it creates duplication of resources and weakens confidence in national regulatory authorities'.[54] Regulatory uncertainty is undesirable and negates the principles of the rule of law which require that the laws must not only be predictable but certain. This responsibility must reside with one regulator, in this case an independent and reformed BAZ.

Election broadcasts and election advertisements

Under Zimbabwean law, election broadcasts are those contemplated by the provision of Section 2(1) of the Fifth Schedule to the Broadcasting Services Act, while election advertisements are defined in Section 3

(1) and (2) of the same Act. This distinction should only matter when it relates to which of the two is to be provided as a public service programme and which one should be paid for. Ordinarily, political party election broadcasts are free of charge, but Section 2 (2) gives the public broadcaster an option to charge. The Act is silent on the sanctions that may be imposed for violating the law.

Other forms of political party advertising

A phenomenon that has arisen in Zimbabwe is that of political praise songs being produced by choirs such as the Mbare Chimurenga Choir.[55]

In the past, ZANU-PF produced songs that sought to promote their party agenda, for example, 'Nora' by the late Elliot Manyika.[56] These songs focus on praising certain political leaders and are usually given unlimited broadcast time. Any broadcast material that seeks to praise a political leader or political party should generally be banned unless it is during an election period in which event the rules applicable to either political party election broadcasts or election advertisement would apply. This is intended to ensure that no one voice is heard on radio or television that might give unfair advantage to one political party over the others. A prohibition of this nature will be based on equity and fair treatment of political parties. These occurrences in Zimbabwe point to a weak legal and regulatory broadcast framework.

Statutory Instrument Number 33 of 2008

This Statutory Instrument also refers to the concept of 'equitable' treatment of political parties, defining it as 'fair treatment' with respect to news, current affairs and discussion programmes accorded to political parties and candidates.[57] The difficulty that arises from this definition is that the term 'fair treatment' is fluid, relative and lacks concreteness particularly when the Statutory Instrument itself excludes 'equal treatment' of political parties and candidates from its scope of application. This potentially creates a risk of unequal treatment of political parties because they do not necessarily have to have equal access to the broadcasting medium and broadcasting time. The definition provided by the Malawian High Court in *Dr Charles Kafumba and 2 Others v the Electoral Commission and the Malawi Broadcasting Corporation*[58] (supra) that:

if campaign messages are broadcast live at a presidential function, then equal treatment means that campaign rallies of other political parties or at least the presidential candidates be broadcast live. That would give other political parties or at least campaign rallies of other candidates an opportunity to reply to matters raised.

According to this judgment then, 'equal treatment' of political parties is a component of a free and fair election. On the basis of this reasoning, fair treatment minus equal treatment of political parties may negatively affect the standard of a free and fair election as political parties may not have equal opportunity to reach out to the electorate. This may be made worse by a partisan media that is given statutory powers to allocate broadcast times and airtime slots to the political parties during an election period.

Again, Section 4 (1) of the SI 33/2008 requires the public broadcaster to ensure that contesting political parties or candidates are treated 'equitably' in the allocation of airtime for broadcasting election matters. The guidance of what 'equitably' means is in Section 2 (1) of the same Statutory Instrument, as explained before.

Terms such as 'fair treatment' and 'equal treatment' are legal standards that lack precision and must therefore be referenced to some kind of acceptable and agreed standard. In *ADF v United States*, a tribunal pointed out that 'the requirement to accord fair and equitable treatment does not allow a tribunal to adopt its own idiosyncratic standard but must be disciplined by being based upon state practice and judicial or arbitral case law or other sources of customary or general international law'.[59]

The shortcoming of Statutory Instrument (SI) 33 of 2008 is that it does not provide any legal guarantees for equitable access to the public broadcaster. The question then is how is the public broadcaster expected to implement this concept without any agreed or acceptable standard or measure as a point of reference? The downside under Zimbabwean law is that as 'fair treatment' excludes 'equal treatment' from its scope of application, how then can fairness be achieved if contesting parties are not treated equally? While it is commendable that a basis for equitable treatment of political parties with regard to broadcasting election matters exists under Zimbabwean law, the downside of the matter is that there are no guidelines to help in determining the standards of equitable treatment.

The importance of allocating time slots and airtime

Presumably, the answer to how the equitable treatment of political parties may be achieved lies in defining a clear formula for the allocation of time slots and airtime on both radio and television, as this would minimise the dangers of one political party's voice being heard on radio and television simply because it happens to be awash with funds. The opportunity to access broadcast media should be equally available to all political parties registered to participate in an election and the advertising rates be heavily subsidised because of the public interest element attached to national elections. Section 4 (2) provides that a public broadcaster shall, during an election period, allocate advertising airtime on television and radio to a political party or candidate contesting an election upon payment by the party or candidate of the amounts stipulated by the broadcaster of the broadcasting of elections advertisements generally.

Indeed, the court in *R (On Application of Animal Defenders) v Secretary of the State for Culture, Media and Sport* (supra) observed that the democratic playing field of debate cannot be achieved if:

> political parties can, in proportion to their resources, buy unlimited opportunities to advertise in the most effective media, so that elections become little more than an auction. The risk is that objects which are essentially political may come to be accepted by the public not because they are shown in public debate to be right but because, by dint of constant repetition, the public has been conditioned to accept them.[60]

There is a legal lacuna between Sections 4(1) and (2) of SI 33 in that they do not state how election advertising time is calculated or allocated to the participating registered political parties. A defined formula for so doing would guide the public broadcaster in implementing the provisions of Section 4(2) of SI 33.

Section 6 (1) of SI 33 attempts to provide some basis for allocating broadcast airtime by setting aside a total of four hours of purchasable airtime during an election period for election advertisements. However, what remains unaddressed is how to allocate the four hours, especially taking into account that fair treatment of political parties does not necessarily mean equitable treatment. Circumstances of this nature will more often than not lead to one political party being given preferential treatment, thus negating the spirit of equity. Statutory Instrument 33 therefore negates the objective of a healthy plural democracy the Broadcasting Services Act underscores.

In addition, by placing the burden of allocating broadcast airtime to the political parties on the public broadcaster, the ZEC appears to have partially abdicated its constitutional mandate of ensuring free and fair elections. This is not, however, to suggest that the ZEC should itself allocate said airtimes and slots but that it should take a leading role in bringing together all the stakeholders for purposes of agreeing on a formula for so doing during an election period.

The public must be protected from a monopoly of political advertisements of all forms.

The rejection of political party broadcasting programmes

Section 6 (5) provides that:

> A broadcaster may reject an advertisement submitted for transmission and if it does so it shall provide written reasons for the rejection within twenty-four (24) hours to the concerned political party or candidate.

In the first instance, this provision may have a negative impact on access to broadcast media, especially in circumstances where broadcasting standards have not been given upfront by the public broadcaster. Generally, there is nothing wrong in rejecting a particular election advertisement where it does not meet broadcasting standards or potentially violates the law by advocating violence, hatred, racism and other forms of discrimination and prejudices.[61] However, concerns may arise, particularly with regard to broadcasting standards, where the broadcaster does not provide a 'checklist' of what is required.

Another difficulty is that a broadcaster has the right to reject without providing reasons for so doing at the time. Although the delay of 24 hours provided for in SI 33 appears not to be unreasonable, the issue is that being able to reject a broadcast transmission programme without explanation may encourage abuse, especially where a particular broadcaster has a slant over one of the political contestants.

This chapter positions itself as advocating for anti-censorship and as such the right to refuse an election advertisement *prima facie* amounts to pre-publication censorship, which is a violation of Section 20 of the Constitution of Zimbabwe. Tom Lewis observed that political speech in Europe has generally received a high degree of protection from the European Court due to its importance in maintaining democracy.[62]

Because of the importance of the freedom of speech, election advertisements should only be rejected if they violate broadcasting codes, programming standards or the law, and reasons for any rejection must be provided together with the notification of rejection. Broadcast standards must, as argued above, be provided to enable all political parties to ensure their programmes are in compliance. Indeed, Section 24 (1) of the Broadcasting Services Act requires the BAZ to develop a code of conduct and programme standards in consultation with broadcasting licensees. Where there is such a code or set of standards, censorship through biased rejection could be avoided.

The key challenge facing Zimbabwe and the broadcast media is ensuring that this option to reject cannot be abused by the public broadcaster in order to curtail political speech. Political speech lies at the core of forms of speech that require greater protection, unlike speech or expression such as pornography. Tom Lewis argues that:

> there is an apparent hierarchy or gradation of expression, with political or journalistic expression involving public interest at the top.[63]

Although Lewis's views on this matter were rejected by the House of Lords, he nevertheless made a very important contribution to the protection of political speech. The Court of Appeal in *Prolife Alliance* (supra) observed that 'freedom of expression is plainly ... a constitutional right, and its enjoyment by an accredited political party in an election contest must call if anything for especially heightened protection'.[64]

SECTION IV

Recommendations and Conclusion

Media reform is an immediate imperative in this transitional phase. The legal and regulatory framework that exists in Zimbabwe does not fully support the exercise of free political speech by all but allows for abuse by those in government. It is now commonly accepted that free political speech is a necessary condition for a healthy plural democracy. As both the media and the public must discharge this 'political duty', it is vital that all political voices must have equal access to the broadcast media and engage each other in unhindered political discourse. This is the 'safe path' that will secure the stability of the state through protecting plural democracy.

Reforms must start with the Constitution in order to provide for the establishment of an independent media regulator with little or no direct control from the executive. The regulatory design must be such that the regulator will not be entirely dependent on the state for funding but be able to generate its own income from licence fees and other income associated with regulation. The board of the regulator must also be appointed through a transparent public process that involves public participation. Rather than reporting directly to the Minister of Information, it must report to Parliament. The legal reforms must also provide for a clear separation between the policymaking powers of the minister and the regulatory functions of the broadcast regulator.

Similarly, the independence of the public broadcaster must be statutorily guaranteed, including its structural design, which must exclude direct appointment by the minister or the President. The public broadcaster must also account to Parliament. Reforms vis-à-vis the public broadcaster must thus include a restructuring process that removes political appointees from the editorial rooms and curtails ministerial influence over the board of directors and its functions.

The regulation of election broadcasts must come under a new and independent media regulator who should be involved in engaging all the stakeholders, for example, the public broadcaster, all registered political parties, and the ZEC, in order to work out a formula which can be used to allocate airtime amounts and time slots for both political party election broadcasts (not paid for) and election advertisements (paid for). This is necessary in order to give all political parties equal access to the broadcast media. The sanctions for violating election broadcast rules must be clear and appropriately punitive so as to discourage potential abuse.

The inevitable summation of all this is that an independent broadcast media is a precondition for a healthy plural democracy and is among the main challenges for Zimbabwe. Until this is achieved, voices of opposition and of those critical of the government of the day will continue to be shackled and muted through media monopoly and manipulation for political gains, regardless of who is in power.

Notes

1 Lord Bingham of Cornhill, *R (On the application of Animal Defenders International) v Secretary of State for Culture, Media and Sport*, [2008] 3 ALL ER 193 at p. 207.
2 Ibid.
3 *Khumalo v Holomisa* 2002 (5) SA 401 (CC) at paras 21-25.
4 See fn1 (above), p. 207.
5 'Development of Democracy idea in European Traditions'. See www. see-ucoop.net/education_in/pdf/civic_edu_book_part1_bul-enl-107.pdf. Accessed 17 January 2011.
6 274 U.S.357, 375-6.
7 *Khumalo v Holomisa*, paras 21-25.
8 *United States v Associated Press*, 52 F.Supp.362, 372(D.C.S.D.N.Y. 1943).
9 *New York Times Co. v Sullivan,* 376 U.S. 254 (1964). See also *Roth v United States* 354 U.S. 476, 484.
10 Andrew Moyse, 'The Media Environment Leading up to Zimbabwe's 2008 Elections', p. 44. See www.kas.de/upload/dokumente//2010/05/ Defying_3. pdf. Accessed 26 January 2011.
11 'The ogre of Harare', 28 March 2008. See www.ivo.co.za/2008/03/28/ the-ogre-of-harare. Accessed 26 January 2011.
12 *Murphy v Ireland* (2003), 38 EHRR 212 at para 69.
13 'Tsvangirai withdraws from Zimbabwe elections'. See www.eurostep. org/wcm/archive-eurostep-weekly/291-tsvangirai-withdraws-from-zimbabweelections.html. Accessed 27 January 2011.
14 Note 6, above.
15 Media Monitoring Project Zimbabwe, 'Report on the Coverage of March and June 2008 Elections in Zimbabwe'. See www.kubatana.net/docs/media/ mmpz_zbc_election_coverage_080804.pdf. Accessed 17 January 2011.
16 *Freedom of Expression Institute v Chairman, Complaints and Compliance Committee and Independent Communications Authority of South Africa and the South African Broadcasting Corporation* Case No.2009/51933 South Gauteng High Court (Johannesburg) at para 88.
17 Note 15, above.
18 www.mediaombudsmannamibia.org/downloads/Guidelines_and_Princi ples_for_Broadcast_Coverage_of_Elections_in_the_SADC_Region.pdf. Accessed 17 January 2011.
19 Note 16, above.
20 Note 18, above, paras 16-22.
21 Ibid., para 88.
22 *Dr Charles Kafumba and 2 Others v The Electoral Commission and The*

Malawi Broadcasting Corporation, Misc. Cause No. 35 of 1999 (High Court of Malawi).

23 Ibid.

24 Ibid.

25 Section 2A (f) of the Broadcasting Services Act (Chapter 12:06)

26 Professor Frank Chalk, 'Radio Propaganda and Genocide' November 1999, Montreal Institute of Genocide and Human Rights. See www.migs. concordia.ca/occpapers/radio_pr.html. Accessed 28 January 2011.

27 Ibid.

28 Kalinga Seneviratne and Sundeep R. Muppidi, 'Media Pluralism and Editorial Independence: A case study approach to public service broadcasting in Asia'. See www.uhaweb.hartford.edu/MUPPIDI/Media%20Pluralism Introduction%20Final.pdf. Accessed 28 January 2011.

29 Note 6, above.

30 *Retrofit (Pvt) Ltd v Posts and Telecommunications Corporation (Attorney-General intervening)* 1995 (9) BCLR 1262 (Z) at p. 1264.

31 395 US 367 (1969) at 390.

32 Melody, W. H., Policy Objectives and Models of Regulation, Chapter 2 in Melody, W.H. ed., (1997) *Telecom Reform: Principles, Policies and Regulatory Practices.* 1 pp. 11–24 at p. 12 www.lirne.net/test/wp-content/ uploads/2007/02/telecomreform.pdf. Accessed 29 January 2011.

33 Vienna Declaration and Programme of Action (the Vienna Declaration), June 1993, UN Doc. A/CONF. 157/23, Part I [5].

34 *New York Times Co. v Sullivan*, 376 U.S. 254 (1964) at 377.

35 *In Re: Munhumeso* 1995 (1) (ZSC) at 557, 1995 (2) BCLR 125.

36 *Red Lion* Case (supra).

37 Section 1 of the Constitution of the Republic of South Africa No. 108 of 1996.

38 Section 57 (2) and (3) of the Electronic Communications Act No. 36 of 2005.

39 Dr Sarah Miskin and Dr Richard Grant, 'Political advertising in Australia'. See www.aph.gov.au/Library/pubs/rb/2004-05/05rb05.pdf. Accessed 9 February 2011.

40 274 U.S. 357,375-376.

41 2007 (1) SA 512 (CC).

42 Ibid at para 28.

43 Retrofit case (supra).

44 *Red Lion Broadcasting Company Inc v The Federal Communications Commission* 395 US 367, at 386-90.

45 *In re Munhumeso* 1995 (2) BCLR 125 (ZS).

46 Section 4B of the Broadcasting Services Act, Chapter 12:06.

47 Monroe E. Price and Peter Krug, 'The enabling environment for free and independent media: Contribution to Transparent and Accountable

Government', January 2002, p. 5.

48 Rob Atkinson, 'A dissenter's Commentary on the Professionalism Crusade', 74 *Texas Law Review* 259, p. 297 (1995).

49 Irene Wu, 'Traits of an Independent Communications Regulator: A Search for Indicators, With Teaching Module on Ethics and Corruption', see www. ictregulationtoolkit.org/en/Document.2849.pdf. Accessed 21 September 2009.

50 Case No. 20002/08.

51 Ibid., paras 5.9 and 5.20.

52 Section 4B of the Broadcasting Service Act, Chapter 12:06.

53 Section 46 (2) of the Broadcasting Services Act, Chapter 12:06.

54 Liyang Hou, 'Conflicts between Competition Law and Regulation in the EC Electronic Communications Sector: An Analysis of the Institutional Framework', p. 5. See www.papers.ssrn.com/sol3/papers.cfm?abstract_ id=1025403. Accessed 9 October 2009.

55 'Mbare Chimurenga Choir Does it Again!', www.zimpapers.co.zw/ news categories/entertainment/133-mbare-chimurenga-choir. Accessed 4 February 2011.

56 'Elliot Manyika dies in mysterious accident'. Available at www. zimbabwemetro. com/news/elliot-manyika-dies-in-mysterious-accident/. Accessed 10 February 2011.

57 Section 2 (1) of Statutory Instrument 33 of 2008.

58 Note 23 above.

59 *ADF Group Inc v United State of America* (ADF Group), Award, 9 January 2003, 61 CSID Reports, 470, paras 175-8, quoted by Christopher Schreuer, 'Fair and Equitable Treatment in Arbitral Practice', *The Journal of World Investment and Trade*, Vol. 6, No. 3, June 2005, Geneva, p. 365.

60 p. 207 para 28.

61 Section 5 (3) of Statutory Instrument 33 of 2008.

62 Tom Lewis, 'Democracy, Free Speech and TV: The Case of BBC and the ProLife Alliance', Web Journal of Current Legal Issues, [2004] 5 Web JCLI, www.webcli.ncl.ac.uk/2004/issue5/tlewis5.html. Accessed 17 January 2011.

63 Ibid.

64 Tom Lewis, 'Democracy, Free Speech and TV, The Case of the BBC and Prolife Alliance', www.webjcli.ncl.ac.uk/2004/issue5/tlewis5.html. Accessed 2 May 2011. See ProLife Alliance (supra).

References

Atkinson, R. 1995. 'A dissenter's Commentary on the Professionalism Crusade', 74 Texas Law Review, 74, p. 259.

Chalk, F.,. 1999. 'Radio Propaganda and Genocide', Montreal Institute of Genocide and Human Rights. November. Available at www.migs. concordia.ca/occpapers/radio_pr.html

Hou, L. 2009. 'Conflicts between Competition Law and Regulation in the EC Electronic Communications Sector: An Analysis of the Institutional Framework', p. 5. Available at www.papers.ssrn.com/sol3/papers.cfm?abstract_id=1025403

Lewis, T. 2004. 'Democracy, Free Speech and TV: The Case of BBC and the ProLife Alliance', Web Journal of Current Legal Issues, 5. Available at www.webcli.ncl.ac.uk/2004/issue5/tlewis5.html

Melody, W.H. 1997. 'Policy Objectives and Models of Regulation', in W.H. Melody (ed.). 1997. *Telecom Reform: Principles, Policies and Regulatory Practices.* Available at www.lirne.net/test/wp-content/uploads/2007/02/telecomreform.pdf.

—. 1997. 'On the meaning and importance of 'independence' in telecom reform', Telecommunications Policy, Vol. 21, Issue 3, April, pp. 195-9.

Miskin, S. and R. Grant. 2004. 'Political advertising in Australia'. Available at www.aph.gov.au/Library/pubs/rb/2004-05/05rb05.pdf

Moyse, A. 2010. 'The Media Environment Leading Up to Zimbabwe's 2008 Elections'. Available at www.kas.de/upload/dokumente//2010/05/Defying_3.pdf, p. 44.

Price, M.E. and P. Krug. 2002. 'The enabling environment for free and independent media: Contribution to Transparent and Accountable Government', January, p. 5. Available at www. global.asc.upenn.edu/fileLibrary/PDFs/ENABLING_ENV.pdf

Schreuer, C. 2005. 'Fair and Equitable Treatment in Arbitral Practice', The Journal of World Investment and Trade, Vol. 6, No. 3, June, p. Seneviratne, K. and S.R. Muppidi. undated. 'Media Pluralism and Editorial Independence: A case study approach to public service broadcasting in Asia'. Available at www.uhaweb.hartford.edu/MUPPIDI/Media%20Plural ismIntroduction%20Final.pdf

Wu, I. 2004. 'Traits of an Independent Communications Regulator: A Search for Indicators, With Teaching Module on Ethics and Corruption'. Available at www.ictregulationtoolkit.org/en/Document.2849.pdf

Other Internet articles

'The ogre of Harare', 28 March 2008, www.ivo.co.za/2008/03/28/the-ogre-of-harare

'Development of Democracy idea in European Traditions', www.see ucoop.net/education in/pdf/civic_edu_book_part1_bul-enl-107.pdf

'Tsvangirai withdraws from Zimbabwe elections', www.eurostep. org/wcm/archive-eurostep-weekly/291-tsvangirai-withdraws-from-zimbabwe-elections.html

Media Monitoring Project Zimbabwe, 'Report on the Coverage of March and June 2008 Elections in Zimbabwe', www.kubatana.net/docs/media/mmpz_zbc_election_coverage_080804.pdf

'Mbare Chimurenga Choir Does it Again'!, www.zimpapers.co.zw/news categories/entertainment/133-mbare-chimurenga-choir

'Elliot Manyika dies in mysterious accident', www.zimbabwemetro.com/news/elliot-manyika-dies-in-mysterious-accident

Case law

Zimbabwe

Retrofit. Pvt. Ltd v Posts and Telecommunications Corporation. Attorney-General intervening. 1995. 9. BCLR 1262. Z).

In Re: Munhumeso 1995. 1. ZSC. at 557, 1995. 2. BCLR 125.

South Africa

Khumalo v Holomisa 2002. 5. SA 401. CC).

Freedom of Expression Institute v Chairman, Complaints and Compliance Committee and Independent Communications Authority of South Africa and the South African Broadcasting Corporation Case No. 2009/51933. South Gauteng High Court. Johannesburg).

Altech Autopage Cellular. Pty. Ltd vote Chairperson of ICASA, Minister of Communications and Others Case No. 20002/08.

South African Broadcasting Corporation Ltd v National Director of Public Prosecution and Others 2007. 1. SA 512. CC).

Malawi

Dr Charles Kafumba and 2 Others v The Electoral Commission and The Malawi Broadcasting Corporation, Misc. Cause No. 35 of 1999. High Court of Malawi).

United Kingdom

R. On the Application of Animal Defenders International. v Secretary of State for Culture, Media and Sport [2008] 3 ALL ER 193.

R. On the Application of ProLife Alliance. v BBC [2002] EWCA Civ 297; [2002] 3 WLR 1080.

R. On the Application of Prolife Alliance. v BBC [2003] UKHL 23; [2003] 1 AC 185.

R. On the Application of Animal Defenders v Secretary of State for Culture, Media and Sport [2008] 3 All ER 193 [2008] UKHL 15.

European Court

Murphy v Ireland. 2003. 38 EHRR 212.

Vgt Vereingegen Tierfabriken v Switzerland. 2001. 10 BHRC 473, ECtHR.

United States of America

ADF Group Inc v United States of America Award, 9 January 2003, 61 CSID Reports 470.

Whitney v California 274 US 357.

New York Times v Sullivan 376 US 254.

Roth v United States of America 354 US 476.

Red Lion Broadcasting Co. Inc. and Others v Federal Communications-Commission et al. 395 US 367(1969).

United States v Associated Press 52 F.Supp.362.

3

Reflections on the Significance of Constitutions & Constitutionalism for Zimbabwe

Greg Linington

Introduction

What is the significance of a Constitution in the affairs of a state? Section 3 of Zimbabwe's current Constitution provides an answer: 'This Constitution is the supreme law of Zimbabwe and if any other law is inconsistent with this Constitution that other law shall, to the extent of the inconsistency, be void.' In other words, the Constitution is sovereign and all state organs operate *under* it, having only those powers it confers upon them, whether directly or by laws authorised by, and consistent with, it. Parliament, too, is subject to the Constitution. In *Chairman of the Public Service Commission and Others v Zimbabwe Teachers Association and Others*,[1] an important judgment handed down in 1996, Zimbabwe's Supreme Court said: 'Zimbabwe, unlike Great Britain, is not a parliamentary democracy. It is a constitutional democracy. The centrepiece of our democracy is not a sovereign parliament but a supreme law (the Constitution).'[2] In another Supreme Court decision, *Smith v Mutasa NO and Another*,[3] Enoch Dumbutshena, then Zimbabwe's Chief Justice, said: 'The Constitution of Zimbabwe is the supreme law of the land. It is true that Parliament is supreme in the legislative field assigned to it by the Constitution, but even then Parliament cannot step outside the bounds prescribed to it by the Constitution.'[4] Parliament can enact laws, but only because it is empowered to do so by the Constitution. Moreover, when exercising this power, Parliament must follow the procedural requirements set out in the Constitution.

The President is also a creature of the Constitution, at least as far as the law is concerned. That document establishes the powers of the office and the parameters within which they ought to be exercised. Those powers are currently vast and for the most part not subject to meaningful constitutional restraints.[5] Such restraints as do exist are often not upheld or enforced properly. This is a problem that lies at the heart of Zimbabwe's constitutional crisis and ought of course to be addressed during the Constitution-making process. Whether this will in fact happen remains to be seen.

The point was made above that laws inconsistent with the Constitution are void. This implies the existence of a mechanism for determining whether such inconsistency is present. That mechanism is the judiciary. In the course of deciding whether impugned laws are inconsistent with the Constitution, the courts – and particularly the Supreme Court – perform (or ought to perform) the broader function of acting as the guardians of the Constitution. Of course, in order to perform this function properly the judiciary must be a genuinely independent institution, manned by competent judges who conscientiously address matters brought before them. Ensuring that a truly independent judiciary is established and maintained is central to the Constitution-making process. In fact, the absence of an independent judiciary would in itself undermine the credibility of a new Constitution.

By assigning duties and responsibilities to government organs, a Constitution transforms *naked* power into *lawful* power.[6] The way in which the exercise of this power is limited and controlled is known as constitutionalism. That is, constitutionalism restricts *what* governments can do, and *how* they go about doing what they are authorised to do. The relationship between constitutionalism and democracy is not always an easy one, principally because a Constitution entrenching a particular system of constitutionalism is usually very difficult to change or amend. Normally, a legislature will only be empowered to amend a Constitution if it follows a special procedure involving a super (rather than a simple) majority. This does not sit easily with the idea that democracy means the rule of the majority. How are we to justify constitutionalism when it seems to thwart (at least on some issues) the will of the majority? This is what is known as the counter majoritarian dilemma.

Stephen Holmes, a proponent of the counter-majoritarian position, says that 'the basic function of a Constitution is to *remove* certain decisions from the [ordinary] democratic process, that is, to tie the community's hands'.[7] Citing American Supreme Court justice Robert Jackson in *West Virginia State Board of Execution v Barnette*, he says:

> The very purpose of a [Constitution is] to withdraw certain subjects from the vicissitudes of political controversy, to place them beyond the reach of majorities and officials and to establish them as legal principles to be applied by the courts. One's right to life, liberty and property, to free speech, a free press, freedom of worship and assembly, and other fundamental rights may not be submitted to vote: they depend on the outcome of no elections.[8]

Constitutionalism seeks to limit governmental power. As politicians – and the electorate – are often emotional and immature, it makes sense to prevent the fundamental values of a nation from being changed – or abolished – easily. If change is to occur it should only happen after mature reflection and debate, and with the support of a *large* (rather than simple) majority of the electorate.

Finally, a word about the 'rule of law'. The phrase is well-known, but what does it actually mean? Obviously, it alerts us to the fact that laws exist in a particular society. But it also indicates a legal system that incorporates certain standards. Thus, the rule *of* law means more than simply rule *by* law. Legal certainty, equality before the law, the absence of arbitrary power and the protection of basic human rights are all attributes of the rule of law.

What follows below is a discussion of a selected number of constitutional issues. The aim is to examine the extent to which constitutionalism operates in Zimbabwe, and to suggest how things could be improved under a new constitution. Of course, the discussion is not comprehensive, but it does at least draw attention to some of the very real problems that currently beset Zimbabwe's constitutional order.

How a new constitution will come into force

The government has declared that once the draft of a new Constitution has been completed, it will be submitted to a referendum. A similar procedure was followed in 1999 in respect of the draft produced by the then 'Constitutional Commission'. It is important to understand that while such a referendum may well be a *politically* significant event, it is not *legally* significant. In other words, whatever the outcome of the referendum, Parliament will be free to decide whether or not to pass the Draft Constitution into law.[9]

No new Constitution can come into force unless the requirements of section 52 of the current Constitution are complied with. That is the provision that deals with the procedure for amending the Constitution. It stipulates that a Constitutional Bill may not be introduced into either House of Parliament unless it 'has been published in the [government] *Gazette* not less than thirty days before it is so introduced'.[10] Constitutional Bills must receive affirmative votes from at least two-thirds of the entire membership of each House of Parliament.[11] (If the Senate fails to pass such a Bill, the House of Assembly can override the Senate,[12] hence the Senate's power is really just limited to delaying its passage).

What happens if the President fails to assent to a Constitutional Bill passed by Parliament? Section 51 of the Constitution, which deals with the exercise of legislative powers in general terms, states that 'a Bill' not assented to by the President must be returned to the House of Assembly. That will be the end of the Bill unless, within six months of receiving it from the President, the House resolves by the affirmative votes of at least two-thirds of its members, that the Bill should again be presented to the President.[13] If this happens, 'the President shall assent to the Bill within twenty-one days of the presentation, unless he sooner dissolves Parliament'.[14] The question that has to be considered is whether 'Bill,' as used in section 51, includes Constitutional Bills, or refers only to ordinary (i.e., non-Constitutional) Bills. A careful reading of section 51 seems to indicate that 'Bill' is a generic term that covers *all types* of Bills. Section 51 (3) says: 'Where this Constitution provides that a Bill of a specified description shall not be presented to the President for assent unless it is accompanied by a certificate, the President shall not assent to such Bill unless it is accompanied by the said certificate.' Ordinary Bills may be presented without such certificates, but Constitutional Bills *do* require certificates. Thus it is abundantly clear that section 51 covers *all* Bills. This is important because it means that the refusal of presidential assent can be overcome by the House of

Assembly. (It is, of course, rather absurd for the House to have to pass a resolution by a two-thirds majority vote to overturn a presidential veto of a Bill it had already passed by the same majority.)

The pardoning power

Section 31 I of Zimbabwe's current Constitution bears the heading 'Prerogative of Mercy'. The word 'prerogative' connotes a power that is immune to judicial scrutiny. Prerogative powers do not therefore sit easily with concepts like constitutionalism and the rule of law. In fact, 'prerogative' is an ugly word that has no place in a modern Constitution. It does, for example, not appear in the South African Constitution. Section 84 (2) (j) of that document simply says that 'the President is responsible for pardoning or reprieving offenders and remitting any fines, penalties or forfeitures'. The way in which the South African President has exercised his pardoning power has actually been subjected to constitutional litigation. In *President of the Republic of South Africa and Another v Hugo*,[15] the Constitutional Court held that the judiciary has the power to determine whether the South African President has acted lawfully when issuing pardons or remissions of sentences. The facts were that President Mandela had granted remission of sentence to all mothers in prison on 10 May 1994 with children under the age of 12. Hugo was a male prisoner and a widower with a son who was 11 years old when the remission was granted. He had successfully obtained an order from a lower court declaring the President's act of remission unconstitutional on the ground that it discriminated against him on the basis of gender. The President then appealed to the Constitutional Court, which set aside the order on the basis that the – undoubted – discrimination was *not* unfair. (This was because the court found that as women were a group that had historically been marginalised, some affirmative action in their favour was justified.) However, the Constitutional Court agreed with the principle enunciated by the lower court, that the pardoning power is justiciable. Like other presidential powers and functions, it must be exercised in a way that is consistent with the rest of the Constitution. The South African Bill of Rights proscribes state action that discriminates unfairly. Thus, had the court found on the facts that the pardoning power was exercised in a manner that discriminated unfairly, it would have confirmed the lower court's order.

It is important that the power to pardon be made justiciable in any new Zimbabwean Constitution, since it is a power that has often been abused. Pardons and remissions ought to be issued only when 'deserving circumstances' are present. Therefore, it might be a good idea for the pardoning provision in a new Constitution to specify the criteria the President must take into account when exercising this power. Perhaps a special committee should be established, consisting of eminent lawyers and other appropriate persons, to advise the President accordingly. Most important of all, the word 'prerogative' must not appear in the pardoning provision. It is of interest to note that at present 'prerogative' appears *only* in the heading to section 31 I of the Constitution (the pardoning provision). In *Hewlett v Minister of Finance*,[16] Zimbabwe's Supreme Court held that section headings do not form part of the substantive content of the Constitution. For this reason, it can be argued that the current pardoning provision is not in fact a prerogative power and that the way in which it is exercised may be questioned by the courts.[17] To date, no one has attempted to bring proceedings of this kind before a Zimbabwean court. It is to be hoped that in a new Constitution 'prerogative' will appear neither in the heading nor the substantive portion of the pardoning provision.

Access to the courts

A Constitution can only be said to be sovereign and supreme in reality if its provisions are enforceable. Obviously, this means that easy access to the courts is vitally important in a modern constitutional state. Zimbabwe's current Constitution establishes – either expressly or implicitly – a number of ways in which constitutional litigation can be initiated. The relevant provision is section 24. Sub-section (1) allows for direct access to the Supreme Court where the applicant 'alleges that the Declaration of Rights has been, is being or is likely to be contravened in *relation to him*' (my emphasis). The only exception is where a constitutional application is brought on behalf of a detained person.[18] The purpose of direct access 'is to provide, in a proper case, speedy access to the final court in the land'.[19] Generally, direct access is a good thing, although it may sometimes have the (unintended) effect of retarding the development of a country's constitutional jurisprudence. This is because a constitutional issue is more likely to be determined correctly by the Supreme Court if it has first been considered by a lower court. In *Bruce and Another v Fleecytex Johannesburg CC and Others*,[20] a judgement handed down by the South African Constitutional Court, President of the court Chaskalson said: 'It is ... not ordinarily in the interests of justice for a court to sit as a court of first and last instance, in which matters are decided without there being any possibility of appealing against the decision given. Experience shows that decisions are more likely to be correct if more than one court has been required to consider the issues raised. In such circumstances, the losing party has an opportunity of challenging the reasoning on which the first judgement is based, and of reconsidering and refining arguments previously raised in the light of such judgement.'[21]

Constitutional litigation may also commence in the High Court. Section 81 (1) of the Constitution provides that the High Court 'shall have such jurisdiction and powers as may be conferred upon it by or in terms of this Constitution or any Act of Parliament'. According to sections 13 and 23 of the High Court Act, the High Court has full original civil and criminal jurisdiction over all matters in Zimbabwe. The words 'civil case' are defined in section 2 of the Act as referring to 'any case or matter which is not a criminal case or matter.' This obviously includes constitutional cases. Moreover, it is a fact that over the years, the High Court has handed down numerous decisions pertaining to constitutional issues. However, this did not prevent High Court judge Ndou ruling in 2003 in *Nyamandlovu Farmers Association v Minster of Lands, Agriculture and Rural Resettlement and Another*[22] that the High Court lacks constitutional jurisdiction – a decision that was clearly wrong. The Supreme Court confirmed in *Capital Radio (Private) Limited v Broadcasting Authority of Zimbabwe and Others*[23] that the High Court is entitled to rule on Constitutional issues.

Sometimes, during proceedings before the High Court or the Magistrates Court, the issue of whether the Declaration of Rights has been contravened may suddenly arise. As has been made clear above, the High Court (but not the Magistrates' Court) has constitutional jurisdiction. In addition, section 24 (2) of the Constitution provides that if a 'Declaration of Rights issue' arises during proceedings in the High Court (or even the Magistrates' Court) then it may refer the issue to the Supreme Court. It is important to understand that the actual proceedings are not transferred to the Supreme Court, only the Declaration of Rights issue. A referral may be made at the request of one of the parties or on the initiative of the presiding judge or magistrate.

Constitutional proceedings, whether in the High Court or directly before the Supreme Court, may only be instituted by persons who have *locus standi* (the right of standing). As has been shown above, a person will not have *locus standi* to approach the Supreme Court directly unless he/she can show that the Declaration of Rights has been contravened in relation to him/her. The *locus standi* threshold is lower in the High Court. In *Capital Radio (Private) Limited v Broadcasting Authority of Zimbabwe and Others*,[24] the Supreme Court said: 'In a constitutional application in the High Court all that a litigant is required to show to establish *locus standi* is a substantial interest in a matter.'[25] That sounds fine, until one realises that in practice the 'substantial interest' test has often been interpreted in a very restrictive manner that has made Constitutional litigation difficult.

This is a very real problem that a new Constitution ought to address. There are various options here. First, the requirements of the 'substantial interest' test could be defined in the Constitution. It might even be a good idea to drop the word 'substantial', since it implies a *high* interest threshold, and substitute instead the word 'sufficient'. Moreover, 'sufficient interest' ought not to be limited to 'personal interest' but should also include elements of the public interest. In other words, persons not personally directly affected by an alleged breach of the Declaration of Rights should nevertheless be allowed to institute constitutional litigation – in appropriate circumstances – in order to vindicate the public interest. Of course, the wording of a provision providing for public interest constitutional litigation must be phrased carefully in order to avoid swarms of busybodies swamping the courts with trivial applications.

An alternative – or additional – approach would be the adoption of a provision that makes it clear that constitutional litigation can also be based on the 'supremacy clause' of the Constitution. Some explanation is needed here. In a constitutional democracy, the Constitution is sovereign and supreme. In Zimbabwe, this is made clear by section 3 of the Constitution, which says: 'This Constitution is the supreme law of Zimbabwe and if any other law is inconsistent with this Constitution that other law shall, to the extent of the inconsistency, be void.' The concept of constitutional supremacy necessarily implies the existence of a right to challenge the constitutionality of laws before the courts.

In Canada, the courts have accepted that a person may challenge the constitutionality of a law by invoking *either* the supremacy or enforcement provisions (sections 52 (1) and 24 (1) respectively) of the Canadian Constitution Act of 1982. Section 52 (1) states: 'The Constitution of Canada is the supreme law of Canada, and any law that is inconsistent with the provisions of the Constitution is, to the extent of the inconsistency, of no force or effect.' Section 24 (1) says: 'Anyone whose rights or freedoms, as guaranteed by this Charter, have been infringed or denied may apply to a court of competent jurisdiction to obtain such remedy as the court considers appropriate and just in the circumstances.'

Canadian constitutional scholar Peter Hogg says:

> [The] supremacy clause gives to the Charter overriding effect. Since the Charter is part of the 'Constitution of Canada', any law that is inconsistent with the Charter is 'of no force or effect'. Since it inevitably falls to the courts to determine whether or not a law is inconsistent with the Charter, s. 52 (1) provides an explicit basis for judicial review of legislation in Canada.[26]

He adds that 'the Charter contains its own remedy clause, namely s. 24'.[27] The latter 'is applicable only to breaches of the Charter of Rights; s. 52 (1) is applicable to the entire Constitution of Canada, including the Charter of Rights. Secondly, s. 24 (1) is available only to a person whose rights have been infringed; s. 52 (1) is available in some circumstances to persons whose rights have not been infringed'.[28] A few pages later, Hogg emphasises his point thus: 'Section 24 (1) is not the exclusive remedy for a breach of the Charter of Rights .... [The] supremacy clause of s. 52 (1) ... renders "of no force or effect" any law that is inconsistent with the Constitution of Canada.'[29] He notes that '[s]tanding to apply for a remedy under s. 24 (1) is granted to "anyone" whose Charter rights "have been infringed or denied". This implies stricter requirements of standing ... [and] contemplates that it is the applicant's own rights that have been infringed or denied'.[30]

However, in *R v Big M Drug Mart Ltd*[31] the Supreme Court of

Canada held that the fact that a corporation had no standing under section 24 (1) to challenge a law was irrelevant. The challenge was based on the supremacy clause, section 52 (1). The court said: 'Where ... the challenge is based on the unconstitutionality of legislation, recourse to s. 24 is unnecessary and the particular effect on the challenged party is irrelevant.'[32] Of this, Hogg says:

> Sometimes a person, motivated by public interest, wishes to make a Charter challenge to a statute that does not even apply to the challenger. This cannot be done under s. 24 (1). However, in Minister of Justice v. Borowski,[33] the Supreme Court of Canada granted standing to an anti-abortion activist to bring an action for a declaration that the Criminal Code's abortion provisions were unconstitutional. Those provisions could never actually be applied to the applicant, who was neither a doctor nor a woman, but he was granted standing nevertheless. This illustrates that the availability of a declaration of invalidity under the general law is governed by more generous standing requirements than are the remedies authorised by s. 24 (1).[34]

In *Ferreira v Levin No and Others and Vryenhoek and Others v Powell No and Others*,[35] a South African Constitutional Court judge may have adopted a similar – though slightly narrower – approach towards allowing constitutional challenges to be based on the supremacy clause.[36] O'Regan J held that where it is alleged that the Bill of Rights has been contravened, the challenge must be based on the enforcement provision.[37] She then implied that other Constitutional litigation should be based on the supremacy clause.[38]

Laurence Tribe, in *American Constitutional Law*,[39] notes that the American Constitution does not expressly confer upon the federal courts the 'power to refuse to give effect to congressional legislation if it is inconsistent with ... the Constitution'.[40] However, in *Marbury v. Madison*[41] Marshall CJ inferred the existence of such a power:

> All those who have framed written Constitutions contemplate them as forming the fundamental and paramount law of the nation, and consequently the theory of every such government must be that an act of the legislature, repugnant to the Constitution, is void.... [Thus] [i]t is emphatically the province and duty of the judicial department to say what the law is.[42]

He added:

> Those, then, who controvert the principle, that the Constitution is to be considered, in court, as a paramount law, are reduced to the necessity of

maintaining that courts must close their eyes on the Constitution, and see only the law. This doctrine ... would declare, that if the legislature shall do what is expressly forbidden, such act, notwithstanding the express prohibition, is in reality effectual. It would be giving to the legislature a practical and real omnipotence, with the same breath which proposes to restrict their powers within narrow limits.[43]

Since Canadian and American courts have been able to infer constitutional jurisdiction from the notion of constitutional supremacy, there is no reason why Zimbabwean courts should not do likewise. Moreover, even if the restrictive approach towards *locus standi* enunciated in *Tsvangirai v Registrar General of Elections and Others*[44] applies to all constitutional litigation brought in terms of section 24 of the Constitution (a view which ought to be rejected), and not just to applications brought under subsection (1) of that provision, there are no grounds for holding that such a restrictive approach ought to apply where the constitutional challenge is founded on section 3 of the Constitution.[45] This emerges clearly from the Canadian decisions referred to above. Hence, a person who alleges that a law contravenes a provision in the Declaration of Rights need not show that the impugned law applies to him, provided that the action is founded on section 3 and not on section 24.

In addition, constitutional challenges framed on the basis of section 3 of the Constitution need not allege that a provision in the Declaration of Rights has been infringed. Such an allegation need only be made where the challenge is framed in terms of section 24. That provision is concerned exclusively with the jurisdiction of the courts in respect of the enforcement of the Declaration of Rights.[46] Section 3 is broader in that it justifies challenging the constitutionality of any law, regardless of whether or not it is alleged that the impugned law has violated a provision in the Declaration of Rights. In *S v Gatsi; S v Rufaro Hotel (Pvt.) Ltd*,[47] the High Court considered the constitutionality of the Presidential Powers (Temporary Measures) Act. It was not alleged that the Act violated any of the provisions of the Declaration of Rights and the court did not explicitly state the basis upon which it was entertaining a constitutional challenge. However, a reference to section 3 at page 14 of Adam J's judgement implies that the court founded its jurisdiction on the concept of constitutional supremacy established by that provision.

Few people in Zimbabwe are aware that the Constitution's supremacy provision confers upon the judiciary a constitutional jurisdiction separate and distinct from that contained in section 24. A new Constitution ought to contain a provision that makes this clear. This would facilitate public interest litigation and would enable the courts to uphold and enforce those constitutional provisions situated outside the Declaration of Rights.

The President's unilateral legislative power

The doctrine of the separation of powers ought to be built into the fabric of all good modern Constitutions. This means that executive, legislative and judicial powers must operate within distinct spheres. Moreover, the powers themselves should be vested in different persons or bodies. However, in Zimbabwe the President, in addition to having vast executive powers, has the power to unilaterally enact primary[48] legislation. This concentration of powers in one office is cause for concern. It is to be hoped that a new Constitution will prohibit Parliament from delegating the power to make primary legislation to other persons and authorities.

As indicated by the last sentence of the above paragraph, the Constitution has not directly conferred law-making powers on the President. Section 32 of the Constitution says:

(1) The legislative authority of Zimbabwe shall vest in the legislature which shall consist of the President and Parliament.

(2) The provisions of subsection (1) shall not be construed as preventing the legislature from conferring legislative functions on any person or authority.

The meaning of sub-section (2) is not entirely clear. Since it does not expressly refer to 'primary' legislative functions, the provision is probably limited to authorising delegation of *subordinate* legislative power, that is, the power to create rules and regulations inferior in status to an Act of Parliament. This is of course justifiable, since neither the Constitution nor Acts of Parliament can regulate in sufficient detail all of the many and varied functions performed by government. As subordinate legislation will be invalid if it is inconsistent with the Constitution or an Act of Parliament, it does not threaten the operation of the separation of powers doctrine. Moreover, subordinate legislation has to function within a framework established by the relevant enabling Act of Parliament.

The President's primary law-making powers derive from the Presidential Powers (Temporary) Measures Act, a statute passed by Parliament in 1986. There has always been controversy about whether or not the Act is constitutional. At the time of its enactment, sub-section (2) of section 32 of the Constitution was not yet in existence; even if it had been, the constitutionality of the Act would still be questionable given that the meaning of sub-section (2) is contested.

However, the validity of the Act was upheld by the High Court in *S v. Gatsi; S v Rufaro Hotel (Pvt.) Ltd*. The court took the view that Parliament had not abrogated its legislative responsibilities because laws enacted by the President under the Act are temporary in nature (they expire after six months). The President cannot renew the law concerned until the expiry of a further six-month period. In addition, the court noted that laws created by the President must be tabled before Parliament within eight days of being enacted. Parliament may, by resolution, invalidate any such law. All of this meant, according to the court, that Parliament remained in overall control of the legislative process.

The correctness of this decision is doubtful. Faced with a similar question, the South African Constitutional Court in *Executive Council of the Western Cape Legislature and Others v President of the Republic of South Africa and Others*[49] held that the South African legislature may only confer subordinate law-making powers on the South African President. Chaskalson P said:

> the legislative authority vested in [the South African] Parliament under section 37 of the Constitution is expressed in wide terms – 'to make laws for the Republic in accordance with this Constitution'. In a modern state detailed provisions are often required for the purpose of implementing and regulating laws, and Parliament cannot be expected to deal with all such matters itself. There is nothing in the Constitution which prohibits Parliament from delegating subordinate regulatory authority to other bodies. The power to do so is necessary for effective law-making. It is implicit in the power to make laws for the country and I have no doubt that under our Constitution Parliament can pass legislation delegating such legislative functions to other bodies. There is, however, a difference between delegating authority to make subordinate legislation within the framework of a

statute under which the delegation is made, and assigning plenary legislative power to another body, including ... the power to amend the Act under which the assignment is made.[50]

In arriving at its decision in the *Western Cape Legislature* case, the court was applying what has come to be known as the 'delegation doctrine'. The doctrine derives from the separation of powers theory and has been developed over the years by courts in the United States. Basically, the doctrine holds that law-making is a function properly left to the legislature and that accordingly excessive legislative powers should not be delegated to the executive.[51] In applying the doctrine in the context of South Africa, Chaskalson P noted:

> Parliament can no longer claim supreme power subject to limitations imposed by the Constitution; it is subject in all respects to the provisions of the Constitution and has only the powers vested in it by the Constitution expressly or by necessary implication.[52]

To this, he added:

> The supremacy of the Constitution is [established] in section 37 in two respects. First, the legislative power is declared to be 'subject to' the Constitution, which emphasises the dominance of the provisions of the Constitution over Parliament's legislative power ... and secondly laws have to be made 'in accordance with this Constitution'.[53]

Accordingly, the court ruled that delegation to the executive of the power to create primary legislation (i.e., the power to amend or repeal Acts of Parliament) would amount to a subversion of the Constitution.[54]

The reasoning of the South African Constitutional Court is to be preferred. The fact that Zimbabwe's Parliament still continues to 'supervise' (at least in theory) the way in which the President uses the primary legislative power purportedly conferred upon him does not change the fact that Parliament had no right to confer such power upon him in the first place.[55]

Constitutionalism and Parliament

The implications of constitutional supremacy and constitutionalism for Zimbabwe's Parliament are best illustrated by the Supreme Court's decision in *Biti and Anor v Minister of Justice, Legal and Parliamen-*

tary Affairs and Anor,[56] a case it decided in 2002. Sadly, with the changes that have taken place on the bench since then, it is unlikely that the case would be decided in the same way today. It is a pity that *Biti* has not been widely discussed by legal academics because it is a groundbreaking decision. In fact, the majority judgment in the case is probably the finest contribution Zimbabwe's judiciary has made to the development of constitutionalism in relation to the powers of Parliament. A courageous and principled bench was able to uphold the rule of law and stop Parliament from abusing its powers. It is for this reason that the case is discussed in some detail below – the first proper analysis of the case that I am aware of.

Are self-imposed restraints on Parliament's legislative powers valid?

Is Parliament bound by self-imposed restrictions on its legislative powers contained in Acts of Parliament or parliamentary Standing Orders? In the United Kingdom it has been said that Parliament is entitled 'to make or unmake any law whatever'.[57] This means that in that country Parliament may legislate in respect of any subject matter without restriction. It has also been held to mean that Parliament is not bound *procedurally* by any manner and form restrictions that may have been enacted by an earlier Parliament. Thus, in terms of this 'orthodox' understanding of the British Parliament's powers, it may ignore legislation requiring it to follow a special voting procedure – for example, a two-thirds majority – when enacting legislation concerning a specific subject. Subsequent legislation passed by a simple majority will therefore be valid.[58] The existence of this 'fundamental rule' of British constitutional law arises from the concept of parliamentary sovereignty. The idea that Parliament can fetter its own powers has been held to be inconsistent with the sovereign status it has in the United Kingdom.[59] This 'fundamental rule' of British Constitutional law is itself a rule of the common law. However, unlike ordinary common law rules, it apparently cannot be amended or abolished by legislative action. In other words, the rule that says that all legislated rules can be repealed or amended cannot itself be changed or amended. For this reason the rule has been described as the '*Grundnorm*' or 'ultimate rule of recognition' of the British Constitution.[60]

The position in Zimbabwe

The position in Zimbabwe is rather different, due to the fact that it is the Constitution, not Parliament, which is sovereign and supreme. In *Smith v Mutasa NO and Another*,[61] Dumbutshena CJ, writing for a unanimous Supreme Court bench, said: 'The Constitution of Zimbabwe is the supreme law of the land. It is true that Parliament is supreme in the legislative field assigned to it by the Constitution, but even then Parliament cannot step outside the bounds of the authority prescribed to it by the Constitution.'[62] *Smith* was concerned with the issue of Parliamentary privilege *not* the legislative process. It was not until the Supreme Court's landmark decision in *Biti* that the full implications of the *Smith* case became clear.

In *Biti*, the question before the Supreme Court was whether the General Laws Amendment Act 2002[63] had been validly passed by Parliament. After the Bill had been introduced into Parliament it was sent to the Parliamentary Legal Committee. It then passed through the first and second reading stages as well as the committee stage. Thereafter, the Minister of Justice, Legal and Parliamentary Affairs moved the third reading. However, when a division was called, the question was defeated by 36 votes to 24. The next day the Minister gave notice that he intended to move a motion that Parliament rescind its decision on the third reading in terms of Standing Order 69:

> The House may, by resolution after notice, direct that any motion submitted and any resolution or other vote, or entry in the journals, shall be expunged or discharged from the order paper or rescinded during the same session, or at any time thereafter. Such motion shall be moved only by a Vice-President, a Minister or by the member who had been in charge of the business concerned.

He also gave notice that he would move to suspend the provisions of Standing Order 127 in respect of the General Laws Amendment Bill. According to Standing Order 127:

> Subject to the provisions of the Constitution, 'no Bill shall be introduced which is of the same substance as some other Bill which has been introduced during the same session and which has not been withdrawn.' The Minister later stated that he was also acting in terms of Standing Order 190 (1) which provided that 'save as is provided in Standing Order no. 21, any Standing or Sessional Order or Orders of the House may only be suspended upon motion moved after notice'.

On the following day both motions were debated by Parliament and affirmed. Thereafter Parliament decided, by a vote of 62 to 49, that the Bill be read a third time.

The opposition Movement for Democratic Change (MDC), victors of the first third-reading vote, challenged the validity of the second third reading.[64] The MDC argued that the manner in which the second third reading was undertaken violated section 18 (1) of the Constitution.[65] This was because the process adopted failed to afford them due process and protection of law, in that provisions of the Constitution and Standing Orders were breached. The MDC opposed the passage of the General Laws Amendment Bill because it contained provisions amending the Electoral Act which it believed would 'completely undermine the validity and legitimacy of the [forthcoming presidential] election and ... deny the electorate their Constitutional right to elect a President of their choice'.[66]

Were the applicants entitled to approach the Supreme Court in the circumstances?

Mkhululi Nyathi, a critic of the Supreme Court's decision in *Biti*, has said that 'there is nothing [in] ... the judgement to suggest that applicants' rights were violated. Neither are the specific rights mentioned'.[67] With respect, it is impossible to take this charge seriously. Ebrahim JA, writing for the majority, states clearly that the court was sitting 'to determine the issue whether section 18 (1) of the Constitution has been breached'.[68] Section 18 (1), a provision in the Declaration of Rights, stipulates that 'every person is entitled to the protection of the law'. The learned Judge of Appeal said that 'the right to protection of law ... includes the right to due process'.[69] He also drew attention to the fact that members of Parliament, like anyone else, are entitled to the protection of the Declaration of Rights.[70] He referred with approval to a passage in *Smith v Mutasa NO and Another*,[71] where Dumbutshena CJ said:

> The independence enjoyed by Parliament in the control of its internal affairs does not prevent its members from defending their fundamental rights should they believe that Parliament has wrongfully abrogated or infringed them. Section 24 of the Constitution ... enables such members to apply to the Supreme Court for redress.[72]

As indicated above, both the MDC and Mr Biti had a valid interest in preventing the passage through Parliament of the General Laws Amendment Bill. If the Bill was passed unlawfully, in violation of the Constitution and Standing Orders, it must follow that a denial of due process and the protection of law occurred. In other words, the MDC and Mr Biti were prejudiced by the illegal procedure adopted by Parliament. They were denied the fruits of their victory in the earlier – and lawful – third reading vote.

Nyathi has also argued[73] that the courts have no jurisdiction over the internal proceedings of Parliament and that the court in *Biti* was in error in enforcing Standing Orders. In support of this view he referred to *Chikerema and Others v UANC and Another*,[74] a decision of the old Rhodesian Appellate Division where MacDonald CJ, after referring to British parliamentary practice, said that Parliament's control 'over its internal proceedings is absolute and cannot be interfered with by the courts'.[75] However, *Chikerema* was a pre-independence case decided in terms of the old Constitution of Zimbabwe–Rhodesia, 1979. Nyathi says[76] that the approach enunciated in *Chikerema* was followed in *Smith v Mutasa NO and Another*.[77] In fact, a careful reading of *Smith* shows that it follows *Chikerema* only in a very limited sense.

While acknowledging that Parliament has the right to manage its internal affairs,[78] Dumbutshena CJ said in *Smith* that should Parliament 'disregard its own laws it falls upon the judiciary to say so and to pronounce the breach'.[79] Thus, the power of Parliament to regulate its own affairs is subject to the power of the judiciary to determine whether Parliament has acted in accordance with the Constitution and the law. In *Chikerema*, the question the court had to consider was whether or not a member of Parliament had become disqualified from sitting in the House. The case was not concerned with restraints on Parliament's legislative powers. MacDonald CJ said that Parliament may 'divest itself of all or part of [its] exclusive jurisdiction [to determine the question] by conferring jurisdiction upon a court of law to determine whether a member has become disqualified'.[80] By the time of the *Biti* case, Parliament was operating under a different Constitution with a justiciable Declaration of Rights. In that context, it had *impliedly* divested itself of the exclusive power to determine whether its legislative procedure was lawful by enacting Standing Orders that transformed its procedures into legally binding rules. Schedule 4 of

the Constitution makes compliance with Standing Orders mandatory, while section 18 (1) stipulates that the protection of law is a
constitutional right. Moreover, constitutional supremacy means that
Parliament is a creature of the Constitution.

In *Biti*, Ebrahim JA said that 'common sense dictates that Parliament is required to comply with its own laws regarding the enactment
of legislation'.[81] He added that '[i]n other jurisdictions, the courts
have applied the principle that legislation which is enacted by a legislative body without compliance with the existing law in respect to
the enactment of legislation will be declared void by the courts, even
where the Constitution provides for a parliamentary democracy form
of government'.[82] Moreover, like Dumbutshena CJ in *Smith v Mutasa*,
Ebrahim JA in *Biti* emphasised that as Zimbabwe is a constitutional
democracy, 'it is the courts, not Parliament, that determine the lawful-
ness of actions of bodies, including Parliament'.[83] Thus, for all of the
reasons cited above, Nyathi is wrong in contending that the courts
cannot question the internal procedures of Parliament.

Were Standing Orders violated?

(1) Standing Order 127

As has been seen already, Standing Order 127 prohibited the introduction of a Bill 'which is of the same substance as some other Bill which
has been introduced during the same session and which has not been
withdrawn'. In order to deal with the problem, Parliament purported
to suspend Standing Order 127. The court ruled that the purported
suspension was invalid. Ebrahim JA drew attention to the language of
Schedule 4, paragraph 1 (1) (a), of the Constitution which stipulates
that the power to introduce Bills into Parliament or move motions for
debate is 'subject to the provisions of this Constitution *and Standing
Orders*'[84] (my emphasis). He also noted that section 57 (1) of the Constitution authorises Parliament to make Standing Orders 'subject to the
provisions of this Constitution and any other law'.[85] For this reason,
Standing Orders were held to have constitutional standing.[86] In other
words, Standing Orders are law because the Constitution says so.
Ebrahim JA then said:

> There is therefore merit in the submission that, having made such a law,
> Parliament cannot ignore that law. Parliament is bound by the law as much
> as any other person or institution in Zimbabwe. Because Standing Orders

arise out of the Constitution, and because the Constitution mandates Parliament to act in accordance with Standing Orders, they cannot be regarded merely as 'rules of a club'. Standing Orders constitute legislation which must be obeyed and followed.[87]

In some jurisdictions Standing Orders have indeed been regarded as 'rules of a club' and as such not binding on Parliament. In the United Kingdom, for example, the House of Lords ruled in *Pickin v British Railways Board*[88] that 'the court has no concern with the manner in which Parliament or its officers carry ... out its Standing Orders'.[89] A similar position prevails in Canada.[90] However, allowance must be made for the fact that Britain is a parliamentary democracy, not a constitutional one, and that the Canadian Constitution does not contain language similar to that used in Schedule 4 of Zimbabwe's.[91]

Was Standing Order 127 validly suspended? The court ruled that it was not. Ebrahim JA said:

> Parliament, having set the rules in terms of section 57 of the Constitution *cannot suspend those rules for the expedience of a party*[92] (my emphasis).

The judgement does not state expressly *why* a suspension in such circumstances is unlawful. Ebrahim JA appears to *imply* that a suspension based on the expedience of a party is *unfair* and therefore, in the circumstances, a violation of the right to the protection of law guaranteed by section 18 (1) of the Constitution. In this connection it is worth noting that the applicant's heads of argument[93] made reference to section 56 (1) of the Constitution, which states that 'save as otherwise provided in this Constitution, all questions proposed for decision at a sitting of Parliament shall be *determined* by a majority of the votes of the members present and voting' (my emphasis). The applicants therefore argued (correctly in my opinion) that the Constitution 'does not permit of a manipulation to allow matters to be voted upon continually until such time as a majority is obtained by one or other side in the House'.[94] The word 'determined' connotes finality. Given that the *Concise Oxford Dictionary* defines 'determine' as meaning 'bring to an end ... settle, decide ... come to a conclusion', implicit in it is the idea that once a matter has been 'determined' it cannot be considered again.

It may be, therefore, that to 'suspend' Standing Order 127 in order to reintroduce a Bill whose fate had been determined when it was lost at the third reading is *ultra vires* section 56 (1) and, thus, of section 18 (1) as well.[95] It is also important not to lose sight of the status of Standing Order 127. In the words of Ebrahim JA, 'not only does Standing Order 127 embody a convention, it is the rule or law applicable by virtue of section 57 (1) (a) of the Constitution[96] in relation to the passing of Bills.'[97]

Standing Order 127 stipulated that the prohibition on reintroducing a Bill 'of the same substance ... during the same session' was 'subject to the provisions of the Constitution'. As Ebrahim JA correctly observed, this was a reference to section 51 (3a) of the Constitution, which states that if the President withholds his assent to a Bill, it must be returned to Parliament. Commenting on this provision Ebrahim JA said: 'It seems to me that the only Bill that may be re-introduced into Parliament during the same session is one where the President has withheld his assent to the Bill.'[98] It would appear that he was interpreting section 51 (3a) in accordance with the principle of *expressio unius est exclusio alterius* (express mention of one thing excludes another). If in fact section 51 (3a) sets out the *only* circumstances under which a Bill may be reintroduced in the same session, it must follow that the purported suspension of Standing Order 127 was *ultra vires* section 51 (3a).[99]

(2) Standing Order 69

In an effort to rescind Parliament's 'first' third reading decision, the Minister purported to move a motion in terms of Standing Order 69. That Order stated that Parliament may 'direct that any motion submitted or any resolution or other vote ... be ... rescinded'. The court ruled that recourse to Order 69 would *not* enable Parliament to rescind its decision at the third reading stage of the legislative process. Ebrahim JA said: 'It is clear that this provision refers only to *motions*. It is made in terms of section 57 (1) (d)[100] of the Constitution, and finds its place in Standing Orders in relation to what is termed *public business*, Standing Orders 31-81, and not in relation to *public Bills*, Standing Orders 101-128.'[101] Earlier in his judgement, Ebrahim JA recognised that 'the Constitution distinguishes between a Bill and a motion'.[102] He noted that both Schedule 4 and section 57 of the Constitution make it clear that Bills and motions are quite different things. Accordingly, he held that the 'first' third reading decision was not validly rescinded. In other words, Standing Order 69 could only be used to rescind votes on *motions* not votes on Bills.

*Suspending Standing Orders does not mean Parliament
can ignore legislative procedures established by the Constitution*
Parliament must adhere to those legislative procedures established by the Constitution, regardless of whether or not Standing Orders have been validly suspended. Ebrahim JA said:

> Even assuming that Parliament was entitled to suspend Standing Order 127 and allow a second Bill in terms thereof to be introduced in the same session, that Bill must be introduced and dealt with in terms of the Constitution.[103]

Thus the Bill concerned would have to be introduced into Parliament and sent to the Parliamentary Legal Committee, in accordance with the requirements of Schedule 4 of the Constitution. Moreover, all other Standing Orders not suspended must be complied with. Reintroducing the Bill does not mean that parliament can ' go straight into debating [it] at the point where it had been negatived'.[104] In other words, even if Standing Order 127 had been validly suspended, the General Laws Amendment Bill could not have been reintroduced at the third reading stage. Rather, it would have had to have been introduced at the beginning of the legislative process, as if it were a new Bill.[105]

In considering this issue, it is important to bear in mind that Parliament has no inherent power of its own. In the words of Ebrahim JA, 'Parliament can only do what is authorised by law and specifically by the Constitution.'[106] He referred with approval to a South African decision, *De Lille and Another v Speaker of the National Assembly*,[107] where Hlophe J (as he then was) said at 449:

> The National Assembly is subject to the supremacy of the Constitution. It is an organ of State and therefore it is bound by the Bill of Rights. All its decisions and acts are subject to the Constitution and the Bill of Rights. Parliament can no longer claim supreme power subject to limitations imposed by the Constitution. It is subject in all respects to the provisions of our Constitution. It has only those powers vested in it by the Constitution expressly or by necessary implication or by other statutes which are not in conflict with the Constitution. It follows therefore that Parliament may not confer on itself or on any of its constituent parts, including the National Assembly, any powers not conferred on them by the Constitution expressly or by necessary implication.[108]

When the matter went on appeal,[109] Mahomed CJ said that '[n]o Parliament ... can make any law or perform any act which is not sanctioned by the Constitution'.[110] This means that Parliament – both in Zimbabwe and in South Africa – cannot do something simply because it is not prohibited. Rather, it can only do what it is authorised to do. This is an important distinction.

Parliamentary procedure and the Privileges, Immunities and Powers of Parliament Act,[111] *as considered in the Biti judgment*

Section 3 of the Privileges, Immunities and Powers of Parliament Act says that:

> Parliament and members and officers of Parliament shall hold, exercise and enjoy –
>
> (a) the privileges, immunities and *powers* conferred upon Parliament, respectively, by this Act or any other law; and
>
> (b) all such other privileges, immunities and *powers*, not inconsistent with the privileges, immunities and *powers* referred to in paragraph (a), as were applicable in the case of the House of Commons of the Parliament of the United Kingdom, its members and officers, respectively, on the 18th April 1980. (my emphasis)

What this provision means is that Zimbabwe's Parliament has the powers of the British House of Commons, as at 18 April 1980, to the extent that those powers are not inconsistent with Zimbabwean law. Thus, even if Standing Order 127 was validly suspended, Parliament would still be precluded from reintroducing a Bill in the same session, since such a reintroduction is not part of British parliamentary practice. While British parliamentary practice may not be judicially enforced in the United Kingdom – there it only has the status of a constitutional convention – British practice *is* legally binding in Zimbabwe, because the Privileges, Immunities and Powers of Parliament Act makes it so.

In *Biti*, Ebrahim JA said:

> Nowhere in [the Privileges, Immunities and Powers of Parliament Act] is it provided that Parliament can bring for the second time the third reading of a Bill; nor is it provided that a matter that has been negatived may be brought again before the same session. Indeed, by virtue of section 3 (b) of that Act, such would be inconsistent with the powers of the House of Commons as at 18 April 1980, and therefore also inconsistent with the law of Zimbabwe. Section 3 of the ... Act itself expressly forbids what was done

in the present case ... [and] provides succinctly that our parliamentary practice is guided by practices in the House of Commons. The 'Bible', on parliamentary practice of that body, is enshrined in Erskine May ... and the editors of that work have no doubt that a negatived Bill should not be reintroduced in the same session of Parliament.[112]

Malaba JA's dissenting judgement in Biti

Whilst Sandura JA, Cheda JA and Ziyambi JA concurred with Ebrahim JA's judgement, Malaba JA dissented. He agreed with the majority that 'Standing Orders have constitutional standing and are binding on Parliament until repealed'.[113] His stance was that by the time the first third reading vote had taken place, the General Laws Amendment Bill had already passed. With respect, Malaba JA's contention is quite incredible and untenable. The whole point of that vote was to determine whether the Bill had been read a third time. A Bill cannot be said to have been read a third time unless an affirmative vote to that effect takes place.

Has the Supreme Court's decision in Biti been affected by its subsequent decision in Quinnell v Minister of Lands, Agriculture and Rural Resettlement and Others?[114]

In *Quinnell,* the applicant challenged the validity of the Land Acquisition Amendment Act[115] on a number of grounds, one of which was that the Bill was 'of the same substance' as section 27 (1) of the General Laws Amendment Bill that had been introduced and not withdrawn during the same session, contrary to Standing Order 127. By a four to one majority the Supreme Court ruled that the Land Acquisition Amendment Act had been validly enacted. Writing for the majority, Malaba JA said: 'There was, of course, a violation of Standing Order 127 although it was of a technical nature. I do not accept the general proposition that presentation of a Bill in contravention of Standing Order 127 in all circumstances spells as its necessary consequence invalidity in the resultant Act.'[116] He stated that the effect of amendments and additions made to the Bill subsequent to its introduction into Parliament 'cure[d] the effect of the irregularity that may have been occasioned by its introduction.'[117] This was because, he went on to say, they 'produced a Bill which was substantially different from section 27 (1) of the General Laws Amendment Bill. [Thus] despite non-compliance with the provisions of the Standing Order at the time the Bill was introduced ... there was substantial compliance with its general object'.[118]

It is difficult – to put it mildly – to understand the majority judgement in *Quinnell*. It cannot be reconciled with *Biti* in a number of respects, although it is set out in language which indicates that the court did not intend – at least expressly – to overturn *Biti*. In short, the *Quinnell* judgement is confusing and logically inconsistent. For example, Malaba JA says in *Quinnell*:

> The court must, of course, take into account the fact that Standing Order 127 is couched in language which imposes a negative duty. It is couched in mandatory terms. Does this mean, as appears to have been accepted by the majority in *Biti*'s case, that in every case of breach of Standing Order 127 the intention of the makers thereof is that the resultant act must be declared invalid? I do not think so. Courts in other jurisdictions faced with the same question have considered the provisions of Standing Orders as directory rather than mandatory.[119] (my emphasis)

So, Malaba JA began by accepting that Standing Order 17 was worded 'in mandatory terms' but then went on to say that it was directory in nature!

In support of his proposition, Malaba JA referred to two Australian cases: *Clayton v Heffron*[120] and *Namoi Shire Council v Attorney-General for New South Wales*.[121] The circumstances in *Clayton* were quite different from those in *Quinnell*. A careful reading of the *Namoi* case shows that it is also not really relevant in the context of the *Quinnell* situation. Section 15 (2) of the Constitution (1902) of New South Wales, Australia, states that once Standing Orders have been enacted they 'shall become binding and of force'. This can hardly be described as emphatically mandatory language. It is quite different from the language used in paragraph 1 (1) of Schedule 4 of the Constitution of Zimbabwe which says: 'Subject to the provisions of this Constitution and Standing Orders ... a Minister ... may introduce any Bill into ... Parliament' (my emphasis). In *Chinamora v Angwa Furnishers (Pvt) Ltd and Another (Attorney-General intervening)*[122] Gubbay CJ said: 'The phrase "subject to" ... subjects the provisions of the subject section to the control of a master enactment or the common law.'[123] This means therefore that compliance with Standing Order 127, which was a Standing Order concerned with the introduction of Bills, was a mandatory requirement, because the Constitution itself stipulates that a

Bill may only be introduced if such an introduction is permitted by Standing Orders. Specific and imperative language such as 'subject to' does not appear in Section 15 (2) of the Constitution Act (1902) of New South Wales. The somewhat vague and general language of the latter may, arguably, be directory in nature. The same cannot be said of Schedule 4 of the Constitution of Zimbabwe, which imposes a specific mandatory obligation (compliance with Standing Orders) on specific persons (Ministers) in respect of a particular function (the introduction of Bills into Parliament).

The language of Standing Order 127 was itself mandatory (or peremptory). This can be seen from the use of the word 'shall' in the Standing Order. According to Christo Botha,[124] 'words with an imperative or affirmative character indicate a peremptory provision (e.g. the words "shall" or "must")'.[125] In *S v Takaendesa*[126] the court said: 'Where a statute prohibits the doing of something unless something else is done as a precedent to doing the thing prescribed, it is a general rule of interpretation that the provisions of the Act are obligatory and not directory' (my emphasis).[127] This fits well with the scenario set out in Order 127, which prohibited the re-introduction of Bills of the same substance unless the earlier Bill was withdrawn.[128] Accordingly, any failure to comply with Order 127 was fatal to the validity of any purported legislation emerging from such a flawed procedure.

The changes made to the Land Acquisition Amendment Bill during its passage through Parliament were relatively minor. It therefore remained a Bill 'of the same substance'. However, even if the effect of the changes was to render it a substantially different Bill, such changes cannot 'cure' the original illegality, i.e., the fact that when it was re-introduced it was substantially the same Bill. According to Standing Order 127, the decisive consideration was the form the Bill took at the time of its re-introduction. If the Minister did not have the power to re-introduce the Bill, then it matters not that Parliament subsequently purported to change the content of the Bill. If Parliament did not have the power to proceed with the Bill in the first place, no amount of subsequent 'curing' can make the process lawful. In *Executive Council of the Western Cape Legislature and Others v President of the Republic of South Africa and Others*,[129] a decision of the South African Constitutional Court, Chaskalson P said: 'The only way in which Parliament can confer power on itself to act contrary to the Constitution is to amend the Constitution.'[130] The same principle must apply in Zimbabwe. Unless and until the Constitution or Order 127 were amended, Parliament had to comply with Order 127.[131]

In *Quinnell*, Malaba JA also attempted to justify his decision by arguing that 'the propriety of [re-] introducing the Bill was not raised by any of the members of the House.'[132] He added: 'Objections to the [re-]introduction of the Bill on the grounds that it contravened the provisions of Standing Order 127 should have been taken ... before the second reading.'[133] In fact, the question of whether objections were raised by Members of Parliament is quite irrelevant. The absence of objections does not mean that Parliament can ignore Standing Order 127, since it is bound to comply with that Order. Malaba JA also said that '[t]he object of Standing Order 127 is to protect Parliament from the embarrassment of having to debate the same question twice in one session.'[134] This is not correct. In the *Biti* case the majority judgement made it clear that the real purpose of the Standing Order is to require 'the majority to abide by a decision regularly come to, however unexpected, and that it is unfair to resort to methods, whether direct or indirect, to reverse such a decision.'[135] In this way, the rights of the minority are protected.[136]

By the time the *Quinnell* case was heard, the composition of the Supreme Court had changed and Justice Ebrahim was no longer on the bench. In *Quinnell*, Sandura JA (who had been part of the majority in *Biti*), wrote a dissenting judgement in which he adhered to the approach the Supreme Court had adopted in the earlier *Biti* case. He said: '[O]nce it is accepted, as it obviously must be, that the Amendment Bill was introduced in violation of Standing Order 127, *cadit quaesto* [end of inquiry]. That is the end of the matter. The Amendment Act is invalid and of no force or effect.'[137] Thus, in the opinion of Sandura JA, Order 127 was a mandatory provision that was binding on Parliament. For the various reasons given above, his approach is to be preferred to that of Malaba JA.

Conclusion

An effort has been made to explain the significance of constitutions and constitutionalism. A number of 'constitutional issues' have been discussed, partly in order to illuminate constitutionalism, but also to point to some of the things that ought to be addressed in the constitutional reform exercise. Many of the problems that beset Zimbabwe today have their origins in the breakdown of constitutionalism and the rule of law. Yet producing a new and (hopefully) better Constitution is not enough. Even the best Constitution is just a piece of paper. What is also needed is the development of a culture of constitutionalism. This will only begin to happen if the people as a whole believe in the values contained in the Constitution.

Notes

1 1996 (9) BCLR 1189 (ZS).
2 Ibid., at 1198.
3 1989 (3) ZLR 183 (S).
4 Ibid., at 192.
5 Although, since the 19th amendment came into force on 13 February 2009, the President's power to dissolve Parliament and make important appointments has to be exercised 'in consultation with' the Prime Minister. 'in consultation' is defined in section 115 (1) of the Constitution as meaning 'after securing the agreement or consent of the person so consulted'.
6 Greg Linington (2011) 'Constitutions and Constitutionalism', in *Mukai-Vukani*, No. 57, August, p. 5.
7 Stephen Holmes (1993) 'Precommitment and the Paradox of Democracy', in Elster and Slagstad, *Constitutionalism and Democracy*, p. 196.
8 319 US 624, at 638, quoted by Holmes at 196.
9 After the Constitutional Commission's Draft was rejected by voters in 1999, large portions of it were nevertheless made part of the current Constitution through a constitutional amendment. At the Constitutional Commission's final plenary session to consider whether to adopt the text of the Draft, the relevant item on the agenda posed instead the question of whether the *Daft* Constitution should be adopted! Whether this was a genuine mistake or a Freudian slip has never been resolved.
10 Section 52 (2) of the Constitution.
11 Ibid., section 52 (3).
12 Ibid., section 52 (4).
13 Ibid., section 51 (3a).
14 Ibid., section 51 (3b).
15 1997 (6) BCLR 708 (CC).
16 1981 ZLR 571 (S).
17 It is true that section 31 K of the Constitution states that 'a court shall

not ... inquire into ... the manner in which the President has exercised his discretion'. However, a distinction must be drawn between the *manner* in which a discretion is exercised, which is one thing, and the *nature* and *extent* of the discretion concerned, which is another. An exercise of the pardoning power that is inconsistent with the Declaration of Rights would fall *outside* the lawful parameters within which the power must be exercised. Thus, the courts would not be violating section 31 K if they invalidated such a purported use of the power. On the requirement that discretionary powers must be exercised lawfully, see *PF ZAPU v Minister of Justice (2)* 1985 (1) ZLR 15 (S) at 18.

18 Section 24 (1) of the Constitution.

19 *Mandirwhe v Minister of State*, 1986 (1) ZLR 1 (S) at 7.

20 1998 (4) BCLR 415 (CC).

21 Ibid, at 419, paragraph 8.

22 Judgment no. HB 19/2003.

23 Judgment no. SC 128/02.

24 Ibid.

25 Ibid, at 4-5.

26 Hogg (2003) *Constitutional Law of Canada*, vol. 2. at 37-2.

27 Ibid.

28 Ibid., at 37-3.

29 Ibid. at 37-21.

30 Ibid., at 37-22.

31 [1985] 1 *SCR* 295.

32 Ibid., at 313.

33 [1981] 2 *SCR* 575.

34 Hogg (2003) at 37-23.

35 1996 (1) *BCLR* 1 (CC).

36 See the comments of Chaskalson P at 98-100 (paragraphs 166-168).

37 Ibid, at 117, (paragraph 223).

38 Ibid. See Jonathan Klaaren 'Judicial Remedies' in Chaskalson et al., *Constitutional Law of South Africa* (1999) at 9-28c (paragraph 9.6). He interprets O'Regan J's comment as a reference to the supremacy clause.

39 Third edition, 2000.

40 Ibid., at 207-208.

41 5 US (1 CRANCH) 137 (1803).

42 Ibid., at 177-178.

43 Ibid., at 178.

44 Judgement no. SC 20/02.

45 It has already been noted above that in *Capital Radio (Private) Limited v Broadcasting Authority of Zimbabwe and Others (supra)*, the Supreme Court ruled that a less demanding test for *locus standi* applies when the Supreme Court exercises its common law constitutional jurisdiction.

46 Of course, section 18 (1) of the Constitution, a provision in the Declaration of Rights providing for the protection of law could be used, in some circumstances, as a means of enforcing constitutional provisions outside the Declaration of Rights.

47 1994 (1) ZLR 7 (H).

48 That is, the power to enact legislation equivalent in status to an Act of Parliament.

49 1995 (10) BCLR 1289 (CC).

50 Ibid., paragraph 51, pp. 1311-12.

51 See Chaskalson et al. (1999) (Revision Service 5, 1999 update), pp. 3-4.

52 *Western Cape* case (n. 52 above) at paragraph 62, p. 1317.

53 Ibid.

54 Ibid. See also the concurring judgement of Mahomed DP, who said at paragraph 141, p. 1347, that the impugned legislation 'goes too far and effectively constitutes an abdication of Parliament's legislative function ... leaving the President absolutely free to change the entire structure and policy of the Act in his or her absolute discretion. [Accordingly, the impugned legislation] is unconstitutional'.

55 For a more detailed discussion of this issue see Greg Linington (2001) *Constitutional Law of Zimbabwe*, pp. 556-8.

56 2002 (1) ZLR 177 (S).

57 Dicey (1965) *The Law of the Constitution* (10th edition), p. 39.

58 Suppose an Act of Parliament states that subsequent legislation relating to a specified matter must, in addition to receiving the assent of both Houses and the Monarch, be approved by the people in a referendum. Would such an Act constitute an attempt by Parliament to change the manner and form through which legislation is enacted? Or could it more accurately be described as a purported redefinition of Parliament? A redefinition is surely consistent with parliamentary sovereignty, even if manner and form procedural restraints are not. For a good discussion of this issue see Patrick Fitzgerald, 'The "paradox" of parliamentary sovereignty', *Irish Jurist* (1972) 28.

59 See, for example, *British Railways Board v Pickin* [1974] AC 765.

60 George Winterton (1976) 'The British Grundnorm: parliamentary supremacy re-examined', 92 *Law Quarterly Review* 591 at 591. However, in *Thoburn v. Sunderland City Council* [2002] 1 *CMLR* 50 at 59. Laws LJ said that the rule can in fact be modified by the evolution of the common law. In other words, the courts can change the rule. It remains to be seen whether the House of Lords will follow this approach.

61 1989 (3) *ZLR* 183 (S).

62 Ibid., at 192.

63 Act 2 of 2002, promulgated on 4 February 2002.

64 The first applicant, Tendai Biti, was (and is) an MDC member of Parliament.

The MDC itself was the second applicant.

65 Section 18 (1) of the Constitution says: 'Subject to the provisions of this Constitution, every person is entitled to the protection of the law.'

66 At 181, quoting affidavits filed by the applicants.

67 Mkhululi Nyathi (2002) 'The Constitution, Parliamentary Standing Orders and the "constraints" on law-making: an analysis of the Supreme Court's decision on Tendai Biti and Anor v the Minister of Justice, Legal and Parliamentary Affairs and Another SC 10/02 [unreported]', *Law Society of Zimbabwe Magazine*, no. 11, p. 6.

68 At 181.

69 Ibid., where he referred with approval to the High Court's decision in *Marumahoko v Chairman of the Public Service Commission and Another* 1991 (1) ZLR 27 (H) at 42-44.

70 2002 (1) ZLR 177 (S) at 185.

71 1989 (3) ZLR 183 (S).

72 Ibid., at 208, quoted by Ebrahim JA in *Biti* at 184.

73 Nyathi (2002) p. 7.

74 1979 RLR 291 (AD).

75 Ibid., at 303.

76 Nyathi (2002) p. 7.

77 1989 (3) *ZLR* 183 (S), at 195.

78 Ibid., at 201.

79 Ibid., at 194.

80 1979 RLR 291 (AD) at 303.

81 2002 (1) ZLR 177 (S) at 189. He referred with approval to two decisions of the South African Appellate Division: *Harris and Others v Minister of the Interior and Another* 1952 (2) SA 428 (A) and *Minister of the Interior and Another v Harris and Others* 1952 (4) SA 769 (A).

82 2002 (1) ZLR 177 (S) at 303. He referred with approval to: *Attorney General of New South Wales v Trethowan* [1932] AC 526 (PC, Australia); *Bribery Commissioners v Ranasinghe* [1965] AC 172 (PC, Ceylon); *R v Mecure* [1988] 1 SCR 234 (Supreme Court of Canada); and *RE Manitoba Language Rights* [1985] 1 SCR 721 (Supreme Court of Canada).

83 2002 (1) ZLR 177 (S) at 190.

84 Quoted by Ebrahim JA at 185.

85 Ibid., at 186.

86 Ibid.

87 Ibid.

88 [1974] AC 765.

89 Ibid. For a discussion of the case see Paul Jackson and Patricia Leopold (2001) *O. Hood Phillips and Jackson Constitutional and Administrative Law*, 8th edition, p. 50, paragraph 3 – 017.

90 See Hogg (2003) pp. 12-13, paragraph 12.3 (b). He says that while

the federal and provincial legislatures may impose manner and form restrictions upon themselves, such restrictions must be contained in Acts, not in internal rules of parliamentary procedure.

91   I believe, however, that even in the United Kingdom and Canada it can be argued that Parliament is bound by Standing Orders. This is because Standing Orders act as 'rules of identification' which enable one to determine whether Parliament has in fact 'acted' in a particular instance. If these 'rules of identification' are not enforceable, the validity of a Bill that has not been passed by a majority could not be challenged. This cannot be right.

92   At 187.

93   Applicant's Heads of Argument, p. 3, paragraph 9.

94   Ibid.

95   This is not stated explicitly in the judgement, but seems to be implied.

96   Section 57 (1) (a) of the Constitution says: 'Subject to the provisions of this Constitution and any other law, Parliament may make Standing Orders with respect to ... the passing of Bills.'

97   At 187.

98   Ibid.

99   This is – perhaps – implied in Ebrahim JA's judgement, but is not stated expressly. See also the comments made by MDC Member of Parliament David Coltart in Parliamentary Debates, volume 28, no. 40, at 3830, where he said: 'Standing Order 127 is very different to most Standing Orders. It deals with substantive matters not procedural matters. What we need to turn to is ... section 51 of the Constitution [which] ... makes [it] ... quite clear there is only one circumstance in which a Bill can be reintroduced and that is where the President has not given his assent and then when that Bill comes back, it will have to secure [a] two-thirds majority.'

100 Section 57 (1) (d) authorises the making of Standing Orders 'with respect to the regulation and orderly conduct of proceedings and business in Parliament'.

101 At 188. He added that the Order 'deals with motions, not with the passing of Bills'.

102 Ibid., at 185.

103 Ibid., at 188-189.

104 Ibid.

105 Nyathi, *supra*, appears to overlook this point (see p. 7 of his article).

106 Ibid., at 193.

107 1998 (3) SA 430 (C).

108 Quoted at page 18 of the cyclostyled judgement.

109 *Speaker of the National Assembly v De Lille and Another* 1999 (4) SA 863 (SCA).

110 Ibid., at 868, paragraph 14.

111 [Chapter 2:08].

112 2002 (1) *ZLR* 177 (S).at 193-194.

113 Ibid., at 194.

114 Judgement no. SC 47/04.

115 Act no. 6 of 2002.

116 *Quinnell*, at page 14 of the cyclostyled judgement.

117 Ibid, at 18.

118 Ibid, at 19.

119 Ibid, at 17.

120 (1960) 105 CLR 214.

121 (1980) 2 NSWLR 639. It may be that Malaba JA did not have access to the judgement itself, since he does not quote from it, but simply makes mention of an article which discusses the case in the 1981 Commonwealth Law Bulletin. I was myself only able to obtain a copy of the judgement through the kindness of Professor Cheryl Saunders of Melbourne University, who emailed me a copy.

122 1997 (2) BCLR 189 (ZS).

123 Ibid, at 207.

124 Christo Botha (1998) *Statutory Interpretation*, 3rd edition.

125 Ibid, at 135.

126 1972 (4) SA 72 (RAD).

127 Ibid, at 78.

128 In *Quinnell* Malaba JA attempted to support his view that Standing Order 127 was directory by saying at page 15 of the judgement: 'The makers of the Standing Order could by express language have declared that the happening of an event such as the breach of its provisions shall have as its effect the invalidation of the resultant Act.' With respect, this is a very weak argument. If the language of the Standing Order is imperative then it must follow logically that it is imposing a mandatory obligation. The Order does *not* have to state that invalidity will result in order to qualify as mandatory.

129 1995 (10) BCLR 1289 (CC).

130 Ibid, at 1319, paragraph 64.

131 In *Mulaudzi and Others v Chairman, Implementation Committee and Others* 1994 (4) BCLR 97 (V), at 132-133, the Supreme Court of Venda held that a failure by a legislative authority to comply with procedural requirements for the enactment of legislation set out in a statute, rendered the purported legislation concerned invalid.

132 See *Quinnell*, at page 8 of the cyclostyled judgement.

133 Ibid.

134 Ibid, at p. 16.

135 See *Biti*, at page 12 of the cyclostyled judgement, quoting Erskine May

(22nd edition) at 370.
136 Ibid.
137 See *Quinnell*, at page 39.

References

Botha, C. 1998. *Statutory Interpretation: An Introduction for Students.* 3rd ed. Kenwyn: Juta.

Chaskalson, M. et al. (eds). 1999. *Constitutional Law of South Africa.* Revision Service 5, 1999 update). Kenwyn: Juta.

Dicey, A.V. 1915 (republished 1982). *The Law of the Constitution*, 10th ed. Indianapolis: Liberty Fund.

Erskine May. 1997. *Parliamentary Practice. The Law, Privileges, Proceedings and Usage of Parliament*, 22nd ed. London: Butterworths.

Fitzgerald, P. 1972. 'The "Paradox" of Parliamentary Sovereignty', *Irish Jurist*, 28-47.

Hogg, P. 2003. *Constitutional Law of Canada.* Loose-leaf edition, vol. 2. Scarborough, Ontario: Carswell.

Holmes, S. 1993. 'Precommitment and the Paradox of Democracy' in Elster J. and R. Slagstad, *Constitutionalism and Democracy.* Cambridge, UK: Cambridge University Press, pp. 195-240.

Jackson, P. and P. Leopold. 2001. *O. Hood Phillips and Jackson Constitutional and Administrative Law*, 8th edition. London: Sweet and Maxwell.

Klaaren, J. 1999. 'Judicial Remedies.' Chapter 9 in Chaskalson et al., *Constitutional Law of South Africa.* Revision Service 5, 1999 update). Kenwyn: Juta. pp. 9-1 to 9-32.

Linington, G. 2001. *Constitutional Law of Zimbabwe.* Harare: Legal Resources Foundation.

— 'Constitutions and Constitutionalism.' *Mukai-Vukani* no. 57, August 2011, pp. 5-8.

McIntosh, E. ed. 1951. *The Concise Oxford Dictionary.* 4th ed. Oxford: Clarendon.

Nyathi, M. 2002. 'The Constitution, Parliamentary Standing Orders and the "Constraints" on Law-Making: An Analysis of the Supreme Court's Decision on Tendai Biti and Anor v The Minister of Justice, Legal and Parliamentary Affairs and Another SC 10/02 [unreported]', *Law Society of Zimbabwe Magazine*, No. 11: 6-7. Parliamentary Debates,. 2002. vol. 28, no. 40. Harare: Parliament of Zimbabwe.

Tribe, L. 2000. *American Constitutional Law*, 3rd ed. Vol. 1. New York:

Foundation Press.
Winterton, G. 1976. 'The British Grundnorm: Parliamentary Supremacy Re-Examined', *Law Quarterly Review*, vol. 92: 591-617.

Cases

Attorney General of New South Wales v Trethowan [1932] AC 526 (PC, Australia).

Biti and Anor v Minister of Justice, Legal and Parliamentary Affairs and Anor 2002 (1) ZLR 177 (S).

Bribery Commissioners v Ranasinghe [1965] AC 172 (PC, Ceylon).

British Railways Board v Pickin [1974] AC 765.

Bruce and Another v Fleecytex Johannesburg CC and Others 1998 (4) BCLR 415 (CC).

Capital Radio (Private) Limited v Broadcasting Authority of Zimbabwe and Others Judgment no. SC 128/02.

Chairman of the Public Service Commission and Others v Zimbabwe Teachers Association and Others 1996 (9) BCLR 1189 (ZS).

Chikerema and Others v UANC and Another 1979 RLR 291 (AD).

Chinamora v Angwa Furnishers (Pvt.) Ltd and Another (Attorney-General intervening) 1997 (2) BCLR 189 (ZS).

Clayton v Heffron (1960) 105 CLR 214.

De Lille and Another v Speaker of the National Assembly 1998 (3) SA 430 (C).

Executive Council of the Western Cape Legislature and Others v President of the Republic of South Africa and Others 1995 (10) BCLR 1289 (CC).

Ferreira v Levin No and Others and Vryenhoek and Others v Powell No and Others 1996 (1) BCLR 1 (CC).

Harris and Others v Minister of the Interior and Another 1952 (2) SA 428 (A).

Hewlett v Minister of Finance 1981 ZLR 571 (S).

Mandirwhe v Minister of State 1986 (1) ZLR 1 (S).

Marbury v Madison 5 US (1 CRANCH) 137 (1803).

Marumahoko v Chairman of the Public Service Commission and Another 1991 (1) ZLR 27 (H) at 42-44.

Mulaudzi and Others v Chairman, Implementation Committee and Others 1994 (4) BCLR 97 (V).

Minister of Justice v Borowski [1981] 2 SCR 575.

Minister of the Interior and Another v Harris and Others 1952 (4) SA 769 (A).

Namoi Shire Council v Attorney-General for New South Wales (1980) 2

NSWLR 639.

Nyamandlovu Farmers Association v Minster of Lands, Agriculture and Rural Resettlement and Another Judgment no. HB 19/2003.

PF ZAPU v Minister of Justice (2) 1985 (1) ZLR 15 (S).

Pickin v British Railways Board [1974] AC 765.

President of the Republic of South Africa and Another v Hugo 1997 (6) BCLR 708 (CC).

R v Big M Drug Mart Ltd [1985] 1 SCR 295.

R v Mecure [1988] 1 SCR 234 (Supreme Court of Canada).

RE Manitoba Language Rights [1985] 1 SCR 721 (Supreme Court of Canada).

S v Gatsi; S v Rufaro Hotel (Pvt.) Ltd 1994 (1) ZLR 7 (H).

S v Takaendesa 1972 (4) SA 72 (RAD).

Smith v Mutasa NO and Another 1989 (3) ZLR 183 (S).

Speaker of the National Assembly v De Lille and Another 1999 (4) SA 863 (SCA).

Thoburn v Sunderland City Council [2002] 1 CMLR 50.

Tsvangirai v Registrar General of Elections and Others, not yet reported, judgement no SC 20/02.

West Virginia State Board of Execution v Barnette 319 US 624.

4

Transitional Justice & Security Sector Governance
Combating Sexual & Gender-Based Violence in Zimbabwe

Annie Barbara Chikwanha

Introduction: the implications of the trajectory for women's liberation on Zimbabwe's democratic transition

Zimbabwean women's tribulations pre-date the Third Chimurenga (2000 to date) and paint a rather sombre vision of the future if ameliorative action on combating sexual and gender-based violence (SGBV) is not taken by all key actors on the political landscape. Generally, survivors of SGBV in post-conflict areas face many interlocking barriers to justice. These include cultural barriers, amongst them the marginalised role of women in their families and a social stigma attached to survivors of sexual violence; legal barriers, from informal customary law, formal justice processes such as discriminatory judicial processes and legal procedures that discriminate against women and afford them few legal rights; and systemic barriers such as a lack of infrastructure, government resources and personnel.[1] Together, these barriers make it very difficult for a survivor of SGBV in Zimbabwe to seek and obtain justice. Though the current transition arrangements make provision for addressing some of these issues, political will is clearly lacking, as evidenced by the pace of delivering justice to victims of SGBV in the country.

The discussion in this chapter is thus shaped by three key questions that have implications for the transition processes: What opportunities does the current transition under the Inclusive Government

(IG) formed under the Global Political Agreement (GPA) present for eradicating or minimising SGBV? How has the country tackled the general environment of discrimination, which leads to violence against women, generally of a sexual nature, perpetrated by the state, by the community and even by those we trust the most in the private sphere? Why have the post-conflict management processes, plans and policies in the country remained 'gender blind' in theory and practice?

From 1890 to date, each successive generation of Zimbabwean women has struggled for dignity and inclusion into the formal governance systems that have gone through various transformations. These struggles cannot be separated from the political phases that have shaped and continue to colour the country's sociopolitical history. In 2008, the Minister of State in the Organ of National Healing, Reconciliation and Integration, Sekai Holland, herself a victim of state-sponsored violence, publicly acknowledged the acts of state-sponsored violence on citizens who dared to hold opposing views to the political elite at each successive phase in the history of the country.[2]

The initial resistance to colonisation in 1890 (the First Chimurenga) gave rise to one popular heroine, Mbuya Nehanda Nyakasikana, who became an inspiration for the participation of women in the liberation struggle that started in the 1960s. During this Second Chimurenga (1966–1980), women enjoyed an elevated status (rhetorically) and considered themselves as equals in the liberation struggle. This populism was essential to sustain the struggle, especially in the battlefield, where the support of women was essential for logistical supplies, information and shelter. And although women also fought alongside the male combatants, their importance as freedom fighters has never been given much prominence. Campbell (2003) accurately captured the patriarchal attitudes inherent in black society at the time:

> The victory of the guerrillas in the independence struggle had been a joint effort by all [women and men], but in the post-independence period, African males who had celebrated women in combat called on the same women to return to the family to carry out their 'respectable' role as mothers.

Bond-Stewart (1987:15, 17) cites Cornelia Nkomo, a woman freedom fighter who lamented the neglect of female combatants after the war:

> When my father gave me an education, people said that I would learn

prostitution and yet they never said that with boys. I started thinking 'What's wrong with my being a woman? There were promises of equality but there were times when men were regarded as bosses. For example, very few women were trained in the air force and artillery. Why? I wanted to .... Teurai Ropa Nhongo was very skilled in military work. Why was she not made the Minister of Defence? ... [W]hy are women in lower ranks?'[3]

The transition to democratic rule after independence in 1980 carved little room for female voices to provide an input into the restructuring and sensitisation of the security sector. Other than having women in the army, as is the case in most democratic countries, mechanisms that could have drawn gender-sensitive reforms into the new post-independent security institutions were not considered. Opportunities presented by this independence transition period were thus lost and the nation-building that occurred laid the foundation for the neglect of women's security needs. The new post-liberation war security sector thus evolved along the same old male-dominated lines, with the security sector's orientation towards handling females' security issues remained unchanged. The mere presence of women in the force appears to have been enough appeasement for both the women and the men at the time.

The democratic consolidation phase, from the mid 1980s to the mid 1990s, left women to their own devices in terms of security provision and obtaining justice, particularly against gender-based violence, even though the broad reforms called for by this neo-liberal paradigm could have been used to reformat Zimbabwe's security sector in a way that increased access to justice for all citizens. Women's security needs, such as a criminal justice system responsive to both domestic and politically related violence and access to resources that would eradicate freedom from fear and want, remained unfulfilled by the new political dispensation, preserving the dominant patriarchal culture that was pervasive in formal institutions and at the domestic level. Unfortunately, the economic hardships brought about by this neo-liberal phase, and its attendant calls for multi-party democracy, worsened the plight of women in the country as they once again became victims of the political squabbles between the ruling party and the opposition.[4]

Worse was yet to come. With the onset of the Third Chimurenga (2002 onwards), resistance to opposition players in the political arena was acted out on women's bodies. The same liberation war logic – that you hurt somebody's family in order to intimidate them into switching loyalties through fear – was applied again, as wives of opposition political parties were raped, beaten and maimed in order to force their husbands into submission. Given this background, the key actors in Zimbabwe's GPA ought to have seized the chances offered by the transition to emphasise reform of the security sector in a way that would eradicate such mindsets and inculcate new human rights-oriented values.

This chapter briefly scrutinises the course of Zimbabwean women's struggle for that seemingly elusive dignity and liberation throughout different phases in the country's history. It discusses the security sector's orientation towards women and the missed opportunities presented by these various transitions for security sector reforms that could have been a blueprint for gender-sensitive security governance both nationally and regionally. More importantly, it attempts to identify opportunities for reforming the security sector to be gender-sensitive under the transitional GPA. The aim is not to portray women simply as the proverbial victims of security agents' exploitative practices, but also as victims of the patriarchal attitudes of African society and bureaucracies in general. Accordingly, the development of a 'safe security' apparatus for women is thus paramount for a successful transition.

Methodology

In attempting to answer the question of whether the GPA addresses issues of SGBV and security sector governance during Zimbabwe's current transition period, the methodology used in collecting data for this paper was determined by the sensitivity of the phenomenon under scrutiny and the problems associated with conducting primary research on a sensitive topic in a generally hostile environment. The data was collected through secondary sources and relied to some extent on anecdotal evidence from the print and electronic media, especially victims' narratives. Police statistics on these victims' experiences are impossible to obtain, as is evidenced by the narratives of many of the victims who could not report to an institution that was directly involved in much of the post-2000 political violence.

A review of relevant academic literature and NGO documents on

SGBV at country, regional and global levels was carried out in relation to the sub-regional, regional and international conventions, standards and protocols used to provide guidelines on combating SGBV. Of particular importance was whether these provisions have been signed, ratified or domesticated by the national governments. Relevant national policy frameworks designed by relevant authorities were also reviewed.

The data was analysed using content analysis and the narrative approach was adopted with the intention to recite facts as told 'in the first person'.

Defining SGBV

SGBV is the specific violence that is targeted at women, and sometimes children, in both the public and private spheres. It includes both physical and emotional harm as well as threats to inflict deliberate, pre-defined harm. Many forms of abuse fall into this category: rape, assault, enslavement, confinement, the denial of basic provisions, verbal abuse and domestic violence.[5] Women all over the world suffer different forms of SGBV and according to Unifem one in three women experience one or more of them. Though SGBV exists in all societies, the combination of different issues in Zimbabwe's current political environment make the situation unique. While security institutions mandated with safeguarding the sanctity of human life and a ministry dedicated to enhancing the quality of women's life exist, they have largely turned a blind eye to the atrocities carried out from 2000 onwards. Instead, it is civil society organisations (CSOs) who have been the main actors stepping in to help victims, albeit in an ad-hoc fashion.

Since 2000, Zimbabwe's women have suffered SGBV almost continuously, with election time being peak season for such abuse and atrocities. All types of conflict inflict suffering on everyone, but the short- and long-term effects particularly affect women. Sexual assault and exploitation are frequently employed as tools of political violence throughout Zimbabwe. This type of victimisation leads to isolation, alienation, prolonged emotional trauma and unwanted pregnancies that often result in abandoned children.[6]

Male-dominated political structures, a patrilineal system designed not to question male authority,[7] a compromised criminal justice system that was clearly loyal to the ruling party and a harsh economic environment that demanded more attention to basic survival needs left countless women vulnerable to abuse by predatory actors. The current domestic legal framework covering SGBV is inadequate as far as protecting women from SGBV, especially of a political nature, is concerned. Legal frameworks such as the Legal Age of Majority Act (1982) and the Domestic Violence Act (2007) cannot be argued to cover politically motivated violence, and without the domestication of the relevant international legal frameworks, there is little room for victims to obtain justice. Actors such as the Research and Advocacy Unit (RAU), the Institute for Democracy in Africa, the Zimbabwe Women Lawyers Association and the International Center for Transitional Justice have all made significant contributions to triggering dialogue on the problem.

Transitional justice mechanisms for security sector reforms in Zimbabwe – an analytic framework

This section briefly discusses select transitional justice mechanisms that could contribute to stabilising Zimbabwe and enhancing human security for women. Moreover, these changes could have been implemented during the GPA transitional phase: prosecution, truth and reconciliation, documentation, memorialisation and reparations. A quick glance at the transitional justice processes in Zimbabwe shows that the country seems to have opted for reconciliation, which is mostly about forgiveness without punishment, even though prosecution, one of the transitional justice mechanisms under the GPA, has provision for investigations and prosecution of perpetrators of political violence. The GPA offers opportunities for correcting the past whilst moving into a new era, yet no action has been taken on effecting some transitional justice mechanism that would begin the much-needed national healing process. In any case, with the limited forensic facilities in the country, prosecution will not deliver justice to many of the perpetrators, as there will not be evidence to nail them down. It also becomes even more questionable whether this would be the right approach in the absence of a revamped security sector since many of the rank and file in the police, the rag-tag youth militia and soldiers were all allegedly involved in committing many of the atrocities.

Would truth and reconciliation be a better option then? Some owning-up to these atrocities is essential, because of the nearness of the perpetrators to the victims, yet there appears to be a reluctance to move in this direction. In any case, the history of Zimbabwe is laden with memories of buried horrors and the tensions continue to smoulder. The Gukurahundi massacres in Matebeleland in the early 1980s are one such example.

Truth and reconciliation commissions have made a mark on the continent's post-conflict healing processes. They hinge on the concept of conditional amnesty: that perpetrators ought to take responsibility for their actions and fully admit to the atrocities they committed, facing prosecution if their testimonies are found wanting. However, truth commissions have mostly been used by countries that were largely involved in outright civil war, which perhaps raises questions as to the suitability of the model for Zimbabwe. Though they make it possible to transcend the past, their real value is in generating public empathy for victims who narrate their experiences, in the process both publicly acknowledging and symbolising the pain of the wronged.[8]

Documentation is a part of many transitional justice mechanisms and is of immense value to healing communities. This is currently being done by different actors both inside and outside Zimbabwe. Ensuring that the history of human rights violations is always remembered keeps citizens on their guard with regard to watching out for the erosion of civic freedoms. Another mechanism, memorialising the dead through films and poetry, is important where impoverished communities cannot afford compensation or where the scale of atrocities was so great that the damages appear to be irreparable and this is yet to be done. Scars certainly do take longer to heal when memories are continually refreshed, but it also makes it easier to accept the past and deal with it constructively. Gender sensitivities can be woven into the memorialisation process, and though the issue of stigma is high for rape victims in particular, the 'shame' of being named as a perpetrator outweighs this. It also tends to tarnish the names of the relatives of perpetrators, hence more people will be compelled to assume responsibility to prevent their kith and kin from committing such crimes.

Reparations, which pin moral responsibility on the state, allow for political stability and are an obligation under international law which states that 'reparation must, as far as possible, wipe out all the consequences of the illegal act and re-establish the situation which would, in all probability, have existed if that act had not been committed.'[9] This is contained in the Draft Basic Principles and Guidelines on the Right to a Remedy and Reparation for Victims of Violations of International Human Rights and Humanitarian Law (4) (Draft Principles on Reparation). This is particularly important where prosecutorial capacity is lacking and is unlikely to be pursued. With emphasis on support for healing, they allow victims to move on with reconstructing their lives. The direct benefits to victims can make governments increase protection for the vulnerable citizens. The Nairobi Declaration on Women and Girls' Right to Remedy and Reparation underscores the importance of this mechanism, especially with its emphasis on a progressive scale according to the gravity of the situation. If governments know that they will be held financially accountable, the violation of human rights would doubtless be minimised.

Though the current emphasis is on reconciliation and healing that is to be achieved through forgiving, as was the case after the liberation war in 1980, Zimbabwe's experiences are such that it would benefit from a combination of the various modes of transitional justice. This is partly because the message that is being portrayed is that forgiveness does not include punishment and this is covered up with celebrating reconciliation as the chosen mode of justice. However, because of the nature of the atrocities committed, much more needs to be done: reparations and compensation ought to be paid, the wrongs acknowledged, documenting the atrocities so that they become an official and public part of the nation's history; and prosecuting some of the 'mass' rapists/ killers who are a danger to society. Many damaged communities will be unable to properly heal until the perpetrators of the crimes committed against them are tried, found guilty and punished. All these approaches aim, to varying extents, to restore relations between victims and offenders within the community, but will only work when there is goodwill on the part of both offenders and victims.

The re-education of Zimbabwean women

The patriarchal model of the liberation struggle was the basis upon which the African government was couched and 'had been entrenched into law' at the Lancaster House negotiations (Campbell, 2003:285).

This section analyses the trajectory of Zimbabwe's women's fight for justice and inclusion that would encourage more state protection for the more vulnerable sex. It also discusses the patriarchal attitudes that were masked by the liberation rhetoric and how these have continued to impinge on security sector reforms that would be gender-sensitive. The struggle for liberation was also couched in terms of seeking dignity for women but this failed to materialise. As with all revolutionary processes, women fighters had to go through an orientation process in which they were re-educated about their role in the struggle for independence and were prepared for their post-liberation roles in the building of an egalitarian society. This decolonisation of the mind did not adequately prepare them for demanding gender-sensitive reforms as the political jargon emphasised equality between the sexes. This created an unhealthy euphoria in these women, who felt their security needs would be catered for by the processes of the revolution and would spill over into the post-liberation phase. What the women misunderstood was that the liberation would not be of them as women, and certainly not from future authoritarian regimes or the patriarchy inherent in the society, but only of the country from colonialism.

Space for women to put themselves on an equal footing with men was largely carved out by the ruling party. Security and development issues that touched on women were thus a separate agenda, as evidenced by the emphasis of separate structures for these within the Ministry of Women's Affairs created in 1981. Women were expected to organise within these structures if they were to get state resources, silencing many of those who could have championed their causes for inclusion as they did not subscribe to the ideology of the dominant party. As a result, women's economic security had little opportunity to flourish. This partly explains the confinement of the women's security discourse to the ruling party in the early years of independence.

The behaviour of the female combatants almost 30 years after the war revealed the oft-neglected, uncelebrated aspects of the war: their suffering of internal violence, gender inequality and sexual harassment, among other negative experiences. The few women who were in the ZANU-PF leadership hierarchy during the struggle, such as Teurai Ropa Nhongo (Joyce Mujuru) (Central Committee) and the late Sheba Tavarwisa (High Command) earned their positions from their participation in combat activities after receiving the very same military training as their male colleagues in exile and proving themselves equally capable. Though all former female fighters are naturally proud of their contribution to the liberation struggle, their pride is nonetheless tinged with bitterness:

> I would never recommend my daughter to follow my example if such a situation arose again. (Kachere in Zimbabwe Women Writers, 2000:191)

Tsuneo Yoshikuni raised an important point in his book about women ex-combatants. He asked, 'what a country would be like if the agenda and the priorities were governed by women: would war be a priority?' (Ibid.:xiii). He answers his own question by quoting a feminist argument, 'Whatever you are fighting for, in the end, it's just a matter of removing one regime and replacing it with another similar regime.' The new regime that came in did not push for the advancement of women according to the liberation struggle's promises. The absence of the female combatants at the negotiations that ended the liberation war, and in the new security apparatus, show how Zimbabwe's struggle clearly relegated women's interests and security issues to the background, from independence onwards.

As already mentioned, although the new political and governance environment that emerged after the struggle offered possibilities for gender-sensitive reforms and processes, none were ever taken. Hence, human rights-oriented security governance reforms remain in a state of permanent flux. Post-independence state institutions set up to deal with women's affairs were weak and followed a strict political agenda that paid lip service to women's security concerns. The mere fact that women are still not part of the upper strata of the entire security apparatus is illustrative of this fact. The non-governmental organisations (NGOs) that emerged in the immediate post-war phase were equally weak and had low networking capacity, as the ruling party demanded organisation within its structures. The Ministry of Women's Affairs was manned by party cadres pushing a socialist agenda in line with the principle of democratic centralism in which the party hierarchy is supreme and all party decisions are the *de facto* law. When former combatants began to push for adequate compensation and for inclusion in governance structures, female ex-combatants were subsumed under the national war veterans' structures, which mirrored those of ZANU-PF. This effectively left women without a voice to criticise the governance style and patterns within the security sector.

In Zimbabwe, the women's movement against SGBV thus emerged in a fragmented manner, with each trying to carve out its own legitimate space within the political setting and this was largely a reaction to the increasing levels of violence that were being perpetrated against women. As a result, resisting the impositions of a domineering party and an insensitive security apparatus became the central issue that shaped the women's agenda. Collecting and collating information on women's concerns and needs became a priority as women's groups scrambled to influence policies. Organisations such as Women and Law in Southern Africa and the Zimbabwe Women's Resource Centre and Network were at the forefront of this effort, which almost became an end in itself as very little action was directed at preventing violence. It was only in the early 2000s that new organisations sprang up as a reaction to the politically related violence that was increasingly being directed at women. The more traditional organisations such as the Young Women's Christian Association of Zimbabwe remained on the sidelines until the excessive violence prompted them to be more active. Coalitions such as the Women's Coalition of Zimbabwe that also formed in response to the depravity were a welcome development, but still proved inadequate in terms of action. Agency on the Zimbabwean security landscape is still quite fragile as many voices have remained on the periphery, confining themselves to sporadic demonstrations of anger.

The second re-education of re-educated Zimbabwean women: (the Third Chimurenga)

Zimbabwe's political culture has been dominated by violent action rather than dialogue, bargaining and compromise. Partly an import from the liberation struggle and the general silence surrounding violence, it has acted against several generations of women, creating the room for sexual violence to become the key weapon in political suppression. After the advent of an effective opposition party in late 1999, the ZANU-PF party felt the time was ripe to re-educate the people of Zimbabwe on the meaning of a people's struggle as well as on the consequences of shifting loyalties to any party that was contesting for inclusion into a highly shrunk political space occupied by the liberators.

From 2000, politically related violence increased whilst the economy dwindled due to an inappropriate governance style. By 2007, Zimbabwean men's life expectancy averaged 37 years and for women it was lower, at 34 years. Male protesters faced widespread human rights abuses, but female activists quoted in Amnesty International's 2006 report, 'Between a Rock and a Hard Place – Women Human Rights Defenders at Risk', described disturbing brutal treatment at the hands of the police: 'Detained women human rights defenders have been subjected to sexist verbal attacks, and denied access to food, medical care and access to lawyers.'[10] Many examples abound to back up this claim.

From 2003, women belonging to the human rights organisation, Women of Zimbabwe Arise (WOZA), have been repeatedly arrested by the police. Many of the women were arrested and later released without charge, with some being charged under the Public Order and Security Act (POSA). Some were charged under the Miscellaneous Offences Act (MOA) especially under the general provision where their actions could be interpreted as causing a breach of the peace. This manipulation of the law comes about when the police cannot charge activists under POSA. Both local and international civic groups believe that this persecution was part of the government's plan to silence the opposition prior to the March 2005 election. This culminated in the proposed legal ban on international human rights groups and foreign funding of local organisations. WOZA refused to be intimidated into silence and continued to stand up in demand of democracy and violated all the restrictions on freedom of association, assembly and expression, the fundamentals of any democratic society. The systematic build up of violence eventually turned into an orgy of state-orchestrated violence.

The security system was increasingly involved in the political repression acts. One such case of abuse of the security system to deter women from demanding justice occurred in July 2008 when two leaders of WOZA, Jennifer Williams and Magodonga Mahlangu, who had been arrested the previous month, were finally granted bail by the Harare Magistrate's Court.[11] Their bail conditions required them to report to the nearest police station twice a week and not to interfere with state witnesses. Strangely enough, the state witnesses were non-existent as the accused had not seen them. The security agents' behaviour contradicted Article 1 of the United Nations (UN) Declaration on Human

Rights Defenders, adopted by the General Assembly of the United Nations on 9 December 1998 which states that 'everyone has the right, individually and in association with others, to promote and to strive for the protection and realisation of human rights and fundamental freedoms at the national and international levels'.

Rape increasingly became the ultimate punishment for women associated with the opposition and those who were seen to be resisting the hegemonic status of the ruling party. According to evidence collected by human rights organisations from the victims, the rapes were all systematic and co-ordinated. Likewise, the language used by the perpetrators was similar and clearly meets some of the criteria for the definition of crimes against humanity.

The following disturbing incidences recorded by Stubbs (2008) support these observations:

> A 13-year-old girl told how she was abducted from her home in exchange for a goat. She was then held in a youth militia camp where she was repeatedly raped and beaten. In another case, a 60-year-old woman was raped by 18 militia members who told her they wanted her to have a ZANU PF baby. Human rights activists told stories of women having pesticides forced into them for failing to reveal the location of opposition leaders.

According to one victim, after being raped, the ZANU-PF soldiers made her crawl on her belly to a bored bureaucrat holding a list and sitting nearby. He found and ticked her name on the list to acknowledge that she had been given her punishment. 'Mine was the fourth name on the list for that day,' she said. Her name was crossed off and the militia forces moved on, presumably to locate their next victim.

The YWCA[12] of Zimbabwe experienced first-hand the political violence church leaders reported when a youth militia entered the property and threatened to behead the 120 displaced women and children who had found refuge at the hostel for four weeks. Many of the women and children had already witnessed torture and murders when they initially fled their homes were left traumatised and terrified.

For example, a 23-year old woman was captured by government youth militia in north-eastern Zimbabwe and dragged to their camp near Mount Darwin, where she was gagged and gang-raped by ten young men who were high on drink and drugs in a horrifying night of sexual abuse and beatings.

In the weeks immediately after the June 2008 presidential elections in Zimbabwe, human rights activists were overwhelmed with reports from women associated with the opposition party, the Movement for Democratic Change (MDC), who had been raped by members of the ruling party, ZANU-PF youth militia, agents of Zimbabwe's Central Intelligence Organisation (CIO), and people who identified themselves as veterans of the liberation war (known as war veterans) in a vicious campaign to intimidate voters and emerge victorious in the presidential election. Aids-Free World (2009) points out correctly that the 300 testimonies revealed that patterns recurred throughout the testimonies of the 70 survivors and two witnesses and cannot be coincidental.

A 30-something-year-old woman identified as Memory recounted how the youth militia raped her:

> When I arrived at the base, they removed all my clothes and I was raped by three men, one after the other.

When she went to the police to report the incident, she was told that they would not accept her statement. The policeman told her:

> We are not dealing with political violence cases. The time will come when we will deal with them.[13]

Another woman recounted:

> A man called M was a very senior war veteran. He was in his fifties. Sometime at the beginning of January 2002 he came to my home and asked my mother if I could 'go with him'. My mother said that I was far too young for him. This angered M. He pulled me to him and began to fondle my breasts in front of my mother. I was scared, ashamed and embarrassed. He then dragged me to his car and pushed me inside .... M drove me to a farm, I was very scared during the drive and did not speak at all .... M took me to a room in the farmhouse. He pushed me on to the bed. He pulled my skirt up and raped me. His hand covered my mouth. I was in a great amount of pain. He was very rough and I was a virgin .... After 24 hours M came back to the room. He said he wanted a 'last one' and then proceeded to rape me again. (Stubbs, 2008)

Estimates put the number of women raped in militia camps between May and July 2008 at more than 2000. During this period, the law enforcement agencies refused to accept reports of politically motivated violence in the country and women reporting rape encountered doubting law enforcement agents and hostility hence many did not make a report due to the stigma attached to rape victims in Zimbabwe. This concurs with the well-known assertion that in all situations of conflict, merely by virtue of their gender, women are both primary and secondary victims of violence. The Constitution of Zimbabwe itself is a drawback for addressing gender issues. Section 23[14] still allows for black women to be dealt with according to 'customary' law when it comes to family, marriage, divorce, inheritance and other customary issues belonging to the private sphere, the space where women are most violated and oppressed. This negates the Bill of Rights in Section 11 of the Constitution. As John Hatchard (1993:41) rightly argues, 'a right is meaningless when it is impossible for a person to exercise it either directly or indirectly', thus the fight for a new Constitution for the women of Zimbabwe is also a fight for protecting basic rights.

The increased militarisation of the Zimbabwean government that took place from 2002 exposed women to higher risks of abuse, yet the government adamantly defended using security and intelligence personnel to oversee the revival of the economy. In March 2006, a new economic and food security revival body known as the Zimbabwe National Security Council, which includes officials from the CIO, the army, police, prison services and the Registrar-General's office, was set up to oversee and enhance the capacity of government ministries. The Minister of National Security supported the action and emphasised that the deployment of security personnel to civilian ministries was to ensure that 'things would move' and that the government needed to closely monitor the performance of all sectors of the economy to ensure that the goal of recovery was met:

> There is nothing sinister with involving security force personnel in areas like the economy and food security: the government is doing what is best for Zimbabwe. Any complaints to the contrary are only meant to rubbish a genuine economic revival and food security programme.[15]

Collaboration to end SGBV in Zimbabwe

Women are victims at three levels, the domestic, the state and the international. Failing to place them at the centre of the security discourse at the domestic level makes them even more vulnerable at the national level, as the case of Zimbabwe illustrates. Even when they flee their own countries to escape sexual violence, they often end up as victims in the hands of their supposed protectors in refugee camps and of the security agents they encounter when negotiating safe passage.

How can Zimbabwean women now push for justice against the perpetrators of politically motivated sexual violence? Testimonies from victims of sexual violence and gang rapes by leading members of ZANU-PF have been collected by AIDS-Free World and other human rights organisations, and these can be used in truth and reconciliation hearings to help heal the victims and work out adequate compensation packages. Although the latter will not necessary eradicate their mental and/or physical suffering the psychology behind it may help to alleviate their anguish. The passage of the United Nations (UN) Security Council Resolution 1820 in June 2008 relayed strong signals that sexual violence as a weapon of conflict will not be tolerated. However, this seems to matter little to GNU authorities, as it has failed to take steps to bring to book any of the perpetrators of such crimes. With the stigma of rape exacerbated by the fear of retribution for reporting it, the number of instances are hugely under-reported. The president frequently pardons political criminals, and one way to encourage victims to come forward and make reports would be to exclude sexual crimes from amnesty provisions and have security institutions ensure full compliance with obligations for prosecuting persons responsible for such acts.

UN Security Council Resolution 1820 is an important step forward for women because it makes sexual violence a state security issue and places it on the same political footing as other crimes against humanity in conflict situations. It also provides an additional channel through which victims can seek legal redress and prosecution in the International Criminal Court and other international forums. However, Resolution 1820 is yet to be used in a court of law and the case of Zimbabwe does provide an opportunity for doing so. Does this mean then that Zimbabwean women can seek redress in the Southern African Development Community (SADC) Tribunal instead? How can we facilitate recourse to justice by the SGBV victims through the African and international human rights protection mechanisms? After all, the perpetrators themselves are very much a part of the entire security system. Unlike with the Economic Community for West African States (ECOWAS), where individuals can automatically take their grievances to the ECOWAS Community Court of Justice, the SADC Tribunal has to ensure that domestic justice channels have been exhausted before it can take up cases.

Though it is unlikely that most of the Zimbabwean judiciary will defy the will of ZANU-PF, a precedent was set in October 2008 when a female regional magistrate, Esther Muremba, convicted the commander of a ZANU-PF youth base for violently raping the wife of an MDC supporter. The magistrate openly condemned the use of sexual violence during the 2008 elections and stated that raping a defenceless woman under the guise of political campaigning was a serious offence. She handed the offender a 20-year jail sentence. This clearly illustrates the power the judiciary does have to combat sexual violence as a political weapon. However, the judiciary itself is in need of reform, so that it can become the impartial professional institution it is supposed to be and begin enforcing all existing laws, inadequate as they are. The GNU provides an opportunity for infusing new blood into the system and instilling a new culture of human rights that has justice at its core. So doing would make it possible for Zimbabwe to conform to Articles 1 and 12.2 of the UN Declaration on Human Rights Defenders, adopted by the General Assembly of the United Nations on 9 December 1998, which states that:

> the State shall take all necessary measures to ensure the protection by the competent authorities of everyone, individually and in association with others, against any violence, threats, retaliation, *de facto* or *de jure* adverse discrimination, pressure or any other arbitrary action as a consequence of his or her legitimate exercise of the rights.

Women celebrated and welcomed the GPA[16] that formed the GNU as it acknowledged the equality between men and women and recognised the role women have played in nation-building and the abuses they have suffered in the process. However, it is important to point out that women's needs and issues were subsumed under sweeping statements in the preamble of the GPA. For example, the two statements below fail to recognise the need to protect women from political violence in particular:

> RECOGNISING, accepting and acknowledging that the values of justice, fairness, openness, tolerance, equality, non-discrimination and respect of all persons without regard to race, class, gender, ethnicity, language, religion, political opinion, place of origin or birth are the bedrock of our democracy and good governance.

> DETERMINED to build a society free of violence, fear, intimidation, hatred, patronage, corruption and founded on justice, fairness, openness, transparency, dignity and equality.

Though the historic agreement aimed to put an end to the political and economic crisis and politically motivated violence, women continue to suffer their effects. The failure to be specific on securing the lives of women points to the absence of their strong inclusion in the drafting of the GPA. Indeed, only one woman, Priscilla Misihairabwi-Mushonga, a member of parliament from the Movement for Democratic Change (the Mutambara faction) was part of the group of people who drafted the GPA.

The pattern of the struggle for women's dignity in Zimbabwe shows the importance of the linkages needed between local groups and international forces. Issues of sovereignty can be used to mask violent repression, and this further marginalises women and increases their distance from security institutions that in any case fail to protect them. This points to the need to have various kinds of coalitions that transcend individual groups' agendas. No transitional process can be effective unless it addresses the issues raised by those affected and acknowledges the evidence collected on these atrocities against women. All attempts at national healing and reconciliation without justice will simply deflect attention and provide a short-term remedy to the seemingly resolved political conflict.

Missed opportunities – UN Resolution 1325

In most cases, gender-related issues are addressed through the principle of non-discrimination stipulated in scattered international conventions (for example, UN Resolution 1325 passed October 2000 on Women, Peace and Security[17]) and it is important to track the extent to which Zimbabwe deviates from these norms and standards. Resolution 1325 recognises the importance of women's participation in the prevention and resolution of conflicts and provides a series of specific measures aimed at women's full participation in decision-making in the area of peace and security. This is a must for Zimbabwe if there is to be everlasting peace and stability.

The working hypothesis here is that the country has taken 'a justice avoidance and evasion' mechanism, especially when it comes to addressing the plight of victims of SGBV victims. Transitional justice mechanisms such as truth commissions, reparation packages and other reconciliation initiatives could have been part of institutional reforms that would have resulted in the establishment of fair, effective and transparent public and security institutions to safeguard against the future abuse of women and other vulnerable groups. Justice avoidance takes place through the failure to domesticate international protocols, standards and agreements and evasion occurs when the legal instruments remain silent on the horrors perpetrated against women's bodies.

Since independence, Zimbabwe has failed to take advantage of many opportunities for reforming the security sector. During the changeover from the colonial regime the emphasis was on Africanisation, and the chance to infuse a human rights gender-sensitive culture was missed. The replacement of white officials with black Africans was essential as it brought about a representative bureaucracy, but the quality of the bureaucrats left a lot to be desired. At the regional level, much of the focus was still on liberation and the content of the liberation outcomes did not feature on the SADC agenda, which was also in its formative stage when Zimbabwe achieved independence in 1980. The case of Zimbabwe could have given SADC all the ammunition it needed to deal with women and security sector governance and reform in this new African state.

Nor did the post-independence one-party state formulate new laws and norms that complied with international legal tools, despite having signed and ratified many of them. In this phase, civil society was marginalised and discouraged, and hence developed along parallel lines and did not contribute to governance. Even when the political space opened up a little, the ZANU-PF regime still chose not to benefit from the support civil society could provide.

This situation is no different now. The opportunities offered by the GPA could also have been used to change the insensitivity of the police force, judiciary and prisons so that female victims of violence can obtain satisfactory degrees of justice. The government has yet to adhere to the GPA by returning the country to the rule of law, bringing all perpetrators of violence to book, eradicating all discrimination based on gender, ensuring community integration and national healing and involving women at every stage of the transitional process, especially on issues that relate to them as women.

The National Constitutional Assembly has contested the Constitution-writing process since March 1999, when President Robert Mugabe set up a constitutional commission that was made up of 400 persons, including the 150 members of parliament. With only 52 (13 per cent) of these commissioners being women, women's concerns were unlikely to get the attention they deserved from the outset. Although it is still a considerable challenge for them to successfully table their agenda, the Constitution-building process has created a convergence point for women. It offers them an opportunity for forming strategic alliances with other coalitions, making it possible to have a co-ordinated voice for lobbying to infuse gender concerns into the mainstream of political contestation in Zimbabwe. The long-neglected gender inequalities in the Constitution can thus be addressed in a co-ordinated manner.

The ongoing under-representation of women in almost all government structures of power and decision-making, not to mention their lack of leadership positions in political parties, is a key challenge that requires a concerted effort by the women's movement in the country. The Constitution is silent on such issues and a change to facilitate the inclusion of women in decision-making is of paramount importance, as it will shift all decision-making from the institutions themselves. The electoral system too – constituency-based, first past the post, winner take all – is a barrier to women's contestation for parliamentary positions as they very often lack the resources to campaign.

Recommendations

The following recommendations come up as a result of this narrative of Zimbabwe women's violent experiences:

- Female representation on the Zimbabwe National Security Council needs to be broadened and its civilian oversight role over civil–military relations strengthened, as do the complaints and grievance mechanisms within this institution.

- Domestic security with international standards, protocols and norms (especially UN Resolution 1325) needs to be aligned and justice services need to be delivered in a manner consistent with international standards and human rights.

- With the inclusion of women, a security sector reform strategy needs to be mapped out, one that harmonises the traditional state security sector with the contemporary human security discourse, and which emphasises the responsibility to provide human security in all its dimensions to all of Zimbabwe's people.

- Zimbabwe needs a method for healing the women who were brutalised in its political processes. Though forgiveness is imperative, it does not mean that there will be no punishment for deliberate pain caused to victims. The Organ on National Healing, Reconciliation and Integration has begun the difficult but vital task of social peace-making. The security sector will have to acknowledge the violence against civilians over the past four decades, or sustainable peace will remain elusive.

- Design and infuse a human rights curriculum into the education system at all levels.

- Ongoing orientation training for the criminal justice system, including traditional structures and rural citizens on human rights and their importance for their development and democratisation, needs to be instigated.

- Gender-sensitive training needs to be added to the security curriculum and introduced into the education system.

- Mechanisms for enforcing and monitoring international instruments for the protection of women's rights in post-conflict contexts need to be established.

- Local-level peace education programmes need to be designed and nationwide reporting systems for sexual abuses that have provided the resources for monitoring and enforcing these mechanisms need to be established.

Conclusion

Zimbabwe requires a security sector that puts humans, not the state, at the centre of security provision. To address SGBV, the security sector reforms that need to be undertaken in the country must be all-embracing, addressing policies, legislation, and structural and behavioural patterns to ensure that they uphold the rule of law and respect human rights. This requires the long-overdue re-alignment of all security policies, legislation, structures and administrative behaviour with democratic tenets that emphasise the adherence to the principles of accountability, transparency and good governance. In particular, combating the interconnectivity problems of the security sector, that is, the military, immigration officials, intelligence services, justice, penal systems and government bodies that monitor and manage the security sector, poses a major challenge for any reform attempts. The security sector as a whole has been greatly tarnished by tumultuous political strife.

Whilst radical changes are very often essential to infuse a new culture of respecting human rights, the reality is such that only incremental change is possible. There are a number of reasons for this. Four dimensions of security sector reform all have to start with a dialogue amongst all the stakeholders: the public, parliamentarians, civil society groups and the security agents themselves (Sanam and Conway, undated). Unfortunately for Zimbabwe, where there have been gross human rights violations across all institutions, these dimensions – the political, based on the principle of civilian control over the military and security bodies; the institutional, which caters for the technical requirements all organisations need to perform effectively; the economic, which sees to the finances for security activities; and the societal, which sells out the modalities for civil society engagement in exercising oversight control – all need to be addressed and this brings in the question of inadequate institutional capacity for steering and managing the reforms.

Successful reform hinges on the presence of a conducive institutional framework. Nowhere in Africa have any of the actions outlined in the many declarations on enhancing the safety of women in conflict zones been fully implemented. Many African countries have failed to domesticate the concrete actions that would minimise SGBV, namely, the UN Convention on the Elimination of all Forms of Discrimination against Women (1979), UN Security Council Resolution 1325 (2000), and the 2006 Brussels Call to Action to the Peace and Security Agenda as set out by the African Union.

The bottom line is that the transitional government must make significant security sector reforms in order to provide SGBV survivors greater access to justice. These include training police officers to properly and adequately protect survivors of violence, providing training and resources to improve the accessibility and effectiveness of the court system and reforming the law so that rape and adultery are no longer treated as sub-categories of the same crime. More importantly, it needs to set up more victim-friendly facilities. This would require a review of the gender and legal framework on Zimbabwe women's rights and how their access to justice can be improved.

The current power-sharing agreements under the GPA and the hesitancy caused by the frailty of the GNU are going to shape both the political momentum for reform and potential scope of reforms. It is thus fundamental that as part of Zimbabwe's ongoing stabilisation and reconstruction, security sector reforms incorporate actions and policies with which to combat SGBV.

Notes

1 This same situation also prevails in South Sudan. See 'Gender-Based Violence in Southern Sudan: Justice For Women Long Overdue'. A study for the Enough Project by the Allard K. Lowenstein International Human Rights Clinic at Yale Law School.
2 See allafrica.com/stories/200905111533.html. Accessed 3 February 2010.
3 K. Bond-Stewart (1987) *Independence is not only for one sex.*
4 RAU (2010a) 'Women, Politics and the Zimbabwe Crisis'.
5 A.B. Chikwanha (2008) 'Security Sector Reforms for Managing Sexual and Gender Based Violence'.
6 D.T. Agbalajobi (2011) 'The Role of Women in Conflict Resolution and Peacebuilding'.
7 RAU (2010b) '"When the going gets tough the man gets going!" Zimbabwean Women's Views on Politics, Governance, Political Violence, and Transitional Justice'.
8 Sam Garkawe (2003) 'The South African Truth and Reconciliation Commission: A Suitable Model to Enhance the Role and Rights of Victims of Gross Violations of Human Rights?'.
9 See Gabriela Echeverria, 'The draft Basic Principles and Guidelines on the Right to Remedy and Reparation: An effort to develop a coherent theory and consistent practice of reparation for victims', www.article2.org/mainfile.php/0106/60/, Asian Legal Resource Centre, posted on 17 January 2003.
10 See Amnesty International Report, 'Between a Rock and a Hard Place – Women Human Rights Defenders at Risk', www.news.bbc.co.uk/2/hi/africa/6914778.stm
11 Defending Women-Defending Rights (2008) 'Release on Bail of Two leaders of Women of Zimbabwe Arise (WOZA)', www.defendingwomendefendingrights.org/zimbabve_release_on_bail.php.

Accessed 7 February 2008.

12 www.worldywca.org

13 The documentary 'Hear Us – Zimbabwean Women Affected by Political Violence Speak Out' and accompanying report 'Putting it Right: Addressing Human Rights Violations Against Zimbabwean Women', present the findings of the RAU's study and call for action on the issue of politically motivated violence against women. Peace Women Women's International League for Peace and Freedom Zimbabwe: NGO Documents Women Abuse, 9 May 2009.

14 Republic of Zimbabwe (1999) 'Constitution of Zimbabwe', Government Printers, Harare.

15 See IRIN News-Zimbabwe: 'Govt denies militarising state, goal is economic rescue' (12 April 2006). Available at www.irinnews.org/report. aspx?reportid=58728, . Accessed 3 February 2010.

16 The GPA is the agreement between ZANU-PF and the two Movement for Democratic Change formations (MDC-T and MDC-M) on resolving the challenges facing Zimbabwe. It was signed on 15 September 2008.

17 UN Doc S/Res/1325 (31 October 2000). For the full text of the resolution see www.un.org/events/res_1325e.pdf

References

Agbalajobi, D.T. 2011. 'The Role of Women in Conflict Resolution and Peacebuilding', Institute for Security Studies, monograph no. 173, Pretoria.

Aids-Free World. 2009. 'Electing to Rape: Sexual Terror in Mugabe's Zimbabwe'. Available at www.humansecuritygateway.com/docum ents/AFW_SexualTerrorMugabe_Zimbabwe.pdf. Accessed 7 February 2010.

Amnesty International. 2006. 'Between a Rock and a Hard Place – Women Human Rights Defenders at Risk'. Available at www.amnesty.org/en/ library/info/AFR46/017/2007

Bond-Stewart, K. 1987. *Independence is not only for one sex.* Harare: Zimbabwe Publishing House.

Campbell, H. 2003. *Reclaiming Zimbabwe: The exhaustion of the patriarchal model of liberation.* Cape Town: David Philip.

Chikwanha, A.B. 2008. 'Security Sector Reforms for Managing Sexual and Gender Based Violence' in *Unfinished Business: Transitional Justice and Women's Rights in Africa*, ACORD, Occasional Paper No. 1. Defending Women-Defending Rights. 2008. 'Release on Bail/Judicial Proceedings'. Available at www.defendingwomen-defendingrights.org/zimba

bwe_release_on_bail.php

Echeverria, G. 2003. 'The draft Basic Principles and Guidelines on the Right to Remedy and Reparation: An effort to develop a coherent theory and consistent practice of reparation for victims'. Available at www.article2.org/mainfile.php/0106/60/, Asian Legal Resource Centre, posted on 17 January 2003.

Garkawe, S. 2003. 'The South African Truth and Reconciliation Commission: A Suitable Model to Enhance the Role and Rights of Victims of Gross Violations of Human Rights?', *Melbourne University Law Review*, Vol. 27, No. 2. 2003), p. 338.

Hatchard, J. 1993. *Individual Freedoms and State Security in the African Context: The Case of Zimbabwe*. Harare: Baobab Books.

Lyons, Tanya. 1997. 'Women The Forgotten Soldiers: Women In Zimbabwe's Liberation War', *Southern Africa Report* (SAR), Vol. 12, No. 2.

Ranger, Terence. 2004. 'The Narratives and Counter-Narratives of Zimbabwean Asylum: Female voices'. Paper presented at 'Connecting Cultures' conference, April 2004, Kent University. Available at www.kubatana.net/html/archive/refug/040430tr.asp?sector=REFUG

Republic of Zimbabwe. 1999. *Constitution of Zimbabwe*. Harare: Government Printers.

Research and Advocacy Unit (RAU). 2010a. *Women, Politics and the Zimbabwe Crisis*. Report produced by the Institute for Democracy in Africa, the International Center for Transitional Justice, the Research and Advocacy Unit, and the Women's Coalition of Zimbabwe. Harare: RAU, May.

— 2010b. '"When the going gets tough the man gets going!" Zimbabwean Women's views on Politics, Governance, Political Violence and Transitional Justice'. Report produced by the Research and Advocacy Unit, the Institute for Democracy in Africa and the International Center for Transitional Justice. Harare: RAU, November.

Sanam, N.A. and C.P. Conway. n.d. 'Disarmament, Demobilisation and Reintegration, particularly in Civil Wars and Internal Conflicts'. Available at www.international-alert.org/sites/default/files/library/TK SecuritySectorReform.pdf

Schirch, Lisa and Manjrika Sewak. 2005. 'The Role of Women in Peace Building'. Available at www.gppac.net/uploads/File/Resources/ GPPAC%20Issue%20papers/The%20Role%20of%20Women%20 in%20Peacebuilding.pdf

Stubbs, Rebecca. 2008. 'Combating the use of sexual violence as a weapon of conflict in Zimbabwe'. Available at www.namibian.com.na/index. php?id=28&tx_ttnews[tt_news]=1432&no_cache=1.

Zimbabwe Women Writers. 2000. 'Women of Resilience: The Voices of Women Ex-Combatants'. Zimbabwe Women Writers: Harare, 2000.

5

Exorcising the Spectre of Electoral Authoritarianism in Zimbabwe's Political Transition

Eldred V. Masunungure & Jabusile M. Shumba

Introduction and a brief methodology

Zimbabwe's recent political trajectory has been a source of much frustration to many citizens and promoters of democratic polity. Its democratisation seems to be moving at a glacial pace. The reality, though, is that its transition from authoritarianism was never going to be easy, nor was it going to be linear. As it is, the transition is occurring in bits and pieces, forward and backwards, up, down and sideways, and the outcome remains inherently indeterminate. Zimbabwe's case also reinforces those who question the notion that transition is unidirectional; rather, it is moving in multiple directions that add complexity and great confusion to the whole political drama.

Andreas Schedler's (2006:1) 'spectre of electoral authoritarianism' has haunted Zimbabwe since independence in 1980. Post-2000, it hardened into what Michael Bratton and Eldred Masunungure (2008:42) have called a 'militarised form of electoral authoritarianism'. This will no doubt be the greatest, though not necessarily intractable, challenge that the country's transition trajectory will face as it painstakingly moves to another set of elections that will hopefully deliver a credible and indisputable outcome. However, as of May 2012, the spectre is stubbornly resisting exorcism.

This chapter analyses Zimbabwe's political transition from the standpoint of efforts to craft the road map to democratic elections. We proceed from the premise that transparent, free and fair elections are of central importance to the country's transition and can be a vehicle for further democratic development. One of our core arguments is that unless the ghost of electoral authoritarianism is exorcised, elections in the country will be a mere replay of previous ones, that is, *elections without a choice*, which are a mere institutional facade of democracy.

Methodologically, the chapter relies on a combination of research instruments, principally desk-based research, survey data and findings from focus group discussions. Where applicable, key informant interviews were conducted to enrich the study. For the past ten years, one of the authors has been privileged to be associated with a research institution that has been at the forefront of collecting both quantitative and qualitative data on a range of governance issues in the country, including on elections. Substantial literature on electoral politics in Zimbabwe has also accumulated over time and this will be referred to in order to inform the study. Lastly, both authors are keen watchers of the unfolding political drama in the country and their 'participant observation' is invaluable in a study of this kind.

Electoral authoritarianism

The chapter does not embrace the simplistic and naive equating of elections with democracy but rather recognises that elections are a critical and irreplaceable component of modern democracy. We endorse Bratton's dictum that 'while you [can] have elections without democracy, you can't have democracy without elections' (Bratton, 1998:52). Indeed, V.O. Key regards elections as a defining feature of a democratic polity when he writes:

> Perhaps the basic differentiating characteristic of democratic orders consists in the expression of effective choice by the mass of the people in elections. The electorate occupies, at least in the mystique of such orders, the position of the principal organ of governance; it acts through elections. (Key, 1955:3)

In sum, without elections, democracy loses its very essence. Zimbabwe easily fits into the category of electoral authoritarian states with the added post-2000 feature of being a militarised one. Considerable literature is now available on electoral authoritarianism and most accounts agree that such a regime occupies a zone in between electoral democracy and 'closed' autocracies that 'refrain from staging multiparty elections as the official route of access to executive and legislative power' (Schedler, 2006:5). According to Schedler, electoral authoritarianism is where elections are broadly inclusive as well as minimally pluralistic, minimally competitive and minimally open.

Empirical evidence suggests that under electoral authoritarian rule, the incumbent regime (variously called 'semi-democratic', 'quasi-democratic', 'competitive authoritarian', 'hybrid regimes', among others) delineates the elective offices and allows some of them to be successfully competed for by the opposition while fencing others off as reserved for the regime. Put another way, the elective political offices are arranged in concentric circles, with the outermost circle occupied by local government, the legislature occupying the next inner circle, with the executive office/s at the centre. An electoral authoritarian regime allows its opponents to capture some (even the majority, but not all) of the local government offices, and it also allows the opposition to win many legislative seats (though rarely a majority and never a large enough majority to enable the opposition to drive constitutional changes on its own). However, the regime draws a red line when it comes to the innermost circle, i.e., the presidential office. Of course, this analytical model assumes that the political system is a presidential or hybrid one where the three (or more, for example, in a federal system) circles of power are all directly elective, which is the case in Zimbabwe.

The logic of this is that considerable competition is allowed in respect of the local government and legislative elections; more competition for the former than the latter. On the other hand, it appears the inner sanctum, i.e., the presidency (or State House, in the case of Zimbabwe) is a preserve where competition is highly constrained and all sorts of spanners are thrown at opposition candidates to prevent them from capturing the throne. In other words, the competitiveness of the electoral game diminishes the closer the contest gets to the centre, where the flagship prize is. We would also expect that contestation for posts is more intense and uncivil the closer one moves towards the centre in this concentric model. Where politically motivated violence and/or intimidation are a characteristic of electoral campaigns, the logic of this model also dictates that the violence and intimidation are sharply focused and concentrated around the presidential electoral contest. In sum, the electoral authoritarianism takes a more hardened form as the contest moves from the outer to the inner circle of contested power positions.

The defining feature of electoral authoritarianism is that it has the juridical trappings of democracy but not the practice. Empirically, it mimics democracy – and even then, often poorly so. The mimicry is designed to deceive for the purpose of obtaining the much-needed political legitimacy. In short, electoral authoritarianism has two faces: the democratic face, which exhibits itself in the array of institutions common in electoral democracies; and an authoritarian face, which expresses itself at the empirical level and mostly in the form of draconian restrictions to political freedoms and civic liberties. Thus, the same regime may be characterised by some as a 'diminished' form of democracy, while for others it is a 'diminished' form of authoritarianism.

Zimbabwe bears all the hallmarks of electoral authoritarianism, with the added dimension that since 2000, when the electoral competition became intense as a result of the emergence of a robust and credible opposition to the ZANU-PF regime, the authoritarianism became hardened and took on militaristic tendencies. At first, the militarisation of the electoral arena was covert, with the security organs (the military, police and intelligence) playing a supportive or back-up role to the ZANU-PF party militia and war veterans of the armed struggle allied to the then ruling party. This made the June 2000 parliamentary election campaign the most violent compared to the preceding two decades. However, the violence escalated drastically in the run-up to the 2002 contest for the presidency. Stephan Mair and Masipula Sithole capture the intensity of the contest for the inner circle:

> Zimbabwe's constitution provides for universal, free, equal and secret elections. The elections of 1990, 1995, 1996 and 2000 were, however, significantly marred by manipulation and violence committed by the ruling party. Moreover, ZANU-PF has never hesitated to misuse state resources and its control over the public media for its campaigns. The campaign for the presidential election in 2002 represents, nevertheless, a new quality in this regard. The systematicness [sic], comprehensiveness and intensity of manipulation as well as intimidation was not known in Zimbabwe before. (Mair and Sithole, 2002:25)

This militarisation of electoral authoritarianism was put on open display in the run-up to the June 2008 presidential run-off election, described by Masunungure (2009:1 and chapter 5) as 'the most controversial and violent election since Independence in 1980'. If, as the literature suggests, electoral authoritarianism couples both formal democratic institutions and procedures (multi-party elections, for example) with authoritarian practices, the said run-off was an election only in name as it dispensed with any trappings of liberal democratic practices. Tsvangirai's withdrawal from the contest was ample evidence that the regime was determined to fence off State House from the electoral competition and thus block the 'access to power' dimension of electoral authoritarianism. At best, the June 2008 episode was a display of what Larry Diamond and others call 'pseudodemocracy', i.e., regimes that 'lack an arena of contestation sufficiently open, free, and fair so that the ruling party can readily be turned out of power if it is no longer preferred by a plurality of the electorate' (2002:24; see also Diamond et al. 1990). If the regime merits to be labelled 'competitive authoritarianism' – the preferred term by Steven Levitsky and Lucan Way (2002) – the emphasis ought to be on the authoritarian rather than the competitive dimension of this label. In the 2008 presidential run-off, the Mugabe regime clearly recognised the supreme importance of legitimising its rule via the electoral process but could not stomach the open competition and level playing field that go with electoral democracy.

No one who witnessed the June 2008 saga at close range would have been in any doubt that the regime was moving away from electoral authoritarianism toward a closed autocracy. Perhaps this would have been the country's destination were it not for the intervention of the tripartite Global Political Agreement (GPA) of September 2008, about which much has been written so far. Suffice it to say the GPA is a political pact that has two pillars: one is a fairly comprehensive and laudable package of policy reform measures, the other a mechanism to manage the transitional period and steer the reform process.

For our purposes, the importance of the GPA is that it is a governance framework dedicated to 'charting a new political direction for the country' (Article 2), at the core of which are steps that the three parties agreed to take leading to competitive, free, fair and credible elections. The GPA rightly notes previous elections were 'divisive and often times confrontational' and implicitly admits that one of the central issues to be addressed by the coalition government is to ensure that future elections are neither divisive nor confrontational.

Another key aspect of the GPA – already noted in the introduction to this volume – is that it is at heart a transition charter, and to the extent that a transition is about changing the rules of the game so as to guide the country from the old to the new order, it is in effect a regime change charter. The challenge that the coalition government faces is treating elections as a key mechanism in political transition and the extent to which the rules of the game will be changed to avoid muddled elections that produce muddled and disputable results. Based on the performance balance sheet of the Inclusive Government, is Zimbabwe on the road from electoral authoritarianism to a democratic polity? If not, what is to be done? The chapter poses these and other questions and seeks, on the basis of empirical evidence, answers to them.

The context: The muddled elections of 2008

In March 2008, the country held tripartite national elections, the flagship being the election for the post of executive president. The other elections were for the bicameral legislature (the 210-member House of Assembly and 60 elective Senate seats) and 1,958 rual and urban local government seats. The parliamentary and civic elections were relatively unproblematic and the results were not only announced within reasonable time but they were also largely accepted. It was the hotly contested presidential elections that generated high drama and triggered the series of events that culminated in the September 2008 political pact between the three major political gladiators. Accordingly, we will focus predominantly on the presidential component of the March 2008 elections.

According to official results, the presidential election did not produce an outright winner as per the legal framework, that is, neither of the presidential candidates received more than 50 per cent of the total votes cast. Robert Mugabe, the candidate for the long-ruling Zimbabwe African National Union Patriotic Front (ZANU-PF), received 43.2 per cent against 47.9 per cent of Morgan Tsvangirai of the Movement for Democratic Change (MDC-T). The electorate, traumatised by violence and intimidation and after anxiously waiting for the results that had been frozen by the Zimbabwe Electoral Commission (ZEC) for five weeks, subsequently proceeded to an electoral run-off in June of the same year.

The run-off-election campaign, pitting Mugabe and Tsvangirai, was characterised by intense and unprecedented state-sponsored violence and intimidation that instilled deep and pervasive fear in the electorate throughout the country and later forced the withdrawal of Tsvangirai just a few days before polling.[1] This effectively eroded the credibility of the election, with Mugabe running a one-man show in which he was the only contestant and the only possible winner. But his pyrrhic victory and quick coronation impressed few. Indeed, virtually all local, regional and international observers failed to express a vote of confidence in what to many was clearly a pre-determined electoral outcome. For instance, the SADC Election Observer Mission (SEOM) categorically said that 'The elections did not represent the will of the people of Zimbabwe' (SOEM Preliminary Statement, 29 June 2008) while the African Union (AU) also emphatically stated that 'it is the considered view of the African Union Observer Mission that the Election process fell short of accepted AU standards' (AU Preliminary Statement, 29 June 2008).

For our purposes, the salutary significance of the GPA political settlement is that it *formally* launched Zimbabwe's political transition. We say 'formally' because we firmly hold the view that the country's political transition predated the GPA and can even be traced back more than a decade.[2]

The relatively successful March and the disastrous June 2008 elections actually interrupted a regional dialogue process that had been running since early 2007. This was when, for the first time, the Southern Africa Development Community (SADC) summit held in Tanzania in March 2007 acknowledged Zimbabwe's deepening political crisis and mandated President Thabo Mbeki of South Africa to facilitate dialogue between the major political protagonists in Zimbabwe with a view to finding a sustainable political solution to the multi-layered crisis. It must be noted that to most domestic political and civic actors, a negotiated political settlement would certainly not have been the best-case outcome. However, regional and international pressures coupled with a deepening syndrome of crises – political, social and economic – exerted irresistible pressure on the domestic political actors to dialogue and reach a settlement. Only the three prominent parties represented in Parliament, i.e., ZANU-PF and its MDC rivals – MDC-T of Tsvangirai and MDC-M of Arthur Mutambara – were involved in the SADC-led dialogue that deliberately excluded civic society.

After bitter and protracted negotiations, the parties first signed the Memorandum of Understanding in July 2008 and the GPA two months later. The GPA became the framework for power-sharing under a self-styled Inclusive Government.

The GPA broadly defines the key milestones towards the holding of free and fair elections, including a new constitution and the reform of key state organs. In the following sections, we examine progress towards reform of critical electoral institutions and processes, and identify the pivotal players in the electoral game, and attendant dynamics and their consequences for the transition path. They are informed by the question: What needs to be done to ensure that the road to credible and indisputable elections is freed of the now legendary impediments and booby-traps?

The litmus test for free and fair elections

Zimbabwe needs to pass a number of tests if it is to be able to hold free and fair elections and ensure a peaceful and effective transfer of power to the winner. Credible elections depend on a number of institutional factors: a non-contested constitutional system, a competitive party system, consensus on the electoral system, and a credible election management system that ensures, among other things, a violent-free electoral environment where citizens freely exercise their power to vote and their vote counts. There have been incessant calls for electoral reform in Zimbabwe, mainly from opposition parties, civil society and the donor community. These demands include accuracy and integrity of voters' rolls and reform of electoral observation regulations, capacity and appointments to the electoral management body.

There are major institutional challenges hindering competitive multi-party democracy in Zimbabwe, among them being the proper role and conduct of the security forces and the state-controlled media. ZANU-PF has perennially been accused of manipulating the state media against its political competitors and abusing the powers of the security forces to orchestrate terror campaigns and persecute opposition political parties and civic activists. The broader democratic movement has thus called for comprehensive security sector reforms to guarantee a free and fair poll and effective transfer of power. All these institutional factors are an essential component of free and fair elections. In this regard, the key question then is, to what extent has Zimbabwe progressed in preparing ground for a credible election followed by a trouble-free power transfer should a non-ZANU-PF candidate win the presidential contest?

As we write, the country is in the advanced stage of a highly contentious and often chaotic constitution-making process. Countrywide incidents of violence during the 2010 outreach programme tainted the credibility of its outcome. An IDAZIM survey conducted in November 2010 (towards the end of the constitution consultation process) showed that only a small majority of 53 per cent were 'happy' about the constitutional reform process[3] as compared to 39 per cent who were not. Nearly four in ten respondents (38 per cent) reported lack of transparency, a quarter (24 per cent) bemoaned blocked participation, whilst a fifth (21 per cent) feared that the final draft document may not reflect people's opinions;[4] 15 per cent reported that people were afraid to voice their personal opinions. For our purposes, it is important to note that Zimbabweans do link the eagerly envisaged new constitution to the electoral process. This was vividly illustrated in the Freedom House survey of December 2010, which reported that:

> Zimbabweans link the emerging constitution to hopes (where they exist) for better safety in a next election – 83 per cent say that a constitution that guarantees rights of freedom of belief, expression and association would make them feel 'very safe' (56 per cent) or 'safe' (27 per cent) come the time of a next election. 13 per cent felt indifferent on the matter (March 2010, pp. 38-9).

Given the above, the main challenge to a credible, free and fair election in the country lies in reforming electoral institutions and dismantling the infrastructure of state-led violence. As such, our ensuing analysis will mainly focus on these two variables.

Reforming electoral institutions

By mid-2010, the parties to the Inclusive Government had agreed to the reconstitution of the Zimbabwe Electoral Commission (ZEC), the elections management agency. The ZEC board has since been reconstituted. Its former chairperson, Justice George Chiweshe (a Brigadier-General in the military courts) was replaced by Justice Simpson Mutambanengwe, formerly a High Court judge in both Zimbabwe and Namibia, as an agreed compromise candidate. The credibility of the ZEC regime under Justice George Chiweshe was irretrievably impaired by the way it managed the two 2008 elections, especially the inordinate and suspicious delay in announcing the results of the March elections and the way it mishandled the subsequent run-off. Although the reconstruction of the ZEC Board was a positive (albeit insufficient) step forward in meeting some of the key milestones, for many local and international observers the reform and implementation of electoral laws is key to guaranteeing its effectiveness. In July 2010, the parties agreed to amendments to the Electoral Act but, 12 months later, they had yet to be debated in Parliament.

We turn now to the proposed principal changes. One of the principal proposals in the electoral law reform process is that election results are made public no more than five days after polling. The parties agreed to amend the Electoral Act so that the ZEC is obliged to declare presidential election results within this time frame. This proposal was informed by the post-March 2008 debacle whereby the ZEC took nearly five weeks to announce presidential electoral results, raising well-founded fears that the results were being manipulated to produce a desirable outcome. The proposed amendment represents a helpful development that will hopefully ensure timely announcement of results in the future. In addition, parties agreed to amend the Electoral Act and provide for an audit of presidential results to make sure that the numbers add up and to ensure more transparency. However, while this is another commendable step forward, it is necessary to set timeframes within which such audits must be done.

The parties also consented to proposals that the ZEC be empowered to summon candidates, election agents or parties accused of engaging in political violence. The proposed legislation is silent on what happens thereafter. Under the proposed amendments, the ZEC will be able to admonish candidates, election agents or parties implicated in acts of political violence and to set up a special court at magistrate level to try such cases. The Attorney-General (AG) will set up a special unit in his office dedicated to prosecuting cases of political violence committed during elections. In this regard, the parties further agreed that upon conviction by special courts, the court can make a special order banning candidates from further participation in the election process. The Electoral Court will be given powers to review administrative decisions taken by officers of the ZEC in terms of the Electoral Act. The Court will be empowered to hear appeals on election matters against special decisions of special courts. All disputes that are election-related will be presided over by the electoral court and it will have monopoly jurisdiction and its judgments, orders and terms will be enforceable in the same way as judgments, orders or directions of the High Court.

It is noteworthy though that the current AG, Johannes Tomana, is himself a contentious factor in relation to the ongoing interparty negotiations. The credibility of the AG has been seriously challenged by pro-democracy civil society, the MDC formations, the legal fraternity and other informed observers, not only due to his alleged irregular appointment but also because of his self-declared partisan affiliation to the former ruling ZANU-PF.[5] Thus, while the proposed amendments may provide for a framework to deal with electoral violence, there is lack of confidence and trust in the AG to exercise impartiality in the execution of his duties. Indeed, it has been argued the Inclusive Government 'will not achieve its goal of producing undisputed elections, unless the present Attorney General is replaced with a professional legal officer'.[6]

Voter registration has been a persistently contentious issue during every election season since the 1985 general elections, when the voter register was first compiled and used. The process has been replete with onerous bureaucratic and administrative requirements that clearly act as disincentives to voters who want to register. The most irksome is the requirement for 'proof of residence', a requirement that disenfranchised many Zimbabweans from voting as they are sometimes denied the supporting letters from prescribed persons if they are perceived to have different political alignments. On this, the GPA parties agreed that ZEC should come up with a set of documents that can be accepted as proof of residence, for example, an affidavit for the person intending to vote or a set of persons with authority in the community who can vouch for the person. This leaves it to the ZEC's discretion as to which persons they will deem will have such authority.

Voter education, another controversial and chronic issue, remains under the preserve of the ZEC, an agency which traditionally has not had the capacity to adequately conduct voter education ahead of national elections. The agency has been reluctant to invite non-governmental actors to assist in setting this very critical cog in the electoral machine in motion. It is important to 'liberalise' this arena by opening up space for civic society and non-governmental organisations to provide nonpartisan, accurate and timely voter education to the electorate so that they can make informed decisions.

Although a number of proposed amendments are laudable, the autonomy of the ZEC and violence – the major factors affecting the holding of a free and fair poll in Zimbabwe – still need to be more firmly addressed. The proposed amendments do not guarantee the ZEC autonomy, which is fundamental to the running of free and fair elections. The reconstitution of the decision-making layer of the ZEC without addressing related fundamental and structural problems (for example, its secretariat) to guarantee its operational independence is insufficient to restore the integrity of the ballot in Zimbabwe. The autonomy and integrity of the ZEC is critical for running credible elections that produce indisputable results. Admittedly, and especially in a highly polarised and confrontational environment such as Zimbabwe's, the de-politicisation of electoral governance is a difficult and delicate task. However, one of the most effective ways of achieving it is through the establishment of an independent electoral management body. Institutional independence does not mean total disconnection from government; rather, it means that as a state institution, the ZEC remains accountable to both the state and the public through Parliament, the representative organ of the people. The fact that the ZEC's functions are to a large extent subject to ministerial approval limits its operational independence. An independent electoral body is key to levelling the political field and ensuring that *all* political actors comply with the law.

In addition, while the proposed electoral legislation makes provisions that proscribe various types of offences such as intimidation, preventing political parties and candidates from campaigning, undue influence and bribery that could be the basis for crafting a code of conduct for political parties and candidates, it appears that these agreed reforms were based on the assumption of the existence of the rule of law in Zimbabwe. On the contrary, Zimbabwe is yet to institutionalise the respect for the rule of law as evidenced by the continued selective application of the law and loss of confidence in the impartiality of key law enforcement institutions such as the police and the judiciary.

The GPA parties should consider and institute wide-ranging reforms, including those of the judiciary, security sector organs and media, in order to deal decisively with politically motivated violence. Security sector reform is one hotly disputed issue that needs to be addressed to ensure an electoral environment that promotes democratic proc-esses leading to free and fair elections whose outcome is indisputable. Furthermore, the electoral reforms did not address issues on media plurality and equitable access to media for political parties during elec-tion time; this has been another contentious issue due to deliberately biased and partial reporting, especially by the state-controlled media. In addition, the electoral environment is constrained by the draconian Public Order and Security Act (POSA) and Access to Information and Protection of Privacy Act (AIPPA) and other pieces of legislation that collectively infringe upon fundamental political freedoms and civic liberties that are vital components of a democratic society. The repeal of these Acts is critical to providing and expanding the space for effec-tive participation in elections.

The security sector: spoilers in the transition?

Credible elections and effective power transfer are central planks in any democratic transition and both are either explicitly stated or implied in the GPA. This section examines more closely the role and conduct of the security forces and the need for reform, not only to ensure peace-ful and credible elections, but also to insulate security organs from the whims of partisan actors and their interests. Since 2000, the security services sector has allegedly been at the epicentre of organising and unleashing violence against real and/or perceived opposition and civic leaders and their supporters. The integrity of security organs like the Zimbabwe National Army (ZNA), the Central Intelligence Organisa-tion (CIO) and the Zimbabwe Republic Police (ZRP) has been degraded due to their actions and/or inactions that have undermined the rule of law (Hendricks and Hutton 2009). ZANU-PF has been accused of manipulating and perverting the security services sector to serve its narrow partisan interests. The formation of the Inclusive Government provides an opportunity to consider and, where feasible, implement fundamental reforms in the provision of impartial and professional security and justice services to the people.

Knox Chitiyo and Martin Rupiya (2005) observe that, from March 2000, the state recreated the settler-colonial Joint Operations Command (JOC) as a high-level decision-making body by bringing together the Commander of the Zimbabwe Defence Forces (ZDF), the Commissioner-General of the ZRP, the Director-General of the Department of State Security (otherwise known as the CIO) and representatives of the Zimbabwe National Liberation War Veterans Association (ZNLWVA). The body was formed to co-ordinate the security sector activities aimed at resolving the perceived threats stemming from both external and internal forces. The military began to organise internally along the lines of operational zones to control the growth and development of the opposition and maintain the hegemony of ZANU-PF. The security apparatuses began to play a supporting role in ZANU-PF's unorthodox political campaign, especially the provision of logistical support to the war veterans and youth militia and targeting real and perceived anti-regime elements, specifically leaders and supporters of the opposition MDC. This marked the increased militarisation of politics, state, and society in Zimbabwe, alongside the politicisation of the military and other security organs.

Indeed, the JOC has been the dominant strategic force in Zimbabwe's political universe in the last decade but its intrusion into the political domain has become more overt and intrusive under the coalition government. Its mission has been to work out a military strategy to ensure ZANU-PF's survival. Initially, the JOC operated under the tacit management of the party, but by the time of the 2005 elections it was clear that it was no longer just an instrument of the party-state. It had become an *alternative* to the state, and was, in effect, a *parallel government*.

By 2008, the securocrats had appropriated most of the levers of state power and there were some new faces at the JOC meetings. The 'front rank' of executive decision-makers within the JOC up to January 2009 included those noted above plus the Commissioner of Prisons and the Minister of Defence. Behind the front rank are the 'advisers' who sit in at meetings and whose advice is sought but who are not decision-makers. They include the Governor of the Reserve Bank of Zimbabwe (RBZ), the leader of the ZNLWVA, the Cabinet Minister in charge of National Security and the Minister in the President's Office.

The partisanship of the military was clearly put on public display in January 2002, just before that year's March presidential elections, when General Vitalis Zvinavashe, then Commander of the Zimbabwe Defence Forces, issued a thinly veiled threat of a military coup were opposition leader Morgan Tsvangirai to win the March 2002 elections. Zvinavashe thundered:

> Let it be known that the highest office in the land is a straitjacket whose occupant is expected to observe the objectives of the liberation struggle. We will, therefore, not accept, let alone support or salute anyone, with a different agenda that threatens the very existence of our sovereignty, our country and our people.[7]

General Constantine Chiwenga, Zvinavashe's successor, also reiterated this just before March 2008:

> Elections are coming and the army will not support or salute sell-outs and agents of the West before, during, and after the presidential elections .... We will not support anyone other than President (Robert) Mugabe, who has sacrificed a lot for this country.[8]

To send the message home in no uncertain terms, the Commissioner of Prisons, retired Major-General Paradzai Zimondi, instructed his prison officers: 'I am giving you an order to vote for President Mugabe.'[9]

More recently, the Commander of 3 Brigade, Brigadier-General Douglas Nyikayaramba, labelled Prime Minister Tsvangirai a 'national security threat' that 'can only be dealt with by people in uniform'. He further said the security forces and ZANU-PF were inseparable and the security forces 'will die with him [President Mugabe] to make sure he remains in power'.[10] Such unguarded and unprofessional statements naturally sent shock waves through the political, civic and regional community. These statements speak eloquently in defence of the crying need for reform in Zimbabwe's security sector if the country is to ensure a peaceful and transparent election, the transfer of power to a legitimate government and that the security sector organs confine themselves to their professional duties. Survey evidence also shows that there is still a modicum of support for the security forces, with more Zimbabweans (55 per cent) expressing trust in the national army than distrust (39 per cent);[11]this also suggests that popular opposition to security sector reform is unlikely.

Other security organs have also become embroiled in partisan politics. For instance, the ZRP has a history of deployment for political ends, as evidenced in their paramilitary involvement in the Gukurahundi in Matabeleland/Midlands in the 1980s, Operation *Murambatsvina* in 2005, Operation *Mavhotera Papi* in 2008 and numerous allegations of human rights violations, including arbitrary arrest, illegal detention, torture and general brutality. The ZRP has therefore been accused of the institutionalised perversion of the rule of law and of being a partisan police force, a charge it vigorously denies. The partisan policing has been integrally linked to the AG, who allegedly takes orders from the ZRP and, according to Beatrice Mtetwa, 'For as long as Tomana [the AG] is there we will continue to have a partisan police force.'[12] No wonder only a minority [44 per cent] of Zimbabweans say they trust the ZRP and a full 50 per cent say they do not.[13]

As for the CIO, it has historically been labelled as the most vicious and partisan of the state security agencies and is perceived to have pervasively infiltrated all levels of society, its operations surrounded by the cloak of secrecy, including use of its public resources. The spy agency has also faced allegations of widespread abuses, including unwarranted detention, interrogation and torture, infringements on rights to privacy, freedom of association and freedom of movement. It has allegedly used both hard methods (for example, kidnapping, detention and interrogation with torture) and soft approaches (for example, the control and interception of internal and external flows of information) (see Chitiyo 2009).

The need to restore a democratic governance system and enabling environment for free political activity are major imperatives for security sector reform. However, it appears that the kind of reform required is probably the most complex and difficult of those embodied in the GPA. It is now increasingly evident that the most significant issue during the transition should be reorienting the security sector, reducing the potential for abuse, and institutionalising a system of checks and balances. In the first place, it is necessary that the security sector acts as one of the drivers rather than the spoilers of the democratic transition to re-establish professionalism, not partisan politics, as the institutional ethos of the military.

In March 2009, and as a first cut at security sector reform, the coalition government passed the National Security Council Act, establishing the National Security Council (NCS) to give policy direction to the security sector. According to clause 4 of the Bill's memorandum, the Council 'will be responsible for reviewing national policies on security, defence, law and order and recommending or directing appropriate action'. The NSC comprises the President as chairperson; the two Vice-Presidents; the Prime Minister; the two Deputy Prime Ministers; the ministers responsible for Finance, the Defence Forces, the Police Force and Prisons Service; one minister nominated by each of the three political parties who are signatories to the Interparty Political Agreement; the Minister of State in the President's Office responsible for National Security; the Chief Secretary to the President and Cabinet; the Chief Secretary to the Prime Minister; the Commander of the Defence Forces; Commanders of the Army and Air Force; the Commissioner-General of Police; the Commissioner of Prisons; and the Director-General of the Department of State for National Security.

The NSC had its inaugural meeting at the end of July 2009, the first meeting since the formation of the Inclusive Government.[14] To many observers, the establishment of the NSC was a positive step towards initiating security sector reforms. However, more than two years later, the NSC has met only at irregular intervals and progress has stalled. If anything, there are clear signs of regression if statements from senior military officers – serving and retired – like then-Brigadier-General Douglas Nyikayaramba are anything to go by (he was promoted to Major-General earlier this year). This lends more credence to reports to the effect that JOC is in fact alive and well, despite being officially declared dead and replaced by the NSC. This no doubt prompted the MDC-T to call for the placement of the security sector on the SADC mediation agenda, a move that ZANU-PF strongly and predictably resisted. Without broad and deep security sector reform, it is doubtful if the country will be able to hold meaningful and credible elections whose results are beyond dispute.

It should also be recognised that, given the delicacy of the matter, realigning the country's civil–military relations (or, more broadly, undertaking the much talked about security sector reform) will neither be easy nor be carried out in the short term. Our analysis persuades us to the conclusion that this type of reform is better confidently done by a legitimately elected government with a popular and uncontested mandate to govern, including negotiating this kind of sensitive reform in the most strategic institution of the state. Presently, one of the defining features of the country's civil–military relations is almost total lack of trust between the security sector (especially the military) and the non-ZANU-PF component of the coalition government. Seldom can sustainable security sector reform be achieved without a high level of mutual trust between the top military and political hierarchies. This is a reality that many of those concerned will find distasteful.

Given the above discussion, it is tempting to conclude that the spectre of electoral authoritarianism in Zimbabwe is reducible to the problem of civil–military relations. Indeed, the security sector – and its political disposition and actions – represents the master spanner in the works. However, it must be appreciated that this sector is only one cog – albeit the central one – in the wheel of the *party-state*. The phenomenon of the party-state started much earlier than the problem of civil–military relations. Building the party-state was an early post-independence project, and by the end of the first decade it had been completed and the party-state consolidated. The civilian state bureaucracy – including local government and parastatals – was the first target and was captured via the policy of Africanisation, whose thrust was the de-racialisation of the white-dominated civil service and other state institutions. This was an unavoidable imperative that was also provided for in the 1979 independence Constitution. But Africanisation soon became politicisation and this legacy is part of the spectre of electoral authoritarianism. In other words, dealing with the problem of Zimbabwe's difficult civil–military relations also requires confronting the problem of the party-state. The party-state must be dismantled alongside the reconstruction of 'objective civil–military relations'.

The centrality of the party-state for ZANU-PF's regime maintenance was amply demonstrated in the period after the GPA but before the installation of the coalition government, when the party irregularly hired up to 75,000 party-aligned youth into the country's public service. This was about one-third of the total strength of the service.[15]

The importance of these irregularly hired workers to the former ruling party's survival and its desire to recapture power is illustrated by the stiff resistance the party is mounting against their removal, even when they were illegally recruited.

In sum, the party-state can be said to constitute *the* problem, while the security sector, because of its strategic location at the centre of the party-state, represents the larger and more intractable *part* of the problem. The security sector and ZANU-PF also seem to be awash with diamond-generated revenue, which has strengthened the spoilers and buoyed their political confidence. We turn now to this morale-boosting bonanza that threatens to be a curse to Zimbabwe's political transition.

The Chiadzwa diamonds bonanza: the political game changer?

The story of Chiadzwa in Marange in eastern Zimbabwe is yet to be fully told but already the name is now synonymous with diamonds and high-level corruption. However, the political impact of the diamonds bonanza has not been adequately analysed. The discovery and exploitation of diamonds[16] in the area introduces another key dynamic in the titanic struggle for power on the political landscape. This is particularly so given the widespread and persistent reports that the military is directly involved in and benefiting from the diamond sales and circumventing the Treasury. The companies that operate in the diamond fields (for example, Mbada, chaired by a retired Air Commodore, and Canadile[17]) are controlled by the military; the ZRP is reported to also operate its own diamond claim. Some watchers of the Zimbabwe diamond debacle see Chiadzwa as the political game changer in that it has provided both the security chiefs and ZANU-PF with a large source of revenue that they can deploy in the power game.

For instance, Human Rights Watch writes:

> Army brigades have been rotated into Marange to ensure that key front-line units have an opportunity to benefit from the diamond trade ... the enrichment of soldiers serves to mollify a constituency whose loyalty to ZANU-PF, in the context of ongoing political strife, is essential. (Human Rights Watch, 2009:3)

The *terradaily*[18] article is even more categorical, asserting that:

> Mugabe is dependent on diamond exports, including large amounts smuggled out by his generals, to stay in power. First and foremost, Mugabe, 86, needs the funds to keep the military and the ruling ZANU-PF party behind him.

Even before the Kimberley Process Certification Scheme approved trade in Zimbabwean diamonds, they were already being traded through agents in Mumbai, Tel Aviv, Moscow, Windhoek, Amsterdam and Dubai, amongst other centres. It is feared that the proceeds from the sales of diamond outside the legal framework do not only prejudice the Treasury but are being used to build a war chest for the former ruling party's electoral and other political activities. The access to diamondsgenerated funds seems to be one of the reasons behind ZANU-PF's otherwise inexplicable appetite for elections in 2011; it probably is awash with easy money from what the Kimberley Process watchdog calls 'blood diamonds'.

Diamonds in Zimbabwe seem to confirm the natural resource curse thesis whereby resources are siphoned off by warlords to finance conflict and other predatory projects, as was the case in countries like Angola, the Democratic Republic of Congo, Liberia and Sierra Leone. To this extent, all stakeholders need to quickly rein in the industry and establish accountability in diamond mining to ensure a level playing field and that the resource is used for developmental rather predatory purposes.

A roadmap to credible elections

We reiterate that the GPA process is about political transition, at the centre of which are elections. Crafting the framework under which the next elections will be conducted has gripped the GPA stakeholders, particularly the GPA parties and SADC. As elections are about power, the rules under which they will be held, not to mention their timing, have consumed the energy and efforts of these stakeholders. Numerous regional level meetings were held by the GPA negotiators and their principals, involving both the SADC summits and that of the SADC Organ Troika on Politics, Defence and Security Co-operation (hereafter referred to as the 'Organ').

The lack of progress generated considerable fatigue and frustration at the SADC level, an attitude that was first overtly expressed at the Summit of the Organ held in Livingstone, Zambia, on 31 March 2011. There, the Summit 'noted with disappointment insufficient progress' and 'expressed its impatience in the delay of the implementation of the GPA' (clause 15 of SADC Troika communiqué). It also 'noted with grave concern the polarisation of the political environment as characterised by, inter alia, resurgence of violence, arrests and intimidation in Zimbabwe' (Ibid., clause 16). Apart from recommending 'an immediate end of violence, intimidation, hate speech, harassment, and any other form of action that contradicts the letter and spirit of GPA', the Organ implored the coalition government to 'complete all the steps necessary for the holding of the election' that will be 'peaceful, free and fair' (Ibid., clauses 17 (c) and (d)).

Subsequent to the Livingstone meeting, the three GPA partners and the SADC Facilitation Team met in Cape Town, South Africa, in May 2011, where there was a multi-party consensus on a number of key issues. Among these were agreements that elections would not be held in 2011 and that the ZEC should be reconstituted. The ZANU-PF supreme decision-making body, the Soviet-style politburo, later renounced these agreements, insisting instead that elections be held in 2011 and without fail and that the composition of the ZEC was not a GPA issue. The adverse reaction of ZANU-PF to the consensus already struck by the negotiators – including its own – appears to suggest that the top party leadership – especially Mugabe himself – had decided on a two-track strategy: the first track being that its GPA negotiators would adopt a seemingly co-operative and 'rational' approach to the dialogue and the second where the party *qua* party would take a militant line that entailed repudiating everything the GPA negotiators had agreed on. This way, it maintained its populist image as a radical and consistent party that brooked no 'nonsense'. This explains why, despite its chief GPA negotiator, Patrick Chinamasa, conceding that elections were not possible in 2011 but 'next year or 2013'. ZANU-PF dismissed this position, saying Chinamasa was expressing his personal views and that the party still stood by the Mutare People's Conference resolution that elections be held in 2011.[19]

By September 2011, and notwithstanding ZANU-PF's two-track strategy and associated grandstanding, the three parties had agreed on a roadmap to elections and had even specified timelines. Yet there were also areas of discord and deadlock. The political roadmap covered up to eight issues and several activities within these issues. While there was total tripartite agreement on four of the issues (sanctions, the constitution, media reform and legislative agenda and commitments) there was continued sharp disagreement on various aspects of the remaining four issues (electoral reform, the rule of law, freedom of association and assembly, and the actual election).

With specific reference to elections, the parties agreed on the following activities:

- Enactment of agreed electoral amendments – this activity was to be executed within 45 days from 6 July 2011
- Voter education and mobilisation of voter registration – to be done within 30 days
- Voter registration – allocated 60 days
- Preparation of new voters roll – to be done within 60 days
- Inspection of voters roll – allocated 45 days
- Clean up of voters roll and production of final voters roll – to be done within 45 days.

The most substantive contentious issue pertaining to elections was the staffing of the ZEC. The three parties offered their own preferences: the MDC-T preferred the fresh recruitment of ZEC staff; the MDC-M more or less preferred the same position as MDC-T, insisting on non-partisanship and transparency in the recruitment of ZEC staff; ZANU-PF argued that there should be no changes to ZEC staff and that its suitability should be the prerogative of the ZEC.[20]

Subsequent to the agreed roadmap, ZANU-PF again contested it, particularly the set timelines. It argued that 'some of the timelines in the roadmap are not acceptable. Days that had been assigned to deal with some of these issues are too long'.[21]

The demand by the two MDC factions to have ZEC staff replaced or professionalised was a response to long-standing allegations of the stuffing of the electoral agency with serving and retired CIO and military personnel. It is vital that all elections stakeholders have full confidence and trust in the electoral management body in order to prevent, or at the very least mitigate, possibilities of unfair practices and rigging that had previously been sources of bitter disputes and accusations. On the rule of law, both MDC formations are calling for the security sector to publicly pledge to 'unequivocally uphold the Constitution' in the lead-up to the referendum and the subsequent elections. ZANU-PF on the other hand, flatly rejects this proposal, arguing instead that the matter 'is not an election issue' despite the fact that, from January 2011, and as already noted, service chiefs have been issuing threatening statements to the effect that they would not salute a president without liberation war credentials.

In addition, the MDC formations are also calling for an end to military and police abuse of the rule of law and an end to all forms of state-sponsored violence, even though ZANU-PF denies the existence of such abuse. The two MDC factions are also calling for the demilitarisation and redeployment of military personnel back to barracks and the withdrawal of the regular and irregular armed forces from partisan campaigns. ZANU-PF again denies the existence of militarisation of politics and of politicisation of the armed forces.[22] In addition, the MDCs are calling for legislation to regulate the operations of the CIO, while ZANU-PF again contends that this is not an election issue. Clearly, there is a litany of disagreements amongst the three parties on the most contentious issues that have spoiled previous elections.

By September 2011, the ball was in the principals' court, but time was also running out, particularly for ZANU-PF, which had declared strongly and openly its preference for an early election, i.e., before the end of 2011. It was increasingly clear that an election in 2011 was a practical improbability, not only because of the intractable outstanding issues, but also because the implementation of even those agreed issues was not feasible before the end of the year. For instance, although the constitution-making was staggering towards an end, it was still rather ambitious to expect that process to be concluded and a new constitution enacted before December 2011. Further, and as one of our interlocutors stressed, the MDC-T would not participate in any election if disagreement around key issues remained. The party reiterated this position at the end of July 2011 when Tsvangirai insisted that the key elements in the elections roadmap are *security of persons during and after elections*, *secrecy of the vote*, and *respect of the result of the vote*:

> These are the three key issues in the election roadmap. Once these have been guaranteed we will then sit down after the Constitution and decide when to hold election, *but that will not be this year.*[23]

For its part, ZANU-PF insisted on sanctions being lifted before elections were held, a prospect that was highly unlikely given the mood of those countries that had imposed the controversial sanctions.

A glimmer of hope is that the unilateral route that ZANU-PF had taken previously to declare election dates was closed, thanks to the role of SADC in the matter. Though the former ruling party's top leadership has a legendary profile of risk-taking behaviour, it would be profoundly reckless and foolhardy to unilaterally declare an election date against the wisdom of SADC. The salient question that arises is whether SADC can finally exorcise the spectre of electoral authoritarianism in its midst. The events up to September 2011 strongly suggest that the fatigue factor now looms large in SADC deliberations in respect of the protracted Zimbabwe problem. After all, the crisis has been running almost uninterrupted for more than a decade. With the exception of Angola, Swaziland and Zimbabwe, the political leadership in all other SADC countries has changed hands. With the Zimbabwe problem still firmly at the top of the organisation's agenda, the image, robustness and general integrity of the regional body are being seriously questioned. Naturally, the organisation would be keen to redeem its image in Africa and the rest of the international community, particularly given the unfavourable but justified comparisons being made between SADC and the Economic Community of West African States (ECOWAS) in West Africa, especially given the latter's no-nonsense approach to the post-election crisis in Côte d'Ivoire.

In September 2011, Robert Mugabe and his party finally (but reluctantly) conceded that elections were out of the question in 2011 but that the delay 'cannot go beyond March next year (2012)'. Further, Mugabe exposed the risk-taking unilateralist streak in him when he thundered:

> I will definitely announce that [election] date. It does not matter what anyone would say. Once I announce the date, everyone will follow. I have the Constitutional right to name an election date with the GPA or no GPA.[24]

Our analysis of this development is that Mugabe wanted to simultaneously concede defeat on the timing of the elections while reassuring his support base that he was still fully in charge by claiming that he would act unilaterally and 'everyone will follow'. This way, he could assure his supporters that he still had punch in his fist. It remains to be seen whether his threatened unilateral action will be implemented, especially as it is highly unlikely that the impediments to a peaceful, transparent and credible election will have been removed.

Conclusion

Electoral authoritarianism is a cunning and perfidious type of governance. It wants the legitimacy and international acceptability that comes with elections and it creates the formal institutions that give the appearance of an electoral democracy. Whilst the juridical infrastructure may deceive many, the empirical reality betrays the authoritarian content of the regime; it is an authoritarian wolf in electoral clothing. Zimbabwe's electoral authoritarianism is as old as its independence but it was of a soft type in the first two decades. It thereafter hardened to produce the current militarised electoral authoritarianism. This is in the context of a party-state that was established and consolidated over the past three decades.

The country's democratic transition via the electoral route is being blocked by a small clique of old regime hardliners at the apex of the security sector and the former ruling ZANU-PF party. SADC, the regional guarantor of the tripartite political pact, is playing a salutary role in trying to unblock the transition and exorcise the spectre of electoral authoritarianism in Zimbabwe. It has scored some spectacular successes, not the least its taming of ZANU-PF's penchant for risk-taking unilateralist political behaviour. Skilful handling and sufficient stakeholder support may well see SADC succeed in exorcising the spectre that has for long haunted Zimbabwe's political agora.

Notes

1 The Catholic Commission for Justice and Peace (CCJP) Gokwe Diocese described the 27 June 2008 election period as follows: '[It] was characterised by a wave of intimidation, torching of houses, beatings, abductions, ceaseless meetings and many other forms of violence. The pre-election period to this election left the people of Gokwe in total fear and psychological stress' (Masunungure 2009:88).

2 An elaborate defence of this position is beyond the scope of this chapter. Suffice it to note that President Robert Mugabe was compelled, in early 1999, to institute a constitutional reform process by appointing a Constitutional Commission. This was in response to intense civil society pressure for a new supreme law for the country.

3 A month later, after the consultations were completed, a Freedom House (2011) survey showed that a larger proportion (62 per cent) felt the

constitutional outreach process had been meaningful; only eight per cent felt it was devoid of any meaning.

4   In the Freedom House survey referred to in note 4, above, 'only 42 per cent reckon that citizens' views will be reflected in a new constitution'.

5   In June 2011, the AG reaffirmed and defended his partisan affiliation: 'I do not see anything wrong in me supporting ZANU-PF. Is it a crime to do so?' See 'Tomana threatens MDC', *Daily News*, 15 June 2011, available at www.dailynews.co.zw/index.php/news/53-top-story/2906-tomana-threat ens-mdc.html. Beatrice Mtetwa, a former Zimbabwe Law Society president and well-known human rights defender, accused the AG of abusing the law by using it 'as a political tool against perceived political opponents'. See Peta Thornycroft, 'Partisan Zimbabwe Police Flourish Under Attorney General', VOA, May 26, 2011, available at www. voanews.com/english/news/africa/Partisan-Zimbabwe-Police-Flourish-Under-Attorney-General-122666289.html.

6   Thornycroft, VOA.

7   *Daily News*, 'Army backs Mugabe', 10 January 2002.

8   IRIN News, 12 March 2008. 'Zimbabwe: Military rattle sabres in support of Mugabe'. Available at www.irinnews.org/Report/77254/ZIMBABWE-Military-rattle-sabres-in-support-of-Mugabe.

9   *The Herald*, 29 February 2005.

10 'Brigadier-General Nyikayaramba responds to Tsvangirai', *The Herald*, 23 June 2011. Available at www.herald.co.zw/index.php?option=com_content& view=article&id=13369:generals-respond-to-tsvangirai&catid= 37:topstories&Itemid=130.

11 Afrobarometer survey, May 2009.

12 Quoted in Thornycroft, VOA, May 26, 2011.

13 Afrobarometer survey, October 2010.

14 *The Herald*, 'National Security Council Meets', 31 July 2009.

15 The consequences of this on the salary bill have been dire, largely accounting for the poor remuneration of the rest of the public service.

16 It has been widely considered (and not disputed) that the diamond field is 'one of the richest in the world, producing six million carats a year worth up to $100 million a month' (Mugabe depends on diamonds for power'. See www.terradaily.com/reports/Mugabe_depends_on_diamonds_for_power_999.html.)

17 Canadile, a joint company of the state-controlled Zimbabwe Mining Development Corporation and Core Mining, a South African company, had its mining licence cancelled in late 2010, allegedly for fraudulently acquiring mining claims at the Chiadzwa fields. Core Mining, however, accused some ZANU-PF leaders of staging a hostile takeover of the firm's mining claims.

18 See note 7.

19 See 'Zanu-PF Spokesman blasts Chinamasa', *The Zimbabwe Mail*. Rugare Gumbo, ZANU-PF spokesman, said, 'The party's conference made a clear resolution, endorsed by the Politburo and the Central Committee … so I don't understand why our negotiator Chinamasa failed to consult the party which has given him the trust to represent it.' Available at www. thezimbabwemail.com/zimbabwe/8021-zanu-pf-split-imminent-over-elections. html.

20 It must be noted that public opinion does not hold the ZEC in high regard, extending very low trust to the institution. For instance, in May 2009, public trust in the ZEC was as low as 30 per cent, with up to 60 per cent expressing distrust. By October 2010, public trust in the ZEC had declined to 25 per cent, while distrust held steady (and even slightly increased) at 61 per cent (Afrobarometer surveys, May 2009 and October 2010). The electoral agency clearly needs to put its house in order.

21 'Call to review poll timelines', *The Herald*, 14 July 2011. Available at www.herald.co.zw/index.php?option=com_content&view=article&id=15 395:call-to-review-poll-timelines&catid=37:top-stories&Itemid=130.

22 The military chiefs have also persistently denied that their soldiers do political work for ZANU-PF. Just before the Heroes' Day holiday in August 2011, the ZNA commander, Lieutenant General Philip Valerio Sibanda, defended army presence in districts across the country saying the soldiers would be 'doing training … and some of them will be assisting in various Government departments like health and agriculture'. He dismissed as 'utter nonsense' the allegations that the army's presence in rural areas was in order to campaign for ZANU-PF. (*The Herald*, 1 August 2011, see www.herald.co.zw/index.php?option=com_content&view=article&i d=17017:army-presencein-countryside-normal-zna-chief&catid=38:local-news&Itemid=131.)

23 *NewsDay*, 1 August 2011, my emphasis. Available at www.newsday.co.zw/ article/2011-08-01-we-wont-bow-to-zanu-pf-persecution-tsvangirai.

24 'Poll next year, says President', *The Herald*, 3 September 2011. Available at www.herald.co.zw/index.php?option=com_content&view=article&id= 20235:polls-next-year-says-president&catid=37:top-stories&Itemid=130.

References

Afrobarometer surveys – May 2009, October 2010.

AU. 2008. *Preliminary Statement of the African Union Observer Mission*, 29 June.

'Agreement between the Zimbabwe African National Union-Patriotic Front. ZANU-PF and the two Movement for Democratic Change

(MDC) formations, on resolving the challenges facing Zimbabwe.'
Harare, 15 September 2008.

Bratton, Michael. 1998. 'Second Elections in Africa', *Journal of Democracy*, 7:51-66.

Bratton, Michael and Eldred Masunungure. 2008. 'Zimbabwe's Long Agony', *Journal of Democracy*, 19, 4:41-55.

Chitiyo, K. 2009. 'The Case for Security Sector Reform in Zimbabwe,' Occasional Paper, Royal United Services Institute. Available at www. rusi.org Accessed 23 June 2011.

Chitiyo, K. and M. Rupiya. 2005. 'Tracking Zimbabwe's political history: The Zimbabwe Defence Force from 1980 –2005'. Available at www.iss.co.za/pubs/Books/Evol_Revol%20Oct%2005/Chap13.pdf. Accessed 24 June 2011.

Daily News. 2002. 'Army backs Mugabe', 10 January.

— 2011. 'Tomana threatens MDC', 15 June. Available at www.dailynews. co.zw/index.php/news/53-top-story/2906-tomana-threatens-mdc.html.

Diamond, L. 2002. 'Thinking about Hybrid Regimes', *Journal of Democracy*, Vol. 13, No. 2: 21-35.

Diamond, L., Juan J. Linz, and Seymour Martin Lipset (eds). 1990. *Politics in Developing Countries: Comparing Experiences with Democracy*. Boulder and London: Lynne Rienner Publishers.

Freedom House. 2011. *Changing Perceptions in Zimbabwe – Nationwide Survey of the Political Climate in Zimbabwe*. Report compiled by Susan Booysen, Johannesburg, March.

Hendricks, Cheryl and Lauren Hutton. 2011. 'Providing security and justice for the people: Security Sector Reform in Zimbabwe'. Available at www.iss.co.za. Accessed 23 June 2011.

Herald. 2009. 'National Security Council Meets'. Available www. business.highbeam.com /437651/article-1G1-204889274/nationalsecurity-council-meets. Accessed 26 June 2011.

— 2011. 'Brigadier-General Nyikayaramba responds to Tsvangirai, 23 June. Available at www.herald.co/index.php?option=com_content& view=article&id=13369:generals-respondto-tsvangirai&catid=37:top-stories&Itemid=130

— 2011. 'Call to review poll timelines', 14 July. Available at www.herald. co.zw/index.php?option=com_content&view=article&id=15395:call-to-review-poll-timelines&catid=37:top-stories&Itemid=130

— 2011. 'Army presence in countryside normal – ZNA chief', 1 August. Available at www.herald.co.zw/index.php?option=com_con tent&view=article&id=17017:army-presence-in-countryside-normal-znachief&catid=38:local-news&Itemid=131

— 2011. 'Poll next year, says President', 3 September. Available at www. herald.co.zw/index.php?option=com_content&view=article&id=202 35:pol ls -next-yearsays-president&catid=37:top stories&Itemid=130

Human Rights Watch. 2009. 'Diamonds in the Rough: Human Rights Abuses in the Marange Diamond Fields of Zimbabwe'.

IDAZIM. 2010. 'Summary of Results Public Attitudes to the Global Political Agreement (GPA) and Political Transition in Zimbabwe'. Harare: IDAZIM.

IRIN News. 2008. 'Zimbabwe: Military rattle sabres in support of Mugabe', 12 March. Available at www.irinnews.org/Report/77254/ ZIMBABWE-Military-rattle-sabres-in-support-of-Mugabe

Key, V.O. 1955. 'A Theory of Critical Elections', *The Journal of Politics*, 17, 1:3-18.

Levitsky, S. and L. Way. 2002. 'Elections Without Democracy: The Rise of Competitive Authoritarianism', *Journal of Democracy*, 13, No. 2. April): 51-66.

Mair, Stefan and Masipula Sithole. 2002. *Blocked Democracies in Africa: Case Study of Zimbabwe*. Harare: Konrad-Adenauer-Stiftung.

Masunungure, E.V. 2009a. 'Introduction', in Masunungure, E.V. (ed.) (2009) *Defying the Winds of Change: Zimbabwe's 2008 Elections*. Harare: Weaver Press.

— 2009b. 'A Militarized Election: The 27 June Presidential Run-Off', in Masunungure, E.V. (ed.) (2009) *Defying the Winds of Change: Zimbabwe's 2008 Elections*.

Newsday. 2010. 'Zimbabwe needs 20bn to fix and modernise infrastructure'. 13 September. Available at www.newsday.co.zw. article/2010-09-13-zim-needs-20bn-to-fix-modernise-infrastructure-idbz. Accessed 20 January 2011.

— 2011. 'We won't bow to ZANU-PF persecution – Tsvangirai'. Available at www.newsday.co.zw/article/2011-08-01-we-wont-bow-to-zanu-pf-persecution-tsvangirai

Ogunsanya, K. 2005). 'Benchmarks for credible elections in the SADC region'. Available at www.google.co.za/#hl=en&q=Institutional+facto rs+for+a+credible+election&oq=Institutional+factors+for+a+credible+ election&aq=f&aqi=&aql=1&gs_sm=e&gs_upl=46654l60430l0l607 33l49l46l0l24l0l0l7o6l776l8l4.4.1.3.3.6.1l22&fp=90e7b8f8b9d5966d &biw=1366&bih=610. Accessed 20 May 2011.

Rupiya, M. 2010)'Diamonds are Forever'. Unpublished policy brief submitted to IDAZIM, 10 August 2010.

SADC Election Observer Mission. 2008. 'Preliminary Statement presented by the Hon. José Marcos Barrica, Minister of Youth and Sports of the

Republic of Angola and Head of SOEM, on the Presidential Runoff and House of Assembly By-elections', 29 June, Harare.

SADC. 2010. Communiqué. Summit of the Southern Africa Development Community Heads of States and Governments Meeting, 17 August 2010, Windhoek, Namibia.

Schedler, Andreas (ed.). 2006. *Electoral Authoritarianism: The Dynamics of Unfree Competition.* Boulder: Lynne Rienner Publishers.

terradaily. 2011. 'Mugabe depends on diamonds for power', 3 March. Available at www.terradaily.com/reports/Mugabe_depends_on_dia monds_for_power_999.html

Thornycroft, Peta. 2011. 'Partisan Zimbabwe Police Flourish Under Attorney General', 26 May. Available at www.voanews.com/english/ news//africa/ Partisan-Zimbabwe-Police-Flourish-Under-AttorneyGen eral-122666289.html

ZBC. 2010. 'Cabinet endorses proposed amendments to Electoral Act', 13 June. Available at www.zbc.co.zw/news-categories/top-stories/1459-cabinet-endorses-proposed-ammendments-to-electoral-act.html. Accessed 20 May 2011.

Zimbabwe Mail. 2011. 'Zanu PF Spokesman blasts Chinamasa', 9 May. Available at www.thezimbabwemail.com/zimbabwe/8021-zanu-pf-split-imminent-over-elections.html

6

Fiscal Space Challenges, Policy Options & Zimbabwe's Economic Recovery

Jabusile M. Shumba & Mohammed Jahed

Introduction and background

The Zimbabwe economy experienced a precipitous decline between 1999 and 2008, cumulatively losing at least 48 per cent of GDP (Government of Zimbabwe (GoZ), 2009). By March 2007, the economy was operating in a hyperinflationary environment,[1] largely because of over-printing money as one of the major sources of financing the budget deficits, but without a corresponding growth in output of goods and services (Makochekanwa, 2007). Industry failed to cope with the rising costs of inputs due to the depreciation of the local currency. National output dropped against declining industrial capacity utilisation[2] to levels below ten per cent across the economy (GoZ, 2009). The sustained effects of spiralling inflation brought by quasi-fiscal activities of the Reserve Bank of Zimbabwe (RBZ) and the contraction of output undermined the country's capacity to collect revenue (IMF, 2010). By 2008, Zimbabwe had fallen into a state of almost complete economic and social collapse characterised by poor public services, especially in the areas of primary healthcare, the provision of clean water and electricity and shortages of basic commodities.

In September 2008, the country's political adversaries agreed on a new path forward and signed an inter-party agreement known as the Global Political Agreement (GPA). This agreement defined the framework for the new government formed in February 2009. In line with

Article 3.1(a)[3] of the GPA, the new government introduced a new macroeconomic policy framework – the Short-Term Emergency Recovery Programme (STERP) – whose main key goals were to stabilise the economy, recover the levels of savings, investment and growth and lay out the basis of a more transformative mid-to-long-term economic programme that would turn Zimbabwe into a progressive developmental state (GoZ, 2009). In addition to the multi-currency framework being part of the new economic path, a number of measures were also introduced, among them being fiscal prudence measures such as cash-budgeting, RBZ reforms such as abolishing quasi-fiscal activities and strengthening public finance with the introduction of the Public Finance Management Bill. Suspending the use of domestic currency and introducing a multi-currency trading system limited the RBZ's discretion to 'create' money by extending credit to the government or the banking system and eliminating the possibility of inflationary financing. This and other fiscal policy measures managed to tame hyper-inflation and restore some form of economic stability.

Revenue collections from taxes recovered against the backdrop of reform measures, rising from US$4 million in February 2009 to close out the year at a total of US$973 million, accounting for 18.6 per cent of GDP (Ibid.). The improvement in revenue collections continued in 2010, and the government revised the projection during the mid-year fiscal policy review from US$1.440 billion (26 per cent of GDP) to US$1.750 billion (31.7 per cent of GDP) based on the strong performance seen during the first half of the year. However, revenue collections have yet to reach the levels seen prior to the decade of economic decline and the challenge of restoring of social services and infrastructure remains. The government is thus faced with the task of creating fiscal space in order to stimulate the public spending instrument in promoting economic growth. It is against this background that this chapter outlines Zimbabwe's fiscal space challenges, argues for public expenditure reforms and discusses some policy options for increasing fiscal space for growth-enabling priorities.

Defining the concept of fiscal space

In its broadest sense, fiscal space can be defined as the financial capacity of a government to provide budgetary resources for a desired purpose, without prejudicing the sustainability of its financial position (Heller, 2005). It is necessary that the manner in which a government raises revenue be sustainable, ensuring that it does not fail to meet its debt obligations.

There are several ways in which a government can create fiscal space:

- Changes to taxation: Taxes are charges/fees imposed on an individual or entity exacted pursuant to legislative authority by a government. They vary in form, ranging from tolls, customs and excise duty, valued-added tax and taxes on personal income. A government can raise additional resources by increasing taxes, broadening the tax base and/or strengthening the tax administration system. However, due consideration must be made depending on the specific circumstance of a given country, particularly as this relates to tax increases and broadening the tax base. Taxation policy is a balance between the pursuits of various government objectives such as maximising state revenue, improving distributional equity, encouraging increased investment and reinvestment or fostering specific industry or sector, deterring pollution and environmental degradation or discouraging the consumption of tobacco and alcohol products (UNDP, 2009)

- Reducing lower-priority expenditures such as existing subsidy programmes, cutting back on defence and internal security, reducing official foreign travel or embassy expenses, rationalising those elements of the civil service that are of low (or zero) productivity and eliminating overstaffing (Heller, 2005). However, any reprioritisation of expenditure must ensure that the government's obligations can be met in the longer term

- Increasing official development assistance (ODA) through foreign aid or debt relief (UNDP, 2009). However, the key challenge here is ensuring predictability and sustainability. As the receiving country has no control over the latter, this can pose a major problem, particularly if only short-term grants are awarded, as the receiving government may scale up expenditures in the expectation of ongoing grants. Other challenges include absorption capacity, the reduced incentive of governments to improve their revenue mobilisation efforts, thus creating dependency and rent-seeking effects within government bureaucracies, exchange rate appreciation and impact on the export sectors (Heller, 2005).

- Borrowing: Government may borrow money from domestic and/ or international markets. As the monies must be repaid, this raises the question of whether the return on the expenditure justifies the cost of borrowing, and, perhaps more importantly, if the spending will enhance government revenues to finance the repayment of the borrowing or trap the country in a debt

- Seigniorage: This refers to printing money via the country's reserve bank in order to lend it to government. However, clear limits to printing of money to create fiscal space need to be set due to its negative effects of pushing inflation. Given the money multipliers in most developing countries, the scope for additional expenditure that can be financed in principle by money creation is rarely above one per cent of GDP, unless a clear and relatively quick supply-side impact can be obtained from the higher level of expenditure (Heller, 2005). In the absence of a quick supply-side response, the jaws of inflation may reverse the economic gains sought through the effects of inflation.

For Zimbabwe, as a country emerging from hyperinflation, printing money may not be the best option as market inflation expectation can easily trigger additional inflation. The domestic market remains illiquid, which renders domestic borrowing very costly, given the displacement effect it may have on the private sector. Zimbabwe lost its international credit worthiness after defaulting on its foreign debt obligations from 2000 onwards – the country's debt overhang is estimated at over 60 per cent of GDP.

And although there is scope for reprioritising public expenditure and increased ODA, the United Nations Development Programme (UNDP) (2009) has cautioned that any forthcoming debt relief may not translate into increased fiscal space as the country has no savings. Zimbabwe should therefore focus on reprioritising public expenditure, mobilising domestic revenues and normalising relations with the international community in order to attract further – and much-needed – ODA.

Theoretical foundations

A subject of intense contestation amongst economists and policy-makers is the extent to which government should intervene in the economy. The classical school of economic thought emphasises the *laissez-faire* approach to economic growth and believes markets should be left alone to attain equilibrium. It views government as inefficient and less important in the pursuit of growth. Keynesian economists argue a different school of thought, advocating that in order to attain economic growth, government is essential to induce aggregate demand and so raise national output (Keynes, 1936).

Keynesian economics argues for government intervention, particularly in times of crisis, to stimulate growth. Government could reverse economic downturns as it can borrow money from the private sector and inject it into the economy through various spending programmes in order to stimulate growth. Indeed, Keynesian economics successfully served as the dominant model during the Great Depression, the Second World War and post-war economic expansion between 1945 and 1973 (Hazlitt, 1959). The advent of the current global crisis has also seen the resurgence of Keynesian economics, as the endogenous growth models by Barro (1991) and King and Rebelo (1995, cited in IMF, 2010) amongst others, further substantiate the positive impact of government expenditure in driving economic growth. Empirical findings on the positive impact of public capital investment on growth by Aschauer (1989) and Canning (1999), amongst others, are further instructive to this study.

The implication is that fiscal policy *is* an important and influential factor in relation to economic growth. If a government directs its money towards capital investment, education, research and development, there will be a positive – and sustainable – impact on economic growth.

International experiences of post-hyperinflation the case of Argentina

Reconstructing economies in recession is a major task and warrants political consensus and commitment for reform. In the absence of political consensus and a deliberate and purposeful course of action for reform any country's road to recovery will be long and painful for its citizens.

The Argentine economy faced severe recession during the 1980s. Growth of real output stagnated, financial markets collapsed, prices rose as the currency steadily depreciated, and capital fled the country in pursuit of safer havens. Most public enterprises were running large deficits, and the external debt kept mounting. The central government, hampered by low tax collections and desperate for revenues, turned to the central bank for finance through the taxation of deposits and money creation. Inflation, which had risen gradually over the previous three decades, soared – reaching average annual rates of 2,600 per cent in 1989 and 1990. In the face of these developments, the banking system practically disappeared. Although it tried a number of times to bring inflation under control, the central government was unable either to balance its budget or to escape its reliance on inflationary financing. The hyperinflation of 1989 and 1990 finally provided the impetus for reform, which began with the Convertibility Plan of 1991.[4]

The major elements of Argentina's Convertibility Plan included financial system and far-reaching public sector reform such as substantially reducing the scope of the public sector by privatising some of the country's major public enterprises. As a result, the latter's efficiency and provision of services improved dramatically, thereby creating some much-needed fiscal space (IMF, 2000). New and stronger laws increased the government's ability to control tax evasion and accelerated economic growth and increased public revenues, while the public pay-as-you-go pension system was replaced by a combination of public transfers and private capitalisation. These measures resulted in a dramatic change in the composition and prices of goods available to the Argentine public and the cumulative effect enabled the country to head down a sustainable path of recovery and growth.

The role of fiscal space and Zimbabwe's economic recovery

A crucial element of Zimbabwe's economic recovery is the creation of fiscal space for growth-enhancing economic activities. Here, we review expenditure and revenue trends in an attempt to not only highlight

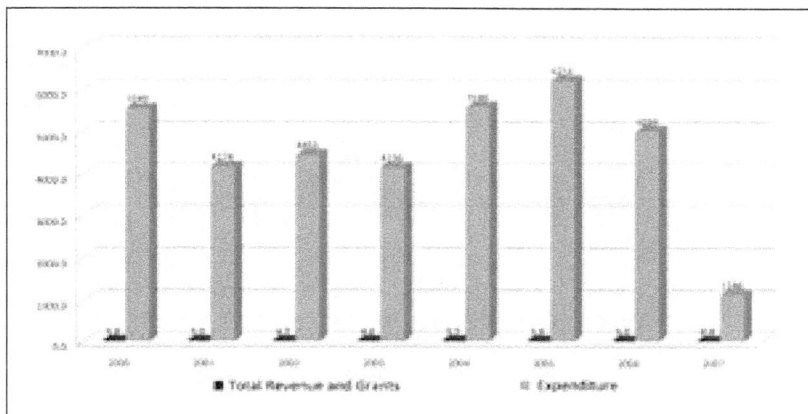

Figure 1: Zimbabwe's total revenue and expenditure performance, 2000 to 2007 *(figures adjusted to 1990 prices in Z$ millions) (Source: Various budget estimates:* Blue Book, *published by the Ministry of Finance)*

Zimbabwe's fiscal space challenges in this area but also explore opportunities for reform. We also discuss some policy options on improving fiscal management.

During the period 2000 to 2007 revenues accounted for far less than one per cent of total expenditures (Figure 1). Following its suspension by the International Monetary Fund (IMF) in 1999, deficit financing was largely achieved by domestic borrowing through seigniorage. This led to hyperinflation that crippled all facets of the economy. At the end of 2009, total public and publicly guaranteed debt amounted to US$6.9 billion or 157 per cent of GDP. The high level of public debt and relatively high scheduled debt service payments, not to mention the inability to generate primary surplus, resulted in the persistence of a public debt ratio above sustainable levels. Low revenues coupled with the huge public expenditure bill[5] left no room for capital expenditure and saw infrastructure severely deteriorate, which further undermined the capacity to generate economic growth.

In 2009, following the adoption of a new economic path, revenue collections improved from US$4 million in February 2009, closing out the year at US$973 million (18.6 per cent of GDP). Significant revenue contributions during the period came through value-added tax (VAT), pay-as-you-earn (PAYE) and customs duties. In 2010, the largest revenue contribution came from VAT, which contributed

161

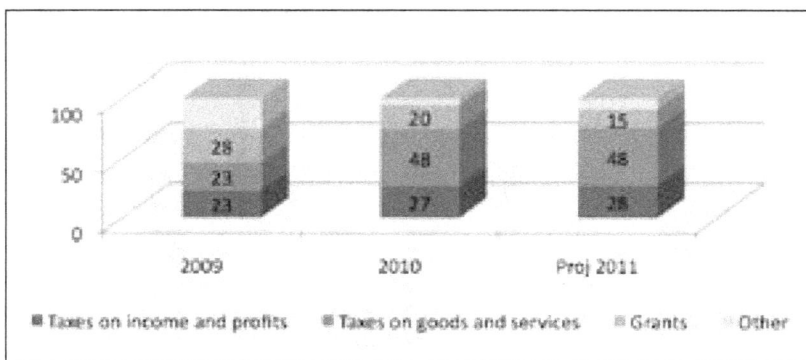

Figure 2: Revenue contributions over the period 2009–2010 (current figures in US$) (*Source: ZIMSTAT, Finance Statistics Report, 2010*)

48 per cent, mainly from domestic sales (55.5 per cent of total VAT) (GoZ, 2010) (Figure 2). The increases in VAT could be attributed to increased capacity utilisation of some of the manufacturing sub-sectors. PAYE also increased significantly in 2010, something which is largely attributable to positive wage and salary reviews as a result of increasing turnover. The increase in the volume of imports in 2010 saw a corresponding increase in revenue from customs duty. However, the performance of other revenue heads which have great potential to contribute to total revenue, for example, companies, non-tax revenues and domestic dividends and interest, remain weak. This is due to poor capacity utilisation, tax evasion and poor tax administration.[6]

Revenues are projected to remain below 26 per cent of GDP over the medium to long term (IMF, 2010) and domestic borrowing via open market operations remains very expensive due to liquidity challenges, while dollarisation implies that the country cannot finance its expenditure from seignorage revenue. The huge external debt ($6.9 billion or 103 per cent of GDP, which is far above the international debt sustainability benchmark of 60 per cent) impairs the country's capacity for international borrowing.[7] All told, these factors leave no major room for financing growth-enhancing capital expenditure.

A review of public expenditure: 2000–2011

In a study showing a sectoral analysis of government spending from 1980 to 1998 it was revealed that the government of Zimbabwe

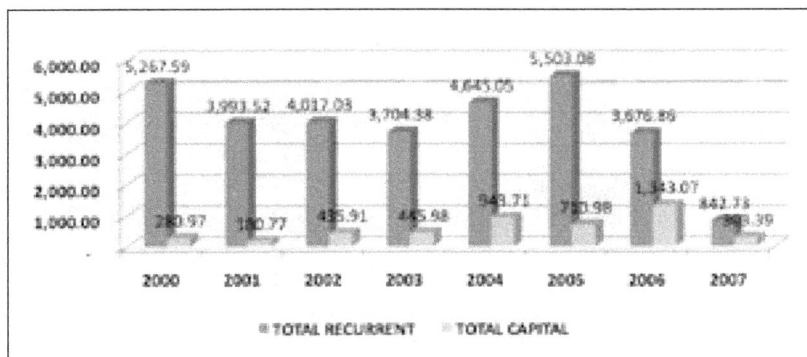

Figure 3: Recurrent and capital expenditure, 2000–2007 (figures adjusted to 1990 prices in Z$ millions) *(Source: Various budget estimates Blue Book, published by the Ministry of Finance)*

spent a total of Z$4,734,873,800.23 (27 per cent) on the economic sector, Z$6,481,569,373.54 (38 per cent) on the social sector and Z$4,512,257,078.51 (26 per cent) on the safety and security sector (Shumba, 2010). The safety and security sector allocation was largely dominated by non-productive military expenditure that included a decade of military support to Mozambique (1982–1992) and one year to the Democratic Republic of Congo (DRC) in 1996. Zimbabwe's involvement in the war in the DRC alone is estimated to have cost the country US$281.5 million since 1996.[8]

Spending in the social sector was characterised by investments in education and health, while support to the economic sector was largely directed at supporting maintenance works, with very limited replacement of worn-out machinery and equipment. By consequence, the country continued to suffer underinvestment in most of its infrastructure, with parastatals unable to raise their own resources to fund capital projects. Even today, most parastatals are struggling with aged equipment that is very costly to maintain.

Over the period 2000 to 2007, recurrent expenditures remained predominantly high and accounted for a significant share of the budget. By contrast, capital expenditures averaged less than ten per cent between 2000 and 2007 (Figure 3), which severely impacted the infrastructure sectors (Shumba, 2010) and continued to undermine the country's capacity to crowd-in private investment and achieve sustained economic growth.

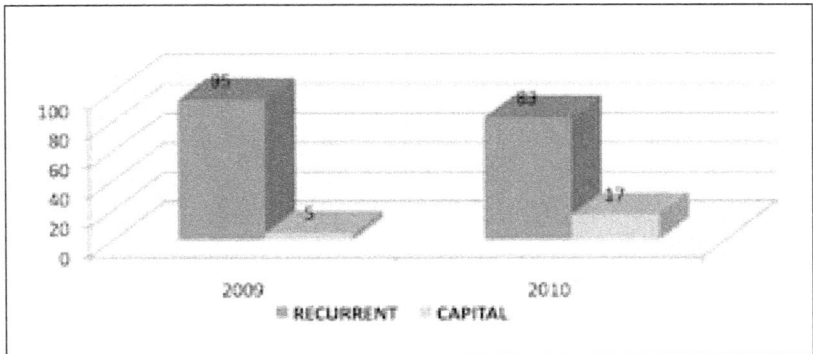

Figure 4: Recurrent and capital expenditure for 2009 and 2010 (percentages)
(*Source: Ministry of Finance, Budget Statements for 2009 and 2010*)

At its inception, the Inclusive Government was unable to signifi-cantly alter this trend due to limited fiscal space against the backdrop of huge non-discretionary expenditure. This is apparent in the 2010 budget, where 82 per cent of total expenditure was recurrent, of which 46.3 per cent went to employment costs. In the 2011 budget, 70 per cent of all revenue was spent on recurrent expenditure, with the largest percentage taken up by salaries and wages for civil servants, includ-ing foreign trips consisting of very huge delegations (a major driver of expenditure in Zimbabwe),[9] even though Zimbabwe desperately needs to rehabilitate its infrastructure and rebuild its education and healthcare system. Figure 4 presents recurrent and capital expenditure expressed in percentage terms over the period 2009–2010.

Of the 133 countries surveyed by the Global Competitive Report, Zimbabwe's economic infrastructure was ranked 101, with the qual-ity of electricity rated amongst the top five worst in the world (IMF, 2010). Only 18 per cent of Zimbabwe's 85,237 kilometres of high-way is paved, while the communications system, once considered the best in Africa, now suffers from poor maintenance and only supplies 247,000 telephones to a population of 10.9 million.[10] In addition, the country's legacy of investing in human capital development is under threat after years of decline due to poor funding. The Infrastructure Development Bank of Zimbabwe, a government-controlled develop-ment finance institution, says the country needs about US$20 billion to fix and modernise its infrastructure, of which US$12 billion is required for maintenance.[11]

In 2010, the government allocated US$25,921,000 towards capital investment in healthcare, which accounted for 14.9 per cent of the total budget allocation to the Ministry of Health. This was also complemented by off-budget capital support from donors; in 2009 they financed US$156 million in off-budget capital expenditures in health and education (IMF, 2010). The government currently spends about US$9 per person on health, which is much less than the US$34 recommended by the World Health Organisation's Macroeconomic Commission on Health. A total of US$609,750,400, accounting for 22.21 per cent of the 2010 budget,[12] is directed towards the education sector. While meeting the Abuja Declaration commitment of 20 per cent budget allocation towards education, Zimbabwe nevertheless needs to inject more funds into the education sector to rehabilitate infrastructure, and attract and retain qualified staff rather than continuing to lose them to 'brain drain'.

Budget allocations to the Ministry of Energy stood at US$16,526,842 in 2010. Lending and equity participation to the Zimbabwe Electricity Supply Authority (ZESA) accounted for the greater share (90 per cent) of the budget allocations, mainly covering the rehabilitation of the Hwange and other, smaller thermal power stations, standing at 90 per cent in both 2010 and 2011. Again, Zimbabwe needs to invest considerably in its electricity suppliers in order to support the recovery of manufacturing and industry.

The Ministry of Transport and Infrastructure Development received an allocation of US$28,938,518 in 2011. Capital expenditure allocations stood at 90 per cent in 2010. A significant share of the capital budget is directed towards road maintenance activities (49 per cent). The allocations to transport and infrastructure are still falling short of requirements to rebuild the transport system and attract investment. Zimbabwe will need a significant capitalisation project to dualise its paved main roads and expand the road network access in order to improve its transport network. The challenge is discouraging because investments in transportation and telecommunication, especially road development, contribute immensely to growth and poverty reduction, yet road and infrastructure development remains poor in Africa (Fan, Mogues and Benin, 2006).

The overall trend between recurrent and capital expenditure is an impediment to Zimbabwe's recovery as it does not aid infrastructure rehabilitation. The current levels of public capital investment fall far short of the levels required to rehabilitate and develop infrastructure in the transport and energy sectors, and rebuild the education and health sectors. Zimbabwe will therefore need to urgently alter this trend to re-orient the economy towards sustained growth. In the next section we discuss policy options to create fiscal space for growth-enhancing activities.

Policy options for Zimbabwe

Zimbabwe is confronted with the difficult task of economic recovery against the background of limited public resources for growth-enhancing public expenditures. Recent experiences of the global financial crisis show us that more needs to be done through in-country, domestic efforts. While we recognise the limitations of the current transitional context, reflected mainly in the lack of policy consensus among the coalition partners, Zimbabwe will have to do more within its internal confines if it is to lay a more robust foundation for economic recovery and sustained growth. In this section we discuss viable policy options through which Zimbabwe's policy-makers can create much-needed fiscal space in financing economic recovery and growth.

Public expenditure reform

Typical public expenditure reductions include cutting down the public sector wage bill, trimming or eliminating subsidies and reducing transfers while simultaneously protecting the share of public investment in the total budget (UNDP, 2009). Zimbabwe's public expenditure is heavily dominated by recurrent spending. Since the 1990s, several budget statements presented before parliament have ignored the need to cut down this spending in order to free more resources for growth-enhancing capital expenditure. Of the 2010 budget, 82 per cent was directed towards recurrent expenditures (GoZ, 2010). Some of the policy options available to Zimbabwe for reforming its public expenditure in order to optimise the impact of limited public resources by investing in growth-enabling capital expenditures include the following:

Cutting down the public sector wage bill – The government currently employs an estimated 250,000 people, generating a wage bill of

US$960 million. This translates to 70 per cent of revenue collections, more than 60 per cent of the total budget and 15 per cent of GDP against regional best practices levels of 30 per cent of the total budget and ten per cent of GDP (Ibid.). In November 2009, the Ministry of Public Service commissioned a civil service audit. While no official position has been issued by the government regarding the status of the report, media reports indicate that the report findings suggest there are over 75,237 'ghost workers' absorbing more than US$20 million from the treasury coffers each month.[13] Other reviews on the public service have noted duplication of duties as a major factor driving the large size of the civil service. Zimbabwe should seriously consider downsizing its civil service in order to make it more affordable, whether by merging some ministries and/or retrenching employees. So doing would enable some of the country's limited public resources to be rechanneled towards more productive ends.

Cutting down safety and security sector spending – Zimbabwe spends significantly more on the security and safety sector than it does on the productive sectors of the economy; overall, this sector accounts for more than 26 per cent of public spending (Shumba, 2010). Measures targeted at reducing government-sponsored military interventions and cutting down the size of the security and safety sector are critical to freeing resources towards growth-enhancing expenditures. Defence expenditures can only be productive if they are supporting, for example, an enterprise for exporting military equipment, something that has not been the case for Zimbabwe. Notwithstanding the need to protect citizens, the huge spending on defence has also impacted negatively on recovery and growth. Reducing its defence budget would enable the government to redirect resources towards infrastructure rehabilitation, which is vital to increasing investment and stimulating economic growth.

Parastatal reforms

Since independence, and in the face of expectations of large inflows of developmental aid after promises by international donors at the occasion of the Zimbabwe Conference on Reconstruction and Development (ZIMCORD) (GoZ, 1984), the government has allocated very limited statutory support towards major parastatals, including, among others, the now-disbanded Zimbabwe Iron and Steel Company, Cold Storage

Commission, ZESA, National Railways of Zimbabwe, Post and Tele-communications Corporation, Cotton Marketing Board and the Dairy Marketing Board. However, the expected inflows of external capital have fallen far below expectations (GoZ, 1986). The statutory support that has been provided has thus been largely directed towards maintenance. With the overarching thrust of reducing public expenditure, the ESAP adopted in the 1990s marked the further dwindling of the budgetary allocations towards parastatals. The Public Sector Investment Programme (PSIP) was reduced, and parastatals were required to finance their capital projects from their own resources. The ESAP reforms crippled many productive sectors of the economy, including agriculture, mining and manufacturing, as the anticipated private sector injection to the economy was not forthcoming. Against the backdrop of ageing capital equipment and infrastructure, the reduced allocations to parastatals had drastic effects across the economy.[14]

Today, most parastatals in Zimbabwe are heavily undercapitalised, sit on huge debt overhang and are running at a loss. Given that the government does not have the technical and financial capacity to recapitalise these entities, there is serious need for policy reform. Privatisation, however, is not the best option. The UNDP (2009) has argued that privatising loss-making parastatals would not generate substantial revenue for the state because most are in debt or technically insolvent. We argue that the government should therefore seriously consider public–private partnerships (PPPs) or commercialisation[15] to make these entities productive rather than an ongoing drain on the system.

Forming public–private partnerships (PPPs)
Zimbabwe requires at least US$22 billion to finance infrastructure rehabilitation and development (internal Standard Bank report, cited in UNDP, 2009). Given its limited resource capacity, the government should consider forming PPPs for rehabilitating and developing infrastructure in the transport and energy sectors. This approach has shown positive results within SADC, including South Africa, where PPPs have been used effectively in the development of the transport sector. Policies such as indigenisation, at a time when the country is struggling from undercapitalisation, may not be the best option as a major challenge to growth and development is the historically born mistrust of the government in implementing redistributive policies in

a transparent manner. The government of Zimbabwe needs to do much more to ensure policy consistency, the implementation of the rule of law and forging international investment agreements if it is to attract private investment in these sectors (Brenthurst Foundation, 2009).

Tax reform

Zimbabwe's global economic freedom score is 26.3, making its economy the 178th freest out of 179 countries in the 2012 World Index. Within sub-Saharan Africa it is the second least free of the 46 countries in this region.[16] This low ranking is partly due to its high tax rates and complicated tax system. For example, companies must make 52 payments a year, which typically involves 256 hours of work and an overall tax rate as a percentage of profits of 63.7 per cent (World Bank cited in UNDP, 2009). Zimbabwe should therefore consider substantial reforms to reduce and simplify its tax administration system. The UNDP (2009) has noted several comprehensive tax reforms in recent years, including simplifying the tax system, broadening the tax base while reducing tax rates, abolishing tax breaks, the on-line filling and filing of tax returns, combining taxes where the tax base is the same (wages, salaries, profits or property taxes) and tax consolidation, thereby reducing the number of taxes and simplifying the payments and collections system. With the informal sector[17] in Zimbabwe being estimated as representing more than 60 per cent[18] of the economy in 2008 but remaining largely untaxed (Zimbabwe Papers, 2009), there remains further scope for mobilising previously untapped resources by putting in mechanisms to tax the informal sector.

Creating an enabling business environment

Business regulations in Zimbabwe are currently confusing, arbitrary and costly; they inhibit business start-ups, repel foreign investment and reduce productivity (Zimbabwe Papers, 2009). With Zimbabwe ranked 159 out of 183 in the World Bank 2010 study in terms of the ease of doing business, there is need for the government to open up the economy and create an environment more conducive to domestic and foreign investment. Key investors have, since the mid-1990s, considered Zimbabwe's property rights system illegitimate, the legal system having fallen victim to political whims and in so doing failing in terms of resolving disputes. Well-defined, readily enforceable and transferable property rights are crucial for economic development; strong property rights have long proved necessary to underpin flourishing economic growth around the world (Ibid.). Zimbabwe should thus restore its political commitment to the rule of law in order to promote an enabling business environment for private investment.

Conclusion

The government of Zimbabwe faces challenges in the prioritisation, focus and management of government expenditure to influence the economy towards sustainable growth. However, confronted with the most obvious difficult challenge of reconstructing the economy after a long period of recession, Zimbabwe has no option but to reform its budget and financial management and move away from political grandstanding, instilling strong fiscal controls and procedures instead. Political consensus and commitment are foundational imperatives for the economic recovery agenda. Given the limitations of the country's fiscal space, current levels of investment in productive sectors continue to fall far short of the levels necessary to realise spin-off effects and stimulate economic growth. A comprehensive public and recurrent expenditure review must preoccupy Zimbabwe's policy-makers in order to create this much-needed fiscal space. Hence, any policy reform agenda should target public sector reform and the reprioritisation of expenditures towards growth-enabling public expenditure on infrastructure and the health and education sectors.

Notes

1   Hyperinflation is defined as a monthly rate of inflation that exceeds 50 per cent.
2   Capacity utilisation is a concept in economics that refers to the extent to which an enterprise or a nation actually uses its installed productive capacity as opposed to the potential output which 'could' be produced, if capacity was fully used (Berndt and Morrison, 1981).
3   This article states that 'The parties agree to give priority to the restoration of economic stability and growth in Zimbabwe. The Government will lead the process of developing and implementing an economic recovery strategy

and plan. To that end, the Parties are committed to working together on a full and comprehensive economic programme to resuscitate Zimbabwe's economy which will urgently address the issue of production, food security, poverty and unemployment and the challenges of high inflation, interest rates and the exchange rate.'

4 IMF (2010).

5 Zimbabwe's public expenditure wage bill accounts for more than 75 per cent of recurrent expenditures by 2009. Source: Central Statistics Office (now ZIMSTAT), income statements (various).

6 www.zimra.co.zw.

7 RBZ monetary policy statement, January 2011 (GoZ, 2011a).

8 IRIN News (2000) 'Zimbabwe: DRC war figures disputed', 31 August 2000.

9 Ministry of Finance, 2011 Budget Statement (GoZ, 2011b).

10 Schinder (1998).

11 *NewsDay*, 13 September 2010.

12 Higher and tertiary education was allocated US$156,767,400 and education co-ordination and development and primary and secondary education were allocated a total of US$453,983,000.

13 SW Radio Africa (2011).

14 Some parastatals, including the Dairy Marketing Board and the Cold Storage Commission, were privatised under ESAP in the early 1990s.

15 This involves transforming parastatals to operate as commercial entities free from government interference and intervention. The parastatal will be allowed to charge commercial rates and its management and operation will be by private sector standards with its performance being measured using market standards and trends.

16 Heritage Foundation (2012).

17 Informal economies have been defined as economic activity that is neither included in a nation's data on gross domestic product nor subject to formal contracts, licensing, and taxation. These businesses generally rely on indigenous resources, small-scale operations and unregulated and competitive markets.

18 Tetrad Holdings, quoted in the *ZimDaily Newspaper* on 13 August 2010.

References

'Agreement between the Zimbabwe African National Union–Patriotic Front (ZANU-PF) and the two Movement for Democratic Change (MDC) formations, on resolving the challenges facing Zimbabwe'. 2008). Harare, 15 September.

Aschauer, D. 1989. 'Is Public Expenditure Productive?', *Journal of Monetary Economics*, 23, pp. 177-200.

Barro, R.J. 1991. 'Government Spending in a Simple Model of Endogenous Growth', Working Paper No. 2588, National Bureau of Economic Research.

Berndt, E.R. and C.J. Morrison. 1981. 'Capacity Utilisation Measures: Underlying Economic Theory and Alternative Approach', *American Economic Review*, Vol. 71, No. 2, May, pp. 48-57.

Brenthurst Foundation. 2009. 'Strengthening Africa's Economic Performance'. Discussion paper 4/2009 prepared in consultation with Genesis Analytics. Johannesburg, South Africa.

Canning, D. 1999. 'Infrastructure's Contribution to Aggregate Output', World Bank, Policy Research Working Paper No. 2246. Available at www.econ.worldbank.org/external/default/main?pagePK=64165259&theSitePK=469382&piPK=64165421&menuPK=64166093&entityID=000094946_99122006330269

Fan, S., T. Mogues and S. Benin. 2006. 'Achieving Sustainable Food Security: New Trends and Emerging Agenda'. Available at www.resakss.org.

Government of Zimbabwe (GoZ). 1984. Budget Statement. Ministry of Finance: Government Printers.

— 1986. Budget Statement. Ministry of Finance: Government Printers.

— 2000–2007. Budget statements. Ministry of Finance: Government Printers.

— 2009. Short-Term Emergency Recovery Programme (STERP): Get Zimbabwe Moving Again. Ministry of Finance and Economic Development, March. Available at www.mofed.gov.zw

— 2010. Budget Statement. Ministry of Finance: Government Printers.

— 2011a. Monetary policy statement (Reserve Bank of Zimbabwe). January. Harare: Government Printers.

— 2011b. Budget statement. Ministry of Finance: Government Printers.

Hanke, H.S. 2008. 'How to Kill Zimbabwe's Hyperinflation'. Institute for Global Dialogue. Johannesburg: Acumen Publishing Solutions.

Hazlitt, H. 1959. *The Failure of the 'New Economics': An Analysis of the Keynesian Fallacies*. Princeton: D. Van Nostrand. Available at www.mises. org/books/failureofneweconomics.pdf.

Heritage Foundation. 2012. Country Index Ratings: Zimbabwe. Available at www.heritage.org/index/country/Zimbabwe, Accessed 26 January 2012.

Heller, P. 2005. 'Understanding Fiscal Space', IMF Policy Development Paper 05/4. Washington DC: IMF.

— 2007. Fiscal Policy for Growth and Development: The Fiscal Space Debate. Paper presented at G20 workshop on fiscal policy, Istanbul.

Howard, M. 2001. Public sector economics for developing countries. Kingston: University of the West Indies.

International Monetary Fund (IMF). 2000. *Zimbabwe: Challenges and Policy Options after Hyperinflation.* Washington DC: IMF Publication Services.

— 2010. 'Argentina's Structural Reforms of the 1990s'. Available at www.imf.org/external/pubs/ft/fandd/2000/03/pou.htm.

IRIN news. 2000. 'Zimbabwe: DRC war figures disputed'. 31 August. Available at www.irinnews.org/Report.aspx?reportid=2202.

Keynes, M. 1936. *The General Theory of Employment, Interest and Money.* London: Palgrave Macmillan.

Makochekanwa, A. 2007. 'A Dynamic Inquiry into the Causes of Hyperinflation in Zimbabwe'. Department of Economics Working Paper Series. University of Pretoria.

NewsDay. 2010. 'Zimbabwe needs 20bn to fix and modernise infrastructure', 13 September. Available at www.newsday.co.zw/article/2010-09-13-zim-needs-20bn-to-fix-modernise-infrastructure-idbz.html.

Shinder, L. 1998. 'Zimbabwe's informal sector – Zimbabwe's solution to joblessness may be in underground businesses', *Monthly Labor Review,* March, 1998. Available at www.findarticles.com/p/articles/mi_m1153/is_n3_v121/ai_20655063/.

Shumba, J.M. 2010. *Analysis of Government Expenditure in Driving Economic Growth in Zimbabwe between 1980 and 1998.* London: Lambert Academic Publishing.

SW Radio Africa. 2011. 'Civil Service Audit Awaits Cabinet Debate Before Release'. 25 February. Available at www.allafrica.com/stories/201102280205.html.

United Nations Development Programme (UNDP). 2009. 'Fiscal Space, Economic Recovery and Poverty Reduction in Zimbabwe'. Working Paper 7.

Zimbabwe Papers. 2009. 'A Positive Agenda for Zimbabwean Renewal'. Available at www.freemarketfoundation.com/downloads/Zimbabwe_Papers_A_Positive_Agenda_for_Zimbabwean_Renewal_19_May_2009.pdf. Accessed 10 September 2010.

ZimDaily. 2010. 'We are being too cautious about recovery – Tetrad'. 13 August 2010. Available at www.newsday.co.zw/article/2010-08-13-we-are-being-too-cautious-about-recovery-tetrad.

ZIMSTAT. 2010. Finance Statistics Report.

7

Migration & Development
Issues & some lessons for Zimbabwe

Daniel Makina

Introduction and background

In 2009, the United Nations Development Programme (UNDP) reported that every year more than five million people cross international borders to go and live in a developed country. The UNDP estimates that as of 2008, 214 million people or 3.1 per cent of the world's population live and work outside their land of birth (UNDP, 2009). This figure may be an underestimate, since such figures often fail to capture what is termed 'irregular migration', that is, those who are undocumented and not reflected in national censuses. The UNDP further estimated that while 37 per cent of current international migrants move from developing to developed countries, around 60 per cent move between either developing or developed countries and three per cent from developed to developing countries. One interesting trend that is observed from data is that the vast majority of people migrate to a country with a higher Human Development Index (HDI) than their own. This is particularly so in the case of migrants from developing countries. Over 80 per cent of all migrants from developing countries relocate to countries with a higher HDI and, more interestingly, not to developed countries but rather to other developing countries with better employment prospects and living standards (Ibid.) than their own. The southern African migration experience would seem to fit into this pattern of movements. The major destination of African migrants is South

Africa which, although being a developing country, has a relatively higher HDI than other African countries. Thus, more often than not, a higher HDI is synonymous with better employment prospects.

The Zimbabwean experience also seems to fit this movement pattern. The major destination for Zimbabwean migrants is South Africa, the continent's economic powerhouse. Destinations also include neighbouring southern African countries as well as New Zealand, Australia, Canada, the UK and the USA. Estimates currently put the number of Zimbabweans living outside their homeland at between three and four million (UNDP, 2010).

Out-migration as a result of economic collapse has had a negative impact on Zimbabwe's human capital base, particularly on national training institutions. Since Independence, Zimbabweans have benefited from high standards of education, and receiving countries have been quick to seize upon the opportunity to make use of the skills Zimbabweans have acquired. Medical doctors, nurses, teachers, engineers, as well as large numbers of semi-skilled and unskilled workers, are now working in the diaspora. Despite the ongoing out-migration, which has continued despite the formation of the Government of National Unity (GNU) in February 2009,[1] it is widely acknowledged that once the political and economic climate in Zimbabwe normalises, the skills base currently in the diaspora could play a key role in helping to rebuild the country. It is also expected to play a developmental role in the transition to democracy.

It is against this background that this chapter explores the migration–development debate in the context of Zimbabwe in transition.

The migration and development debate

Migration can affect economic development through three mechanisms, namely, changes in labour supply; changes in productivity; and migrants' remittances. It is increasingly being recognised that such development gains are significant not only to origin countries but also to destination countries where migrant workers provide their labour. However, the extent of the development benefits from labour migration depends on the degree to which the migrants are protected and empowered both by the country of origin and the destination countries. In other words, development gains from migration for the countries involved and the protection of migrant workers' rights are inseparable.

Migration contributes to development in origin countries by, among other things, alleviating pressures on labour markets, enabling the flow of remittances home, skills acquisition and investments by migrants, all of which help to reduce poverty. In destination countries, migrants contribute to development by meeting the demand for workers, increasing the demand for goods and services, particularly where they receive decent wages, and contributing their entrepreneurial skills.

The most visible and tangible link between migration and development relates to the impact of remittances. There has been a notable increase in the global flow of remittances to developing countries over the years, the amount having risen from US$76 billion in 1999 to over US$300 billion by 2009. According to the World Bank, officially recorded remittances in 2009 stood at US$316 billion, down six per cent from US$336 billion received in 2008 because of the global financial crisis. However, the decline has been smaller than that experienced in private or official capital flows. Remittances have remained more resilient relative to other categories of resource flows to developing countries and have thus become more important as a source of external financing in many developing countries. One key explanation for such resilience is that while portfolio flows may cease completely for a time, remittances tend to be a small part of the income of migrants who will continue to remit, even if at a lower level than previously. The World Bank has also observed that the more diverse the migration destinations, the more resilient are remittances (Ratha, Mohapatra and Silwal, 2010).

On a global basis, Figure 1 (overleaf) shows that recorded remittance flows to developing countries have overtaken official development assistance flows in the past decade.[2]

Although globally recorded remittance flows to developing countries have overtaken official development assistance (ODA) flows, in sub-Saharan Africa (SSA) the general flow of ODA is still significantly higher than recorded remittances (see Figure 2).

The tenuous link between remittances and development has been aptly expressed in a diagram by Carling (2004) (Figure 3). In essence, then, if remittances are spent on immediate consumption, then future

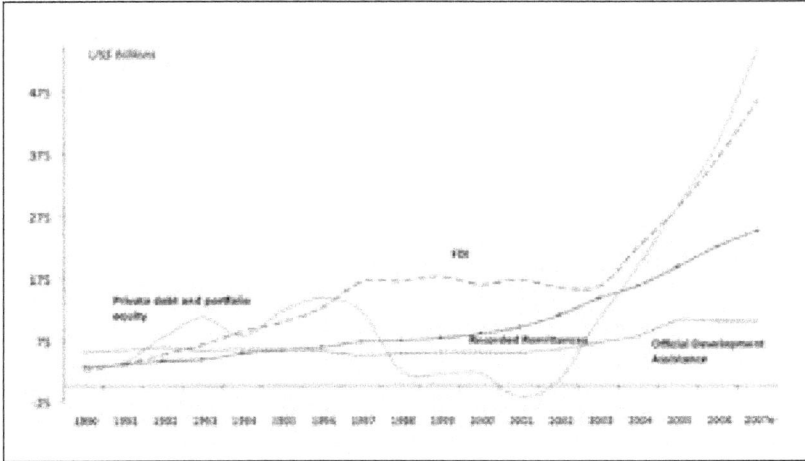

Figure 1: Remittances, FDI, private debt and portfolio equity, and ODA trends, 1990–2006 (*Source: Global Economic Prospects 2006 –World Bank*)

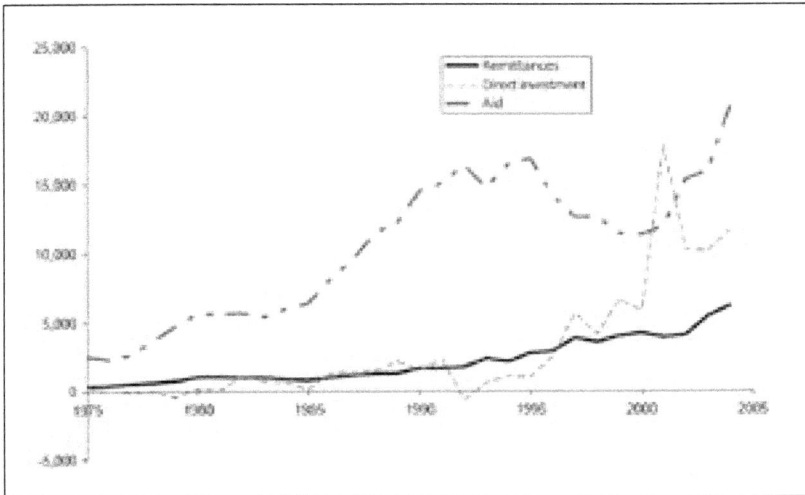

Figure 2: Remittance flows to sub-Saharan Africa, 1975–2004 (in US$ millions) (*Source: Gupta et al. 2007*)

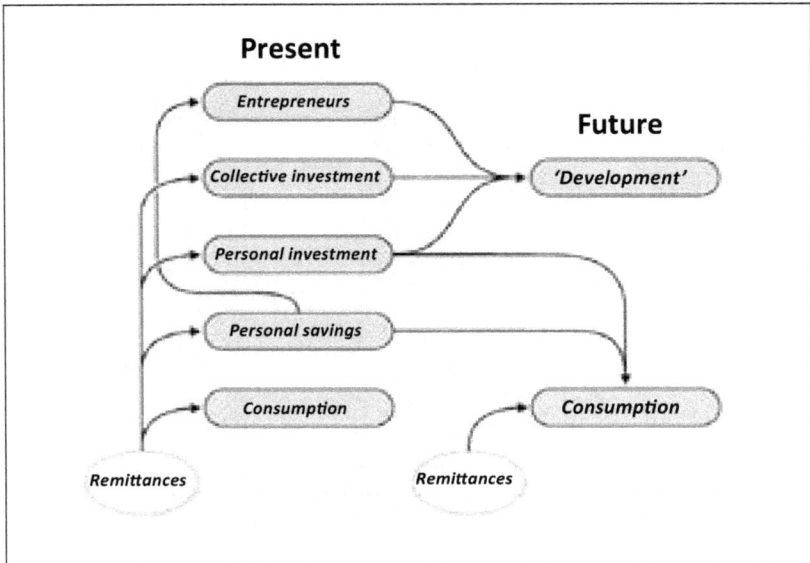

Figure 3: Remittances–development linkages (*Source: Carling 2004*)

consumption has to be financed by future remittances or other sources of income. However, if remittances are invested or saved in financial institutions, they can be used to finance future consumption and can lead to development. It is also possible that remittances could be applied in ways such that future livelihoods do not depend on future remittances. For example, a World Bank policy paper argued that '[i]n a community now largely dependent on income from migrant remittances, development would mean building local enterprises that would not live off remittances directly or indirectly (via the multiplier) so that local jobs could be sustained without continuing migration and remittances' (Ellerman, 2003).

The benefit of financial intermediation of remittances is that money transferred through banking institutions enables both senders and recipients to gain access to other financial products and services offered by these institutions. The banking relationship that ensues affords recipients the ability to establish credit histories that should enable them to access credit. Banks, on the other hand, are given the opportunity to develop products and services to specifically cater for remittance senders and recipients.

However, in poor developing countries (including Zimbabwe) the developmental impact of remittances is often illusive because of lack of financial access by both migrants and recipients of remittances. In a study that examined the state of access to financial services by Zimbabwean migrants in South Africa and the intermediation of remittances, it was observed that migrants generally use informal channels to intermediate remittances. A minute two per cent of migrants surveyed reported using official banking channels to send remittances to their home countries. The remainder utilise informal channels such as taxi/bus drivers and friends and relatives visiting home. While this phenomenon can technically be attributed to immigration laws and the financial regulatory environment, there are other factors such as cultural inertia at play (Makina, 2010a). Furthermore, some remittance-receiving countries have underdeveloped financial systems, especially in rural areas, so that informal channels become the readily available means of transferring remittances to recipients.

On the other hand, in countries in transition, as Zimbabwe is, where credit markets are either inefficient or non-existent, remittances have helped local entrepreneurs to bypass lack of collateral or high lending costs and to engage in productive investment. Thus, remittances can be a positive substitute for an inefficient financial system in that they ease liquidity constraints.

While positive impacts have been widely emphasised in the literature, remittances have also been observed to have negative effects in certain instances. Substantial remittances could have the negative effect of producing the 'Dutch disease'[3] associated with all other kinds of transfer, including ODA. In countries receiving substantial remittances, there is a tendency for the real exchange rate to appreciate, which penalises non-traditional exports, thereby hampering the development of the tradable goods sector. In this way remittances can lead to greater vulnerability to external shocks by increasing imports and reducing the incentive to develop exports (Bourdet and Falck, 2006).

Relying too heavily on remittances can also delay structural changes in the domestic economy. For instance, in the Philippines, a country with a remittance-maximising strategy, Graeme Hugo (2006) has observed that remittances have discouraged modernisation in the agricultural sector and also diverted attention from the need to attract foreign direct investment (FDI) in manufacturing. The tendency to channel remittances into conspicuous consumption activities is also seen as undermining the potential of remitting to promote sustainable economic and social change (see Magunha et al., 2009).

Another possible negative effect is that remittances can fuel inflation in a country suffering from supply-side constraints. This could be acute in crisis countries, including Zimbabwe, where economic production has broken down and residents often largely rely on remittances from relatives who have migrated. For instance, Raymond Parsons (2007) has postulated that remittances in the presence of rapid declines in aggregate supply in Zimbabwe could have been one of the contributory factors that fuelled inflation in the country.

Contemporary migration trends of Zimbabweans

A study by the Southern Africa Migration Project (SAMP) (2002) showed that, within the southern African region, Zimbabwe's migration history is unusual. Historically, southern African countries have either been recipient or sending countries for migrants. However, Zimbabwe has always been unique in being both. Many Zimbabweans left their home country to work abroad, primarily in South Africa.[4] At the same time, Zimbabwe was a recipient of labour migrants from countries such as Zambia, Malawi and Mozambique. At the time of the 1951 census, there were 246,000 foreign Africans in Zimbabwe (40 per cent of whom were from Mozambique). In this regard, Zimbabwe was a source, destination and transit for labour migrants. The pattern of migration significantly changed during the second half of the twentieth century, however, when Zimbabwe became more of an emigration country.

Historically, five overlapping phases of out-migration from Zimbabwe beginning in the 1960s can be identified (Pasura, 2008). These phases are illustrated in Table 1 (overleaf). The first phase involved the migration of political exiles to neighbouring countries (Botswana, Mozambique, Tanzania and Zambia), and labour migration to South Africa to work in the gold mines. The migration of refugees and exiles from Zimbabwe to Botswana, Zambia and Mozambique during the liberation war reached its peak in the period between 1977 and 1978 such that by 1979 it was estimated that there were over 210,000 Zimbabwean refugees in these countries (Makanya, 1994).

Period	Nature of migrants	Size of migrants based on secondary sources	Main destinations
Phase 1: 1960–1979	Migration of political exiles; labour migration to South Africa	210,000 political exiles 75,000 labour migrants to South Africa	Zambia, Mozambique, Botswana, Tanzania, South Africa
Phase 2: 1972–1989	Flight of white Zimbabweans (the war of liberation escalated in 1972)	142,000	South Africa, UK, Australia, Canada, New Zealand
Phase 3: 1982–1987	Ndebele migration following political persecution	5,000	South Africa, Botswana and Britain
Phase 4: 1990–1998	Migration of skilled professionals	200,000	South Africa, Botswana, UK, USA and Australia
Phase 5: 1999–present	Mass exodus following political and economic crisis	Three to four million	South Africa, UK, Botswana, Australia, USA, Canada, New Zealand, etc.

Table 1: Zimbabwe's five phases of emigration (*Source: Pasura 2008:98*)

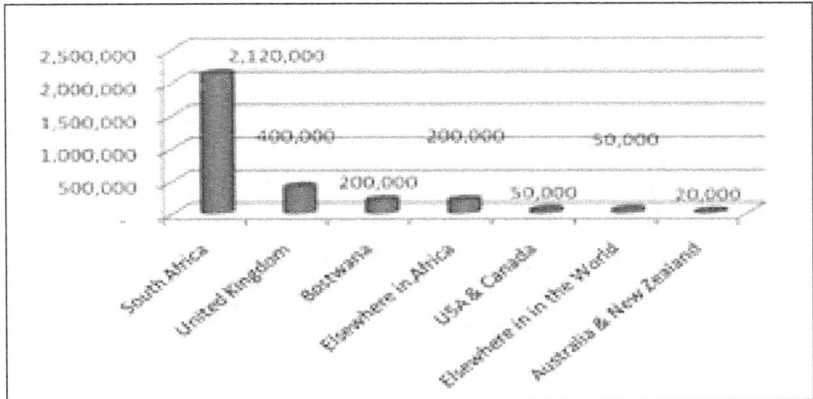

Figure 4: Distribution of Zimbabwean migrants (*Source: UNDP 2010:9*)

The second phase involved white Zimbabweans fleeing the war of liberation, and those who feared retribution on attainment of independence (Selby, 2006). The third phase of migration emanated from the post-independence conflict in Matabeleland and parts of the Midlands between government and armed opposition which led to a military operation known as Gukurahundi. This conflict is estimated to have led to the emigration of 4,000 to 5,000 refugees to Botswana, South Africa and elsewhere (Jackson, 1994). The fourth phase is said to have resulted from the negative effects of the IMF/World Bank Economic Structural Adjustment Programme (ESAP) introduced in 1990. This programme led to widespread economic hardships that led many professionals such as teachers, nurses and doctors to leave the country in search of greener pastures (Tevera and Crush, 2003).

The fifth phase of migration is associated with the large-scale migration to various countries that commenced in 2000 following the violent controversial land reform programme interspersed with a series of disputed elections that triggered a political and economic crisis. In 2010, the United Nations Development Programme (UNDP) estimated that 3,040,000 Zimbabweans were in the diaspora. Migration is so widespread that there is at least one emigrant per household (Tevera and Crush, 2003; Maphosa, 2007). Figure 4 indicates their geographical distribution.

In many respects the Zimbabweans living abroad have all the critical features of a diaspora as traditionally defined, namely, a significant

Organisation	Year formed	Mission/Focus
Refugee diaspora organisations		
Zimbabwe Refugee Association (Johannesburg)	2000s	Upholds the human rights and welfare of Zimbabweans in Johannesburg
Zimbabwe Restoration (formerly Refugee) Association (Durban)	2000s	Originally set up to protect the rights of refugees, it is currently engaged in empowering members to reconstruct/develop a future Zimbabwe through skills-acquisition programmes
Zimbabwe Political Victims Association (ZIPOVA)	2003	Serves the full needs of Zimbabwean refugees, and in addition, services and advocates for the development of the Zimbabwe diaspora
Zimbabwe Exiles Forum	2003	Documents the human rights violations visited upon Zimbabweans inside and outside the country
Professional organisations		
Doctors in the Diaspora	2005	Deals with the problems of registration to practise and lobbies for the free mobility of doctors within the SADC region
Zimbabwe Lawyers Association	2006	Lobbies for the interests of Zimbabwean lawyers in South Africa. In addition, it helps members learn models of democracy to bring back to Zimbabwe
Association of Zimbabwe Journalists	2005	Assists Zimbabwean journalists living abroad to gain skills and build independent media
Cultural organisations		
Mthwakazi Forum	2005	Provides a debating forum for Zimbabweans on sociopolitical issues
Umbrella organisations		
Zimbabwe CSO Forum	2005	Promotes civil society by uniting and strengthening this sector to influence development policy and advocate for a new prosperous and democratic Zimbabwe
Global Zimbabwe Forum (now Geneva-based)	2007	Aims at creating an international platform for all Zimbabweans in the diaspora; mobilising development funds; developing the human capital of the diaspora for the benefit of the development of a future Zimbabwe; preparing the diaspora to plan and influence the future of Zimbabwe
Zimbabwe Diaspora Development Chamber	2008	Facilitate development projects both in the diaspora and in Zimbabwe

Table 2: Some diasporan organisations in South Africa

population of people with a common sense of displacement, both voluntary and involuntary, and who entertain a hope of returning home one day when the conditions that drove them into migration are removed. The desire of at least two-thirds to eventually return home has been reported in three survey studies (Chetsanga and Muchenje, 2003; Bloch, 2005; Makina, 2010b). Various diaspora organisations that engage in cultural, political, social, and economic activities that are Zimbabwe-related have been created in host countries. Some of the diasporan organisations in South Africa and their stated objectives are listed in Table 2.

Beyond South Africa, notable diaspora organisations include the Zimbabwe Diaspora Development Interface (ZDDI) in the UK, the Zimbabwe Global Forum in the US, the Coalition for Change in Canada and the Concerned African Association in Botswana. Many of these organisations are reflective of the refugee nature of out-migration as their main focus is facilitating the granting of refugee status of Zimbabweans in host countries and the protection of their rights. However, after 2007 some diaspora organisations began to take on a more distinctly development agenda, especially the Global Zimbabwe Forum, the ZDDI and the Zimbabwe Diaspora Development Chamber.

The extent of the brain drain

The out-migration from Zimbabwe has severely compromised the country's skills base. In 2003, a study by the Scientific and Industrial Research and Development Centre (SIRDC) showed that in terms of profession, 26 per cent of Zimbabweans abroad were teachers, 25 per cent doctors, nurses and pharmacists, 23 per cent engineers and other scientists, 17 per cent accountants, five per cent farmers, two per cent bankers and one per cent each were clergy and others. Thirty-four per cent had a first degree, 28 per cent had polytechnic education, 20 per cent had a Masters degree, nine per cent vocational training, and two per cent each had diploma level training or none. The largest proportion (40.8 per cent) was in the age group 30-39, followed by the 20-29 age group (25 per cent), the 40-49 age group (23.7 per cent) and those aged 50 or over (10.5 per cent). The SIRDC study was optimistic that a large number may return, given that 66 per cent of all migrants had children in Zimbabwe and 60 per cent owned property there.

The Zimbabwe National Human Resources Survey (2006) reported the extent of the brain drain in terms of the vacancy rates (the mean ratio of vacant posts to established posts) across all sectors of the economy. The study found emigration pressures to be severe, with 70 per cent of those interviewed having intentions of leaving the country. The three common reasons given for wanting to leave the country were economic (80 per cent), wishing to work abroad (39 per cent) and self-advancement (46 per cent). In line with other studies, people with higher qualifications were in the majority of those intending to emigrate: 86 per cent for PhD-holders, 76 per cent for MSc or postgraduate diploma-holders and 76 per cent first degree graduates.

The impact of the brain drain on the economy, especially amongst the professional and technical category, has been marked and has resulted in acute shortages of such personnel. While no sector has been spared by migration, its impact has been most pronounced in the social sectors, healthcare in particular. In 2008 it was estimated that more than 80 per cent of the doctors, nurses, pharmacists, radiographers and therapists who trained since 1980 had left the country (UNDP, 2008). Critical shortages of staff were experienced at major public hospitals, a problem compounded by staff shortages at the university medical training school in Harare. By March 2007, the overall vacancy rate at the medical school was 60 per cent.[5] The results of a survey by Clemens and Pettersson (2006) on the distribution of Zimbabwean medical professionals in nine destination countries is shown in Table 3.

The Chamber of Mines of Zimbabwe estimated that more than half the industry's skilled personnel emigrated from the country between 2007 and early 2008. According to Professor Tony Hawkins (2009), between 480 and 550 university graduates are required in mining disciplines, yet the University of Zimbabwe's maximum capacity of mining-related departments was 124 students per year. Hawkins noted that it would take four to five years to supply existing needs.

The education sector was not spared by the brain drain. Although the proportion of trained teachers improved from 89.3 per cent in 2000 to 96.7 per cent by 2006 at primary school level, at secondary school level it had deteriorated from 97.8 per cent in 2001 to 91.9 per cent by 2006. A situational analysis report on skills development reported

	Doctors	Percentage of total abroad	Nurses	Percentage of total abroad
Total at home	1,530		1,1640	
Total abroad	1,602	100	3,732	100
South Africa	643	40.1	178	4.8
UK	553	34.5	2,834	75.9
US	234	14.7	440	11.8
Australia	97	6.1	219	5.9
Canada	55	3.4	35	0.9
Portugal	12	0.7	14	0.4
Belgium	6	0.4	0	0.0
Spain	1	0.1	3	0.1

Table 3: Distribution of Zimbabwean doctors and nurses in nine destination countries (*Source: Clemens and Pettersson 2006*)

Institution	Current staff levels	Vacancies	Vacancy rate (%)
UZ	385	1,171	67
HIT	37	86	70
ZOU[7]	191	38	16
Polytechnics	1,043	1,587	60.3

Table 4: Vacancy rates at institutions of tertiary education (*Source:* Zimbabwe Independent, *27 November 2009*)

that due to brain drain vocational training centres experienced staff turnovers of around 50 per cent. Harare Polytechnic also had a critical shortage of staff, with 250 vacant staff posts out of 690.

Most of the government-owned tertiary education institutions in the country are understaffed, with the University of Zimbabwe (UZ) and the Harare Institute of Technology (HIT) being the hardest hit (Ministry of Higher and Tertiary Education, 2009).[6] Table 4 shows the vacancy rates at the major tertiary education institutions.

According to the Zimbabwe Institution of Engineers (ZIE), it has a database of close to 3,800 engineers and technicians, excluding student members. It estimates that approximately 930 of these are practising

Destination	No. of ZIE members
South Africa	270
Botswana	295
UK	165
Others	200
Total	930

Table 5: Zimbabwean engineers working abroad (*Source: ZIE 2009*)

engineering outside Zimbabwe (Table 5). The majority of these left the country during the hyperinflationary period (2005–2008).

Brain drain in the engineering industry has negatively affected the operations of major companies which include ZESA, NRZ, Hwange power station and ZISCO steel, as well as consultancy companies such as Murray and Roberts and Kuchi Holdings.

When analysing the Zimbabwean situation, it is important to acknowledge two things. First, the external environment acting on skilled Zimbabweans is very dynamic. In the last decade there have been unprecedented opportunities for skilled Zimbabweans to leave the country for other regional and international destinations. Second, the push-forces, in terms of domestic conditions, have intensified considerably over the last decade. In combination, these have encouraged the skilled to leave in unprecedented numbers. This not only had immediate impacts on the country's public and private sectors but also reduced the ability of the country to institute economic recovery.

Although survey studies indicate that should there be political and economic stability, Zimbabweans in the diaspora aspire to return home and participate in development, realising the latter aspiration is dependent upon many variables. Empirical results cited by the UNDP (2010) show that the chances of re-attracting Zimbabwe's skilled migrants are high if political and economic stability is achieved as they still have strong ties with their home country. The promising observation is that those who left after 2000 are more likely to return than those that left before the crisis. However, militating against return migration will be the widening wage differentials between Zimbabwe and host countries. An important observation was that the higher the income level the migrant earns in the receiving country, the less likely that the migrant will return. Therefore, while skilled migrants might wish to return in order to contribute to the development of the country, they might be dissuaded from so doing by the low wage levels in Zimbabwe[8]. A key policy recommendation would be a return to political normalcy and sustained implementation of economic reforms that narrow the wage differential between Zimbabwe and immigration countries.

The impact of migrants' remittances on sustaining livelihoods

Remittances play a major role in supporting livelihoods in Zimbabwe. A 2007 survey carried out by the Mass Public Opinion Institute on survival strategies employed by Zimbabweans at home found that remittances from friends and relatives ranked as the fourth most important source of livelihood. Remittances were reported to be an alternative source of income in providing for food for 12 per cent, for healthcare for 11 per cent and as cash income for 11 per cent. By 2007, they had become a critical source of foreign currency for the government (MPOI, 2007).[9]

The magnitude of remittance inflows to Zimbabwe is unknown because these flows largely occur through informal channels.[10] Remittances officially reported by the Reserve Bank of Zimbabwe (RBZ) were a meagre US$43.9 million in 2007. Using a range of methodologies, the International Fund for Agricultural Development reported that in 2007 Zimbabwe received US$361 million in monetary remittances, excluding in-kind transfers. This represented 7.2 per cent of the country's 2007 GDP. Following dollarisation in 2009, remittances flowing through formal banking channels increased by 32.9 per cent, with the RBZ reporting that remittances through formal channels in 2010 amounted to US$263.3 million compared to US$198.2 million recorded in 2009. The increase in remittances through official channels is also attributed to the liberalisation of the remittance transfer market, which allowed bureaux de change to effect international transfers in addition to their usual business of buying and selling foreign currency.

An earlier study by Bracking and Sachikonye (2006) found that remittances were contributing to poverty reduction and productive

Remittance use	No. of remittance receiving households	Frequency (%)
Food	79	98.8%
School fees	63	78.8%
Medical expenses	52	65.0%
Livestock	47	58.8%
Building and consumer goods	25	53.8%
Agricultural inputs	43	31.2%
Business	8	10.0%
Other	31	38.8%

Table 6: Uses of remittances (*Source: Maphosa 2007:30*)

accumulation. Pendleton et al. (2006) have shown that remittances have become an essential part of the household budget and have reduced vulnerability at household level in both urban and rural areas. On average, the net contribution of remittances ranges from 80 to 93 per cent of a household's total expenditure About 90 per cent of the 705 migrant households (i.e. households with at least one member resident outside the country) sampled throughout the country reported that family members who have migrated regularly remit cash using both formal and informal channels. With Zimbabwean migrants remitting as much as 50 per cent of their income in order to support their family back home, the significance of remittances to poverty alleviation and development is undeniable.

A study on the uses of remittances by households in rural southern Zimbabwe shows that although immediate consumption tops the list, remittances are also applied to a wide range of other needs (Table 6).

International lessons on managing migration for development purposes

In order to derive maximum benefit from migration, international instruments constitute the most important building blocks for protection of migrant workers. There are eight core International Labour

Organisation (ILO) Conventions that apply to migrant workers, two of which are specific to migrant labour and detail their rights – Convention No. 97 of 1949 on Migration for Employment and Convention No. 143 of 1975 on Migrant Workers (Supplementary Provisions). Furthermore, the UN's International Convention on the Protection of the Rights of all Migrant Workers and Members of Their Families lays out a comprehensive legal framework for migration policy and practice and covers most issues of treatment of migrant workers and of inter-state co-operation on regulating migration. Overall, these three international instruments constitute an international charter on migration.[11] Zimbabwe, however, has not yet ratified any of these Conventions.

The ILO Multilateral Framework on Labour Migration sets out non-binding principles and guidelines for a rights-based approach to labour migration and also gives a practical guide to governments, and employers' and workers' organisations in the formulation, strengthening, implementation and evaluation of labour migration policies that guarantee the rights of migrant workers, reinforcing their protection and enhancing their contribution to development. The Framework comprises 15 broad principles which were either derived or summarised from existing international conventions and labour standards, and the corresponding policy guidelines to give effect to these principles. The four broad themes that underlie the framework as well as underpinning a rights-based approach to labour migration include: (1) decent work for all; (2) management and governance of migration; (3) promotion and protection of migrant rights; and (4) migration and development. This framework serves as a point of reference when drawing up a national labour migration policy that promotes development and beneficial interaction with diasporas.

With regard to emigration countries interacting with their diasporas, empirical analysis by Docquier and Lodigiani (2006) has shown that business networks driven by skilled migration have stimulated FDI inflows in their countries of origin. They give as an example China, where it is estimated that 50 to 70 per cent of FDI originated from the Chinese diaspora. In their sample of 114 countries, they find business network effects to be significant in large countries with large diasporas. An important lesson is that these effects were found to be stronger in democratic countries and in countries with only moderate levels of corruption.

With regard to financial flows, scholars have cautioned that remittances should be treated as private flows so that it might not be advisable to have policies that force them to be channelled into productive investments when the general investment conditions have not been improved. Connell and Brown (2005:48) emphasise a stable macroeconomic environment in the immigrant's country of origin and the necessity to channel remittances through official channels as key considerations that should be factored into the design of policies aimed at stimulating a greater flow of remittances into sustainable investments. Two arguments are often advanced in favour of remittances flowing through formal financial systems. One is that financial institutions have a much wider knowledge of productive investments than individuals, and are thus able to identify investment projects with higher returns. The second is that these higher returns would in turn attract an even higher level of investment than in the case where the financial system is bypassed. However, for these conditions to be met, a well functioning financial system with high levels of intermediation would have to exist, something that is absent in many developing economies.

However, the emphasis on the importance of creating the appropriate conditions so that remitters are willing to send money home through official channels should be accompanied by a note of caution, because the temptation by governments of remittance receiving countries to try and 'control' such sources of foreign exchange is a real one. This point has been argued forcefully by Frankel (2009:2-3), who points out that:

> The sending of remittances is a decentralised decision made by individuals, based on a familiarity with and appreciation for the needs, desires, constraints and opportunities faced by themselves and their families .... Free-market theory says that private agents do a good job of making these decisions .... If the hypothesis is true, then efforts by national governments to harness remittances are likely to be harmful, above and beyond the obvious point that taxing them could 'kill the goose' that is flying the golden eggs in to the country.

Emigration countries that have actively courted their diasporas have employed a number of diverse strategies that, among others, have focused on either maintaining or rebuilding bonds with migrant communities and encouraging patriotic sentiments. In order to strengthen attachment to the home country, some countries have allowed dual nationality/citizenship to members of their diaspora. They have also initiated programmes to maintain cultural ties and provided their diasporas privileged access to business opportunities in the home country.

In an effort to foster a developmental impact from migration, emigration countries have employed strategies that broadly fall into three categories, viz., remittance maximisation strategies, business-oriented strategies and strategies of turning 'brain drain' into 'brain gain'. For instance, the Philippines and Mexico employ remittance maximisation strategies as a means of tapping into the developmental potential of their diasporas. China and India, on the other hand, employ business oriented strategies while Taiwan, Albania and Mali have employed strategies to turn 'brain drain' into 'brain gain'.

The experience of the Philippines

The focus of the development strategy of the Philippines in the area of migration has always been on temporary migration, with policies towards overseas residents focusing on placing and protecting temporary workers and maximising remittances.

Faced with growing unemployment as well as severe balance of payments problems in the 1970s, and drawn by the economic boom of the oil-producing Arab states, the government of the Republic of the Philippines institutionalised labour migration by adopting a Labour Code in 1974 and created the Philippine Overseas Employment Administration (POEA). Today, the POEA regulates and manages the temporary migration process by limiting participation to qualified players, setting minimum standards of recruitment and employment, and formulating rules and regulations to manage the process and maintaining a monitoring system that ensures compliance by all players (Agunias and Ruiz, 2007). Annual deployment has exceeded one million workers since 2005, and as of December 2007 there were 4.13 million Filipinos working abroad, while an estimated 0.9 million were illegally working outside the country. The Middle East remains a major destination, with more than one million Filipinos working in Saudi Arabia alone. It is noteworthy that Filipinos abroad have the right to vote in national elections conditional upon their return within a two-year period.

The Commission on Filipinos Overseas (CFO) promotes and maintains cultural and socio-economic ties with migrant Filipinos who have taken up permanent residence or become citizens of other countries.

In this regard, the agency liaises with overseas Filipino organisations to align migrants' initiatives in various developmental areas with the national government's objectives. Cultural activities include overseas tours of Philippine entertainers, psychological counselling services and the establishments of schools in areas with a high concentration of Filipino migrants that promote 'Filipino values' and a sense of identification with the homeland. The Citizenship Retention and Reacquisition Act of 2003 granted the right of retention of citizenship to all Filipinos who had lost their citizenship by reason of their naturalisation as citizens of a foreign country.

With almost ten per cent of the country's 90 million population employed overseas, the labour export model has no doubt alleviated the unemployment problem in the Philippines, which in 2008 stood at 7.4 per cent. Remittances, mostly from expatriate Filipinos, have buoyed up the current account and alleviated the balance of payment situation. In 2008, US$16.4 billion, (10.4 per cent of GDP) in remittances were received in the country.

At the micro level, evidence also shows that remittances have alleviated poverty in the Philippines. Kelly Bird (2009) of the Asian Development Bank (ADB) estimated that remittances had reduced the poverty head count in the Philippines by five per cent in 2006 alone. In the three months from December 2008 to February 2009, for example, 40 per cent of remittances had been spent on education while 23 per cent had been spent on business activities. There has been a growing trend of entrepreneurship among overseas Filipino households, and Bird estimated that 55 per cent of these households had at least one self-employed entrepreneur in 2006.

The experience of Mexico

In 2009 Mexico was the third-largest recipient of remittances in the world, and its diaspora is largely concentrated in one country, the USA. For many decades, its attitude towards the diaspora was ambivalent, and formal diaspora programmes only began to be put in place in 1990. Outreach to the diaspora has since been strengthened. In 2001, the government established the Presidential Office for Mexicans Abroad that was designed to strengthen ties between Mexican emigrants and their communities of origin. Legislative changes have since been made to allow Mexicans living abroad to maintain dual nationality, albeit without voting rights. The government strategy is two-fold, viz., to expand the opportunities for Mexicans abroad and to facilitate remittances.

The Matricula Consular is issued by the Mexican government to its citizens living outside Mexico as an identity document. The USA acceptance of the Matricula Consular as a valid identity document has enabled illegal Mexican immigrants to open banking accounts and get drivers' licences in various cities and states. This has in turn facilitated the intermediation of remittances through the formal banking system.

Furthermore, Mexico has fostered engagement with the diaspora through 'home town associations'. This has been made possible because residents of the same town or village tend to migrate to the same locality in the USA. Home Town Associations have served the dual purpose of giving social support to migrants and economic support to their town or village of origin. The Mexican Home Town Associations send home various kinds of support that include charitable contributions, funding infrastructure improvements, funding for human development projects and capital investment in income-generating activities (Orozco, 2001).

The experience of China

Though China was the second-largest recipient of remittances in 2009, its strategy is business-oriented. It endeavours to attract direct investment and open trade opportunities using its overseas Chinese communities. Overseas Chinese communities, estimated at over 35 million, are found in virtually every country in the world (MPI, 2004). The government has made efforts to maintain a sense of identity among overseas communities of emigrants and their descendants.

It is estimated that about half of the US$48 billion in FDI that flowed into China in the course of 2002 originated from the Chinese diaspora (Hugo, 2006). The government has encouraged diaspora engagement in FDI and trade, as well as philanthropic contributions and other activities, through preferential policies and stimulating a sense of belonging to China.

The experience of India

Despite India being the world's largest recipient of remittances, it has a multi-pronged diaspora policy aimed at direct investment promotion, portfolio investment, technology transfer, market opening and outsourcing opportunities.

When India conducted nuclear tests in 1998, it was subjected to economic sanctions by a number of countries. In order to counter the impact of these sanctions, the Indian government launched a large sale of five-year bonds named 'Resurgent India Bonds' that were guaranteed by the State Bank of India and available only to non-resident Indians. While the government counted on patriotism amongst the Indian diaspora, significant benefits were added to make the bond sale attractive, such as an interest rate that was two per cent higher in dollar terms than that prevailing on the US bond market, the option to redeem in either US dollars or German marks, and exemption from Indian taxes. According to the Migration Policy Institute (MPI) this bond sale was a major success, raising £2.3 billion in just over two weeks. Two years later in 2000 another bond, the 'India Millennium Deposits' was issued, and over £3 billion was raised.

In order to capitalise on its large diaspora, Indian information technology entrepreneurs and professionals have set up a number of business networks. These networks match experienced entrepreneurs and start-up managers in a mentoring relationship. Furthermore, they back up promising enterprises in both the host country (e.g., the USA) and the home country with venture capital (Kapur, 2001).

The experiences of countries discussed above offer insightful lessons and useful policy direction to Zimbabwe.

Policy implications for Zimbabwe

The need for a national labour migration policy

A labour migration policy is essential for the governance of migration, the protection and empowerment of migrant workers and for ensuring that migration is linked to development and growth. Migration policies must address how to govern emigration, immigration, seasonal migration and refugees (Musonda, 2006).

Good governance of labour migration requires harmony in the areas of legal frameworks, policies and institutional frameworks in order to facilitate labour migration management. For Zimbabwe, an important policy challenge entails the development of a sound labour migration policy, a legal framework and the effective management of labour migration based on international instruments and social dialogue. In order to accomplish this the government of Zimbabwe needs to ratify and domesticate ILO Conventions 97 and 143 and embrace the principles and guidelines provided in the ILO Multilateral Framework on Labour Migration. This should be done in tandem with the drafting of comprehensive legislation and regulatory frameworks that cover the mandates of those ministries and organisations responsible for the administration of labour migration. Furthermore, Zimbabwe should enter into bilateral agreements with the major labour-receiving countries (South Africa, Botswana and the UK). These agreements should be on specific labour issues and be guided by regional and international instruments on labour migration.

Studies have shown that Zimbabwe migrant workers suffer from abuse, malpractice and exploitation, mainly due to the fact that the majority have an irregular status, and lack travel documents and work permits. The result is that the majority fill the 'three D' jobs, i.e., those that are dirty, dangerous and degrading and accompanied by the absence of employment contracts, with exploitative wages, long working hours and neither social protection nor representation. Migrants who are deported have no access to unpaid wages and savings and are often unable to retrieve their personal belongings.

The policy response lies in the adoption of the rights-based approach to protection against abusive recruitment practices as well as the enforcing of laws and regulations in accordance with international labour standards. A rights-based approach also includes the provision of social protection for migrant workers in the host countries. This can be achieved by negotiating bilateral and multilateral social security agreements with countries receiving Zimbabwean migrants to ensure that migrant workers have protection.

Leveraging remittances for development

Labour migration can affect development, growth and poverty reduction through remittances and migrants investing in the home country. Accordingly, remittances have a double impact, at both the household and national levels. In order to harness labour migration for development the following policy responses are crucial:

- Mainstreaming labour migration issues in national policies (fiscal and monetary), national development plans, the National Employment Policy Framework and the Zimbabwe Decent Work Country Programme, among others
- Allowing dual nationality to nationals living abroad so as to enhance national attachment
- Promoting the productive use of migrant workers' remittances and widening remittance channels
- Establishing a recognition system for skills gained from abroad
- Creating a conducive environment that facilitates the participation of migrants in the home country financial system
- Providing return and reintegration services.

Being the most tangible aspect of migration, remittances are the least problematic in terms of policy interventions. Remittance flows pass through unofficial channels because formal services are often unavailable in remote areas or because remitters send money through trusted family and friends to avoid formal or government intervention. It is recommended that the best way to serve the interests of migrants is to improve and expand the banking system rather than to clamp down on the informal system without creating viable alternatives. Furthermore, more players should be involved in money transfer services. Microfinance institutions with the capacity to handle remittances should be encouraged to take on this extra service.

Given a stabilised macroeconomic environment, there would be various mechanisms for leveraging remittances. The government and local financial institutions could issue bonds in foreign currency for its nationals in the diaspora at competitive interest rates and thus create a more attractive instrument for channelling remittances. Private financial institutions could be given incentives to introduce a wide variety of financial instruments for the diaspora.

One policy recommendation is to link remittances to financial intermediation as a strategy for harnessing their development impact. Orozco and Hamilton (2005) and Robinson (2004), among others, have argued that financial intermediation of remittance flows can provide senders and recipients with access to asset-building. Through the provision of remittance services, banks can reach out to unbanked recipients and recipients with limited financial intermediation. The banking relationship that ensues affords recipients the ability to establish credit histories and take advantage of education and health savings plans and many other investments offered by banks.

The lack of legal status denies most people access to financial services. A survey in South Africa found that 60 per cent of Zimbabwean migrants in Johannesburg do not have a bank account because they are undocumented (Makina, 2007). Concerted efforts towards 'formalising' the legal status of migrants would certainly encourage a greater access to a variety of financial services, resulting in the lowering the costs of remittance transfer.

Survey data for South Africa and the UK puts the desire to invest in business as being topmost in the minds of the Zimbabwe diaspora (Bloch, 2005). In this regard, what is required is for government to make the macroeconomic environment conducive for migrants to invest back home. The government should offer incentives such as tax breaks, land and other support services to enable migrants to become an important source of FDI, and one potentially more stable than foreign investors with no intimate connection with the country.

Migration information & engaging with diaspora organisations
The availability of official information and statistics is crucial to developing sound policies on labour migration. It is therefore necessary for the government to set up a comprehensive information and data system – a Labour Migration Information System (LMIS) – which provides information on labour migration trends for policy-making. An LMIS could include information such as definitions on migrant categories and migrant terms, and profiles of migrants by gender, professions, duration of stay, wages and salaries, working conditions, experiences and competencies.

In order to collect migration data, the government needs to interact with diaspora networks. Zimbabwe diaspora organisations are increasingly beginning to engage in activities that play a role in the development of their home country. In order to encourage contribution to development, there is need for an institutional platform for partnership between the government and the diaspora. Embassies, consular offices and trade offices in the diaspora could, for example, be used to provide for communication and the co-ordination of mutually beneficial activities.

Other governments have used a variety of institutional forms to connect with their own diasporan population. For example, Ghana has a Migration Unit in the Ministry of the Interior, Serbia a Ministry of Diaspora and Bangladesh a Ministry of Welfare and Overseas Employment.

Concluding remarks and prospects for the future

If Zimbabwe is to move forward, it is critical that the government develop migration policies that address human resources and technological concerns that are currently retarding development. More often than not development policies are designed separately from migration policies. Sustainable human resource development, however, dictates that the two should be integrated. In order to design credible policies, one needs to understand the nature of the migration flow from the standpoint of human resources and international transfer of knowledge. The nature of the Zimbabwe migration flow is that it has long involved the movement of large numbers of the skilled and unskilled. From a developmental perspective, any country would strive to re-attract the skilled component, which is critical for stimulating development, rather than the unskilled component. However, in the case of Zimbabwe, it may be that the unskilled migrants are more willing to return than the skilled migrants. If this proves to be the case, then the Zimbabwean government needs to actively promote labour-intensive investments to accommodate them.

What must also be taken into account, though, is the fact that the decade-long decimation of industry in Zimbabwe has resulted in far fewer in-country employment opportunities for today's school and college leavers. As a result, in the initial stages of socioeconomic recovery, Zimbabwe's education centres might end up serving the employment needs of foreign countries. Here, imposing a restrictive migration policy in the absence of opportunities in Zimbabwe is thus unadvisable. Instead, the government should harness the potential for return migration by adopting a transitional policy of exporting labour to selected countries with which it has entered into beneficial bilateral arrangements.

Overall, the idea is to formulate appropriate migration policies aimed at facilitating the mobility of all workers in ways that are beneficial to both migrant-receiving countries and the home country. The first building block for harnessing the developmental impact of migration is the development of a national migration policy. This is a task the Government of National Unity should accomplish as part of its transitional arrangements.

(This chapter is based on UNDP Working Paper No. 11 of 2010 – *The Potential Contribution of the Zimbabwe Diaspora to Economic Recovery* – co-authored by Daniel Makina and Godfrey Kanyenze.)

Notes

1   The GNU is a transition government formed by major political parties to carry out specific economic political reforms that will lead to free and fair elections.
2   The remittance data are made up of aggregate worker remittances, compensation to employees, and migrant transfer series from the IMF's Balance of Payments database.
3   'Dutch disease' is the negative impact on an economy of anything that gives rise to substantially increased inflows of foreign currency. The increased currency inflows usually lead to currency appreciation, making the country's other products price competitive on the export market. It may also lead to higher levels of cheap imports and to deindustrialisation as industries are moved to other locations.
4   The SAMP research showed that almost a quarter of adult Zimbabweans had parents and grandparents who have worked in South Africa at some point in their lives.
5   The vacancy rates were as high as 100 per cent in haematology, 96 per cent in anatomy, 95 per cent in physiology, and 88 per cent each in anaesthesia and critical care medicine and histopathology.
6   'Staff shortages hit tertiary education sector', 27 November 2009. See www. theindependent.co.zw/business/24433-staff-shortages-hit-tertiary-education-sector.html
7   Zimbabwe Open University.
8   Since the introduction of dollarisation in January 2009, the average monthly wage in the civil service has risen from US$100 to US$250 (about R2,000). This level is equivalent to the average earned by the lowest paid member of the South African civil service.
9   A government minister once acknowledged as much in a private conversa-

tion with a reporter. Asked how sustainable the economic crisis was, he reportedly stated: 'What's keeping us going is remittances from Zimbabweans who left the country. Without those, 50 per cent of the people who are struggling to survive at the moment would die' ('Lunch with a dissident minister', *The Sunday Times* (UK), 8 July 2007).

10 A survey in South Africa found about 98 per cent of remittances being intermediated through informal channels that included taxi/bus drivers, friends, and other informal means (UNDP, 2008).

11 United Nations High Commissioner for Human Rights, UN Committee on Migrant Workers, 8th Session, April 2008.

References

Agunias, D.R. and N.G. Ruiz. 2007. 'Protecting Overseas Workers: Lessons and Cautions from the Philippines', Migration Policy Institute Working Paper, New York.

Bird, K. 2009. 'Philippines: Poverty, Employment and Remittances – Some Stylised Facts'. Available at www.bsp.gov.ph/events/ircr/down loads/papers/BSP_11_bird_paper.pdf.

Bloch, A. 2005. 'The Development Potential of Zimbabweans in the Diaspora', IOM Migration Research Series No. 17.

Bourdet, Y. and H. Falck. 2006. 'Emigrants' Remittances and Dutch Disease in Cape Verde', *International Economic Journal*, Vol. 20, No. 3:267-84.

Bracking, S. and L. Sachikonye. 2006. 'Remittances, poverty reduction and the informalisation of household well-being in Zimbabwe', GPRG-WPS-45.

Carling, J. 2004. 'Policy options for increasing the benefits of remittances', Paper presented at Workshop B9: Remittances and Development: beyond increasing incomes, at the Ninth International Metropolis Conference, Geneva, 27 September to 1 October 2004.

Chetsanga, C.J. and T. Muchenje. 2003. *An Analysis of the Cause and Effect of the Brain Drain in Zimbabwe*, Scientific and Industrial Research and Development Centre, Harare. Available at www.sarpn. org.za/documents/d0000422/Zimbabwe_Brain_Drain.pdf.

Clemens, M. and G. Pettersson. 2006. 'Medical Leave: A new database of health professional emigration from Africa', CGD Note. Center for Global Development, Washington DC.

Connell, J. and R.P.C. Brown. 2005. *Remittances in the Pacific: An Overview*, Asian Development Bank, March 2005.

Docquier, F. and E. Lodigiani. 2006. 'Skilled Migration and Business Networks', mimeo, Université Catholique de Louvain.

Ellerman, D. 2003. 'Policy Research on Migration and Development', Policy Research Working Paper, 3117. Washington DC: World Bank.

Frankel, J. 2009. 'Are Bilateral Remittances Countercyclical? Implications for Dutch Disease and Currency Unions', Paper presented at Conference on Immigration and Global Development: Research Lessons on How Immigration and Remittances Affect Prosperity Around the World, Washington DC.

Godwin, P. 1993. *Rhodesians Never Die: The Impact of War and Political Change on White Rhodesia*. Oxford University Press: Oxford.

Gupta, S., C. Pattillo and S. Wagh. 2007. 'Impact of Remittances on Poverty and Financial Development in sub-Saharan Africa', IMF Working Paper WP/07/38, International Monetary Fund: Washington DC.

Hawkins, T. 2009. 'The Mining Sector in Zimbabwe and its Potential Contribution to Recovery, UNDP Comprehensive Economic Recovery in Zimbabwe Working Paper Series', Working Paper 1, UNDP, Harare.

Hugo, G. 2006. 'Sending money home to Asia', *insights*, January, Issue 60. Available at www.eldis.org/vfile/upload/1/document/1103/id21%20 insights%2060.pdf.

International Labour Organization (ILO). 2010. *International labour migration. A rights-based approach*, ILO – Geneva.

Jackson, J. 1994. 'Repatriation and Reconstruction in Zimbabwe During the 1980s', in T. Allen and H. Morsink (eds). 1994. *When Refugees Go Home*, London, UNRISD, pp. 126-66.

Kapur, D. 2001. 'Diasporas and Technology Transfer', *Journal of Human Development*, Vol. 2. (2): 265-86.

Luo, Yu-Ling and Wang, Wei-Jen. 2002. 'High-skill migration and Chinese Taipei's industrial development,' in OECD, International Mobility of the Highly Skilled. Paris: OECD.

Magunha, F., A. Bailey and L. Cliffe. 2009. 'Remittance Strategies of Zimbabweans in Northern England', School of Geography, University of Leeds.

Makanya, S.T. 1994. 'The Desire to Return: Effects of Experiences in Exile on Refugees Repatriating to Zimbabwe in the Early 1980s', in T. Allen and H. Morsink (eds). 1994. *When Refugees Go Home*, London, UNRISD, pp. 105-25.

Makina, D. 2007. 'Survey of Profile of Migrant Zimbabweans in South Africa: A Pilot Study'. Available at www.idasa.org/media/uploads/ outputs/files/Survey%20of%20profile%20of%20migrant%20Zimba-

bweans%20in%20South%20Africa%20-%20A%20Pilot%20Study.
pdf.

— 2009. 'Recovery of the Financial Sector and Building of Financial Inclusiveness', UNDP Comprehensive Economic Recovery in Zimbabwe Working Paper Series, No. 5, UNDP, Harare.

— 2010a. 'Zimbabwe in Johannesburg', in J. Crush and D. Tevera. eds. *Zimbabwe's Exodus: Crisis, Migration, Survival*, Southern African Migration Programme/IDRC 2010.

— 2010b. 'The Impact of Regional Migration and Remittances on Development: The Case of Zimbabwe', *Open Space*, Vol. 3, No. 3:35-43.

Maphosa, F. 2007. 'Remittances and development: the impact of migration to South Africa on rural livelihoods in southern Zimbabwe', *Development Southern Africa*, Vol. 24, No. 1:123-35.

MPI. 2004. *Beyond Remittances: The Role of Diaspora in Poverty Reduction in their Countries of Origin*. Migration Policy Institute: Washington DC.

MPOI. 2007. 'Survey Findings on The State of Zimbabwe's Economy and People's Survival Strategies'. Unpublished report commissioned by the National Endowment for Democracy. July.

Musonda, F.M. 2006. 'Migration Legislation in East Africa', International Migration Papers No. 82, ILO, Geneva.

Orozco, M. 2001. 'Globalisation and Migration: The Impact of Family Remittances in Latin America', in Approaches to Increasing the Productive Value of Remittances, papers presented at a conference held at the World Bank, 19 March 2001, sponsored by the Inter-American Foundation, the UN Economic Commission for Latin America and the Caribbean.

Orozco, M. and E. Hamilton. 2005. 'Remittances and MFI Intermediation'. Paper presented at the 2005 Financial Sector Development Conference: New Partnerships for Innovation in Microfinance. Frankfurt, 23 June.

Parsons, R.W.K. 2007. 'After Mugabe goes – The Economic and Political Reconstruction of Zimbabwe'. Presidential Address to the Economic Society of South Africa Biennial Conference, Johannesburg, 12 September.

Pasura, D.M. 2008. 'A Fractured Diaspora: Strategies and Identities among Zimbabweans in Britain'. Unpublished PhD thesis, University of Warwick.

Pendleton, W., J. Crush and E. Campbell et al. 2006. 'Migration, Remittances and Development in Southern Africa', Migration Policy Series, No. 44, SAMP, Kingston.

Ratha, D. 2003. 'Workers' Remittances: An Important and Stable source of External Development Finance', in *Global Development Finance, 2003*. Washington DC: World Bank.

— 2007. *Leveraging remittances for development.* Migration Policy Institute, Policy Brief No. 3, Washington DC. June.

Ratha, D., S. Mohapatra and A. Silwal. 2010. 'Outlook for Remittance Flows 2010–11', Migration and Development Brief 12, Development Prospects Group, World Bank.

Robinson, S. 2004. 'Remittances, Microfinance and Community Informatics – Development and Governance Issues'. Paper presented at the Remittances, Microfinance and Technology Conference: Leveraging Development Impact for Pacific States. FDC, Brisbane, 10 June 2004.

Selby, A.E. 2006. 'Commercial Farmers and the State: Interest Group Politics and Land Reform in Zimbabwe'. Unpublished PhD thesis, Oxford University.

Tevera, D. and J. Crush. 2003. 'The New Brain Drain from Zimbabwe. Southern African Migration Project', Migration Policy Series No. 29. Available at www.queensu.ca/samp/sampresources/samppublications/policy-series/Acrobat29.pdf.

The Independent. Zimbabwe. 2009. 'Staff shortages hit tertiary education sector', 27 November 2009.

United Nations (UN). 2009. *World Population Prospects: The 2008 Revision.* Department of Economic and Social Affairs, UN: New York.

United Nations Development Programme (UNDP). 2008. *Comprehensive Economic Recovery in Zimbabwe: A Discussion Document.* UNDP, Harare.

— 2009. Human Development Report 2009 – Overcoming barriers: Human mobility and development, UN, New York.

— 2010. 'The Potential Contribution of the Zimbabwe Diaspora to Economic Recovery', Working Paper No. 11 of the Comprehensive Economic Recovery in Zimbabwe Working Paper Series, UNDP, Harare.

8

Upgrading Zimbabwe's Bureaucratic Quality

Myo Naing

Introduction

Civilisation and bureaucracy have always gone hand in hand. As soon as the term 'bureaucracy' was popularised, something pejorative and inefficient was associated with it. However, contrary to the popular view, bureaucracy is one of the indispensable and vital organs of state apparatus and bureaux are among the most important institutions in every nation worldwide. Moreover, in spite of popular view, it is not always problematic. Most of the bad news and negative impressions result from a general misunderstanding of bureaucracy, its nature and its constraints. Moreover, the political, social and economic development of a nation depends on it having an effective public sector. No transition will be successful without re-structuring and reforming the latter so that it becomes effective, efficient, responsible and accountable, and all the more so because it plays an important and vital role in rebuilding a nation.

Grounded on this premise, i.e., the significant and indispensable role of bureaucracy in the development of a nation, this chapter examines public sector reform in Zimbabwe. It uses an analytical framework based on Weber's 'Ideal Type' bureaucracy approach, with the aim of identifying the current problems in Zimbabwe's bureaucracy as well as those elements missing from previous public sector reform programmes. The chapter ends with recommendations on what steps the transitional government can possibly take to upgrade Zimbabwe's bureaucratic quality.

Bureaucracy is important for a nation

In spite of the widespread negative image bureaucracy is awarded, the development process of a country depends on the quality of its bureaucracy. Without talented and competent personnel, a civil service would be a useless instrument for implementing a government's development programmes (Quah, 1996:9). Myint (1959:27) points out that 'economic development plans would be unsuccessful when there were no competent men to put them into practice'. Contrary to popular belief, bureaucracy is not necessarily a large sector in an economy. The critical factor is not about quantity, but quality. If its quality, skill mix and accountability mechanisms are good, even a very small civil service can serve a big population (Schiavo-Campo et al., 1997:35).

Law and Bany-Ariffin (2008:549) state that 'bureaucratic quality represents autonomy from political pressures, strength, and expertise to govern without drastic changes in policy or interruptions in government services, as well as the existence of an established mechanism for recruitment and training of bureaucrats'. The World Bank (1993:14) also recognises the impressive success of East Asian economies from an institutional perspective and states that 'the first step these economies had taken was recruiting a competent and relatively honest technocratic cadre and insulating it from day-to-day political interference'. It remarks that 'strong well-organised bureaucracies wield considerable power in Japan, Singapore and Taiwan, China' (Ibid.).

In their cross-national analysis of the effects of 'Weberian' state structures on economic growth, Evans and Rauch (1999) support the World Bank view by stating that the bureaucracy was a key ingredient of the 'miracle'. At the same time, Blunt (1983) and Hyden (1983) argue that the weakness of bureaucracy in Africa helps explain the poor development performance of many countries on the continent. International institutions clearly acknowledge that insulation of the bureaucracy from democratic control is an institutional requirement of poor countries wanting to achieve economic growth and development. Therefore an institutional requirement of poor countries for economic development is to insulate the bureaucracy from political control

Max Weber's Ideal Type of bureaucracy	Zimbabwe's bureaucracy	Findings, discussion and recommendations
• Characteristics • Inherent problems • Human-created problems • Suggested solutions	• Past attempts and reforms to upgrade bureaucracy • Current problems	• Elements missing from past attempts and reforms • Discussion • Recommendations

Table 1: The analytical framework

(Toye, 2007:88). Although bureaucracy is clearly indispensable for any nation, because of its nature, complexity and large size, there are problems inherent in a bureaucracy. While some problems are inherent, some are outcomes of organisational and personal weaknesses.

Analytical framework

The analytical framework of this study is mainly based on Weber's 'Ideal Type' bureaucracy approach (Table 1), which hinges on the premise that although bureaucracy has a negative connotation, in its concrete sense it is not necessarily bad (Toye, 2007:88). Although Weberian bureaucracy has garnered much criticism from different schools for inefficiency, unaccountability and corruption, if properly maintained and managed, it can be a great help in the developmental process of a nation.

Weber's ideal bureaucracy

One of the earliest and the most established theories on public service is Max Weber's (1946) organisational theory on bureaucracy and the concept of the public service. Max Weber defines bureaucracy as 'organisations with a pyramidal structure of authority, which utilise the enforcement of universal and impersonal rules to maintain that structure of authority, and which emphasise the nondiscretionary aspects of administration'.

According to Weber, the bureaucratic nature of an organisation stems from the fact that it operates under a hierarchy of authorities, emphasises meritocracy and not inherited right or ownership, and that the decision-making process follows a chain of command, amongst other characteristics. A most important characteristic of the bureaucratic organisation is its impersonality. Officials within the bureaucratic structure are obliged to follow rules and discard personal emotion. According to Weber, the concept of bureaucracy as an organisational theory is the 'most rational' and 'ideal' solution to the complexities embedded in the procedures of modern organisations (Oyelaran-Oyeyinka, 2006:49). John Toye (2007:88) concludes that 'the essential problem for poor countries is to design the institutional context for a non-bureaucratic bureaucracy'. To do so, it is again necessary to clearly and rightly understand what is wrong with bureaucracy in the abstract sense.

Problems and constraints of bureaucracy

Toye (2007:88-9) provides five complaints laid by those who use 'bureaucracy' as a term of abuse. These complaints include unaccountability to the public whose affairs bureaucracy administers, pervasive inefficiency, a tendency to become corrupt, practise without discretion and judgement, and poor co-ordination among different offices and departments. Although there are five problems associated with bureaucracy, it is important to note that in fact only three are problems and the other two are causes. The three problems are 1) inefficiency, 2) corruption, and 3) lack of accountability to the public whom they are serving. These three problems are caused by another two factors: 1) rigidity of rules and procedures, and 2) poor co-ordination amongst different and related agencies and departments.

Ludwig von Mises (2007) argues that government bureaucracy is inherently inefficient and there is no way to cure this. As a solution to solve it, Niskanen (1968:304), however, proposes to create competition among the bureaucratic agencies. Wilson (1989:115) identifies the other reasons for public servants' ineffectiveness and inefficiency (i.e., poor performance and service delivery). He argues that it is not because they are either unskilful, uninterested, or unprogressive, but because of the constraints they face. Moreover, inefficiency is also an outcome of lack of skills, workload, lack of co-ordination among agencies and departments, red tape, and rigidity of rules and procedures.

The second but probably biggest problem of bureaucracy is corruption. The World Bank (2009:3) defines corruption as 'the abuse of public office for private gain'. The adverse effects of corruption are well established. Corruption hinders policy implementation as scarce resources are wasted on bribes and not on development programmes (Quah, 1996:9). The prime reason of failures in anti-corruption attempts is the fact that the country leadership is not totally committed to fight against corruption and the government itself is not clean at all.

Unaccountability is, according to Toye (2007:88-9) the most fundamental problem of bureaucracy. He states that 'officials are accountable only to their superiors, and not to those whose affairs they administer'. To check the accountability of public service, Peter Evans (2003 cited by Toye, 2007:90) suggests empowering bottom-up democratic participation to check that state action reflects the needs and desires of ordinary citizens. Max Weber also, therefore, advocates a system that uses meritocracy in order to eliminate corruption and inefficiency.

Methodology

The findings presented in the study are largely the outcome of documentary and archival research and a literature review of economic theories on bureaucracy and public administration and the attempts at and outcomes of Zimbabwe's public sector reform of the last 30 years. The major limitation to this study was the difficulty encountered in accessing recent hard empirical data and statistics on Zimbabwe's public bureaucracy, especially in the last three-year transition period, i.e., from 2009 to 2011. Although every possible effort was made to obtain these, there is virtually no reliable and adequate time-series data on wages and salary of public servants. The last year the Zimbabwe Central Statistical Office (CSO) published data on real wages was in 2004. Thus this study could only use and analyse outdated statistics and data previously collected by various researchers and organisations.

To compensate for the scarcity of such data, there was an intensive literature review as well as face-to-face interviews with eleven Zimbabweans: four members of the Zimbabwe African National Union (Patriotic Front) (ZANU–PF), three members of the Movement for Democratic Change led by Arthur Mutambara (MDC-M) and four Zimbabwean students studying at the University of Witwatersrand, Johannesburg.

Zimbabwe's experience

Once the breadbasket of southern Africa, by 2008 Zimbabwe's estimated gross national annual per capita income had dropped to US$360, far below the sub-Saharan Africa average of US$1,428 (AfDB, 2010). In the early 1990s, thanks to a series of successful reforms after independence, Zimbabwe's public service was also one of the best in sub-Saharan Africa, but it has since been severely weakened, compromised by a decade of political and economic crisis (Chimhowu, 2009:8).

Initial attempts to reform the public sector
Reform of the public service in Zimbabwe started in 1981, under Prime Minister Robert Mugabe, who looked to strengthen the capacity of the country's civil servants by conducting customer surveys in order to enhance accountability and assess the conduct of public officials in service delivery and to ensure that services offered are accessible and meet client needs, improving gender mainstreaming mechanisms, establishing an anti-corruption commission, running training and recruitment programmes for the civil servants, enhancing bottom-up participation of other stakeholders in policy formulation, fostering ownership and the successful implementation of programmes and developing and implementing a performance management system.

Mugabe's directives transformed the face of the public sector, bringing it in line with the new social and economic environment, but the colonial rules and regulations governing public administration were unchanged. New, black civil servants were trained at public service training institutes and equipped with necessary skills on how government operated and to understand the rules and procedures governing service delivery. Many highly qualified Zimbabweans returned home after independence, further benefitting the public service delivery, in particular the education and health sectors (Chimhowu, 2009:111).

However, following the rapid expansion in service provision, the budget deficit began to grow. By the end of the 1980s, economic growth was beginning to slow, which had negative knock-on effects on service delivery. Thanks to low public sector salaries and wages and better payments in the private sector and abroad, many competent experienced public officials left for the private sector or went abroad, weakening the capability of the bureaucracy as inexperienced and junior staff were left to manage it on their own (Kavran, 1989). The Public Service Review Commission Kavran Report (1989) revealed that the rules and procedures of bureaucracy were over-complicated and its functions duplicated. Civil servants had poor attitudes towards work, and since there was neither a performance management culture nor transparency throughout the public sector, communication of decisions was poor and staff turnover was high. Overall, bureaucracy was centralised, secretive and inaccessible to the public (Ibid.).

In 1991 an economic structural adjustment programme (ESAP) was introduced with the aim of restructuring the country's economy and its administrative machinery. However, none of its intended outcomes[1] materialised in full. In fact, the economy worsened.

In 1997, having seen the adverse social effects of the ESAP, the government launched a five-year public service reform programme (PSRP). That same year, the National Economic Consultative Forum (NECF) was established in Parliament, with the aim of improving governance and engagement with a disgruntled civil society in policy design and implementation.

The PSRP had two phases. The first phase focused on downsizing and on implementing cost-saving measures to reduce the wage bill and public expenditure measures to improve performance. The second concentrated on 'enhanced performance and service delivery, putting citizens first and promoting good governance'. Recruitment and promotion procedures were professionalised and, in place of internal recruitment and seniority in the service, open competition was exercised in order to attract competent people to the public service (Chimhowu, 2009:115).

In 2004 the Anti-Corruption Commission Bill was enacted and an Anti-Corruption Commission was established with the aim of providing an independent, powerful and high-profile body to spearhead the battle against corruption and provide mechanisms to investigate corruption at all levels and in all sectors (UN, 2004:11). Several cases of misappropriation of state funds were dealt with by the Public Service Commission. However, the UN (2004:11) observed that the investigative mechanisms were inadequate as far as curbing the scourge of corruption in the public and private sectors was concerned.

At the end of 2005, a performance management system was instituted with the aim of improving service delivery. Performance agreements were introduced for the permanent secretary, with individual work plans derived from the organisational strategic plan used to assess individual officers at the operational level. To make public servants more client-focused and accountable, client charters and service delivery targets were also institutionalised as part of performance management. However, there were neither tangible results on impact of these systems in service delivery, nor were permanent secretaries individually assessed for organisational performance (Chimhowu, 2009:114).

Current problems in the bureaucracy

Despite these reforms and programmes, serious problems were still in evidence in 2011. The capability of the bureaucracy remained weak because of the severe 'brain drain' and skills flight caused by the deteriorating economy. The quality of service delivery deteriorated even further. Senior officials were reluctant to make decisions and take risks on outcomes in what was an economically and politically unstable environment. Since the legal framework on corruption was weak, the magnitude of corruption, though not quantified, was unprecedented in all facets of society (Munakiri, 2009). Corrupt public officials used their bureaucratic powers to assist rent-seekers, not the general public. Seldom held accountable for their performance, bureaucrats succumbed to incentives to delay services in order to extract bribes (Mhonderwa, 2011).

By 2010, many public officials were still engaging in illegal private activities in order to supplement their meagre incomes. For example, since teachers' salaries could not cover the costs of accommodation and food, many teachers preferred to stay at home and give private lessons to students who could afford to pay (Pswarayi, 2010).

Although affirmative action was adopted as a strategy for training women and promoting them to senior management positions and gender mainstreaming mechanisms put in place in all ministries, very few women came to hold decision-making positions. By 2006, there were only six women amongst the 32 permanent secretaries and only one female university vice-chancellor out of 13 (Chimhowu, 2009:

111-15). The possibility of reaching the Millennium Development Goal target of 30 per cent occupancy by women by 2015 is thus very low.

Zimbabwe's transition and the role of bureaucracy

When discussing the crisis and issues of Zimbabwe, political reform is seen by many as the *sine qua non*. The focus is too often on its political transition, national politics, power-sharing and ensuring forthcoming elections will be free and fair. Although these issues of political transition and governmental transformation are important for Zimbabwe, on their own they are not enough to rebuild the nation, restructure the economy and alleviate widespread poverty. For without a committed, competent and efficient bureaucracy, policies, projects and strategies will not prove successful.

In this regard, the issue of public administration is equally important. In fact, it is a matter of national security because no society can live in peace and prosperity without an effective public sector (Shafritz and Russell, 2000:177).

The historical experiences of nation-building show that revolution alone is not enough for a nation to be stable and prosperous. After a revolution is accomplished, the role of the bureaucracy becomes important and vital in rebuilding a nation: 'Napoleon not only solidified the French Revolution of 1789 but also reformed the administration and created a merit-based civil service. ... Most recently, in the late 1980s, after the political revolutions, Eastern European countries successfully launched administrative revolutions and made sure a state's economy could function with the greater efficiency' (Ibid.).

In the same vein, the economic success of Botswana is attributed to both politicians and bureaucrats who did not steal revenue from its mineral wealth, especially from diamond revenues, and channelled them into productive investment (Kiiza, 2007:292). Botswana's political leaders were able, early on, to secure a contract with a transnational diamond mining company that gave the government 50 per cent of all export revenues. This, in turn, allowed the government to maintain a reasonably well-paid meritocratic bureaucracy in which 'probity, relative autonomy and competency have been nurtured and sustained' (Parsons in Evans, 2007:45).

Elements missing from in the previous reforms

Even though the government of Zimbabwe enacted many types of reforms recommended by a variety of academic textbooks and research papers and advice and recommendations from the international financial institutions, a huge number of problems associated with bureaucracy still exist in the public service. This is partly because the reforms lacked essential 'ingredients', namely:

- The introduction of meaningful meritocracy.
- The provision of competitive salaries and incentives.
- The creation and implementation of full-grown anti-corruption strategies.
- Fully insulating the bureaucracy from political intervention.
- A monitoring and evaluation system and total quality management.

This section considers the impact of these programmes and measures that were overlooked or unconsidered.

1. The absence of merit-based recruitment and promotion – The merit system is the most important characteristic of bureaucracy. Both Hegel (1976:par. 291) and Weber (1946) stress that recruitment, employment and promotion in the bureaucratic system must be based on qualifications and achievement, internal labour markets and professionalisation. Indeed, all studies and public administration textbooks stress the importance of meritocracy in the bureaucratic system and recommend that the selection of personnel for the public service should be done by the meritocratic system in order to attract only the best and the brightest candidates. Accordingly, competent local civil servants should be promoted to more responsible positions based on merit and not patronage.

There was an introduction of meritocracy in Zimbabwe's public service reform during the last twenty years. Job evaluation and profiling processes were conducted for all public service positions. An assessment and examination centre, and staff development at internal and external training institutions, were established. However, the essence of a real merit system was still lacking. The tripod of faultless selection and recruitment, perfect training and exposure to the highest standards of professionalism and the character to sustain it was lacking in Zimbabwe's previous reforms and programmes. Furthermore, instead of strengthening the merit system, the leadership applied a spoils system.

2. *Failing to provide competitive salaries and incentives* – As with nearly everything else, in bureaucracy you get what you pay for. Generally, 'the more favourably the total public sector compensation package compares to compensation in the private sector, the better the quality of the bureaucracy' (World Bank, 1993:175).

During the last 20-year period, public salaries did increase in Zimbabwe (Table 2). However, with the hyperinflation experienced between 1998 and 2008, the actual buying power of a salary decreased. In 1992 employees in public administration received on average only 38.6 per cent in real terms of what they earned in 1980. For employees in education and health this percentage was 61.4 and 64.8 respectively (ILO, 1993:28-29). Salaries in the public sector remain far lower than those in the private sector and incentive systems are non-existent. For the period 1990 to 2004, real average earnings in all sectors of the economy had virtually collapsed because wage increases failed to match inflation.

Table 2 shows that between 1990 and 2004 the average real earnings index for the whole economy declined dramatically to ten. The average real earnings index of the public administration declined to 14.4 and the education and health sector, to 18.1 and 18.6 respectively (Chimhowu, 2009:24, 77; The Zimbabwe Institute, 2007:29-30). The teaching sector suffered deeply between 2007 and 2008, the period of hyperinflation. In 2008, educational staff, being amongst the least-paid workers, received on average only 12 per cent in real terms of what they had earned in 1990 and 1991 (Table 3). The worst period for the teachers was during October to December 2008, when their average incomes were less than US$10 (Chagonda, 2010:9).

When salaries are too low and not enough for survival, there are only two options left for the people. The first one is to succumb to corruption and the second one is to leave the country. Mostly because of the political and economic crisis, an estimated two million Zimbabweans including many skilled personnel have left the country recently (AfDB, 2010:1). Since most migrants were able-bodied and of working age, it is a major human capital loss and is partly responsible for the

Year	1990	1992	1994	1996	1998	2000	2002	2004
Agriculture	100.0	53.5	57.4	54.0	61.7	51.0	56.0	11.8
Mining	100.0	84.2	77.4	80.7	101.9	82.6	69.1	10.1
Manufacturing	100.0	80.5	71.6	71.0	73.0	66.3	49.6	9.4
Electricity	100.0	84.0	90.9	113.5	194.6	181.2	118.8	7.7
Construction	100.0	72.9	59.5	69.4	86.0	93.5	37.8	4.0
Finance	100.0	95.5	83.0	87.6	94.4	86.5	42.5	3.5
Distribution	100.0	83.4	68.6	73.0	80.1	73.0	41.4	4.0
Transport	100.0	73.6	67.5	62.2	71.0	78.9	37.4	1.9
Public administration	100.0	68.1	57.8	81.0	113.0	167.3	66.8	14.4
Education	100.0	78.4	59.3	75.5	92.0	113.4	53.2	18.1
Health	100.0	75.5	62.0	73.7	110.2	151.7	51.4	18.6
Private domestic	100.0	59.1	37.9	25.4	16.3	6.6	1.6	0.1
Other	100.0	76.4	68.4	71.9	81.5	79.2	44.7	7.5
Total	100.0	75.9	65.3	70.6	86.3	90.7	52.0	10.0

Table 2: Real average earnings index, 1985–2004 (1990 = 100)
Source: The Zimbabwe Institute (2007:29-30)

	1990–91	July 2008
Number of Staff	104,962	117,612
In Z$	12,032	43,176,000,000,000
Index of increase in Z$	100	358,843,085
In US$	4,565	560.73
Exchange rate used	US$1 = Z$2.636	US$1 = Z$77,000,000,000
Index in US$	100	12

Table 3: Average annual education staff salary 1990–91 compared to 2008 in Z$ and US$ (*Source: Chimhowu 2009:77*)

decline in productivity and service delivery (Chimhowu, 2009:9), low staff morale, inefficiency, poor inter-department co-ordination and poor service delivery. Overall, between 1988 and 2011, the position of civil servants deteriorated and levels of efficiency in the public sector plunged.

3. Lack of full-grown anti-corruption strategies – One of the problems that aggravated Zimbabwe's collapse is its unprecedented level of corruption (Munakiri, 2009). Zimbabwe ranks 134 out of 178 countries in Transparency International's Corruption Perceptions Index for 2010. There is widespread corruption in government. In January 2011, the civil service audit revealed that there could be as many as 70,000 'ghost' workers on the government payroll, impacting heavily the state's already dry coffers (*NewsDay*, 2011).

Experience around the world, however, shows that anti-corruption measures can be successful only if the leaders themselves are honest, clean and have a strong commitment to eradicating the corruption. If the leaders themselves are corrupt, there is no way to prevent public services from also becoming corrupt.

4. Failing to insulate the bureaucracy from the political intervention – The World Bank concludes that the success of the East Asian economies is attributable to their institutional traits that insulate the technocrats and bureaucrats from political interference. Economic technocrats and

	Factors				
	Economic efficiency		Political pressures		
Policy	Yes	No	Yes	No	Choice
Raise producer prices	X	X	X	X	Reform
Redistribute land		X	X	X	Stalled reform
Reorient agricultural services	X				Reform
Curb bureaucratic growth					No reform

Table 4: Political and economic factors in agricultural policy choice in Zimbabwe, 1980–1985 (*Source: Bratton 1987:176-7*)

bureaucrats need to enjoy a considerable degree of autonomy to formulate and implement policies in keeping with politically formulated national goals. Lack of such autonomy as well as political interference make them unable to introduce and sustain rational economic policies (World Bank, 1993:167). The bureaucracy therefore should have a tradition of independent policy-making.

The Constitution of Zimbabwe provides for the establishment of commissions to oversee the appointment of public and judicial officials, with the aim of ensuring that the government will have access to a functioning public bureaucracy imbued with the norms of neutrality and professionalism. In practice, however, 'the choice and performance of policy in Zimbabwe has been the result of a different combination of political and economic calculation' (Bratton, 1987:176-7). The determinants of policy choice should be whether a proposed policy measure has demonstrable economic benefit and an organised political constituency. As Table 4 shows, in Zimbabwe, policy choices and decisions are instead a function of the political pressures, rather than economic efficiency.

5. A monitoring and evaluation system and total quality management (TQM) – Although regular customer satisfaction surveys and public service assessment reports were carried out in order to enhance accountability and assess the conduct of public officials in service delivery and to ensure that services offered are accessible and meet client needs, there is no continuous assessment programme and no means to measure performance and customer satisfaction. Moreover, although findings and recommendations provided by surveys and reports were acknowledged and adopted by the Cabinet, none have since been implemented (Chimhowu, 2009:114).

Furthermore, even though almost all necessary programmes and mechanisms are in place, the implementation, monitoring and evaluation processes are weak. Monitoring and assessment teams are neither competent nor committed and their assessments are neither honest nor impartial nor helpful. Nor has there been an introduction of Total Quality Management (TQM), which is one of the ways to improve the performance and service delivery of public service by increasing efficacy and efficiency.

Under TQM, employees are not simply told what to do but are asked to think and to participate in the process of organising work. All members of the institution or body are trained in and expected to analyse work processes and to work together for improvement (Cohen and Brand, 1993:6). In other words, TQM empowers staff to be involved in the decision-making process and to find better ways of performing their duties. The fact that the command chain members of the public sector in Zimbabwe are obliged to follow – and the goals they have to aim for – are directed from outside of their organisation (Wilson, 1989:115) is one of the constraints that has made the country's public sector inefficient and ineffective. Applying TQM can overcome this and boost not only the workers' performance but also their work morale.

Findings of the past reform programmes

Based on the findings of the past public service reform programmes of Zimbabwe, and from lessons learnt from the reforms of other countries, five important issues on leadership, staff morale, and finance need to be discussed.

1. Leadership's failure, lack of political will and lack of rule of law – Leadership plays the greatest role in the development of any country. The quality and integrity of a state's leader(s) is a decisive factor that determines whether the developmental trend of a country will ascend or descend.

In Zimbabwe, the lack of political will and leadership commitment is also responsible for the failure of all bureaucratic reforms and programmes. In an interview[2] with four members of the ZANU-PF Youth League, all of them stated that political interference is high at all levels of the public service and hinders the processing and implementation of national programmes.

The negative effect of political interference on the economy is well observed and documented. Kenya's successful reform experience shows that the political environment should be conducive to success, and that objectives and aims must be clear and uncomplicated. Substantial investment should be made in training and recruiting personnel (Wallis, 1989:188-90). In the same way, the Republic of Korea's experience has shown that excessive government interference in day-to-day management without effective control over the results has hugely negative effects on the performance of nation's bureaucrats (Wallis, 1989:190-2).

It is clear that one of the root causes of Zimbabwe's problems is the absence of the rule of law in the country, and not only in relation to the behaviour of the rank and file. People in power can get away with criminal conduct without reprimand: political office is a talisman for doing wrong with impunity, it is a passport for looting without jail, and it is a passport for vice without corrective action (Munakiri, 2009).

While 80 per cent of the population survive on less than US$2 a day (Chimhowu, 2009:19), people in power and their cronies are wealthy and have opulent life styles.

Before it can attempt any other type of restructuring, Zimbabwe must address these failings and then re-establish the rule of law in the country. Without honest and competent leadership and the rule of law, any attempts at reform are doomed to failure.

2. *Impersonality versus slothfulness* – One of the problems with Zimbabwe's bureaucracy is ever-deteriorating staff morale. Public officials have mostly adopted a 'don't care' attitude to work. The impersonality of the bureaucratic system has been blamed for this. It should be noted that there is a realistic rationale for the impersonality *principle* of the

bureaucracy. Equal – impersonal – treatment of clients and customers is one of the most highly valued characteristics of bureaucracy, as it allows public servants to serve the population with objectivity, consistency, and equality. Treating everyone identically ensures consistency and fairness through equal treatment (Johnston, 1993:28).

There is, however, a wide gap between this definition of impersonality, i.e., being neutral or unbiased, and that of meaning apathy, slothfulness or indolence. Only the former can help move bureaucracy beyond nepotism and favouritism (Pinchot and Pinchot, 1994:28). On the other hand, an unhealthy working environment, low remuneration and a lack of social cohesion – the type of impersonality experienced by Zimbabwe's bureaucracy – do nothing for productivity and morale. Only when they receive a salary that is high enough to allow a reasonable standard of living for their family, will public sector productivity and efficiency really improve.

3. The reasons for public servant's low salaries and allowances – The low salaries and allowances of public servants are the product of political and economic mismanagement and the poor macroeconomic situation. The government should be aware that the foundations of the unstable economic environment were caused partly by the adverse effects of the Economic Structural Adjustment Programme (ESAP) that started in 1991, although two major economic management decisions by the state – the unbudgeted expenditure in the form of payments made to veterans of the war of liberation and involvement in the civil war in the Democratic Republic of Congo – are also responsible (Chimhowu, 2009:17).

As a direct result of the ESAP's social spending reduction scheme, 25 per cent of all public workers were laid off. By 1997, formal unemployment had reached 50 per cent. Moreover, new US$ 3.5 billion loans over five years as a reward for implementing ESAP reforms added to the existing debt of US$2.5 billion and increased interest payments on both foreign and domestic debt (Chimhowu, 2009:17).

Concerning the ESAP, a lesson provided by Kiiza (2007:297) in his study of three successful African economies (Botswana, Mauritius and Uganda) deserves full attention. He states that:

> sub-Saharan African countries that have stifled their post-independence developmentalism and embraced economic liberalism need to rethink

their preferences. Economic liberalism is not necessarily a wrong ideology, but it is simply inappropriate for sub-Saharan Africa at the current stage of development. The 'good' economic strategy for the now-developed countries (NDCs) may be 'bad' for developing countries; and the 'good' institutions (or policies) of the NDCs are not necessarily 'good enough' for developing countries.

Failure of the government's programme to redistribute white-owned commercial farmland to the black majority dramatically accelerated Zimbabwe's economic meltdown. Real GDP has declined by an estimated 52 per cent since the Fast-Track Land Reform Programme was launched in 2000 (USAID, 2007:10). Since then government was also unable to offer public servants good salaries because of the failure of the economy after 2000.

4. Necessity of a financial resource at the beginning – Lack of adequate financial resources is another important reason for the failure of Zimbabwe's attempts at bureaucratic reform at the end of the 1980s. In the early stage of any reform, financial resources are indispensable. They need not be high, but must be adequate to start the programme. International financial institutions and donors understand this necessity and it would not be impossible to get enough financial assistance if the new government of Zimbabwe could demonstrate its honesty, integrity and strong commitment.

5. The 'freedom-fighter curse' or 'liberator syndrome' – Zimbabwe has used various programmes and measures in its failed attempt to upgrade its bureaucracy. While political uncertainty and economic instability are two important factors behind this failure, root causes also include corruption and the failure of the nation's leadership.

There are two risks for most newly independent developing countries. One is the 'resource curse', the other the so-called freedom-fighter curse or 'liberator syndrome' i.e., the problems caused by those who have liberated their countries from the colonies and then gone on to ruin their countries by becoming ruthless long-ruling dictators. Zimbabwe has unfortunately suffered the effects of both since its independence.

As Terence Mashingaidze (2009) rightly states, 'a country could be well endowed with natural resources and human capital but with rascals at the helm people will still suffer. Zimbabwe is in a leadership deficiency mode. Everything that happens in any society is a function of leadership'. The first thing Zimbabwe needs most is not a sound economy but a committed and well meaning leadership.

Bureaucratic reform will not be easy under unsupportive leadership, political uncertainty and an non-conducive policy environment.

Recommendations

Quality bureaucracy is a result of multi-factorial elements. It is the outcome of good practices and programmes and well-structured and organised institutions. Zimbabwe's once excellent public service can be restored if it takes the steps outlined below.

1. *Two aspects of the reform: institutional and attitudinal* – Reform measures to improve bureaucratic quality should have two aspects: addressing the institutional aspects by improving the structure and procedures of the public bureaucracy, and changing the attitudes and behaviour of the bureaucrats in order to promote organisational effectiveness and commitment to national goals. 'Change Management' training, workshops and seminars could be used to change the attitude of the employees.

2. *Public acceptance and good communication* – Decisive reform needs to be all-inclusive, especially in the planning stages. It is very important to include all stakeholders, especially the labour unions and donors, at the early stage of planning. Public acceptance is also critical for the programme to be successful. The best way to see this happens is to ensure the streamlining process is transparent, fair, open and clear. A well-designed and managed communication plan for all the stakeholders is also of critical importance.

3. *Providing continuous training for the public servants* – Continuous training is indispensable to upgrading and improving the standard and performance of public servants. All the best public services around the world provide continuous and extensive quality training to their employees. Training, seminars and workshops are also necessary not only to instil a good attitude and mindset, but also to create better

understanding and social cohesion in the workplace. In Zimbabwe, then, priority should be given to providing training and capacity-building for staff. This is the best way to create a motivated, competent and committed civil service.

The training programmes also need to be contextually relevant and highly advanced in content. Their content needs to be updated annually by experts and made challenging, even for the brightest members of the services.

4. Establishing a full-time assessment committee – Continuous monitoring and evaluation of the performance of a bureaucracy is essential to keeping programmes and reform plans on the right track. It is also necessary to train a pool of assessors to international standards. To enhance accountability and assess the conduct of public officials in service delivery, and to ensure that services offered are accessible and meet client needs, simple, well-administered customer surveys should be conducted regularly. Measurement systems and public reporting centres should also be established.

Setting up a task force is one of the effective approaches to continuously assess, monitor and evaluate the public service. Various task forces could be set up according to the situation; for example, a morale task force could be set up to boost the work team spirit and a 'quality task force' established to assure and upgrade the quality of the public service. A 'mobile assessment team' also needs to be formed.

5. Fighting corruption decisively and devotedly – To minimise all kinds of corruption in the public service, incentives and opportunities for it must be removed by strengthening the existing legislation, increasing the penalties for corrupt behaviour (imprisonment and fines,) and enacting a strictly enforced dismissal policy. The Prevention of Corruption Act, which authorises that a person found guilty of accepting an illegal gratification has to pay as punishment the amount he or she had taken as a bribe in addition to the legal punishment needs to be strictly applied and enforced.

Corrupt public servants should be expelled from the civil service and have their pensions withdrawn. An Anti-Corruption Commission staffed with honest and competent persons with the legal power to investigate any bank, share or purchase account of any person suspected of having committed an offence against the anti-corruption law should also be launched. Further, it must be free from political interference, as should the judiciary and legal institutions, as it cannot be effective if its actions are not supported by the institutions that have the legal authority to punish those who commit crimes (Tanzi, 2000:152).

6. *Establishing meritocracy in bureaucracy* – As previously stated, the foundation of the ideal bureaucracy is the merit system. For Zimbabwe's public service, officers must only be recruited and promoted on merit. Appointments and awards of scholarships must only be given to the best candidates. To this end, an examination system must be set up, one that focuses on key competences, attitudes and behaviour of personnel joining the service.

7. *Paying competitive salaries and offering rewarding long-term careers* – To maintain the quality of public administration, it is absolutely essential to pay competitive salaries and allowances and also to offer rewarding long-term careers. Paying a low salary to ten unproductive employees is more expensive than paying a high salary to one useful productive worker. The quality of bureaucracy is not about quantity, but quality and performance. And no matter how prestigious the civil service, it will fail to retain its talented personnel if an enormous gap between salaries in the public and private sectors remains. Furthermore, there is a relationship between wage levels and the corruption index. This has been tested empirically (van Rijackehem and Weder, 1997; Ul Haque and Sahay, 1996; cited in Tanzi, 2000:128). Cross-sectional data shows that the relationship between corruption and wage levels are statistically significant. Countries that regularly increased bureaucrats' salary are also able to retain and attract more able, productive and honest individuals.

Besides paying competitive salaries, offering rewarding, long-term careers not only increases competencies in the long run, but it also increases corporate coherence and 'reduces the relative attractiveness of the quick returns available from corrupt individual practices'. It also 'help[s] structure the incentives of individual bureaucrats in a way that enhances the ability of the organisations they manage to effectively pursue long-term goals' (Evans and Rauch, 1999:752).

Conclusion

Revolutionaries with their guns can start and win a revolution, but only the administrators that follow in their wake can solidify and complete it. Thus all conquering armies have necessarily been followed by hordes of bureaucrats (Shafritz and Russell, 2000:177).

A strong transition can bring some economic recovery again. The restoration of basic social services will increase Zimbabweans' confidence in taking a natural step forward towards a democratic, post-Mugabe situation (Negin and Ford, 2009:3-5).

While huge, the challenges to upgrading Zimbabwe's bureaucracy are not insurmountable, even though most of its staff are dispirited, demoralised, and disheartened because of the Mugabe regime's abuse, misuse and mismanagement of the apparatus of state, its mechanisms, and resources. Fellow developing countries have already followed the successful path and enough lessons and best practices of other needy states have been studied and documented to guide Zimbabwe along.

However, unless the honesty and competence of the political leadership can be guaranteed, the chance of any reform, no matter how well structured, achieving their aims are very low. Leading by example, and transmitting strong values and principles of good governance, are critical to ensuring that reforms are successful. Thus, the best thing the new government of Zimbabwe can do for its country and its people is to govern the nation with honesty, integrity, and accountability, with the help of a competent, committed and honest bureaucracy. If other countries can do it, why can't Zimbabwe?

Notes

1 Macroeconomic stabilisation, an expanding economy, and increased employment creation, resulting in improved standards of living and a slim, effective and efficient public service.
2 Interview, Pretoria, December 2010.

References

AfDB. African Development Bank. 2010. *Zimbabwe: Country Brief.* Available at www.afdb.org/fileadmin/uploads/afdb/Documents/Project

-and-Operations/Zimbabwe%20Country%20Brief__02.pdf

Blunt, P. 1983. *Organization Theory and Behaviour: An African Perspective*. London: Longman.

Bratton, M. 1987. 'The Comrades and the Countryside: The Politics of Agricultural Policy in Zimbabwe', *World Politics*, Vol. 39, No. 2. January), pp. 174-202.

Chagonda, T. 2010. 'Dollarization of the Zimbabwean Economy: Cure or Curse? The Case of the Teaching and Banking Sectors'. A conference paper read at the Renaissance of African Economies conference in Dar Es Salam, Tanzania, 20-21 December 2010. Available at www. codesria.org/IMG/pdf/papers14.pdf

Chimhowu, A. 2009. 'Moving forward in Zimbabwe: Reducing poverty and promoting growth'. Available at www.bwpi.manchester.ac.uk/ research/ResearchAreaProjects/Africa/Moving_forward_in_Zimba bwe_whole_report.pdf

Cohen, S. and R. Brand. 1993. *Total Quality Management in Government: A Practical Guide for the Real World*. San Francisco: Jossey-Bass.

Evans, P.B. 2007. 'Extending the "Institutional" Turn: Property, Politics, and Development Trajectories', in H-J. Chang (ed.), *Institutional Change and Economic Development*. United Nations University Press: Tokyo. pp. 53-74.

Evans, P. and J.E. Rauch. 1999. 'Bureaucracy and Growth: A Cross-national Analysis of the Effects of "Weberian" State Structures on Economic Growth', *American Sociological Review*, October 1999; Vol. 64, pp. 748-65. Available at www.jstor.org/stable/2657374

Hegel, G.W.F. 1976. *Philosophy of Right* (translated by T.M. Knox). Oxford: Oxford University Press.

Hyden, G. 1983. *No Shortcuts to Progress: African Development Management in Perspective*. Berkeley: University of California Press and London: Heinemann Educational Books.

International Labour Organisation (ILO). 1993. *Structural change and adjustment in Zimbabwe*.

Johnston, K. 1993. *Beyond Bureaucracy: A Blueprint and Vision for Government that Works*. Homewood, IL: Business One Irwin.

Kavran, D. 1989. Report of the Public Service Review Commission of Zimbabwe, Under the Chairmanship of Professor D. Kavran, Vol. 1, Harare.

Kiiza, J. 2007. 'Developmental Nationalism and Economic Performance in Africa: The Case of Three 'Successful' African Economies', in H-J. Chang (ed.), *Institutional Change and Economic Development*. United Nations University Press: Tokyo, pp. 281-300.

Law, S.H. and A.N. Bany-Ariffin. 2008. 'Institutional Infrastructure and Economic Performance: Dynamic Panel Data Evidence', *Transition Studies Review*, Vol. 15, No. 3, pp. 542-57.

Mashingaidze, T.M. 2009. 'It's leadership, stupid!', 11 December. Available at www.newzimbabwe.com/pages/opinion218.14917.html

Mhonderwa, B. 2011. 'Zimbabwe: Cost of Inappropriate Behaviour in Public Sector', *The Herald*, 4 April. Available at www.allafrica.com/stories/201104050035.html

Mises, L. von. 2007. *Bureaucracy*. New Haven: Yale University Press.

Munakiri, T. 2009. 'Corruption, Zimbabwe's biggest enemy'. 11 December. Available at www.newzimbabwe.com/pages/opinion225.14972.html.

Myint, H. 1959. 'Interview with Dr Hla Myint, Deputy-Rector of Rangoon University, 1959', *New Burma Weekly*. Vol. 4, No. 1, January.

Negin, J. and J. Ford. 2009. *Rebuilding Zimbabwe: Australia's Role in Supporting the Transition*. The Lowy Institute for International Policy, Policy Brief, October.

NewsDay. 2011. 'Public service reveals 70,000 ghost workers on payroll'. Available at www.zimbabweonlinepress.com/index.php?news=3215. 28 January.

Niskanen, W.A. 1968. 'The Peculiar Economics of Bureaucracy', *The American Economic Review*, Vol. 58, No. 2, Papers and Proceedings of the Eightieth Annual Meeting of the American Economic Association. May, pp. 293-305.

Oyelaran-Oyeyinka, R.N.I. 2006. *Governance and bureaucracy: Leadership in Nigeria's Public Service*. Netherlands: Universitaire Pers Maastricht.

PE Consulting Group. 1989. *National Salary Survey*. Gauteng: PE Corporate Services.

Pinchot, G. and E. Pinchot. 1994. *The End of Bureaucracy and The Rise of Intelligent Organisation*. San Francisco: Berrett-Koehler.

Pswarayi, G. 2010. 'Zimbabwe's Education System on the Verge of Collapse, Corruption Blamed'. In *Global Press Institute*, 24 November. Available at www.globalpressinstitute.org/print/477

Quah, J.S.T. 1996. 'Wielding the Bureaucracy for Results: An Analysis of Singapore's Experience in Administrative Reform', *Asian Review of Public Administration*, Vol. VIII, No. 1. July-December.

Schiavo-Campo, Salvatore, Giulio de Tommaso and Amitabha Mukherjee. 1997. *Government Employment and Pay: A Global and Regional Perspective*. World Bank Policy Research Working Paper No. 1771.

Shafritz, J.M. and E.W. Russell. 2000. *Introducing Public Administration*

(2nd ed.). New York: Longman.

Tanzi, V. 2000. *Policies, Institutions and the Dark Side of Economics.* Cheltenham: Edward Elgar.

Toye, J. 2007. 'Modern Bureaucracy', in H-J. Chang (ed.), *Institutional Change and Economic Development.* United Nations University Press: Tokyo, pp. 75-94.

United Nations. 2004. 'Republic of Zimbabwe Public Administration: Country Profile', July.

United States Agency for International Development (USAID). 2007. *Zimbabwe Economic Performance Assessment: A Benchmark Study.*

Wallis, M. 1989. *Bureaucracy: Its Role in Third World Development.* London: Macmillan.

Weber, M. 1946. 'Bureaucracy', in H.H. Gerth and C. Wright Hills (eds), *From Max Weber: Essays in Sociology.* New York: Oxford University Press.

Wilson, J. Q. 1989. *Bureaucracy: What Government Agencies Do and Why They Do It.* New York: Basic Book.

World Bank. 1993. *The East Asian Miracle, Economic Growth and Public Policy.* New York: Oxford University Press.

— 2009. *Introduction to Corruption.* Youth for Good Governance: distance learning program. Module III.

Zimbabwe Institute. 2007. *The Labour Market and Sustainable Growth and Transformation in Zimbabwe.* Cape Town: The Zimbabwe Institute.

9

The Role of Local Authorities in Democratic Transition

Norbert Musekiwa

Introduction

Zimbabwe is in the painstaking process of recovering from the decade-long sociopolitical and economic crisis that began in 2000. The support and capacity of local government structures is crucial to seeing this evolve. Following the March 2008 harmonised elections, the results of the local-level elections were largely uncontested. Thus it is arguable that local authorities in Zimbabwe are currently governed by representatives that were democratically elected by the people and that constitutional and democratic transition is already taking place at that level.[1]

Local government can be treated as a legitimate level of government that received an unquestioned mandate in the 2008 elections. Though affected indirectly by the formation of the Government of National Unity (GNU), local authorities have never had to resort to negotiated political settlement or work through the political contestations seen in the current seventh Parliament of Zimbabwe. Accordingly, local authorities should provide spaces that nurture democratic transition.

This chapter analyses the role that Zimbabwe's local authorities as sub-national institutions, and one of the major vehicles for democratic change, are playing in promoting or inhibiting the nation's transition from an authoritarian regime to a liberal democracy. It considers the extent to which local government can be the nucleus of democracy-promoting peaceful transition, how local government can promote democratic consolidation, and the degree to which the country's political institutions and democratic procedures are being legitimised, stabilised and broadly accepted by both political actors and the wider population. It also considers whether the contestations at national level are aiding local democracy or threatening the existing fragile democratic space and asks if Zimbabwe's fledgling local, democratic transitional processes can survive the often disruptive mutual mistrust and conflict.

The data underpinning this chapter was collected through interviews and archival research. During December 2010 and January 2011, in-depth consultations were held with senior personnel from the Ministry of Local Government and the Local Government Board (LGB). Key informants, mostly members of civil society with expertise in local governance, were also interviewed. Key policy pronouncements and relevant legislation were also reviewed.

Defining local government and local governance

Local government can be defined as those statutory sub-national structures of government with general or specific powers devolved to them by a national authority and whose primary purpose is the delivery of service within a geographically defined area in a nation or state (Vosloo, 1974:10; Ismail, Bayat and Meyer 1997:2). Local government can also be viewed as a system of sub-national government dealing with the administration of affairs of a local nature closest to the people, (Sachikonye et al., 2007:75). Local government therefore entails the establishment of participatory and democratically elected structures that can identify with the needs of the people at grassroots level and ensure the translation of those needs into the actual programmes and projects and maintenance of essential services. A local authority is the organisation composed of the elected and appointed officials with a mandate over a specific area (Ismail, Bayat and Meyer, 1997:3).

Increasingly, there is greater emphasis on the concept of local governance (Ibid.:2). Governance entails the process of decision-making and the process by which decisions are implemented or not implemented and can be used in several contexts such as corporate governance, international governance, national governance and local governance.

The concept of governance acknowledges the roles played by the formal and informal actors and structures involved in decision-making and implementing the decisions made. Government, both central and local, is only one of the key actors in governance and other actors are involved in a varied manner depending on the level of government. Actors in local governance include, among others, the influential ratepayers, associations of farmers, co-operatives, non-governmental organisations, research institutes, religious leaders, finance institutions, and political parties. In addition these, the media, lobbyists, international donors, and multinational corporations also influence the decision-making processes.

In Zimbabwe, local government is responsible for the provision of a wide range of services. When the centre failed to provide essential services during the crisis years from 2000 to 2008 the country was held together by the local authorities that delivered the basic services (Musekiwa, 2010). To that extent, the local level democracy can be a bulwark against state failure to deliver basic services and against resistance to democratic transition.

Theoretical framework

There are two main theoretical approaches to the study of local government, namely the centralist and decentralist. The centralist school of thought regards local government as local administration, a mere extension and integral part of the sovereign state, implying that the sovereign has an obligation to supervise the local government to ensure that powers delegated to the sub-national units are not overstepped (Ismail, Bayat and Meyer, 1997:14). Democratic transition within this framework is directed from the centre and not from sub-national levels.

The decentralist school of thought regards local government as deserving 'an autonomous status in the constitutional arrangements guiding the country' (Ibid.:20). The decentralist framework of local government, and specifically the liberal and democratic theories that guide this study, regards local governments as free-standing, nurturing democratic transition through alternation of elected local leadership independent of the centre.

The liberal democratic theory's primary concern is how representative government fulfils the requirements for liberty, equality and fraternity (Ibid.:27). The basic tenets undergirding representative institutions are: 'free elections, majority rule, protection of minorities, subject to the majority's final say and the assumption that government operates on the basis of widespread discussion and responsiveness to an informed public opinion' (Ibid.). Liberal democracy works best when citizens are able to elect, at scheduled times, local representatives under free and fair conditions and when the election result reflects the wishes of the electorate (Commonwealth Local Government Forum, 2005:6). Regular and scheduled elections therefore provide an opportunity for alternation of power among various political parties.

Within the liberal democracy framework, are tenets of democratic transition processes informing this study. States are perceived as existing on a continuum of democracy ranging from authoritarian to liberal democracy (Schedler, 1998:93). Authoritarian regimes demand obedience to the ruler and do not provide for change of leadership. The electoral democracies manage 'to hold (more or less) inclusive, clean, and competitive elections but fail to uphold the political and civil freedom essential for liberal democracy' (Ibid.:93). Liberal democracies are characterised by universal political rights, competitive and inclusive elections with the 'alternation of power being ultimate proof of any democracy' (Ibid.:92). Democratic transition entails a move from authoritarian or electoral democracies regime to more democratic arrangements. In this study democratic transition is conceptualised as the purposeful shift along the continuum from an authoritarian to electoral democracy, or from an electoral democracy to a liberal democracy as demonstrated in Figure 1. It is worth noting that the shift can also be reversed where there is democratic breakdown. In this chapter, such democratic erosion is not regarded as democratic transition.

Zimbabwe is classified as an electoral democracy that had gradually slid into authoritarianism. In that case, the transition back to fully fledged electoral democracy is perceived by the former opposition parties and international community as both welcome and positive to the extent that it is a renewal and a restoration after democratic reversal

---

DEMOCRATIC TRANSITION

AUTHORITARIAN REGIME → ELECTORAL DEMOCRACY →
LIBERAL DEMOCRACY

DEMOMCRATIC BREAKDOWN

AUTHORITARIAN REGIME ← ELECTORAL DEMOCRACY ←
LIBERAL DEMOCRACY

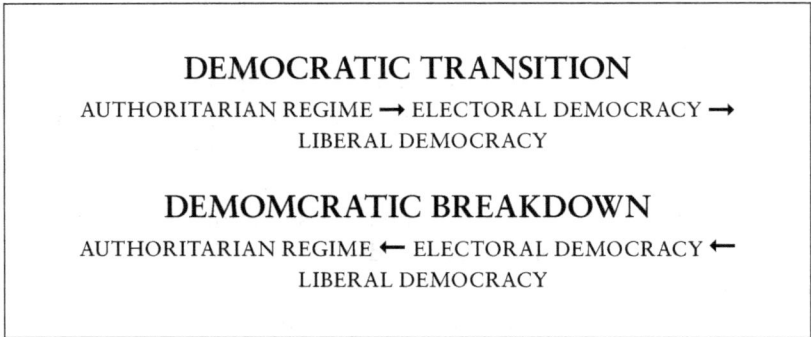

Figure 1: Transition along the continuum of democracy (*Adapted from Schedler 1998:107*)

into authoritarianism (Sachikonye 2007:23). The African Union and the Southern African Development Community (SADC) had a significant interest and role in the democratic transition of Zimbabwe as the SADC-appointed facilitator negotiated the environment for 2008 elections and the subsequent political settlement.

Historically, democratic transition in Africa has followed one of five different routes: government change via national conference, as was typical of Francophone Africa in the 1980s and 1990s; government change via multiparty elections, as was the case in Zambia; co-opted transitions where the incumbent has the maximum advantage of power of incumbency to win the election; guided democracy, where the military controls the transition; and authoritarian reaction or subnational conflict where the incumbent refuses to open up the political system or open conflict precludes such transition (Martin, 1993:6). The democratic transition in Zimbabwe is consistent with the co-opted model where the incumbent has maximum advantage. Indeed, Robert Mugabe employed the power of incumbency to determine the nature of democratic transition by negotiating a political settlement after losing the 2008 elections.

Local government structures in Zimbabwe

In Zimbabwe, elected, appointed and traditional leadership structures constitute the local government sector. The country is divided into ten administrative provinces and split further into 60 districts. Harare and Bulawayo metropolitans are unique in that the administrative district and provincial boundaries are congruous. The number of districts in the remaining eight provinces varies between six and nine. Though an administrative district would normally contain more than one local authority, no local authority boundary cuts across district boundaries. Each local authority is divided into administrative wards, with each ward represented in council by an elected councillor. The number of wards in a local authority ranges from six to 46. A Provincial Governor appointed in terms of the Provincial Councils and Administration Act (1984) heads each of the ten provinces. Though not a member of Cabinet, the Provincial Governor, commonly referred to as the Resident Minister, has ministerial status.

There are four types of local authorities in Zimbabwe: urban councils, rural district councils, provincial councils and traditional leaders. Urban councils are established in terms of the Urban Councils Act (1996) and exist in a hierarchy of cities, municipalities, town councils and local boards, with the city being the highest status and attracting the widest range of mandates and autonomy and the local board having the lowest status. Rural District Councils (RDCs) are provided for by the Rural District Councils Act (1996). As of January 2011, there were 91 local authorities nationwide, of which 31 were urban and 60 rural. Urban and rural district councils in Zimbabwe have a wider range of mandated services than most of their counterparts in sub-Saharan Africa. Zimbabwe's urban councils also enjoy greater operational autonomy and more resources than their rural counterparts (Sachikonye et al., 2007:80). The main function of the ten Provincial Councils is to co-ordinate the activities of the other local authorities operating within their respective provincial boundaries. Composed entirely of mayors and various chairpersons, and devoid of its own staff and budget, they have become a loose co-ordinating body without any meaningful executive powers. Traditional leaders' roles and functions are today now fused with their geographically closest RDC. The Ministry of Local Government superintends all local government activities throughout the country.

However, except for traditional leaders and provincial governors, the legitimacy of these local government institutions is not enshrined in the Constitution. In terms of Section 111(A) of the existing Constitution, an Act of Parliament can provide for the appointment of governors by the state president. Section 111 also provides that 'there shall be chiefs to preside over the tribespeople in Zimbabwe who shall be appointed by the President'. Section 38(b) of the Constitution further states that ten provincial governors, president and deputy president of the Council of Chiefs and eight chiefs representing each of the eight provinces other than the metropolitan provinces shall be members of parliament (GoZ, 2005:56). The governors occupy office with the indulgence of the President and have to vacate office when a new President assumes office (Linington, 2001:205). As a result, the provincial level of local government is therefore vulnerable to changes by a partisan executive. A constitutional provision enshrining local government as a free-standing level of government would enhance the legitimacy of that level of government. It would also insure local government against any whimsical legislative amendments by the national executive that have not followed the proper process. The constitutional recognition of local government would thus provide legitimacy, and all the more so if it were to specify the powers and responsibilities of local authorities over and above establishing a revenue-sharing formula.

Local government in Zimbabwe and its historical roles in transitions

Local government institutions have played a critical role in the history of political transitions in Zimbabwe. During the second Chimurenga,[2] local authorities were often viewed by the nationalist movements as retrogressive and impeding democratic transition. They have also been an effective tool for democratic transition in post-independence Zimbabwe. Remodelled at independence to suit the new socialist agenda, local government reforms turned the idea of majority rule into reality when universal suffrage was introduced. Despite ZANU-PF's arguably secure control of the national governance structures, some local authorities have always been under the control of opposition parties. Chipinge RDC was always controlled by ZANU-Ndonga from 1980 into the early 1990s and the western regions of Matabeleland North and South and Midlands were controlled by PF-ZAPU from 1980 until 1987, when ZANU-PF and PF-ZAPU signed a unity accord merging the two to form one political party. Since its formation in 1999, the

Movement for Democratic Change (MDC) has the majority in terms of the political affiliation of elected councillors in major urban councils. Local governments in Zimbabwe have therefore been partially facilitating democratic transition since 1980, despite the best efforts of the ZANU-PF government to frustrate it.

The local government portfolio has been critical to the ZANU-PF government in realising its mission. Indeed, the Ministry of Local Government (MoLG) continues to be the largest ministry in the history of Zimbabwe, having 12 ministers. It is headed by a cabinet minister and always has a deputy minister. The ministry has a further ten provincial governors and resident ministers who by virtue of their appointment also become members of the senate. All provincial governors are directly appointed and answerable to the President.

After the 2008 harmonised elections, the three parties in the GNU agreed on a formula to allocate the appointment of provincial governors that would have seen the MDC being able to nominate more than half of the ten governors. However, ZANU-PF has refused to honour that agreement and the President has continued to reappoint ZANU-PF cadres as governors. At this level, democratic transition has been stalled by ZANU-PF's intransigency. Robert Mugabe of ZANU-PF has in fact maintained exceptional control and influence over this important ministry. Since independence in 1980, the President has always appointed a minister or a deputy minister for local government from his home province of Mashonaland West, and necessarily someone of Zezuru origin.

The MoLG is one of the few ministries that are represented in all 60 districts. The Minister of Local Government supervises the operations of District Administrators and Provincial Administrators, who head the ministry at the district and provincial level respectively. The one-party dominance enjoyed by the ZANU-PF government has long enabled it to make judicious appointments of key civil servants, especially at sub-national levels (Hodder-Williams c1983:7). As a result, despite the District Administrators and Provincial Administrators being civil servants, their political neutrality is questionable.

The MoLG has wide-ranging powers over local authorities. The minister has the prerogative to approve rates set by local authorities and influence the appointments of senior council staff. He or she directly approves the appointment of senior RDC staff and appoints members of the LGB, which approves the appointment of senior urban council staff. The Urban Councils Act (1996) grants the LGB a wide range of powers with which to determine local authority staffing matters. For example, the LGB is empowered to model conditions of service; model regulations stipulating the qualifications and appointment procedures for senior council officials; and approve the appointment and discharge of all senior council officials. It also has the power to conduct inquiries into the affairs and procedures of council and to exercise any other function that may be imposed on the Board by the Urban Councils Act.

In its first report, the LGB admitted that it had to consult the minister or the permanent secretary for local government 'when urgent issues come up' (LGB, 1998:17). The minister would also approve the conditions of service and salaries for all council staff and councillors. The LGB was established ostensibly to be a referee in the recruitment and dismissal of senior staff in urban councils (Ibid.:20). However, long underfunded, it has had to rely on the MoLG for office space and running costs (Chakaipa, 2010:55). It has never operated independently or been able to hire its own staff – it is run by personnel seconded from the MoLG, a move that compromises its neutrality. Since inception, the workings of the LGB have been subject to influence from its parent ministry:

> there is a great deal of political influence in urban governance, not only by local politicians (the councillors) but by national politicians as well (that is, the ministers, governors and members of parliament). (LGB, 1998:18)

The Minister of Local Government has used the LGB to stall and influence any democratic transition taking place at the local authority level. For example, even though it is largely indirect, the minister's influence on the appointment of senior council staff has been grave, as they are key members of the policy community on whose advice elected councillors rely.

The Urban Councils Act and the Rural District Councils Act (1996) empower the Minister of Local Government to dismiss elected councillors for misdemeanours. In terms of Section 114 of the Urban Councils Act, the minister also has the power to suspend a duly elected councillor from exercising all or any of his or her functions. Section 157 of the Rural District Councils Act equally empowers the President to

Local authority	No. of councillors suspended	No. of councillors dismissed	No. of councillors whose suspensions were lifted
Bindura Town Council	3	2	1
Chitungwiza Municipality	2	2	
Harare City Council	9	6	3
Rusape Town Council	7	5	2
Manyame Rural District Council	1	1	
Total	22	16	6

Table 1: Number of councillors suspended and dismissed and those whose suspensions were lifted between September 2008 and January 2011. (*Source: Ministry of Local Government, March 2011*)

suspend councillors 'if he considers it necessary or desirable to do so in the public interest'. There are no further guidelines as to what constitute reasonable grounds or necessary or desirable conditions. Nor does the legislation provide any recourse for redress for the suspended councillor. The legislative provision allows the Minister to subvert the will of the people without him having to account to any authority for that action. The party in control of government can (ab)use the suspension provision to frustrate democratic transition at the local authority level. The Minister of Local Government has always resorted to those powers to deal with perceived problems in councils. Since the formation of the GNU in February 2009, Ignatius Chombo, the current Minister of Local Government, has suspended 22 councillors (Table 1), of whom 16 have since been dismissed. Only one councillor from ZANU-PF was suspended; the rest were from the MDC.

Prior to the MDC coming onto the local government scene in 2000, ministerial powers to suspend councillors were used to rein in truant ZANU-PF councillors. Lately, the clause has been used to target the MDC-controlled councils. The MDC has responded by forming organisations such as the Democratic Councils Forum and the Elected Councillors Association of Zimbabwe (ECAZ) to resist the 'political meddling' in local authority affairs by the Minister of Local Government (Nyazema and Gama, 2011).

In sum, the MoLG has been used to promote ZANU-PF's partisan interests, not to support and promote local authorities. Without substantive changes to its political culture, this ministry will remain a hindrance to democratic transition in general and the smooth operations of non-ZANU-PF-led local authorities in particular.

Traditional leadership and its role in the democratic transition of Zimbabwe

Traditional leadership is one level of local governance that is enshrined in the Constitution. Traditional leaders are a critical link between citizens and the state as they are active at all levels of government, from the national assembly to the smallest village unit. The hierarchical structure and spread of traditional leadership makes them an effective tool for communication between national leadership and the citizens (Chakaipa, 2010:53). At national level, the chiefs appoint representatives to sit in the Upper House of Parliament. They are also represented as *ex officio* members of all RDCs.

A village is the smallest administrative structure and is headed by a traditional leader. The size of villages varies substantially from five households to over 100 households per village (Musekiwa, 2010:30). The village head chairs the Village Assembly, which comprises all the adult inhabitants of a village. The Village Assembly supervises the Village Development Committee (VIDCO), an elected structure. The village head reports to a headman,[3] a sub-chief who controls several village heads. Several headmen report to a chief. There are often one or more chiefs in an administrative district. Nationally, there are 266 chiefs in Zimbabwe and an average of three chiefs represent traditional leaders in an RDC as *ex officio* councillors. Each province – except for the two metropolitan provinces – appoints one chief who becomes an *ex officio* Member of Parliament. The law disqualifies traditional leaders from standing for election as Members of Parliament or local authority councillors.

Elected institutions also populate the sub-district levels. Several VIDCOs form a Ward Development Committee (WADCO). The

WADCO covers an administrative ward area. The administrative ward boundaries are usually congruous with the headman areas' boundaries. The VIDCO and WADCO structures were conflated with the ruling ZANU-PF party structures, with the same individuals assuming leadership in both the party and elected local government institutions. The district and sub-district structures of the ruling party women and youth leagues and the Zimbabwe National Liberation War Veteran Association (ZNLWVA) members have no legal authority outside that of interest groups but would often exercise power and influence over the sub-district local government structures. As noted by Rutherford (2001:213), VIDCOs are often viewed and treated as vehicles of ZANU-PF.

Traditional leaders co-ordinate development, maintain population records and collect taxes payable to the local authority. They are also empowered to deal with problems of land and natural resources conservation and management in their areas, preserve and maintain rural family life, and punish crimes such as livestock theft and misuse of natural resources. The powers exercised by chiefs extend to administrative, judicial, planning and development co-ordination, traditional culture preservation and policing leaders at village level. On judicial functions, the chiefs have powers to settle minor disputes concerning land, *lobola* (marriage dowry paid by the groom), and the burial of the deceased. The Traditional Leaders Act also gives chiefs 'limited' powers to arrest and report criminals to the Zimbabwe Republic Police. The traditional leadership and elected leadership coexist in a conflictual relationship with contested claims to legitimacy. Traditional leaders' appointments, though following culture and tradition, have to be approved by and can be reversed by the Minister of Local Government.

Traditional leadership has always had a complex relationship with governments, especially those whose legitimacy is threatened and during periods of transitions. During the last years of colonial rule in Rhodesia, traditional leaders were courted by the white minority government when its legitimacy and authority were increasingly challenged by rising African nationalism. Save for a notable few, the liberation movements largely viewed traditional leaders as 'collaborators' with the colonial government and 'sell-outs'. They were regarded as instruments used by colonial government to resist democratic transition. However, Nyambara (2001:781) challenges this conventional wisdom that implied chiefs' compliance with government policies and argues that the position of chiefs was more complex than that of government stooges, for 'while some chiefs complied with and enforced state policies, others used their newly acquired powers to enhance their positions or undermine policy'. The compliance to the state dictates was a pragmatic strategy employed by the chiefs (Ibid.:780). During the liberation struggle, a number of traditional leaders collaborated with the nationalist movements and became agents of democratic transition (Ibid.:787; Makumbe, 2010:92).

At independence the new ZANU-PF-led government had unquestioned legitimacy, having won the 1980 general elections convincingly. The new government had no need for allies in the form of traditional leadership and continued to treat them with disdain. Traditional leaders lost some of their organisational power, such as land allocation, and adjudicative powers to the elected local authorities and the government-appointed judicial system. This changed after the adoption of the economic structural adjustment programme (ESAP) in 1990, which saw increasing suffering and hardship for the majority of the population, who subsequently began to question the legitimacy and authority of ZANU-PF.

In response, like its colonial predecessors, the ZANU-PF government sought – and successfully so – a fresh alliance with a seemingly legitimate traditional leadership in order to prolong its rule and avert democratic transition at the local level. Over the years, traditional leadership has become increasingly aligned with ZANU-PF, largely through the *ex officio* positions it occupies in local government and the National Assembly. Save for a minority, it openly campaigns for ZANU-PF and chiefs in Parliament, while local authorities always vote for ZANU-PF (Makumbe, 2010:93), if only to access benefits or as a survival strategy, bowing to the dictates of a regime in legitimacy crisis in the process.

The confounding factor is that such alliances with forces resisting democratic transition seem not to cause any permanent damage to the legitimacy of the institution of traditional leadership among its subjects. Nevertheless, since the traditional leadership remains a legitimate authority among the people, it is possible to have a government that engages the traditional leadership in democratic transition.

Local authorities and democratic transition and consolidation

Local authorities are the vehicles for delivering democracy. They provide the most essential services and access to public decision-making. Most people rely on local authorities for essential services such as health, education and refuse collection. Through the activities of local authorities, citizens (should) have a good chance of influencing local decision-making and being involved in the appointment of local leadership. Participation in the elections is open to all adult citizens. The council proceedings and records of meetings are open to public scrutiny (Chatiza, 2010:12).

Regular scheduled, free and fair elections are a necessary precondition for democratic transition, for it is through elections that the electorate has an opportunity to change the political slant of local leadership. Since independence Zimbabwe maintained a record of conducting local government elections at scheduled times (every five years). In this respect, the electoral process in Zimbabwe has facilitated democratic transition at the local level. However, the issue of whether these elections have been free and fair is contestable, given ZANU-PF's influence over the election machinery. In this regard, it is worth noting that during the 2008 elections 413 (21 per cent) of the 1,958 seats won were uncontested (Chakaipa, 2010:59).

Moreover, although the outcome of the 2008 local government elections was not contested, there was an inordinate delay in duly elected councillors assuming office. Section 47(c) of the Urban Councils Act states that duly elected councillors shall assume office, 'in the case of a general election of councillors, on the day following polling day'. Section 103 of the Urban Councils Act further indicates that the District Administrator shall chair this first meeting. On this occasion, the District Administrators, who take their cue from the Minister of Local Government and were awaiting the outcome of the national level negotiations, simply delayed calling the meeting until the latter were resolved. The duly elected councillors could therefore not assume office, nor could they elect a chairperson or the deputy. In this case the national-level political contestations unduly affected democratic transition in local government.

Despite this and other delays, democratic transition did occur on a

Province	Local Authority	No. of elected councillors	No. of appointed councillors
Harare Metropolitan	Harare City Council	46	11
	Chitungwiza Municipality	25	6
	Ruwa Town Council	9	2
	Epworth Local Board	7	1
Bulawayo Metropolitan	Bulawayo City Council	29	7**
Midlands	Gweru City Council	18	4
	Kwekwe City Council	14	3
	Redcliff Municipality	9	2
	Shurugwi Town Council	13	3
	Zvishavane Town Council	10	2
	Gokwe Town Council	6	1
Masvingo	Masvingo City Council	10	2
	Chiredzi Town Council	8	2
Mashonaland West	Kadoma City Council	17	4
	Chegutu Municipality	12	3
	Chinhoyi Municipality	15	3
	Kariba Municipality	9	2
	Karoi Town Council	10	2
	Norton Town Council	13	3
	Chirundu Local Board*		
Manicaland	Mutare City Council	19	4
	Rusape Town Council	10	2
	Chipinge Town Council	8	2
Mashonaland Central	Bindura Municipality	12	3

Province	Local Authority	No. of elected councillors	No. of appointed councillors
Mashonaland East	Marondera Municipality	12	3
Matabeleland South	Gwanda Municipality	10	2
	Plumtree Town Council	6	1
	Beitbridge Town Council	6	1
Matabeleland North	Victoria Falls	11	2
	Hwange Town Council	15	3
	Lupane Town Council†		
Total		389	86

**The seven councillors for Bulawayo City Council could not assume office as judgement in a case challenging their appointment in the High Court was still being heard in January 2011.*
Chirundu Local Board has no elected councillors and is run by commissioners appointed by the MoLG.
†*Lupane Town Council had not yet been proclaimed a local authority when Statutory Instrument 94 was gazetted.*

Table 2: Urban Councils – Appointed Councillors, 2010 (*Adapted from Statutory Instrument 94 of 2010 (GoZ, 2010) and MoLG records (2011)*).

substantive scale in local government, for ZANU-PF lost the control of all urban councils and some RDCs to the MDC. Even so, the Minister of Local Government has wide-ranging powers regarding the dismissal of councillors, the appointment of special interest councillors, the appointment of senior local government executives and the setting of conditions of service for councillors and staff. Both the Rural District Councils and the Urban Councils Acts permit the minister to appoint 'special interest' councillors – a number no more than one-quarter of the 389 elected councillors – with no obligation to specify the interests represented by the appointed councillors in the case of urban councils. As a result, most of the appointed councillors for urban councils were ZANU-PF candidates who had lost. In terms of Statutory Instrument 94 of 2010, the Minister of Local Government subsequently appointed 86 additional councillors.[4] Table 2 shows the number of elected and appointed councillors on each urban council.

Although appointed councillors have no voting powers, they do 'participate in the business of the municipal or town council to which they are appointed and perform the same functions and are entitled to the same benefits in every respect as if they were elected councillors'.[5] As a result, appointed councillors have effectively influenced the tempo of debate in councils and affected agenda-setting, even if it meant disrupting council business.

The Minister of Local Government also has the power to appoint a caretaker council where there is no council. The minister can appoint a caretaker council even to replace a council he has dismissed. In a way, the elected council is at risk, for it can potentially be replaced by a caretaker council – a move that effectively limits democratic transition. The last caretaker councils appointed in 2004 for the cities of Harare and Mutare were replaced during the harmonised elections in 2008. Since 2008, the minister has not dismissed any council, preferring to target individual councillors instead.

The wave of these subjective appointments could be interpreted as a strategy by ZANU-PF to counter the effects of democratic transition that had taken place in the aftermath of the 2008 harmonised elections. They are also a recognition, albeit a destructive one, that democratic transition is underway in local government, hence the need to watch over the developments and possibly contain them. Anecdotal data from MDC-controlled councils is that the appointed councillors are perceived as having been deployed to spy on behalf of the Minister of Local Government, protect the interests of ZANU-PF and, to a large extent, make MDC-controlled councils ungovernable. Coordination between the parent ministry and MDC-controlled councils becomes difficult given the perception that part of the minister's agenda is to make the MDC councils fail through the actions of the appointed councillors.

One case that demonstrates that local democracy can function, and that transitions do take place effectively when citizens are permitted to exercise their rights, is that of the Bulawayo city council resident, Billy Ncube, who challenged in the High Court the Minister of Local Government's right to appoint special interest councillors for the city council (Dube, 2008). In his High Court application of 24 September 2008, Ncube argued that the minister had abused provisions of the Urban Councils Act to avert democratic transition by attempting to bring into council ZANU-PF candidates who had lost their seats in the elections (Ibid). In January 2011, more than two years after initial appointment, these special interest councillors still had not assumed office as the case was still being heard, a clear indication that civil society has an influential role in local decision-making and evidence that local government is a distinct sphere of government that is democratising and worth defending against the change-resistant central elements.

Local authorities would be more effective instruments of democracy and promote democratic transition if the Minister of Local Government had no prerogative to appoint special interest councillors. In the event of a need to appoint special interest councillors, the interest groups themselves should nominate candidates to be approved by a neutral organ such as a multiparty parliamentary portfolio committee and not a partisan minister.

Despite the numerous ministerial interventions, local authorities in Zimbabwe are manned by policy-makers duly elected by the people. In that regard, local authorities are effective agents for democratic transition.

Women as drivers of transition in local government

Most of the services provided by local authorities affect women in specific ways (Sachikonye et al., 2007:99). Given the patriarchal nature of Zimbabwean society, women are responsible for securing water for domestic use and often have to walk long distances to fetch water whenever the local authority fails to provide it. Similarly, women are responsible for the disposal of domestic waste and have to find means doing so if this is not provided by the local authority. Waste disposal poses particular challenges in urban areas, where facilities and scope for recycling are limited. Deficits in service delivery – whether of water, healthcare or education – result in women having even less time to invest in civic duties as they battle to secure for their households the essential services the local authorities fail to provide. It is therefore imperative that women hold positions of decision-making in local government in order to influence the allocation of resources in a manner that takes into account women's social and domestic obligations. Evidence from recent elections indicates that though women constitute more than 50 per cent of the population, they remain underrepresented in both the executive and the legislative arms of local authorities. There were only 53 elected women out of 389 urban councillors after the 2008 harmonised elections (Chakaipa, 2010:62). Genuine democratic transition must see a far greater involvement of women in civic organisations and national and local politics. Any national or local authority or governance structure that fails to take into account the interests of half of its population cannot be considered truly democratic.

Conclusion

Liberal democratic institutions and culture are necessary for effective democratic transition. Despite the fact that the fairness of the processes and outcomes has been invariably disputed by the 'losing' contestants, Zimbabwe has had regular scheduled local government elections, thereby providing a theoretical opportunity for a constitutional transition. Though the duly elected councillors had difficulty assuming office after the 2008 general elections, save for the 16 councillors dismissed by the Minister of Local Government all elected councillors have been able to assume office as mandated by the electorate. A democratic transition is therefore taking place at local government level, particularly as ZANU-PF failed to retain control of all the urban councils at the last elections. The government has interrupted the democratic transition through the (ab)use of the clause permitting the appointment of special interests councillors in order to dilute the influence of the MDC-controlled councils and further the interests of ZANU-PF. The Minister of Local Government has frequently resorted to suspending and dismissing elected councillors, and in a way that abrogates the wishes of the electorate and undermines the democratic transition processes.

For democratic transition to take place effectively, Zimbabwe needs to create an enabling legislative framework by enshrining local government in the Constitution and removing most of the minister's powers to suspend councillors and unduly interfere with the operations of legitimately elected councils. The appointment of special interest councillors should, if necessary, be approved by a neutral multi-party parliamentary committee.

Notes

1 The Minister of Local Government, Ignatius Chombo, however, routinely disrupts this democratic transition through various measures, chief among them being the specific appointment of approximately 25 per cent of all councillors to represent 'special interests' and his prerogative to dismiss elected councillors for minor transgressions.

2 Chimurenga is a derived from '*murenga*'. The first liberation war was 'precipitated, inspired and directed' by Murenga, the great high spirit of the Shona religion, in the 1890s in a bid to liberate the country from European colonisers (Chigwedere, 1991:3). The 1966–1979 war of liberation in Zimbabwe drew inspiration from and was considered a continuation of the earlier Chimurenga, hence it became known as the Second Chimurenga. The repossession of white-owned farmland from 2000 was characterised as the third and final Chimurenga.

3 'Headman' is an official title, but Shona tradition dictates that males should occupy the office of traditional leadership.

4 Statutory Instrument 94 of 2010 was issued in May 2010 as a response to the September 2008 challenge made in the High Court application by Billy Ncube of Bulawayo. The High Court application argued among other issues that the Minister of Local Government had not enacted the relevant Statutory Instrument to enable the appointment of special interest councillors. The appointments of councillors representing special interests had initially been done in July 2008 on the basis of a circular letter from the Minister of Local Government and hence appointed councillors in all other local authorities except Bulawayo assumed duty at the same time as elected councillors.

5 Section 4(A)(2) of the Urban Councils Act.

References

Chakaipa, S. 2010. 'Local Government Institutions and Elections', in J. de Visser, N. Steytler and N. Machingauta. 2010. *Local Government Reform in Zimbabwe, A policy dialogue.* Bellville, South Africa: Community Law Centre, pp. 31-70.

Chatiza, K. 2010. 'Can Local Government Steer Socio-economic Transformation in Zimbabwe? Analysing historical trends and gazing into the future', in J. de Visser, N. Steytler and N. Machingauta. 2010. *Local Government Reform in Zimbabwe, A policy dialogue.* Bellville, South Africa: Community Law Centre, pp. 1-30.

Chigwedere, A. 1991. *The Forgotten Heroes of Chimurenga I: Archives Speak*. Harare: Mercury.

Commonwealth Local Government Forum (CLGF). 2005. *Time for Local Democracy, The Aberdeen Agenda: Commonwealth Principles on Good Practice for Local Democracy and Good Governance*. London: The Commonwealth Local Government Forum.

de Visser, J., N. Steytler and N. Machingauta. 2010. *Local Government Reform in Zimbabwe, A policy dialogue*. Bellville, South Africa: Community Law Centre, pp. 31-70.

Dube, L. 2008. 'MDC official challenges Chombo appointments', *Zimbabwe Independent*, 25 September.

Government of Zimbabwe (GoZ). 1984. Provincial Councils and Administration Act. Harare: Government Printer.

— 1996. Rural District Councils Act, Chapter 29:13, Revised edition. Harare: Government Printer.

— 1996. Urban Councils Act Chapter 29:15. Revised edition. Harare: Government Printer.

— 2005. Constitution of Zimbabwe Amendment. No. 17. Act 2005. Harare: Government Printer.

— 2010. Statutory Instrument 94 of 2010. Local Government. Special Interest Appointed Councillors. Amendment. Notice, 2010. Harare: Government Printer.

Hodder-Williams, R. c.1983. *Conflict in Zimbabwe: The Matebeleland Problem*. London: Institute for the Study of Conflict.

Ismail, N., S. Bayat and I. Meyer. 1997. *Local Government Management*. Johannesburg: International Thomson Publishing.

Linington, G. 2001. *Constitutional Law of Zimbabwe*. Harare: Legal Resources Foundation.

Local Government Board. 1998. *First Report of the Local Government Board covering period 15 May 1996 to 25 September 1998*. Harare: Local Government Board.

Makumbe, J. 2010. 'Local Authorities and Traditional Leadership', in J. de Visser, N. Steytler and N. Machingauta. 2010. *Local Government Reform in Zimbabwe; A policy dialogue*. Bellville, Cape Town: Community Law Centre, pp. 87-100.

Martin, G. 1993. 'Preface: Democratic transition in Africa', *A Journal of Opinion*, 21. 1/2, pp. 6-7.

Musekiwa, N. 2010. '"State Failure" in Provision of Education and Health Services in Zimbabwe: Adjustments, adaptations and evolving coping strategies of rural communities, 2000 –2007'. Unpublished PhD thesis, University of Cape Town.

Nyambara, P.S. 2001. 'Immigrants, "Traditional" Leaders and the Rhodesian State: the Power of "Communal" Land Tenure and the Politics of Land Acquisition in Gokwe, Zimbabwe, 1963–1979', *Journal of Southern African Studies*, 27. 4, pp. 771-91.

Nyazema G. and S. Gama. 2011. 'Councillors unite to fight political meddling', *Daily News* (Zimbabwe), 20 January.

Rutherford, B. 2001. *Working on the Margins: Black Workers, White Farmers in Post-Colonial Zimbabwe*. Harare: Weaver Press.

Sachikonye, L., S. Chawatama, C. Mangongera, N. Musekiwa and C. Ndoro. 2007. *Consolidating Democratic Governance in Southern Africa: Zimbabwe*. EISA Research Report No. 30. Johannesburg: Electoral Institute of Southern Africa.

Schedler, A. 1998. 'What is democratic consolidation?', *Journal of Democracy*, 9. 2, pp. 91-107.

Vosloo, W.B. 1974. 'Introduction', in W.B. Vosloo, D.A. Kotze and W.J. Jeppe. 1974. *Local Government in Southern Africa*. Pretoria, Cape Town: Academica, pp. 9-12.

10

Youth in Zimbabwe – A Lost Generation

Mary Ndlovu

With exuberance we saluted them as the born frees, those lucky ones born after 18 April 1980. They would never have to live as colonised subjects. Countless opportunities would open up in front of them, and they would simply have to pluck the fruit that had so long been denied to the majority of black Zimbabweans. Access to education would provide them with a ticket to employment, rising incomes and improved standards of living for the whole family, and ultimately the nation. Together with their parents and their elder siblings, they would build a future of prosperity that would validate the bitter sacrifices of the struggle for independence.

Now, more than 30 years on, the oldest of the born frees should be fully adult, no longer even youths. They might have expected to have concluded their education, settled into stable employment or set up small businesses, or be gradually taking over the heavy work and responsibilities of agriculture from their elders; they could be planning marriage if they are not already married, and raising children with confidence. But this is the privileged position of a minority. For the majority, the reality is very different.

Who are the youth and what is their problem?
Let us consider for a moment those Zimbabweans born between 1980 and 1995 – those now aged 16 to 31. We will call them the youth of today.[1] While the vast majority attended primary school long enough

to become literate – probably more than 80 per cent[2] – fewer than 40 per cent completed secondary school[3] and at most only six to seven per cent of them gained the basic qualifications to secure further training and thus employment.[4] And even for those who did gain a full O-level certificate, i.e. five passes, their qualifications did not lead them to satisfactory jobs. Instead, our young people – both with and without O-levels – hawk air-time on street corners, cross borders in tens of thousands to do almost anything to survive in neighbouring countries, turning deals with the expertise of hardened criminals or, worst of all, are transformed into brutal torture machines in the service of an aging president.

What happened? Why can our young people not succeed with the education they have been given? Why can they not find jobs or generate sufficient income through self-employment? Why do they prefer to confront the risks of illegal emigration rather than remain in their native country? And what of the consequences for them and for Zimbabwe? What can be done to rescue this situation?

The problem is not unique to Zimbabwe; it typifies the position of youth in much of Africa and, more recently, in many nations of the developed world. However, while globalisation and technological and social changes underlie a shared dilemma, the difficulties facing Zimbabwean youth have particular characteristics that need to be understood in the national context if any viable local solution is to be found.

We might also define youth as those young people who are in transition from dependent childhood to self-sustaining adulthood.[5] In order to achieve this transition satisfactorily multiple factors must come together, of which we will focus on three only: the need for an appropriate education, the need for access to employment or some form of income-generation and the need for socialisation by adults into a moral order. In Zimbabwe, there have been failures in all of these three areas, with the biggest problem being a misfit between the first and the second: education has not been adequate to prepare youth for achieving economic independence and the economy has not provided sufficient employment opportunities. When we add to that a lack of appropriate socialisation, particularly in recent years, the outcome for many youth has been devastating.

In this chapter we will look primarily at the inadequacies in educational policy in relation to the performance of the economy and the consequences for the youth. We will also mention more briefly the economic failures and the perversion of the legal and political systems that have been described and analysed at length in many other publications.[6] We will also touch on the failure of appropriate socialisation of youth.

Post-independence developments in education

We can trace much of the problem back to policy failures in the period immediately after independence. The new government faced many dilemmas of transition from an economy geared for the benefit of a racial minority to an economy that would work to benefit everyone. Expectations had been raised as African majority rule was achieved, and promises had been made throughout the liberation struggle, particularly regarding educational opportunities. Realising those promises, however, would not be easy. The relationship between economic development and education is a delicate one and requires a careful balancing act. Although education costs money, it can also generate economic growth if its content is appropriate and its implementation efficient. Too much money invested in education can become a serious drain on the economy, monopolising the state budget and depriving it of the investment inputs to drive development. Too little investment in education can also act as a drag on the economy if insufficient skilled manpower is trained. Thus planning in the two areas must go hand in hand.

Expansion

In 1980 ZANU-PF was in a hurry. There were strong pressures on government to move rapidly to deliver on the promise of their election manifesto to provide free and compulsory primary and secondary education for all children, regardless of race. Rhodesian education had been strictly segregated, with gross imbalances in the provision of schooling for children of different races. Schooling was not compulsory for blacks, nor was it free. Although most black children did attend primary school, of those who reached Grade 7 approximately 80 per cent were forced to end their education at that point because policy dictated that only a minority of educated Africans were required.

Those who proceeded to secondary school were streamed either to academic mission schools (there were some government schools, especially in urban areas) or to vocational schools to learn a trade such as building, brick-laying, dress-making or commercial studies. A second selection process took place after two years, when many were weeded out of the system. White children proceeded to comprehensive high schools, where there were both academic and non-academic commercial streams, or to separate technical high schools. Yet even there, the vocational and technical aspects of education were underdeveloped, since the Rhodesian government had saved expenses by relying on immigrants for skilled labour.[7] Although the achievements of African education were not negligible, they were nevertheless discriminatory, highly unequal, excluded the vast majority from the opportunity to pursue employment other than manual labour and were thoroughly resented by the black majority. One of the many attractions for those teenagers who left home to join the liberation struggle, was the possibility of achieving an education which would be denied at home. In addition, one of the promises of the war was that in a free Zimbabwe racial differences would be eliminated and everyone would have the opportunity to go to school.

Thus a purely political decision was taken, and early in the third school term of 1980 the Ministry of Education announced that as of January 1981 not only would all children in Grade 7 be able to progress to secondary school, they would also be able to do so for free. However, it appears that the ministry had done little to project cost estimates or indeed any other consequences of this decision prior to it being announced. In fact, the new government was in such a hurry that it could not wait for the conclusion of the National Manpower Survey or for the Transitional National Development Plan, the results of which were released in 1981 and 1982 respectively. The injudicious haste with which the government proceeded to embark upon an unprecedented expansion of the education system, without coordinating it with other aspects of economic development, created innumerable problems and ultimately ensured that education would not serve economic development but rather become a heavy drag on it. Instead of taking an incremental approach that could have concentrated on ensuring quality primary education for all, gradually widening the scope of secondary education, government chose to take a quantum leap and divorce the expansion of education from economic and budgetary realities.

The designers of education policy after independence were driven by two complementary compulsions: to correct the racial inequalities of the colonial period and to use education to build socialism. Although their policy statements[8] demonstrated that they clearly understood the need to calibrate education and economic development, the policies they implemented could not, in isolation from overall development plans, take a holistic perspective on education as part of the development process, as an integral component of building an economy. Neither did they apparently plan for the social consequences that would result from a massive expansion in the education sector.

The 1980 resolution to provide free secondary education to everyone went alongside the decision to make primary schooling available to all and to make it free. No more fees – government would provide. Following on from these decisions were several inevitabilities. The most obvious were mammoth programmes to build schools and provide teachers to cope with the doubling of primary school enrolments and a multiplication of secondary school places by a factor of six within the space of six or seven years. With the population growing at a rate of more than three per cent at that time, that meant that the expansion would not come to a stop, it would only slow down after sufficient schools were built and staffed.

In January 1981 there were no new schools, and no new teachers, but there were many new enrolments, as those children who had been out of the country in refugee camps returned home and those who had been out of school looked for Grade 1 places. A makeshift arrangement added classes for Form 1 to existing primary schools, giving them the name 'upper tops'. Teachers were to be drawn from the corpus of primary teachers or from Form 4s who had failed to secure a certificate. The spirit of the refugee camps dictated that some schooling was better than nothing, and 'making do' would be the motto. New training colleges were opened and the old ones expanded and new teacher-training programmes introduced in which students would spend most of their time teaching and only two terms out of four years in lectures (the Zimbabwe Integrated Teacher Education Course or ZINTEC). In that way thousands of new teachers could be produced to staff the new schools and new classrooms. Meanwhile, the construction of secondary schools, mostly in rural areas but also in towns and cities, rushed ahead. By 1983 the number of secondary schools had quadrupled from 197 to 790.[9] By 1989 there were nearly 700,000 children attending secondary school and 2.2 million primary school – an unsustainable number in a population of approximately ten million.[10] They were served by 58,000 primary school teachers and 24,524 secondary school teachers, of whom only 32,000 were fully trained and 7,500 partly trained.[11]

Curriculum change

Alongside the massive expansion programme went changes in curriculum. Just as everyone was to have equal access to education, everyone was to have the same education. The division between academic (F1) secondary schools and vocational (F2) secondary schools for Africans was to be terminated. Vocational schools would be eliminated and all children would follow an academic curriculum, usually with one 'practical' subject appended. They would be given four years only to complete the O-level syllabus – a syllabus designed for the top 20 per cent in British schools.[12] This was a major, critical and ultimately disastrous decision for Zimbabwean education and for Zimbabwean youth. The feeling was widespread that F2 schools were inferior and designed specifically for Africans (which was true) and thus should be abolished. However, those involved in education knew that most children would not be able to manage the O-level curriculum. If F2 schools were to go, then something non-academic should replace them. Nevertheless, those who understood this point gave in to the political pressure to do what was popular rather than what was realistic. Now all children were to take O-levels, including pure science and pure mathematics, and if they failed them, there was no other educational option open to them but to repeat and try again.

This approach to curriculum design originated from the deep resentment towards Rhodesia's racially segregated education, hence the desire to promote racial equality and the socialist idea that differentiated education would inevitably reinforce class inequalities. It was understandable, but it missed two very important points. First, children may all be equal in human value and in the rights they hold, but they are not all endowed with the same capacities, nor do they begin at the same starting line. If a physically fit child with a tennis racquet and a malnourished child without one are given equal opportunity to play tennis, it is obvious what will happen. Second, children offered the same curriculum will not all perform in the same way. Equal opportunity for people who are not equal will not create equality; it will still entrench inequalities. Children unsuited to an academic education, and many of those who were simply facing too many obstacles in their social environment to succeed,[13] were being set up for failure. Furthermore, and equally important, no country can absorb entire cohorts of academically trained youth into white collar jobs to which such an education was originally intended to lead.

Crucially, the academic curriculum led nowhere for most children. If they failed, they came out of school without any skill; if they passed, they could generally proceed to tertiary education or specific training. However, this worked only until 1984, when the first few cohorts of automatic transition from primary school reached the end of secondary school, by which time there were 71,000 school-leavers,[14] most having no O-level certificates, and the numbers would escalate exponentially over the years. By 1990 there were 140,000 leaving at Form 4 level – many more, if drop-outs from lower down the system were included.[15] Only a small proportion could be accommodated in tertiary education – possibly 20,000 at most. What would the rest do in an economy that was creating only 28,000 jobs a year (and by the 1990s was actually losing jobs)?[16]

Quality

Rapid expansion also had significant and long-lasting implications for the quality of the education provided. While one may discount the poor facilities initially used for secondary school pupils (many schools were still being constructed), the importance of having trained teachers cannot be overlooked. By the end of the 1980s still only half of the teachers at both primary and secondary levels were trained. As the new training colleges and programmes came on stream this figure was gradually reduced. Initially, however, their entry requirements had to be lowered in order to attract candidates, many of whom only had O-level certificates. If this gave an opportunity to school leavers with limited qualifications within approximately five years, as more teachers were trained, it became difficult to qualify for entry to a teacher-training college without an A-level certificate. Nonetheless, although it might seem that standards were slowly being raised in this process, lecturers for the training colleges were recruited from among practising teachers – many of whom were not adequately qualified to train teachers – thus reducing the standards of training and creating a domino effect throughout the system. Accordingly, it was inevitable that standards within the schools would fall.

The automatic progression from Grade 7 was soon extended to every grade – every child would move up at the end of the year, whether or not they had achieved the required standard. This was done in the name of equality – everyone is now equal so no one gets extra chances – and in the name of economy – extra years means extra expense. Unsurprisingly, this impacted negatively on the quality as well as the efficiency of education. It no longer mattered for the teacher or for the children if large numbers failed the end-of-year tests, as there was no immediately visible consequence. Some children who failed to grasp the essentials in early years were simply pushed up from one grade to the next, arriving at secondary school barely able to read, let alone perform in other subjects. The inevitable outcome followed – very low pass rates. Sadly, this meant an unforgiveable waste of money, paying teachers to teach children who could not learn at the level they were being taught. We could take an example of a child who enters Grade 1 at the age of five. She is somewhat immature and finds it difficult to learn to read and/or perhaps the teacher is untrained and has problems handling small children. Nevertheless, she proceeds to Grade 2, where the Grade 2 teacher is also inexperienced, resulting in this child (and others like her) falling further behind. By Grade 3, even an experienced teacher would find it difficult to help such children to catch up. By the time they are in Form One they are perhaps only functioning at Grade 4 level, educationally at sea and having lost interest. Had they been allowed to repeat their first year they could well have been rescued. Multiply this case by tens of thousands and the human and economic costs are completely unacceptable. Even those children in Grade 7 who manage to keep up but are not really academically inclined and then find themselves confronted with academic subjects in Form One will struggle to cope. If they fail, they have no option but to go up a form, becoming more and more discouraged in the process. Even if they do not drop out, which many of course did, they will have wasted everyone's time and money and gained a sense of themselves as incapable and failures.

These problems might have been avoided by retaining vocational curricula for those whose strengths were non-academic in nature, and by allowing slower learners to repeat at crucial points. However, with both of these solutions considered against the principle of equality, they were unacceptable. Besides which, allowing repeats would increase expenses as would a vocationalisation of the curriculum.

Education and the economy

Alongside this wastefulness was the relationship between education and the economy, one which caused the biggest problem. While the preponderance of untrained teachers gradually declined over the years, education was becoming a heavy drain on government finances. Despite the fact that there was considerable input from foreign aid donors, especially governments and UN agencies,[17] the costs of building schools, paying teachers, providing teaching materials, sustaining administration and training teachers proved prohibitive. The economy was not growing – in fact in 1982 and 1983 it actually contracted.[18]

By the mid-80s the situation was becoming unsustainable. There was insufficient revenue to support the amount of expenditure needed to continue the expansion and improvement of education, especially secondary education, and there was no gainful employment available to the hundreds of thousands who were flooding out of the schools by the 1990s. The economy had remained sluggish throughout the decade, growing on average at approximately two per cent per annum against a population growth rate of over three per cent. New jobs were certainly not being created for all these school leavers.

Much has been made of the importance of extending basic education to the majority in order to promote economic growth and development as well as gender equity. Educated young girls are inclined to reduce the number of children they will bear and provide better nutrition and care for those they do raise, leading to higher life expectancies and higher levels of productivity.[19] However, the key factor in determining whether the education of rural youth leads to economic development is whether that education contributes toward improved productivity in the rural context, particularly in relation to agriculture, especially when formal sector employment opportunities are not expanding.

Instead of improving it, universal secondary education was in fact having a devastating effect on the rural economy and society. A prodigious effort was made to follow the policy that every child should be able to walk to a secondary school, with the vast majority of new secondary schools having been built in rural areas. In the end, it proved impossible. Many walked up to ten kilometres each way, thus reducing the effectiveness of their time in the classroom, as fatigue would set in. Others decided to camp at their schools during the week, creating informal hostels that were unsupervised by adults and became social disaster areas. Very few of those children benefited from this kind of arrangement and most dropped out before completing, let alone passing and obtaining a certificate.

Most black children who had gone to secondary school before independence had attended mission-run boarding schools. There was a widespread understanding that admission to secondary school implied that one was exiting rural life, that after finishing school one would find a place in the city, either in employment or in further education. It was almost unthinkable for a secondary school graduate to return to life in the village. Those who did not go to secondary school remained at home, assisting with the tasks of subsistence farming and/or domestic life. But what if everyone went to school? Who would help the older generation in the fields? Who would dip the cattle, chase birds off the crops, fetch firewood and help with the harvest? For secondary schoolchildren, only Saturday and Sunday and the school holidays were open for them to help. A significant source of labour was lost to most households. But even when these children finished without passing a single subject, they did not return to the previous pattern – something in their position had changed. Having attended secondary school they felt they no longer belonged in the village, and the academic curriculum they had been offered reinforced this view. They no longer needed to accept the authority of a parent or uncle or grandfather who had never been to school or who only went to primary school. Never mind that they had learned little, and had perhaps passed one or two subjects at most; they needed to go to town to look for a job – a job that was not there.

Inequity and inefficiency

Thus the 1980s ended with a huge expansion in secondary education, but at considerable cost in terms of quality of learning and inefficient utilisation of a substantial portion of the state budget. Furthermore, inequalities persisted as the burdens borne by rural parents outweighed those of urban parents and the quality of education that was offered was lower. In spite of automatic progression, in fact nearly 25 per cent of children dropped out before completing primary school,[20] and this trend, established in the 80s, continued more or less constantly until the 2000s, when the figures began to deteriorate further. Of those who did complete, just over two thirds proceeded to secondary school.[21]

That meant that about 50 per cent of any age cohort entered secondary school, but by the time they reached the end of secondary school, one quarter of them had abandoned schooling,[22] meaning that only slightly more than one third of those entering Grade 1 reached Form 4. The majority of these youth had been taught by untrained teachers for at least a substantial portion of their time at school. The initial cohorts to reach Form 4 performed relatively poorly, with pass rates in 1986 at 11.4 per cent,[23] and as more and more rural schools came on stream O-level pass rates dropped shockingly. In the mid-90s it was being reported that of those students writing five papers, only 1.3 per cent passed them all.[24] Although the pass rate increased according to the number of papers written, the numbers passing five subjects never reached beyond 15 per cent, which translates to five to six per cent of an age cohort.

The greatest effect of drop-outs and low pass rates was felt in rural areas. National averages disguised the fact that in urban areas drop-outs were far fewer and that greater proportions of pupils passed their exams. The results of SACMEQ[25] regional standardisation tests at Grade 6 level in 2007 revealed the stark inequalities between rural and urban schools. Pupils in the Bulawayo and Harare areas were scoring as high as the best countries in the SADC region, while those from rural districts averaged just above the countries scoring lowest in the region.[26] Rural schools, primary and secondary, had fewer qualified teachers and fewer teaching resources of all kinds, including classroom furniture, and rural parents were expected to contribute more in terms of labour for construction.

In the 1980s, hundreds of thousands of young people left school without a single qualification, without a skill, without any interest in raising the levels of rural productivity, and with no prospect of satisfactory employment. Of course, some did manage to secure O-levels after repeating at the private colleges which sprang up in towns to cater for this demand, while others were absorbed into family businesses or secured manual or clerical employment, but the great majority of these were in urban areas, widening the gap between the experience of rural and urban youth. Certainly, an enormous gulf had developed between the capacities and expectations of young people and the ability of the national economy to provide them with gainful occupation. The results were low self-esteem, the inability to work at home or in town, the failure to set realistic goals, depression, sometimes emigration and often entry into a life of petty crime, illegal activities, alcohol and drugs. Rural youth in particular had lost their centre of gravity, alienated from the life they might have expected but not suited for anything else – either to changing the nature of rural productivity or to employment or self-employment. Such signs were already very clear by the end of the 1980s and have continued up to the present.

The government's response

The government was certainly not oblivious to these problems as they unfolded. Their genuine wish to create equal opportunity had, however, led to a dead-end situation for many youth and a negative impact on the economy. There were of course those who had cautioned against rapid expansion in the first place, but political considerations had prevailed. Regarding the curriculum, ZANU-PF's policy statements continued to insist that vocational education should eventually be integrated with academic studies. However, the implementation was relegated to pilot or experimental schemes. The most prominent was under ZIMFEP – the Zimbabwe Foundation for Education with Production – for schools that were directly descended from the refugee schools in Mozambique and Zambia. The foundation attempted to integrate technical and academic learning and combine it with productive activity and it specifically assisted with employment or self-employment of the young people after they left school. Part of ZIMFEP's contribution to educational progress was the development of appropriate syllabuses in technical subjects. However, with only 12 schools in the whole country, and only minimal success on the job creation side, this project had little influence on the wider picture. Similarly, an attempt to introduce a vocational curriculum in 1987 foundered on lack of finance and resistance from parents who still hoped for white-collar jobs for their children.[27] The vocational thrust fizzled out into an attempt to give practical subjects more emphasis. The socialist dream for an integrated polytechnic education, like so many other socialist dreams, faded. And without further development of a curriculum that would teach entrepreneurial skills and business arithmetic rather than pure maths and other academic subjects, and without the provision of low-level credit to school-leavers to help them establish small businesses or invest in technologies to improve rural agriculture, little progress would be made.

The origins of the problems of today's youth can be traced, then, to these decisions taken in the excitement of independence, when politics triumphed over careful planning and economic common sense. Those policies created an army of poorly educated young people with no skills and low self-esteem due to their exam failures and who were unprepared for life, rural or urban. If there were no jobs for these young people to find in towns, they should have been prepared for a more productive and more satisfying life in the rural areas. Or at least the expansion should have been more gradual, allowing the outputs of the education system to contribute to a growing economy rather than becoming a weight on it. But once the pattern was set it became politically impossible to reverse, as the government itself acknowledged in 1985 when the Prime Minister had to quickly counter an announcement made by the Ministry of Education that selection would be re-introduced for children entering Form 1 from the following year.[28]

Politics had been at the root of the post-independence restructuring of education, and politics would prevent government from backtracking. Education, at least judging solely by numbers, was a miraculous achievement rightly praised by many. Certainly, politicians could not go back on their promises to the people.[29] Rather than admit publicly the serious problems that had arisen, the inequalities, the inefficiencies, the serious mismatch between education and economic realities, government, quite understandably, and as all governments do, chose to emphasise the positives and ignore the negatives. And so was born the myth of education as a great success story. Statistics of growth in enrolment figures, of numbers of schools, of production of qualified teachers were impressive and were constantly reiterated. Extremely favourable comparisons were made with other SADC countries, especially in terms of participation rates, pupil–teacher ratios and progression to secondary education.[30] Conveniently, the inefficiencies, the huge gap between rural and urban educational provision, the unacceptably high drop-out rates and the extremely low pass rates at O-level were left out of most government information. Statistics could also be selected in a way that told only part of the story; pass rates at O-level were always given as percentages of those writing, which is fair enough, but what was rarely mentioned was that only just over a third of any given age cohort was sitting such exams. While the 'school-leaver problem' was frequently discussed by critics, no realistic solutions were presented or implemented, either in terms of educational change or employment opportunities.

Thus, during the first decade of independence the pattern was set for a national failure in fulfilling the responsibilities towards youth. Whilst education was offered to the vast majority, it was an inappropriate one; the mismatch between education and the economy meant that the means of securing employment or generating an income was available only to a small proportion of youth, and finally, the socialisation of youth, particularly rural youth, began to falter as they were growing up with unrealisable expectations fuelled both by their optimistic parents and unrealistic government programmes.

Retreat under ESAP

And yet government was soon forced into a partial retreat by economic realities. The generation of revenues from the economy had not kept pace with the enormous expenditure demands of free schooling and healthcare. Government could not cover its deficits in the domestic budget or in foreign exchange flows. As a result, it was forced to accept an IMF structural adjustment programme of 'cost recovery'.

One of the prices of support from international financial institutions was to introduce user fees for social services. In other words, parents would have to make a contribution to cover the ever-expanding costs of education. School fees were introduced in urban primary schools that had hitherto been free, although a welfare net ensured that most of those who could not pay would have their fees paid through a social dimensions fund, hence the numbers of children in school in the 90s did not decline. Education costs continued to increase as untrained teachers were gradually replaced by trained teachers, with the figure of 100 per cent trained teachers all but reached by the end of the decade. Less money was made available for building and resourcing schools, so although better teaching could be expected, learning resources were depleted as the annual per capita grant to schools was eroded by the inflation which took hold and lasted through the decade.

The introduction of fees was the major substantive change to education policy in the 1990s, but it had little effect on the system itself, and even less on the inappropriate preparation of young people for participation in the economy. Percentages of children in school dropped slightly, but with population still increasing, absolute numbers did not decline, and inexorably the accumulated totals of unoccupied school-leavers reached into the millions. Annually, tens and eventually hundreds of thousands of children walked out of the school doors after up to 11 years of automatic advancement from one year to the next, without having had to achieve any standard of performance at all.

Despite the problem of semi-educated and unemployable youth that was already evident in the 1980s, nothing was done to change the academic curriculum, to provide pupils with any type of trade or skills-based training while in school, or to provide such training for those who had left school. The ongoing political imperatives continued to frustrate those who pushed for substantive change in the curriculum, the reality being that any kind of vocationalisation would not only be unpopular with some but would also be prohibitively expensive – as indeed would any major adjustments requiring the retraining of teachers and the purchase of vast amounts of equipment and materials. The system which had been built was a colossus, and once established, any significant change would require a prodigious effort as well as massive financing. So nothing meaningful was done.

The vast pool of youth grew by a gradually increasing number each year, aggravated by the fact that structural adjustment was a spectacular failure in terms of stimulating economic growth. Throughout the decade the economy contracted steadily; from 1991–96, economic growth had slipped to an annual average of 1.8 per cent and employment growth rates to 0.7 per cent against a population growth rate calculated at just over three per cent,[31] meaning that the problem of joblessness began to extend even to those who had completed tertiary education. Those millions who had left school without a single O-level certificate were now having to compete with university and college graduates. The trickle of emigration of the youth to South Africa and Botswana – which had begun as early as the 1980s, before the end of apartheid – began to pick up. Other youths were seeking survival and occasional windfalls by digging for gold in various parts of the country, still others began cross-border trading or petty trading on street corners. Only those with comparatively affluent parents could afford the journey overseas to seek their fortunes in Europe, North America or Australia.

By the late 90s, the education system had passed its peak of development and, under-resourced due to the declining economy and the constraints of structural adjustment, lost quality at a faster rate even with trained and experienced teachers found in most classrooms. Considerable numbers of parents no longer found it worthwhile or possible to find the money for school fees, especially for secondary schooling, when the investment appeared to bring so little return. Worse, net enrolments[32] in primary schools dropped from 86 per cent in 1990/91 to 83 per cent in 2001/2002[33] and in secondary to 40 per cent.

Warning voices about the catastrophe facing youth became so loud that the President finally acted and in 1998 he appointed a presidential commission to look into the problems of education and make recommendations. The resulting Nziramasanga Report was highly critical of almost every aspect of the education system. Key among its recommendations was that the secondary school system should be vocationalised, with a three-path approach adopted to allow children after Form 2 to follow academic, technical or commercial streams. Primary school syllabuses also needed to be made more functional and entrepreneurship needed to be introduced very early to assist those who would leave school without any chance of formal employment. The report also pointed to declining moral leadership on the part of teachers and a lack of discipline and focus by pupils. It recommended that civic education and guidance and counselling be incorporated into school programmes and curricula and greater administrative attention be paid to disciplining teachers who were setting a poor example for pupils.[34]

The recommendations were educationally and socially sound, but of course they would require finances that were at the time certainly unavailable, not to mention the political will, which was definitely lacking. The truth was that the contents of the report reflected very badly on the political and administrative leadership of the Ministry of Education. As a result, the report was simply hidden from the public and discussed nowhere other than within the ministry itself. Lip service was paid to some of its recommendations, but no major changes were made to the education system, and thus no improvements in the prospects for youth could be expected.

The future for the vast majority of Zimbabweans who had left school during the 1990s was thus very bleak. Without any sense of direction of where their future lay or of any realistic goals, they were left blowing in the wind, looking for any opportunity which might come their way. Their adult mentors often could not guide them, themselves at a loss after their hopes for their children had been dashed. The pattern set post-independence continued, with none of the needs of youth which could take them confidently into adulthood satisfied.

Disaster in the new millennium

If the situation at the end of the 1990s was abysmal, what was to follow was many times worse. As the deteriorating economic situation threatened its power position, ZANU-PF threw all caution to the wind. For the next decade politics and the need to remain in power would be given priority over any considerations of economic performance or the genuine needs of Zimbabwe's youth. With the beginning of the officially sanctioned land invasions in February 2000, the government began a wholesale onslaught on commercial agriculture, the most significant sector of the economy, destroying the productive employment of hundreds of thousands of farm workers, not to mention the farms themselves, in the process eliminating a major source of government revenue. This was followed in 2005 by an attack on the informal sector – petty trading, illegal small mining, small manufacturing enterprises, even housing – to which so many of the unemployed, youth as well as others, had retreated to eke out a meagre income. Soon after that came an unprecedented assault on the formal retail trading sector. Until 2008, the process was accompanied by the manipulation of the currency to create hyperinflation on a scale hardly known anywhere in the world and was punctuated by violent elections and subversion of the rule of law designed to prevent the political opposition, the MDC, from wresting power from ZANU-PF.

The wholesale dismantling of the productive economy brought the nation to its knees. What effect did it have on the youth still struggling to gain an education and become economically engaged? Of course, the first effect was to shrink the economy even further, so that even many of those who did have jobs lost them, particularly in agriculture and manufacturing. With the continued harassment of traders, the informal economy could no longer be seen as a viable alternative. No one in government seemed to care about what happened to education: it was further starved of funds, teachers deserted their posts as salaries became worthless and in rural schools they frequently became the targets of violent gangs accusing them of supporting the MDC. All efforts to reform the system were abandoned. By 2003 the percentage of children who had enrolled in Grade 1 and reached Grade 5 had dropped to 70 per cent.[35] By 2005, participation rates in primary school had dropped to 82 per cent and to 34 per cent in secondary schools.[36] Moreover, these figures represent the situation before the substantial collapse between 2007 and the beginning of 2009 when schools became dysfunctional and little learning was taking place.

The social effect on youth was traumatic. It was, indeed, traumatic for the whole nation, as the steady flow of job-seekers to South Africa and Botswana became a rush. Adults temporarily abandoned their families in the hope of being able to earn enough outside to send home to keep them fed. Many young people were either left in the care of neighbours, maids or relatives or simply had to fend for themselves and wait for remittances to arrive. Others left their families to become breadwinners themselves, sending home money and groceries to look after their parents, grandparents and siblings.[37]

The normal situation of young people following in the footsteps of parents from whom they learn appropriate social behaviour was reversed. Adults were following their children into exile, and into the streets to earn a living instead of being their role models. Where was the socialisation, the guidance from their elders that children needed? Displacements during the farm invasions and Operation Murambatsvina uprooted many families, rendering them ultimately confused, disoriented and with no plans for the future other than bare survival. Traumatised adults seeking to adapt could no longer meaningfully advise their children. More than a quarter of children of primary school age and nearly two thirds of those of secondary school age were no longer experiencing the discipline of school life; for those in school, teachers' attention was diverted elsewhere, as they too joined the monthly trek across borders to secure food and add to ever more meaningless salaries through trading. Many children who were still enrolled in school were also supplementing family incomes through petty trading, gold mining and even prostitution, attending school when they could, frequently being chased away when they failed to pay fees on time. Attendance figures diverged widely from recorded enrolments. Churches provided a social and moral haven for some, more than 50 per cent of the population being active churchgoers,[38] but religion could not make up for the absence of direction in the family and the school.

In the midst of this collapse and disorientation came a new and dangerous set of negative moral values demonstrated by members of the ruling elite as they proceeded to manipulate every aspect of public life, not only to serve their continued stay in power, but to appropriate for themselves the little wealth remaining in the country. Greed and self-interest became the driving force of public figures, who projected themselves to the nation with hate speech and intolerance of anyone with differing views, boasting of their achievements and displaying their newly acquired wealth through conspicuous consumption – and trumpeting the supremacy of violence over respect for the rule of law.[39] How could the youth, and in fact the whole of society, fail to be affected by such a display? The head of the fish was rotten, and the rot began to spread to its body, undermining the moral fibre of what had once been a hard-working society.

Everyone was affected by this wholesale deterioration; the defence of necessity led to cheating and deception in order to survive. But the effect on the youth was greater than on their seniors. Adults who had experienced employment and stability may have been disoriented and forced to abandon a settled life for the time being, but at least they had the benefit of having been acquainted with regular work and family life. In contrast, most of the youth had never experienced the discipline of steady employment and had learned habits of survival that included constant changes of direction, opportunism and short-term focus with no thought of the future.[40] At an age when they might have been settling into long-term relationships with future partners many engaged in uncontrolled sexual activities, which reflected only a need for immediate gratification.[41] At an age for establishing and confirming an identity with which they could be satisfied, no such achievement was possible – they would be anything that the situation dictated. For boys, this lack of identity could be more serious than for girls. The girls at least could and did settle into motherhood at a young age – with a high percentage becoming mothers even in their teens.[42] They could then develop a focus to their existence in terms of mothering and trying to provide for their children. Unmarried and unattached, boys took little responsibility for their offspring and could not make them a focus of their existence. The youth were at sea in a world of violence and confusion with no guideposts to direct them along the route to a stable and satisfying life.

Vulnerable as they were, government had still worse in store for some – they could be turned into the unsophisticated shock troops of a violent regime desperate to impose itself on a hostile population. Thus was born the so-called National Youth Service.[43] Billed at its launch in August 2001 as a programme to inculcate 'patriotism' and provide trade and vocational training to youths, it was not contained within the Ministry of Education but within the Ministry of Youth, Gender and Employment Creation, a more politicised ministry purporting to cater for youth. The rapidly established residential training centres quickly became centres for ZANU-PF political indoctrination. They were also militarised, with most instructors either serving or retired army officers or war veterans, and weapons training was included in the programme. Without the appropriate supervision of responsible adults trained in handling young people, many youths became victims of sexual exploitation and brutal treatment. Policy pronouncements changed in regard to this youth programme, so that at times it was said

to be compulsory for all school-leavers, with a certificate of completion required for post-secondary education or jobs in the civil service,
while at others it was said to be voluntary. During election periods
in the early 2000s, there were cases of abduction and kidnapping to
recruit reluctant youths to the centres. It was apparent that few in
government intended to provide a genuine training facility for youth,
and certainly no new employment opportunities were being created to
absorb them. Rather, there came chilling reports of the brutal treatment of these youths at the centres, demonstrating the classic tactic of
the despot – first brutalise those you wish to use to brutalise others.
Youth from these centres then became ripe for recruitment into the
violent ZANU-PF militia, where they were given petty rewards of
small amounts of cash, food, alcohol and drugs for committing violent
acts against white commercial farmers or against what was perceived
as a disloyal electorate.[44] It was a most cynical betrayal of the nation's
young people, seducing them with promises of jobs and money. It is
well known that some of the 'graduates' were eventually squeezed into
the civil service without proper qualifications or any clear public service to perform. And there they remain, drawing salaries that cannot
be justified and utilising funds that are badly needed to assist the
recovery of the economy. Many are permanently tainted, scarred by
their experiences as perpetrators of violence, forever imprisoned in the
clutches of ZANU-PF unless they want their crimes exposed. A small
but significant number, having been induced to commit crimes and
even atrocities with which they could not square their consciences,
escaped into exile.[45] Others fled before they could be forced into the
camps, contributing another strand to the mass exodus. They joined
the hundreds of thousands of other Zimbabwean youth, moving from
piece job to piece job, dependent on charity and bribing police, some
ultimately sinking into crime or prostitution.

Whilst the picture painted above does not of course describe the
plight of all youth, it does reflect the reality for the vast majority.
Having embarked on schooling made available by the expansion of
the 1980s, the youth found that even if they managed to continue to
the end of secondary school they nevertheless emerged ill-equipped to
participate meaningfully in economic activity. Social guidance and the
moral examples they should have gained from the combined effort of
social institutions – family, school, church and political leaders – were

fragmented and inadequate. Political leaders were taking them in the direction of blind obedience and the commission of violent acts for personal gain. None of the prerequisites for young people to transition to responsible adulthood ready to establish and support their own families were present. As a result, a whole generation of youth has been left staring into a dark hole.

Current realities and future possibilities

The formation of the Government of National Unity in 2009 gave hope to many that the nation's nightmare might come to an end and allow young people a chance to create for themselves 'normal' lives. However, while it is possible that the worst may be over, the way back will be long and tortuous. The trek has barely begun and remnants of the decade of chaos and destruction continue to poison Zimbabwean society.

What is the position of the youth today? In addition to the many who completed secondary school with no hope of finding gainful employment, there are now significant numbers of those who left school at a very early age, before they gained functional literacy and numeracy, and many others who may have completed primary school or even secondary school, but in the chaos of the years 2007–2009, which meant that they actually learned very little.[46] Alongside them are those still in South Africa or elsewhere in the region who are now beginning to return home, either forcibly or by choice, given difficult circumstances in exile. Jobs available in the formal sector are even fewer than they were before. There are, however, possibilities in the informal sector again, and some have realised that they can indeed survive at their rural homes if they commit themselves to hard work and can adapt to find new niches. Yet the problem of lack of skills continues, as does the separation of families and loss of direction from elders. The unseemly bickering and greediness of many politicians across the party spectrum continue to set a poor example of responsible adult behaviour, and even some churches have been hijacked or divided by politicians and charlatans. Public morality still has a long road to travel to return to decency, with the state-controlled media bursting with hate speech and outright untruths, ever attempting to brainwash and manipulate people's thinking. Back in their classrooms, many teachers have become the latest abusers of youth, especially in urban areas, punishing children when they fail to pay levies (incentives) that supplement their meagre salaries. The law continues to be flouted by those in power, and violence, threats of violence and spurious arrests are ongoing. Youth are still being used and abused by ruling party militia, deceived into thinking that the use of violence and lawlessness can bring them riches through the indigenisation of established enterprises.

But there are signs of hope. Many youth organisations and programmes have sprung up throughout the country, some run by youth themselves and others functioning as NGOs or supported by churches.[47] Their activities vary widely, but many are engaged in peacebuilding and conflict resolution programmes aimed at giving youth an understanding of how to resolve issues without the use of violence. Some attempt to teach the principles and behaviour of democratic leadership, encouraging service rather than domination and cronyism. Foreign donors have in many places established vocational training for young people who have left school without skills or job prospects, the better programmes including entrepreneurship and micro-finance to assist them in setting up income-generating projects related to the dominant activity in their community.[48] Still, these are few compared to the great need, and ultimately income-generation will not succeed unless the macro-economy grows sufficiently to see the circulation of more cash to support the products and services offered.

The black hole into which Zimbabwe's youth have been staring can only be reformed over time and when a stable, legitimate and dedicated government is in place to guide a determined recovery. For youth, that recovery must include a complete overhaul of the education system, positive growth of the economy's formal and informal sectors, the cessation of state-sponsored violence and a return to public and private morality and the rule of law.

It is not proposed to offer comprehensive solutions to the problems here. Rather, we wish to suggest some basic principles that might guide the policies as we attempt to reconstruct a functioning society and an economy that offers appropriate education, economic opportunities and positive social guidance and examples for the youth – a society in which every youth has a fair chance of transitioning to adulthood and earning an honest living.

The basic premises are as follows:

- Before we can imagine solutions we have to accept that meaningful change for the majority of Zimbabwe's youth will only begin when we have leaders of government who look beyond their own self-interest and desires to what is beneficial for the nation as a whole.

- Solutions must be holistic. Education for the youth must be developed in the context of policies for economic development and employment generation so that the two can work together.

- The pace of change must be dictated by economic realities, not political daydreaming. Zimbabweans must accept the limitations of the economic position and face the reality that they simply cannot have everything they want. Priorities will have to be identified, for education as for other expenditure.

- Democracy requires that the people agree with the policies of government, but similarly it is the responsibility of government to help the people understand what is and is not possible. Zimbabweans have learned from the ongoing crisis and are likely to be prepared to accept such solutions as vocational education as long as it holds out real possibilities of a meaningful existence. In fact, many parents are now demanding it.

Education policies:

- Some system of education will have to be devised that is built around learning basic skills and attitudes that will prepare both urban and rural children for a future of productive work, not petty trading or destructive violence. This will require an overhaul of the curriculum and the retraining of teachers.

- We will need to accept that a productive future for a large proportion of youth can only be found within the rural economy, and as such devise a curriculum that recognises this reality.

- At the same time an effort needs to be made to ensure that education introduces new ideas to rural production and makes use of new technologies.

- The youth need to be exposed to peace-building education and conflict-resolution skills as the beginning of learning a new morality beyond exploitation and greed.

Out-of-school youth:

- Programmes need to be devised for youth who left school before completing their primary education and who may need help with basic literacy.

- Other programmes that teach technical as well as entrepreneurial skills and are linked to specific assistance with job-creation through self-employment are needed for those youth who finished secondary school with no useful skills.

Partnerships:

- The government can multiply its resources by working closely with non-governmental organisations, faith-based organisations and community-based organisations to achieve common goals, and should take advantage of these opportunities.

- Zimbabweans must also be prepared to take the initiative themselves, rather than waiting for government to solve problems.

- The planning for change must involve Zimbabweans as a whole.

Much work waits for those who wish to bring meaningful change, for an entire generation of youth has been corrupted and disoriented. The road to recovery will be long and the journey slow, but with good will and hard work we can rebuild a society where our youth can hope for a useful and relevant education, a steady source of income and moral guidance from their elders. We already have a 'lost generation' – those who we once called the 'born frees'. Unless positive changes are made, we will soon have another.

Notes

1 There is no agreed age range which prescribes who is a youth. UN statistics sometimes indicate age 15-24 as youth, but not always. In Zimbabwe, the ministry responsible for youth takes 30 as the upper age limit.

2 UNDP *Zimbabwe Human Development Report 1998*, Figure 5, p. 50. The primary school drop-out rate has remained over 25 per cent from the 1980s to the present, except for a brief period in the late 80s and early 90s. The majority dropped out in the early years before Grade 5, so it is possible that as many as 20 per cent did not achieve functional and permanent literacy. A very small percentage never entered school, but we

have no precise statistics on this. This pattern continued into the 2000s. For example, 451,583 children enrolled for Grade 1 in 2003 but only 337,000 'survived' to enrol in Grade 4 in January 2006 – a drop-out rate of 25 per cent. (Ministry of Education, Sport, Arts and Culture, 2010). By the time the cohort reached Grade 7 in 2009 they were down to 300,000, meaning that only two thirds of the original cohort entered Grade 7.

3   Ibid., Figure 7, p. 51. In 1995, less than 40 per cent of the appropriate age cohorts were enrolled in secondary school, down slightly from the early 90s. Page 271 of the *Human Development Report 2007/2008* puts the net secondary enrolment rate in 2005 at 34 per cent. Demographic figures from the Afrobarometer Survey of 2009 indicate that approximately 37 per cent of respondents in a population sample covering all ages had at least completed secondary school. The rest had either no formal schooling (six per cent) or had dropped out along the way.

4   The minimum qualification for entering the Zimbabwe Republic Police or the Zimbabwe National Army was until relatively recently five O-levels. The same applied to teacher training and nurses training and most courses offered at polytechnics.

5   'Youth' is an elastic term which could have a variety of meanings and definitions. I have explained here the way I will use it for the purpose of this chapter.

6   Patrick Bond and Masimba Manyanya's *Zimbabwe's Plunge: Exhausted Nationalism, Neoliberalism and the Search for Social Justice* focuses on the 1990s, while Amanda Hammar, Brian Raftopoulos and Stig Jensen's 2003 collection of essays entitled *Zimbabwe's Unfinished Business: Rethinking Land, State and Nation in the Context of Crisis* and Raftopoulos and Savage's *Zimbabwe: Injustice and Political Reconciliation* look at the early 2000s, as does *Post-Independence Land Reform in Zimbabwe,* a collection of essays edited by Medicine Masiiwa. *Zimbabwe: The Past is The Future,* edited by David Harold-Barry, takes a broader view of the whole period. Lloyd Sachikonye looks at the role of institutionalised violence in *When a State Turns on its Citizens,* while *Beyond the Enclave: Towards a Pro-Poor and Inclusive Development Strategy for Zimbabwe,* edited by Godfrey Kanyenze (2011a), takes a sectoral approach to economic policy and brings the discussion almost up to 2010.

7   B. Raftopoulos (1986) 'Human Resources Development and the Problem of Labour Utilisation', in I. Mandaza (ed.) (1986) *Zimbabwe: the Political Economy of Transition 1980–1986,* CODESRIA, p. 276.

8   See, for example, a statement made by Dr Dzingayi Mutumbuka in 1981 that education must serve the development needs of the masses and every school must become a productive centre, and the ZANU-PF 1985 election manifesto which promised that every child would study technical subjects from primary school level 'so that he/she leaves school technically and

technologically prepared for the world of work' (Colclough et al., 1990: 36, 147).

9 R. Zvobgo (1986) 'Education and the Challenge of Independence' in I. Mandaza (ed.) (1986), p. 342.

10 C. Colclough et al. (1990) *Education in Zimbabwe: issues of quantity and quality*, SIDA, pp. 74-5.

11 Ibid., pp. 49, 53.

12 In the pre-independence system white children were streamed according to whether they would need four or five years to complete.

13 For example, having to walk long distances to school, having no capacity to do homework where there is no electricity, carrying out family chores relating to keeping the home or herding cattle, having no books or other relevant resources in the home.

14 R. Zvobgo, p. 344.

15 Colclough et al., p. 51.

16 G. Kanyenze (2004) 'The Zimbabwe Economy 1980–2003: a ZCTU perspective', in D. Harold-Barry (2004) *Zimbabwe: the Past is the Future*, pp. 114, 133.

17 In 1987, for example, the US and eight western European countries provided a total of USD253 million. See Colclough et al., p. 108.

18 The reasons will not be discussed here. Some were external to Zimbabwe, others rooted in the history, while still others reflected inappropriate policies. See G. Kanyenze (2004) 'The Zimbabwe economy 1980–2003: a ZCTU perspective', in D. Harold-Barry (2004) *Zimbabwe: the Past is the Future*.

19 G. Kanyenze (2011b) 'Education and Training', pp. 297-9; (2011c) 'The Labour Market', pp. 251-3.

20 The SACMEQ (Southern and Eastern African Consortium for Monitoring Educational Quality) study shows primary completion rates as 72 per cent for 2000, 68.2 per cent for 2006 and 59 per cent for 2008, but these were years of hardship and reflect a definite downward trend from early years. However, in 1990, Colclough et al. estimated the completion rate as being less than 75 per cent (see p. 72).

21 Colclough et al. p. 73 estimate 70 per cent transition by the end of the 1980s, Makopa Z. 'The provision of the basic classroom teaching and learning resources in Zimbabwean Primary schools: their relationship with Grade 6 pupils achievements in the SACMEQ III Project' 2011 estimates the transition to Form 1 between 67 per cent and 72 per cent from 1995 to 2009. World Bank figures put the 2002 transition rate at 69 per cent. See www.data.worldbank.org/indicator/topic/education.

22 Colclough et al. note that 26.5 per cent of the 1986 Form 1 cohort dropped out before reaching Form 4, and that appears to have been maintained more or less at a constant level. See p. 75.

23 Ibid., p. 97.
24 Ibid., p. 51.
25 Southern and Eastern African Consortium for Monitoring Educational Quality.
26 Z. Makopa (2011) p. 58.
27 Colclough et al., p. 99.
28 B. Raftopoulos, (1986) 'Human Resources Development and the Problem of Labout Utilisation' in *Zimbabwe: the Political Economy of Transition 1980-1986*, in I. Mandaza (ed.) (1986) CODESRIA, p. 300.
29 Ibid., p. 302. Raftopoulos suggests that any back-tracking would have created a 'crisis of state legitimacy'.
30 UNDP *Human Development Report 2004*. Pages 178-9 make the comparisons clear.
31 UNDP *Zimbabwe Human Development Report 1998*, p. 27.
32 Net enrolment estimates those registered in school as a percentage of the number of children of the appropriate age group.
33 UNDP *Human Development Report 2004*, p. 178.
34 C.T. Nziramasanga (1999) *Report of the Presidential Commission of Enquiry into Education and Training*.
35 This is a critical figure, as it is considered necessary to complete four years of education in order to retain functional literacy – assuming of course that literacy is established in those four years.
36 UNDP *Human Development Report 2007/2008*, p. 271.
37 Afrobarometer survey data for 2005 shows that 75 per cent of respondents had never earned a wage or salary. The data for 2009 showed that only 12 per cent had full-time employment, while those who were unemployed, only 39 per cent were looking for jobs.
38 Afrobarometer 2009 survey data, p. 11.
39 Sachikonye (2011) explains this 'coercive accumulation'. See pp. 37-40. A particularly startling example of the boastfulness can be seen in the 15-page *Sunday News Supplement* of 11-17 December 2011 entitled 'Dr Obert Mpofu Graduates with a Doctorate in Policy Studies'. On the first page alone there are five photographs of Mpofu.
40 Of course, this form of social breakdown did not begin after 2000, or even in the post-independence period; social change was ongoing, but the destabilisation became excessive, intensive and far more widespread than at any previous period, except perhaps in some districts during the liberation war and the Gukurahundi.
41 UNICEF's *State of the World's Children, 2011* reports that 97 per cent of Zimbabwean males in the age range 15-19 admitted to having had high-risk sex with a non-marital, non-cohabiting partner in the previous 12 months. The figure for females was much lower, at 24 per cent. Only three per cent of the males and five per cent of the females had undergone an

HIV test and received results in the same period.

42 Ibid. UNICEF indicates that 21 per cent of Zimbabwean females aged 15-19 were married and 21 per cent of females aged 20-24 had given birth before the age of 18.

43 A comprehensive report of the most active years of the National Youth Service was produced in 2003 by Solidarity Peace Trust. 'National Youth Service Training: shaping youths in a truly Zimbabwean manner', www. solidarity peacetrust.org. Other useful reports are O.R. Madondo (2005), 'The Problem of Youth in Mugabe's Zimbabwe' Africa Files, www. africafiles.org/article.asp?ID=6498, and Richard Smith 'Fear, terror and the Spoils of Power: youth militias in Zimbabwe', www.csvr.org.za/index. php?option= com _ content&view= a r ticle&id=2319:fea r-terror-a ndthe-spoils-of-power--youth-militias-in-zimbabwe&catid=139:mediaarticles& Itemid=37.

44 It has not been possible to explore the National Service programmes in detail as they evolved up until the 2008 elections.

45 Much of what has been recorded about the training camps comes from testimonies given by those who fled the country, especially to South Africa. See the Solidarity Peace Trust report for 2003.

46 Of the 164,000 pupils enrolled in Form 4 in 2008 only 20,000 passed five subjects at O-level, i.e. 14.4 per cent of those who actually sat for the exam. The following year, after high exam fees were introduced, less than half of all Form 4s wrote the exams and, not surprisingly, a higher percentage (19.3 per cent) gained one or more certificates. But this was closer to ten per cent of the Form 4 pupils and about three per cent of the age cohort (See Ministry of Education, Sport, Arts and Culture (unpublished statistics) and G. Kanyenze, 'Education and Training' (2011a)). Grade 7 exam passes dropped drastically, falling from 68.3 per cent in 2006 to 39.4 per cent in 2009.

47 Among these are the Youth Initiative for Democracy in Zimbabwe (YIDEZ), which is based in Harare but works in many communities across the country, Youth for Today and Tomorrow, based in Bulawayo and working in Matabeleland, and ENVISION, based in Harare.

48 Examples include Catholic Relief Services, which funds programmes in carpentry and dress-making in Bulawayo and Manicaland, the Norwegian Refugee Service, which works with internally displaced children of farm workers in Chipinge and Chiredzi, the Farm Orphan Support Trust (FOST), which works with youth clubs in Mashonaland Central and Manicaland, and SNV, a Dutch NGO which is developing a pilot programme to teach youth fruit production in Manicaland.

References

Afrobarometer survey data from 2005 and 2009. Available at www.afro baromoter.org.

Bond, P. and M. Manyanya. 2002. *Zimbabwe's Plunge: Exhausted Nationalism, Neoliberalism and the Search for Social Justice.* Harare: Weaver Press.

Chakanyuka S. et al. 2009. The Rapid Assessment of Primary and Secondary Schools conducted by the National Education Advisory Board, July. Harare.

Colclough, C. et al. 1990. *Education in Zimbabwe: Issues of Quantity and Quality.* Stockholm: SIDA, December.

Hammar, A., B. Raftopoulos and S. Jensen (eds). 2003. *Zimbabwe's Unfinished Business: Rethinking Land, State and Nation in the Context of Crisis.* Harare: Weaver Press.

Harold-Barry, D. (ed.) 2004. *Zimbabwe: The Past is The Future.* Harare: Weaver Press.

Kanyenze, G. 2004. 'The Zimbabwe economy 1980–2003: a ZCTU perspective', in D. Harold-Barry. 2004. *Zimbabwe: The Past is the Future.* Harare: Weaver Press.

— 2011a. *Beyond the Enclave: Towards a Pro-Poor and Inclusive Development Strategy for Zimbabwe.* Harare: Weaver Press, in association with Alternatives to Neo-liberalism in Southern Africa, the Labour and Economic Development Research Institute, Zimbabwe, and the Zimbabwe Congress of Trade Unions.

— 2011b. 'Education and Training', in G. Kanyenze (ed.) *Beyond the Enclave: Towards a Pro-Poor and Inclusive Development Strategy for Zimbabwe,* Harare: Weaver Press.

— 2011c. 'The Labour market', in G. Kanyenze (ed.) 2011. *Beyond the Enclave: Towards a Pro-Poor and Inclusive Development Strategy for Zimbabwe,* Harare: Weaver Press.

Madondo, O.R. 2005. 'The Problem of Youth in Mugabe's Zimbabwe', Africa Files. Available at www.africafiles.org/article.asp?ID=6498

Makopa, Z. 2011. 'The Provision of the Basic Classroom Teaching and Learning Resources in Zimbabwean Primary schools: their relationship with Grade 6 pupils achievements in the SACMEQ III Project'. Available at www.sacmeq.org/downloads/theses/Makopa_Z.pdf.

Masiiwa, M. (ed.) 2004. *Post-Independence Land Reform in Zimbabwe.* Harare: Friedrich-Ebert-Stiftung.

Ministry of Education, Sport Arts and Culture, Government of Zimbabwe. Unpublished statistics.

Nziramasanga, C.T. 1999. *The Zimbabwe Report of the Presidential Commission of Inquiry into Education and Training*, Harare: Government Printer.

Raftopoulos, B. 1986. 'Human Resources Development and the Problem of Labour Utilisation' in I. Mandaza (ed.) 1986. *Zimbabwe, the Political Economy of Transition 1980–1986*, Dakar: CODESRIA.

Raftopoulos, B. and T. Savage. 2004. *Zimbabwe: Injustice and Political Reconciliation*. Cape Town: Institute for Justice and Reconciliation.

Sachikonye, L. 2001. *When a State turns on its Citizens: Institutionalised Violence and Political Culture*. Johannesburg: Jacana Media.

Smith, R. 2005. 'Fear, Terror and the Spoils of Power: youth militias in Zimbabwe'. Available at www.csvr.org.za/index.php?option=com_content&view=article&id=2319:fear-terror-and-the-spoils-of-power--youth-militias-in-zimbabwe&catid=139:media-articles&Itemid=37

Solidarity Peace Trust. 2003. 'National Youth Service Training: Shaping Youths in a Truly Zimbabwean Manner'. Available at www.solidaritypeacetrust.org/205/national-youth-service-training.

UNDP *Zimbabwe Human Development Report 1998*. UNDP: Harare.

— *Human Development Report 2004*. UNDP.

— *Human Development Report 2007/2008*. UNDP.

UNICEF. 2011. State of the World's Children 2011.

World Bank. n.d. World Development Indicators (WDI) on education in Zimbabwe. Available at www.data.worldbank.org/indicator/topic/education

Zvobgo, R. 1986. 'Education and the Challenge of Independence', in I. Mandaza (ed.) 1986. *Zimbabwe, the Political Economy of Transition 1980–1986*, Dakar: CODESRIA.

11

The Fast-Track Land Reform Programme
Impacts on the Environment & Agriculture

Vupenyu Dzingirai, Emmanuel Manzungu
and Owen Nyamwanza

Introduction

That many African countries advocate for and have implemented land reform as a part of post-colonial restoration is a much-discussed topic, particularly in relation to southern Africa. Here, the different and sometimes painful drive to land reform has been observed in young post-colonial states. Aware of the importance of land, and its centrality in colonial resistance, countries such as Mozambique, Namibia, South Africa, Zambia and Zimbabwe have prioritised land reform in the name of achieving ethnic and racial equity in land distribution.

However, in the case of Zimbabwe, the impact of land reform on agriculture and the environment and the state of social services in resettled areas is not well known. These are matters that this chapter seeks to address.

The first section deals with the conceptual framework and is followed by a brief description of the fast-track land reform programme. The main section looks at the impact of land reform on agriculture and the environment, and the last section presents recommendations on how Zimbabwe can move forward in the area of land reform.

Conceptual framework

The chapter proceeds from the simple transactional premise dominant in social anthropology that individual interests pervade political and social life (Bailey, 1973; Barth, 1970). Ruling elites want legitimacy and recognition from those they govern. This sought-after legitimation is crucial as it allows ruling elites to preside over resource flows and their allocation. When the legitimacy of these elites is threatened by crisis – be it economic or ecological – such that they can no longer provide basic resources to their agitated followers, who may start to accuse them of being selfish or corrupt and therefore needing replacement, they become more desperate and adopt the following strategies, but not necessarily in the sequence that follows. First, they will adopt pragmatic strategies to survive, using political offices or positions to unlock resources such as arable land to share out among the citizenry (Christodoulou, 1990). Second, they will use procedures such as constitutional reform to access material and control economically valuable resources like land, forestry, wildlife and water to provide these to the disgruntled public. Thirdly, they may also exploit related legislation and policies to obtain those natural resources, e.g., land, that people need for survival. Where such rules and principles do not exist, or where existing principles and rules favour competing groups, politicians and political groups create new ones to disenfranchise them. In the case of Zimbabwe, ZANU PF created new legislation and policy to wrestle land from white settler farmers and give it to black households.

The disenfranchisement of the unfortunate 'other' is ideologised. The expropriation of land, for example, is often justified in normative or ideological terms. It may be presented as redistributive, intended to create an equitable society, even if the resource in question is retained or centralised. It may be presented as corrective, intended to redress the ills of the past. The 'other', in this case the landowners and those connected to them (including farm workers), are vilified and criminalised, making the expropriation seem not only inevitable but justified. This seems to be the case even in South Africa, where land occupations usually precede the criminalisation of Afrikaners (Sihlongonyane, 2005).

In this conceptual scheme then, a delicate equilibrium is reached: politicians remain – at least for a while – legitimate as a result of their populism, and followers celebrate their short-term spoils arising from the support they give. However, ruling elites cannot control how their followers use the resources they acquire in this way. Indeed, for fear of upsetting them, the elites are forced to be more and more chaotic and populist, suspending all rules relating to wise use of the resource in question. Fidelis Kanyongolo (2005) has shown this to be the case in Malawi, where politically nervous politicians have not rebuked land abuse by the landless people.

Using this framework of transactional populism, this chapter considers Zimbabwe and the impact of land reform on the country's land and agriculture in the last ten years, the interests in land by the powerful and the state of social service delivery to new farmers. It uses Zimbabwe as a case study, a country wherein land has suffered decades of manipulation under strategies that are political and populist.

The land question, post-independence reform and FTLR

The struggle over land in Zimbabwe has long been characterised by strategic considerations. With the onset of colonialism nearly 120 years ago, settler authorities casually granted European settlers land without due consideration of their ability to farm it or the needs of the native population. This was made possible by the partial nullification of native rights, and in some cases outright eviction of the existing native 'tenants', sending them to often dry and malarial places on the fringe of the colony such as Gwayi region of Matebeleland (Alexander et al., 2000). This disenfranchisement ultimately gave rise to anti-colonial protests structured along ethnic lines and promises were made of restitution of expropriated land, freedom of association among other hitherto suppressed liberties from the underground nationalist movement to all supporters and those who were prepared to fight for restoration of the country's independence. This was achieved in 1980, after a long and bloody war of liberation.

In respect of land reform and the desire to equally redistribute land and to co-exist with former adversaries, the first decade of independence was tricky for the ruling elite and nationalists. For whilst they longed to redistribute land to the liberation fighters and the displaced native population, they feared upsetting the international community and destabilising their power base in the process, as had happened in Mozambique. In order to remain in power and in international favour, the ruling nationalists devised and presided over a market-led land reform process in the first decade of independence as prescribed by the Lancaster House Constitution of 1979 that privileged settler interests.

Occupation/Status of Beneficiary	Size of farm (ha)	Comment
Former ZANU-PF provincial chairman and former board member in the private sector	1,606	Wholesale farm allocation
Senior Prison services official and a retired top army official	1,028	Consolidation of 14 subdivisions
Senior army official	1,020	Two farms consolidated
Governor of Mashonaland East	941	Wholesale farm allocation
Chairman of ZANU-PF Mashonaland East and chairman of many other private sector boards	661	Farm allocated as whole
Son of a late cabinet minister who was declared a national hero	610	Wholesale allocation of the farm
Senior official in the CIO and former ambassador	432	Wholesale farm allocation
Cabinet minister	400	Consolidation of five plots
Cabinet minister	366	Four subdivisions consolidated
Governor and former cabinet minister	357	Consolidation of three subdivisions
Member of parliament	351	Five subdivisions consolidated
Senior official in the CIO	327	One subdivision
Deputy Director in the Office of the President	211	Three subdivisions consolidated
Senior ZRP official	290	Wholesale farm allocation
Former chairperson of education committee	144	Consolidation of two subdivisions
Cabinet minister	122	One subdivision
Ex Member of parliament, chairperson of ZANU-PF Mashonaland East Women's League	120	Single plot

Occupation/Status of Beneficiary	Size of farm (ha)	Comment
District Administrator of Goromonzi	75	One subdivision
Senior police officer	75	One subdivision
Deputy secretary in a government ministry	45	One subdivision

Table 1 (left and above): Land allocation to members of the governing elite in Goromonzi District: The top 20 cases (*Source: Adapted from Marongwe (2011)*)

This land reform, although it settled some 160,000 landless people, largely benefitted white settlers who were believed to dynamise post-colonial production (Selby, 2006:130).

In the 1990s, the nationalists shifted their position after substantive threats to their power emerged in the form of various groupings affected by the IMF- and World Bank-supported economic reform of the 1990s. These included peasants, workers and land-based social movements with members who were veterans of the liberation war. When the labour movement gave birth to the opposition Movement for Democratic Change (MDC), and with the war veterans increasingly disobedient, the ruling nationalists radicalised their position on land, instituting a programme of fast-track land reform (FTLR).

The chief characteristic of FTLR was captured by the locally charged idiom of *jambanja,* which emphasized participants' unbridled access to the commercial farmland of their choice and the suspension of officialdom. In other words, laws that protected private land rights were disregarded and new ones that encouraged land takeover were hurriedly established. A bureaucratic revision was also started, resulting in all those officials whose interpretation and implementation of the legislation was considered an affront to *hondo yeminda* (war for the land) being threatened or sacked. The interpretation of policies and legislation rapidly shifted to suit nationalist elite and ZANU-PF party desires, resulting in over 4,000 white- and foreign-owned farms being seized for immediate resettlement, with land use plans only to be drawn up after the occupation (Chaumba et al., 2003:7-16). Land was not only given to ordinary people, but it was also given to those perceived as allies to the ruling elite (Table 1), irrespective of whether the recipient could farm or even had an interest in so doing.

Nor did the elite forget to reward themselves with choice farmland. According to an A2[1] land audit carried out by the Ministry of Lands (Government of Zimbabwe, 2006), multiple farms in this category were appropriated by politicians and their cronies. At one point, Masvingo Province had seven cases of multiple farm ownership, Mashonaland West six, Mashonaland East five and Midlands two. Online sources indicate that 2,000 high-ranking government officials own about five million ha, which is equal to almost half of the prime land that was redistributed.[2] This view is supported by Selby (2006:329), who stated that a confidential addendum to the Utete Commission Report exposed a sample of multiple farm grabbings by particular politically well-connected individuals. Farmworkers on these farms perceived to be sympathetic to the white settler were either persecuted or forced to leave, particularly in Mashonaland West (Rutherford, 2001). The same report identified that Mashonaland West province topped the list in terms of the numbers of farmworker households that had been displaced, with 6,285. Mashonaland East had 3,959, Midlands 224, Matabeleland North and Masvingo 56. A second layer of victims who would also be persecuted were the black occupiers, mostly the landless and peasants, whom the elite farmers also regarded as a nuisance and a threat to their operations.

In this power driven and populist seizure of farmland that carried with it observed 'partisan violence' (Alexander, 2006:1), the ruling elite arguably found a lifeline to remaining in power. At least 300,000 supportive households were resettled, together with the economic and partisan military elite that could be counted on to protect the ruling elites. Certainly, these new farmers did not have strong tenure: the 99-year leases could not be used as collateral to obtain lines of credit, resulting in some farmers 'spreading risks' by laying claim to several plots, while still retaining ownership in the old resettlement and communal areas. Still, this was a welcome development from populist stratagems, but it nevertheless hid the impacts that these settlers had on farms. The next section examines this matter.

The environmental cost of fast-track land reform

Fast-track land reform affected Zimbabwe's natural and farmed environments in many ways and to varying degrees. These are discussed by category below.

Forestry-related impacts

Though the degree of destruction to indigenous forests may be difficult to accurately assess due to limited systematic data, these precious resources were certainly affected by farm occupations. Unlike those grown in commercial forests, indigenous trees are slow to regenerate (Matose, 2004), making the environmental cost of their destruction, which was more pronounced in areas where newly resettled farmers cleared virgin land for agricultural purposes, particularly high. Evidence for this comes from Masvingo province where, by 2009, an estimated 6.8 , 13.3 and 23.7 hectares per household had been cleared in model A1 villagised, A1 self-contained and A2 farms respectively (Scoones et al., 2010:78).

An early audit by government revealed the extent of the problem of deforestation by resettled A2 farmers. In Mashonaland East, this was severe in 33 of 1,895 farms, in Matabeleland South seven out of 498 settled farms; in Midlands, five out of 585; Mashonaland West three out of the 840 resettled plots, and Mashonaland West 85 out of 4,087. These figures represent critical cases only.

The timber industry, which once employed 10,000 people, has also fallen victim to jambanja.[3] Representatives of the Timber Production Federation reported that in 2006 alone about 10,000 hectares of commercial woodland were destroyed by fires started by new settlers seeking to frighten and punish commercial plantation-owners still in residence. To date, roughly 30,000 hectares (25 per cent of all commercial forest holdings)[4] have been destroyed by fire. Farm occupiers and workers who were hostile to the plantation owners were responsible for the destruction. In many cases, neither the police nor the government have taken any punitive action.

Commercial and indigenous forest cover is likely to continue dwindling. Sporadic invasions driven by political considerations are ongoing despite the formal conclusion of the resettlement programme.

In Manicaland, for example, war veterans (and those pretending to be war veterans) from Chikukwa, Ngorima and Muusha communal areas in Chimanimani District still invade and start fires on the Charter, Martin and Skyline estates. In every case, the plantations belong to individuals believed to have links with the MDC. And for that reason, neither the police nor the military intervene; the opposition party and its supporters are regarded as a danger to national security and therefore not worthy of public protection.

Why settlers cleared forests

Where politics is not to blame, what is the rationale behind this destruction of forests on settler farms and plantations? Is there some practical significance to widespread tree clearing? The destruction of indigenous and exotic forest resources during and after FTLR has been attributed to factors such as farmland expansion, establishing tenure over a given piece of land and the establishment of new and human settlements. This section considers the veracity of each of these factors.

Expansion of arable land
The most prominent reason given for the widespread destruction of forest resources has been to open up land for crop production. Vast tracts of virgin forest have been destroyed by fires started deliberately by newly resettled farmers intent on clearing land for agricultural purposes. This has been observed in Gwayi and Matetsi conservancy areas (Dzingirai, 2009) and also noted on Fair Range Estate, Chiredzi District, where 3,000 hectares of mopane woodland were fired in order to make way for cotton (Chaumba, 2006). In the eastern highlands, forest clearance was carried out to create fields for potatoes, maize and other subsistence crops.

Reinforcing claims of rights over land
New settlers have cleared indigenous and commercial forests as a way of establishing claims over unsurveyed land (Maguranyanga and Moyo, 2006), a practice that has arisen because of the absence of formal ways of establishing rights over occupied land. A patch of cleared forest belongs to the one who removed the trees, and the land

is removed from the 'market place'. Claims to land through clearance have been observed in Masvingo.

Establishing new settlements

Owing to the colonial and post-colonial radicalised and hierarchical segregation of access to land, the black majority found themselves concentrated in ecologically fragile communal areas while the white minority enjoyed the fruits of the better endowed lands. The rapid population increase in communal lands over the last century (Cumming et al., 2006) has put increasing pressure on the ability of communal land to meet the needs of subsistence farmers. The FTLR came at a time when communal areas had almost reached breaking point in terms of carrying capacity; hence it constituted an outlet valve for land-starved people. New farmers, especially those allocated virgin land, cleared vast expanses of forest as they sought to establish homes. This brought with it an additional reason for cutting down trees: wood for the construction of dwellings and fencing.

Subsistence fuel wood supplies

Forests were also cleared for energy purposes in communal and resettlement areas (Chingarande et al., 2010, Mubvami, 2004). There also came a huge demand for fuel wood in urban areas when national power shortages intensified. Harare in particular seemed to source its supply from the nearby areas of Goromonzi, Seke, Beatrice and Zvimba (Mubvami, 2004; Muyengwa, 2009).

It is not correct to limit energy needs only to subsistence. Even industry was effectively sucked into the practice of the wanton destruction of vegetation. The Reserve Bank incentivised farmers to grow more flue-cured tobacco by establishing a 15 per cent foreign currency retention scheme on sales of tobacco during the 2002/2003 and 2007/2008 agricultural seasons. Accordingly, the numbers of farmers growing tobacco rose. The subsequent increase in production of flue-cured tobacco resulting in the clearance of large tracts of woodland as firewood was sought for furnaces (Dzingirai, 2009). Although coal would have been a viable alternative to wood, it was not readily available to newly resettled farmers because of logistical and pricing bottlenecks. For the 2010/2011 agricultural season over 46,015 ha of forest were stripped in order to cure part of the 127 million tonnes tobacco produced.[5] The economic meltdown of the last decade that saw huge numbers of people laid off from formal employment also led to beneficiaries and non-beneficiaries of FTLR resorting to stripping trees for profit, particularly in Matabeleland North, where rare species were felled and quickly transported to sculptors and wood-carvers dotted along the major tourist highway to Victoria Falls.

Custodians of the environment, the Environmental Management Agency (EMA) and the Forestry Commission, are cash-strapped, poorly staffed and unable to effectively execute their mandate. Moreover, where they try to institute regulatory order, they are accused by politicians of being sympathetic to the country's enemies. Nevertheless, both bodies do try to control poaching and trade in fuel woods by fining offenders they happen to come across.

The impact on wildlife

Land reform has negatively impacted on affected wildlife in two ways: habitat eradication and poaching.

The destruction of wildlife habitats

If there is any matter that has been widely observed since the inception of FTLR, it is wildlife habitat destruction. In many cases, particularly in the south-east Lowveld, resettled people subsequently invaded wildlife conservancies because they partly claimed these lands to be traditionally theirs (Wels, 2003). Over 1,000 households invaded the Save Valley conservancy[6] and a similar number invaded the nearby Chiredzi River conservancy, where a diverse range of wild animal species was put under threat due to reform-induced occupation.[7] Such invasions were not limited to conservancies; occupiers also targeted national parks or game reserves. For example, Gonarezhou National Park, which constitutes part of the Great Limpopo Transfrontier Conservation Area, was invaded by 3,000 Shangani families from the adjoining communal areas and beyond. Private game ranches were similarly invaded, in the case of Matabeleland North with the encouragement of self-interested regional politicians (Dzingirai, 2009). In some cases farmers simply encroached for settlement, nothing more. In others they strategically used their settlements to exploit the neighbouring wildlife.

This land reform-related poaching occurred at two levels: commercial and subsistence poaching.

Commercial poaching

Commercial poaching has long been an issue in Zimbabwe, particularly during the 1990s when foreign poachers networked with local trappers in the pursuit of trophies. This practice peaked during fast-track land reform when the rule of law and wildlife regulations broke down, with the result that invaders targeted high-value wildlife and smuggled the trophies to foreign markets that included South Africa (Dzingirai, 2009:29). So vicious was the poaching that it is estimated that 80 per cent of large game on commercial game reserves was eradicated (Lindsey et al., 2011). The invaders, who became part of an intricate syndicate and were supported by politicians (Selby, 2006; Marongwe, 2011), had firearms such as AK-47s and vehicles for tracking and targeting buffalo, elephant, rhino, zebra and lion. The products of these animals found their way to various international markets in South Africa, Vietnam and China, among others.[8] About 22 black and white rhino were poached in 2010 alone. Such is their arsenal of sophisticated equipment, which can include light aircraft, that it is easy for them to outsmart the national parks authorities, police and army details deployed to safeguard these valuable and often endangered animals.[9] These illegal activities have also had a dramatic impact on the economy. Table 2 indicates the potential losses to the economy as a result of poaching.

Subsistence poaching

Also called 'hunting for the pot', poaching for subsistence purposes also increased as more people found themselves in closer proximity to a valued and much-prized source of food. Between August 2001 and July 2009, the number of illegal hunting incidents recorded in the Save Valley came to 10,520 (Lindsey et al., 2011). In the same period, approximately 84,000 wire snares were removed from conservancies and national parks in the south-east Lowveld. In 2011, over 400 snares and traps were removed by from national and private parks invaded by local communities.[10] The use of snares leads to indiscriminate killing of animals, not all of which are readily suited to human consumption,

Species	Trophy fee	Daily rate	Minimum hunting length	2005		2006		2007		2008		2009	
				No. killed	Lost potential	No. killed	Lost potential	No. killed	Lost potential	No. killed	Lost potential	No. killed	Lost Potential
Cheetah	2,700	850	14	0	0	0	0	0	0	1	14,600	0	0
Leopard	3,500	883	14	0	0	0	0	4	63,448	0	0	0	0
Lion	7450	1,672	20	5	204,450	1	40,890	0	0	1	40,890	0	0
Sable	3528	1,055	12	3	48,564	1	16,188	0	0	1	16,188	5	86,215
Zebra	200			31	6,200	19	3,800	27	5,400	54	10,800	76	15,200
Total					259,214		60,878		68,848		82,478		101,415

Table 2 Lost potential trophy-hunting income ($US) from high-value species killed by unlicensed hunters (*Source: Lindsey et al., 2011)*)

294

Species	Chiredzi River Conservancy	Triangle Estates	Eaglemont Ranch
Buffalo	50	95	0
Bushbuck	60	95	>50
Bush pig	N/A	95	N/A
Eland	50	95	>50
Elephant	40	?	N/A
Giraffe	40	10	>50
Hartebeest	N/A	95	N/A
Hippopotamus	20	66	N/A
Impala	75	95	>50
Klipspringer	60	95	>50
Kudu	80	95	>50
Leopard	30	95	>50
Sable	95	99	>50
Warthog	90	10	>50
Waterbuck	80	95	>50
Wildebeest	40	95	>50
Wild dog	100	100	>50
Zebra	40	95	>50

Table 3: Animals recorded lost to illegal hunting in Save Valley conservancies
(Source: Lindsey et al., 2011)

for example the already endangered African wild dog and bat-eared foxes (Dzingirai 2009).

Table 3 indicates changes to wildlife occasioned by subsistence hunting in three conservancies in the Save Valley.

Poaching has served as an easy route to much-needed protein in areas ravaged by droughts and severe food insecurity (Gandiwa, 2011). The impetus to poach among settlers and communal people is high, given that the reprimand for such acts tends to be, at worst, a slap on the wrist.[11] The land reform programme has thus had hugely negative impacts on the environment, forestry and wildlife in particular. This is largely due to the suspension of regulations and the populism around the land reform. However, the negative effects of FTLR on the environment are not limited to natural resources.

The impact of fast-track land reform on commercial agriculture

There is general agreement that the fast track land reform programme negatively affected commercial agriculture in the country and that this had a contagion effect on the rest of the agricultural sector. This was because commercial agriculture provided valuable goods and services to the agricultural industry at large in the form of seeds for example. In addition the forward and backward linkages to industry were critical – commercial fertiliser and agricultural chemical industries depended on commercial agriculture and when it faltered these faltered as well. Despite this general agreement, there are differences in terms of the magnitude of the impact as well as whether the poor performance of commercial agriculture can all be attributed to the fast track land reform programme. Two narratives – discussed below – can thus be identified, both of which are equally represented in literature and have a life of their own because objective empirical evidence is difficult to get. As such, any data presented as fact when discussing the impact of the fast track land reform programme on commercial agriculture should be read and understood in context.

The first is that the programme caused a significant reduction in agricultural output, resulting in widespread food insecurity and famine. Bill Derman (2006) asserts that the impact of the programme was so severe that Zimbabwe became a shell of itself. Tobacco production plummeted as did maize and other crops, and industry that was linked to agriculture almost disappeared, resulting in widespread shortages of fuel and other commodities. According to Derman, citing various sources, 55 million kg of tobacco was produced in 2004 compared to 240 million kg before the fast track land reform. He also reports of between 1.9 and 4 million people being food insecure. Manzungu (2004: 64-5), also citing various sources, confirms the above downward production trend:

- Maize production plunged from 800,000 tonnes in 2000 to around 100,000 tonnes in the 2002/3 season
- Soya bean production plummeted by 100,000 tonnes between 2000 and 2002
- Tobacco production decreased from 236 million kg in 2000 to 201 million in 2001 to 165 million in 2002 and 75 million in 2003
- Wheat production fell to 150,000 tonnes from normal production of 300,000 tonnes
- Commercial beef herds shrank by more than 600,000 between 2000 and 2002.

These statistics are used to mourn Zimbabwe's status as the so-called 'bread basket' of southern Africa, which contrasts sharply with the present situation, where approximately 45 per cent of the population is malnourished.

A competing narrative perspective is that of Ian Scoones (2010) and other researchers such as Moyo (2006, 2007) who view such a 'doomsday' narrative as lacking proper perspective and tending to mix up 'realities and myths'. It should be expected that such a massive programme will be characterised by such temporary production setbacks, which will be corrected once a significantly greater number of farmers are on the land. It has also been argued that drought and economic isolation have also affected agricultural production. Such an argument is presented in Scoones et al. (2010). This study, based on a survey of 400 households in Masvingo province, painted a picture of good progress being made despite a number of challenges still remaining. A similar outcome was observed by Precious Zikhali (2008), whose study compared FTLR beneficiaries with a group of communal farmers. The former were found to be more productive because of superior input usage; they also achieved higher rates of return.

Irrigation

The fact that between 50,000 and 70,000 hectares of irrigated land were taken out of commission epitomises the impact of FTLR on agriculture.[12] Irrigation has always played an important role in agricultural production because of its contribution to increasing crop yields, crop diversification and better utilisation of the available rainfall. Before

Category	Before 1995	After		
		1999	2011	
	Area (ha)/proportion (%)			
			Dept of Irrigation	FAO
Large-scale commercial farms, including estates	93,565 (82)	98,400 (82)	63,470 (34)	80,854 (47)
ARDA[14]	13,500 (12)	8,400 (7)	17,100 (9)	11,084 (6)
A2	N/A	N/A	60,560 (33)	69,714 (40)
A1 and old resettle-ment	No accurate figures	No accurate figures	30,460 (16)	
Communal areas	6,000 (6)	11,000 (9)	15,000 (8)	11,861 (7)
Total hectarage	113,065	117,800	186,590	173,513

Table 4: The structure of irrigation in Zimbabwe before and after fast-track land reform (Figures in parenthesis refer to percentages) (*Sources: Zawe, 2011; FAO, 2011; Utete, 2003)*

FTLR, the irrigated white commercial farming sector (now A1 and A2 farmland) accounted for 100 per cent of the wheat and sugar cane produced, as well as 70 per cent of coffee, 55 per cent of tea and 45 per cent of cotton. By contrast, traditional field crops like maize and horticultural crops such as beans, tomatoes and vegetables were grown by smallholder farmers with less developed irrigation systems that saw low crop yields. The situation was made worse by the FTLR as the general economy deteriorated. The result was that the financial viability of the many smallholder irrigation schemes was further compromised. Today, many of these schemes cannot operate without subsidies from the government or from donor agencies. As is alluded to below, the fact that a significant part of the country's commercially irrigated land has been taken over by smallholder irrigation has seen the contribution of irrigation to the country's economy fell dramatically.

As already suggested, fast-track land reform changed the face of irrigation dramatically, that of large-scale commercial irrigation in

Irrigation type	Capital costs US$ per ha	Rehabilitation costs in US$ per ha	O&M costs in US$ per ha per year
Surface	10,000	4,500	375
Sprinkler	8,500	3,000	500
Drip	13,000	6,000	250
Average cost per ha	10,500	4,500	345

Table 5: Costs associated with different irrigation systems (*Source: FAO 2011*)

particular (Table 4). Prior to the reform programme, large-scale commercial agriculture (individually owned farms and estates) constituted 80 per cent of all viable land,[13] while the state-owned Agricultural and Rural Development Authority (ARDA) and communal irrigation each accounted for around ten per cent of the remaining area. The irrigated area that now falls under A1 and A2 farmland is facing many operational challenges. There are a number of reasons for this. First, many farmers were required to share irrigation systems that were originally for a single user. Second, no arrangements were put in place for sharing water and electricity costs. Third, the new farmers have yet to gain experience in irrigated agriculture. Meanwhile, the lack of rule of law seems to be apparent as the majority of the new farmers did not care about water permits and were unwilling to pay for water as stipulated in the Water Act and by the Zimbabwe National Water Authority (ZINWA) Act. Even some new farmers were denied servitude of conveying water to their properties by powerful new farmers who also claimed ownership over dams, mainly on A2 farms.

In summary it can be said that FTRL has had a negative impact on commercial irrigation. This is illustrated by the fact that the total area under irrigation has decreased. For example, while ARDA manages a total of 15,000 hectares, only 7,000 are currently being irrigated.

Reviving irrigation development and management in the aftermath of reform is going to be expensive, and thus hugely challenging. The costs of irrigation development and rehabilitation are high. Operational and maintenance (O&M) costs are also high (Table 5).

Availability of social amenities in resettlement areas

The state of social services is the key to the future of the land reform because any meaningful production on the farms is dependent upon the good health of those working on them. It is also dependent upon a good level of education – the basis of all productive training – of those owning or those operationally engaged at these farms. Finally, production is also dependent upon the availability of clean water and good sanitation facilities (Murisa, 2010).

The situation regarding these variables in the resettled areas is poor to desperate. As a result of the haphazard way in which FTLR was executed, little attention was given to the provision of critical social services like education, health, housing, water and sanitation to newly resettled farmers, reflecting few if any set targets. Even a decade ago, the UNDP lamented that 'the provision of roads, schools, clinics and boreholes, etc. was lagging far behind settler emplacement' (UNDP, 2002:21).

Conditions relating to the provision of adequate water and sanitation, health and education services on settled farms will now be examined in sequence.

Water and sanitation

Commercial farms used to provide water and sanitation services to the farm labourers. To be sure, the compound conditions were not perfect, because in some cases there was open defecation and infectious diseases which included TB and HIV (Rutherford, 2001). There was, nevertheless, an attempt by landowners to deal with these issues.

Overall, clean water and sanitation facilities are still lacking in the FTLR programme settlements. Little capital injection has been made towards the establishment of these and other social services in the resettled areas. The situation was further compounded by the breaking down of service delivery institutions such as the District Development Fund, which was responsible for developing water and sanitation facilities in rural and resettlement areas. As a result, newly resettled people may have to travel distances of four to five kilometres to collect drinking water[15] (Masiiwa and Chigejo, 2003). Even then, there is the issue of the quality of water. According to the A2 Audit Report, in Matabeleland South only 44 of the 754 new plots had regular access to clean water. The situation was worse in Mashonaland West, where only 195 of the 4,000-plus had a clean water supply. In Mashonaland East, 105 of 1,895 farms had a safe water supply.

Conclusion

It is clear that agriculture and the environment have been hit hard by the reform process. This destruction arose because the ZANU-PF ruling elite effectively toyed with Zimbabwe's commercial farmland, using it as a tool for securing patronage from the masses. Its power threatened, the way out was to resort to populism and the suspension of law and order. The solution was land seizure, and then allocating that same land, minus title deeds, to marginalised indigenous people who wanted it and to members of the elite deemed supportive to the reform itself and to the state. It was a populist stratagem, but one that ultimately resulted in the death of agriculture as a source of GDP and wholesale damage to the environment and Zimbabwe's flora and fauna as pressure on the land increased to untenable levels.

How can Zimbabwe undo this comprehensive damage? Obviously it is neither possible nor proper to restore the land arrangements of the period prior to the reform. What is needed is a rationalisation of the reform process in such a way that it is more equitable, efficient and beneficial to the environment. This means revisiting the issue of multiple ownership, resolving the issue of beneficiary selection, wise use of the environment, and improving social services.

As we have discussed, multiple ownership emerged as a chief feature of FTLR. This is not just, as it continues to deny a means of living to the poor and landless. It is also inefficient, as land held under multiple ownership is often grossly underutilised. What is required to take Zimbabwe forward is not a commission to establish multiple ownership, since two formal processes led by Parliament have already done this[16]. Rather what is needed is a land commission with the mandate to act swiftly on known cases. Such a commission would have to be bipartisan, made up of men and women of impeccable reputation able to apply the law and policy without favour and incorporating significant social groups and movements involved in the land question.

To date, beneficiary selection has been determined through the criterion of patronage. Land was given to people who were seen to be sympathetic or supportive to ZANU-PF. In many cases this has not been productive as the beneficiaries are disinterested in farming and/or lack the capacity to utilise land beyond asset-stripping. What is needed is a land authority or a commission as intimated above to revise beneficiary selection in a way that results in the maximum use of the land for the good of the country. All farms that are idle or are underutilised should be targeted for review and, where possible, promptly reallocated to motivated and competent indigenous people from the communal areas or to small-scale agriculturalists. Given that some resettled people are not using the land productively, this would cause little disruption.

In this regard, there is need to recapitalise the irrigation sector to allow for currently underutilised irrigable land to be put to use. Efforts should be made to build a common ethos among farmers who access a common facility. Such an ethos should be reflected in shared payment of bills, repair of infrastructure and general co-operation regarding the rehabilitation of irrigation systems.

With settlers, and those who have tried but failed at smallholder agriculture, continuing to strip the land of its resources, wholesale damage of major cultural, economic and social value is being done. In relationship to wildlife and fisheries, it is recommended that the Ministry of Environment, through its allied departments, the Parks and Wildlife Authority and Forestry Commission, step in promptly, putting in place a range of measures to reverse such pillaging. Such measures could include providing control of wildlife and forestry to new landowners, allowing them to commercially benefit from extant resources according to standards set by the authority. The CAMP-FIRE programme and conservancies provide a good example of how a carefully managed incentive-based and locally owned system can encourage local communities to use the natural resources in their jurisdiction wisely.

These are but a few suggestions of how sustainable use of resources can contribute towards enabling Zimbabwe to move towards prosperity and security. However, such steps are only possible where the land reform process is depoliticised or rationalised and where non-state partners potentially useful to the process are welcome. Achieving this will be good not only for the human population – for those in power and for those they govern – but also for the country's flora and fauna.

Notes

1 FTLRP was premised on two resettlement models: Models A1 and A2. A1 was intended to decongest communal lands and was either villagised or self-contained. A1 beneficiaries were selected by the District Lands Committee. A2 was meant to establish black commercial farmers and beneficiaries were selected from applications sent to the Ministry of Lands, Agriculture and Rural Resettlement.

2 Alex Bell (2010) 'Mugabe elite control 5 million hectares of Zim land', 30 November. Available at: www.swradioafrica.com/news301110/ mugselite301110.htm

3 Andew Mambondiani, 'Zanu reforms threaten Zimbabwe's timber industry'. *Think Africa Press,* 18 August 2011. Available at www. thinkafricapress.com/zimbabwe/zanu-reforms-threaten-zimbabwe-timber-industry

4 It is estimated that only 90,000 of 120,000 hectares of the commercial forest of 1999/2000 remain. See Chris Goko and Sydney Saize, 'Timber producers lose US$120 million'. *Daily News,* 7 April 2011. Available at: www.dailynews.co.zw/index.php/business/35-business/2017-timber-producers-lose-us120m.html

5 'Over 46000ha of forests destroyed', *Financial Gazette, 2 August 2011.*

6 Everson Mushava, 'Zim should revisit wildlife land reform programme', *Daily News,* 14 December 2011. Available at: www.dailynews.co.zw/ index.php/news/34-news/5969-zim-should-revisit-wildlife-land-reform-programme.html?tmpl=component&print=1&layout=default&page=

7 Wolmer et al., 2003:12.

8 Barnaby Phillips, 'Poaching threatens Zimbabwe wildlife', *BBC News* 01/10/03. Available at www.newsvote.bbc.co.uk/mpapps/pagetools/print/ news.bbc.co.uk/2/hi/africa/3156604.stm. See also 'Cabinet ministers and Zanu-PF officials making a killing from wildlife conservancies – Wikileaks', *Financial Gazette* 10 October 2011. Available at www. zimbabweonlinepress.com/index.php?news=3846

9 Zimbabwe's Wildlife threatened by poachers, *The National* 08/09/09 www.thenational.com. 'Hunter's footprints of destruction', *Daily News,* 3 May 2011.

10 'What will it bring?', *Tikki Hywood Trust News,* 8 May 2011. Previously available at www.zimbabwe7.wildlifedirect.org/2011/05/08/2011-what-will-it-bring

11 Ibid.

12 Irrigation infrastructure in Zimbabwe in many ways reflects the country's socio-political history. Before independence, irrigation was developed along racial lines, as happened in other economic spheres. On one side was individual/estate commercial-scale irrigation and on the other subsistence-oriented smallholders. The former was developed on the back of a strong state-subsidised funding. While both types received state support, smallholder irrigation has not proved financially viable.

13 After the fast-track land reform programme practically all private large-scale commercial farms were re-categorised as A2 farmland.

14 ARDA and almost all commercial estates have a number of out-growers. This allows smallholder farmers to grow crops they would otherwise be unable to, for example, sugar cane. Research has shown that smallholder farmers can grow what are considered to be hi-tech crops. What seems to be crucial are the rules under which such crops are grown and marketed.

15 Though the supplies tended to be somewhat inadequate, commercial farmers did provide clean water and sanitation facilities in compounds. FTLR farmers lacked these, leading to a decline in health and safety.

16 The government of Zimbabwe instituted at least two processes, the A2 Land Audit by the Ministry of Lands and Land Reform and Resettlement in collaboration with SIRDC in 2006, and the Flora Bhuka Land Reform Audit in 2002.

References

Alexander, J. 2006. *The Unsettled Land: State-Making and the Politics of Land in Zimbabwe 1893–2003*. Oxford: James Currey and Harare: Weaver Press.

Alexander, J., J. McGregor and T. Ranger. 2000. *Violence and Memory: One Hundred Years in the Dark Forests of Matabeleland*. Oxford: James Currey.

Bailey F.G. 1973. 'Debate Compromise and Change', in F.G. Bailey (ed.). *Debate, Compromise and Change, The Politics of Innovation*. Oxford: Basil Blackwell.

Barth, F. 1970. 'Economic Spheres in Darfur' in R. Firth (ed.). *Themes in Economic Anthropology*. London: Tavistock Publications.

Bell, Alex. 2010. 'Mugabe elite control 5 million hectares of Zim land', 30 November. Available at: www.swradioafrica.com/news301110/mugs elite301110.htm

Chaumba, J. 2006. 'Opportunities and Constraints on Crop Production within Zimbabwe's Fast Track Land Reform Programme: A Case Study of Fair Range Estate, Chiredzi District, South Eastern Zimbabwe'.

Unpublished MPhil thesis, University of the Western Cape, Programme for Land and Agrarian Studies. PLAAS).

Chaumba. J., I. Scoones and W. Wolmer. 2003. 'From Jambanja to Planning: The Reassertion of Technocracy in Land Reform in Southeastern Zimbabwe?' Sustainable Livelihoods in Southern Africa Research Paper 2, Institute of Development Studies, Brighton.

Chingarande, S., P Mugabe, K. Kujinga and E. Magaisa. 2010. 'Agrarian Land Reforms in Zimbabwe: Are Women Beneficiaries or Mere Agents?' IDRC Research Paper, Institute of Environmental Studies, University of Zimbabwe.

Christodoulou, D. 1990. *The Unpromised land: agrarian reform and conflict worldwide*. London: Zed Books; New York: Atlantic Highlands.

Cumming, G.S., D.H.M Cumming and C.L. Redman. 2006. 'Scale Mismatches in Social-Ecological Systems: Causes, Consequences, and Solutions', *Ecology and Society* 11 (1):14. Available at www.ecology-andsociety.org/vol11/iss1/art14/

Derman, Bill. 2006. 'After Zimbabwe's fast track land reform: Preliminary observations on the near future of Zimbabwe's efforts to resist globalisation'. Available at www.mpl.ird.fr. Accessed 1 March 2012.

Dzingirai, V. 2009. 'The Impact of Political Crisis on Natural Resources, A Case Study of Zimbabwe', *Africa Insight*, Vol. 39(3), pp. 23-37.

Financial Gazette. 2011. 'Zimbabwe: Jealously guard rhino against poachers', 6 December. Available at www.allafrica.com/stories/2011120 70419.html. Accessed 16 December 2011.

Food and Agriculture Organisation (FAO). 2011. Aquastat, Zimbabwe, FAO, Rome, Italy.

Gandiwa, E. 2011. 'Preliminary assessment of illegal hunting by communities adjacent to the northern Gonarezhou National Park', *Tropical Conservation Science* Vol. 4(4): pp. 445-67.

Goko, C. and S. Saize. 2011. 'Timber producers lose US$120 million'. 7 April 2011. Available at www.dailynews.co.zw/index.php/bus iness/35business/2017-timber-producers-lose-us120m.html. Accessed 16 December 2011.

Government of Zimbabwe. 2006. A2 Land Audit Report, 29 September.

Financial Gazette. 2011. 'Over 46000ha of forests destroyed', 2 August.

Kanyongolo, F.E. 2005. 'Land Occupations in Malawi: Challenging the Neoliberal Legal Order', in S. Moyo and P. Yeros (eds). *Reclaiming the Land: The Resurgence of Rural Movements in Africa, Asia and Latin America*. London: Zed Books, Cape Town: David Philip.

Lindsey P.A., S.S. Romañach and H. Davies-Mostert, 2011. 'Ecological and Financial Impacts of the Illegal Bushmeat Trade in Zimbabwe',

Oryx – The International Journal of Conservation, 45(1), pp. 96-111.

Maguranyanga, B. and S. Moyo. 2006. 'Land Tenure in Post FTLRP Zimbabwe: Key Strategic Policy Development'. Policy brief prepared on behalf of the African Institute of Agrarian Studies, Harare, Zimbabwe.

Mambondiyani, A. 2011. 'Zanu reforms threaten Zimbabwe's timber industry'. Available at www.thinkafricapress.com/zimbabwe/zanu-reforms-threaten-zimbabwe-timber-industry. Accessed 16 December 2011.

Manzungu, E. 2004. 'Environmental Impacts of the Fast Track Land Reform Programme: A Livelihoods Perspective', in David Harold-Barry (ed.). 2004. *Zimbabwe: The Past is the Future*. Harare: Weaver Press.

Marongwe, N. 2011. 'Who was allocated Fast Track land and what did they do with it? Selection of A2 farmers in Goromonzi District, Zimbabwe and its impacts on agricultural production', *Journal of Peasant Studies*, Vol. 38. (5), pp. 1069-92.

Masiiwa, M. and O. Chigejo. 2003. 'The Agrarian Reform in Zimbabwe; Sustainability and Empowerment of Rural Communities Study Report', Department of Agrarian and Labour Studies Institute of Development Studies, University of Zimbabwe.

Masunungure, E. 2008. 'Civil Society and Land Reforms in Zimbabwe: Conceptual Considerations', in S. Moyo, K. Helliker and T. Murisa (eds). *Contested Terrain – Land Reform and Civil Society in Contemporary Zimbabwe*. Pietermaritzburg: S and S Publishers; Harare, Africa Institute for Agrarian Studies.

Matose, F. 2004. 'Trends in forest ownership, institutional arrangements and the impact on forest management and poverty reduction: A case study from Zimbabwe'. Rome: FAO.

Moyo, S. and B Maguranyanga. 2006. 'A review of Zimbabwean agricultural sector following implementation of the land reform: overall impacts of the fast track land reform programme'. Available at www.kubatana.net/docs/agric/aias_land_reform_040513.doc. Accessed 1 March 2012.

— 2007. 'Emerging Land Tenure Issues in Zimbabwe', African Institute for Agrarian Studies Monograph Series Issue No. 2/07.

Mpofu, T. 2009. 'Zimbabwe's Wildlife threatened by poachers', 8 September. Available at www.thenational.ae/news/world/africa/zimbabwes-wildlife-threatened-by-poachers. Accessed 16 December 2011.

Mubvami, T. 2004. 'Impact of Land Redistribution on the Environment' in M. Masiiwa (ed.), *Post-independence Land Reform in Zimbabwe: Controversies and Impact on the Economy*. Harare: Friedrich Ebert

Stiftung and Institute of Development Studies, University of Zimbabwe.

Murisa, T. 2010. 'Social Development in Zimbabwe'. Discussion paper prepared for the Development Foundation for Zimbabwe. Available at www.dfzim.com/wp-content/downloads/Social_Development_in_Zimbabwe_by_Dr_T_Murisa.pdf

Mushava, E. 2011. 'Zimbabwe should revisit wildlife land reform programme', 14 December. Available at www.dailynews.co.zw/index.php/news/34-news/5969-zim-should-revisit-wildlife-land-reform-programme. Accessed 16 December 2011.

Muyengwa, S. 2009. 'Conflicts and Commercialization Pressures over Forest Resources in the Post-Fast Track Land Reform Context in Zimbabwe: A Case of Seke Communal Lands', in B. Mukamuri, J.M. Manjengwa and S. Anstey (eds). *Beyond Proprietorship – Murphree's Laws on Community-Based Natural Resource Management in Southern Africa*. Harare: Weaver Press; Ottawa: International Development Research Centre.

Nkala, O. 2011. 'Hunter's footprints of destruction', 3 May. Available at www.dailynews.co.zw/index.php/features/49-featured/2343-hunters-footprints-of-destruction.html. Accessed 16 December 2011.

Philips, B. 2003. 'Poaching threatens Zimbabwe wildlife'. 1 October. Available at: www.news.bbc.co.uk/2/hi/africa/3156604.stm. Accessed 16 December 2011.

Rutherford, B. 2001. *Working on the Margins: Black Workers, White Farmers in Post-colonial Zimbabwe*. Harare: Weaver Press; New York: Zed Books.

Scoones, I., N. Marongwe, B. Mavedzenge, J. Mahenehene, F. Murimbarimba and C. Sukume. 2010. *Zimbabwe's Land Reform: Myths and Realities*. Harare: Weaver Press.

Selby, A. 2006. 'Commercial Farmers and the State: Interest Group Politics and Land Reform in Zimbabwe'. Unpublished PhD thesis, International Development Centre, Oxford University.

Sihlongonyane, M.F. 2005. 'Land Occupations in South Africa', in S. Moyo and P. Yeros (eds). *Reclaiming the Land: The Resurgence of Rural Movements in Africa, Asia and Latin America*. London: Zed Books; Cape Town: David Philip.

Tikki Hywood Trust News. 2011. 'What will it bring?', 8 May. Previously available at www.zimbabwe7.wildlifedirect.org

Wels, H. 2003. *Private Wildlife Conservation in Zimbabwe: Joint Ventures and Reciprocity*. Leiden: Brill Publishers.

Wolmer, W. 2003. 'Wildlife Management and Land Reform in Southeastern Zimbabwe: A Compatible Pairing or Contradiction in Terms?', Sustainable Livelihoods in Southern Africa Research Paper 1, Institute of Development Studies, Brighton.

UNDP. 2002. 'Zimbabwe Land Reform and Resettlement: Assessment and Suggested Framework for the Future', Interim Mission Report January 2002.

Utete, C. 2003. Report of the Presidential Land Review Committee. Volume II, Special Studies, Harare.

Zikhali, P. 2008. 'Fast track land reform and agricultural productivity in Zimbabwe'. Discussion paper, the Environment for Development (EfD) Initiative and Resources for the Future (RRF), Washington DC, October 2008. Available at www.efdinitiative.org/research/publications/publications-repository/fast-track-land-reform-and-agricultural-productivity-in-zimbabwe/files/EfD-DP-08-30.pdf.

Zimbabwe Broadcasting Corporation. 2010. 'Will education sector improve?' 2 December 2010. Available at www.zbc.co.zw/news-categories/blogs-a-features/4687-education-sector-set-to-improve.html. Accessed 16 December 2011.

Zimbabwe News Online. 2011. 'Cabinet ministers getting richer from conservancies seized from former white commercial farmers', 10 October 2011. Available at zimbabwenewsonline.com/top_news/2380.txt.

Contributors

Vupenyu Dzingirai is a professor of Applied Social Sciences at the University of Zimbabwe. He is also the Chair of the Zimbabwe Forum, an environmental conservation network based in Harare. He has researched and published widely on land and natural resource conflict in southern Africa and is co-editor of *Living on The Edge*, a book published by Earthscan that examines local people and their relationships with protected areas in southern Africa.

Professor Mohammed I. Jahed holds a PhD in Economics. He currently serves at the Development Bank of Southern Africa (DBSA) as Divisional Executive: Policy and Integration. In addition, he sits on various boards, including the National Presidential Advisory Council of Broad-Based Black Economic Empowerment, the Magalies Water Board, Econometrix, and the Small Business Project. Previously, he served as a senior economic planning specialist at the DBSA; Deputy Director General at the Office of the Premier of Limpopo Province; and Chief Economist and Head of Policy, Strategy and Research of the NEPAD Secretariat. He was also a Professor at the Graduate School of Public and Development Management at the University of the Witwatersrand.

Greg Linington is a lecturer in Constitutional Law in the Department of Political and Administrative Studies at the University of Zimbabwe. He is a graduate of the University of Zimbabwe Law Faculty, where he was awarded the BL and LLB degrees. He also has an MSc in International Relations from the same university, and an LLM in Constitutional Law from the University of South Africa (UNISA). He is the author of *Constitutional Law of Zimbabwe* (2001) and numerous articles and book chapters on Zimbabwe's constitutional law.

Daniel Makina is Professor of Finance and Banking at the University of South Africa, where he has been since 2000. Previously, he lectured at the Business School of the University of Zimbabwe. Professor Makina did his undergraduate studies at the University of Zimbabwe, after which he obtained an MSc in Financial Economics at the University of London, and his PhD at the University of the Witwatersrand. He has published extensively in national and international journals, is an editorial referee to several journals, and is a member of the Board of Editors of the *African Journal of Management and Economic Studies*. Professor Makina has been involved numerous consultancy assignments and in the preparation of policy research papers for the UNDP, UNICEF and the ILO.

Dr Emmanuel Manzungu is senior lecturer in the Department of Soil Science and Agricultural Engineering at the University of Zimbabwe. He has researched and published widely. He specializes in research involving water resources, and environmental and land management in Zimbabwe and the southern African region.

Eldred V. Masunungure is a Political Science and Public Administration graduate of the University of Zimbabwe and Dalhousie University (Canada) and teaches in the Department of Political and Administrative Studies at the University of Zimbabwe. His current research interests include political transitions, elections, governance, and policy-making. He edited *Defying the Winds of Change: Zimbabwe's 2008 Elections* and is widely published in local and international journals, including *African Affairs, Journal of Democracy* and *Journal of International Affairs* (Columbia University).

Norbert Musekiwa is a lecturer in political science and public administration at the University of Botswana. He has also lectured in public administration at the University of Zimbabwe. He holds a PhD in Political Studies from the University of Cape Town. Musekiwa has consulted widely in the area of local government and worked for the Ministry of Local Government for a total of ten years, six as a civil servant and four as consultant to a local authority capacity-building programme implemented by the Government of Zimbabwe with assistance from four bilateral donors, the World Bank and the UNDP.

Myo Naing is a Burmese in exile and is currently finishing his PhD, entitled 'Public Sector Reform in South Africa: Necessity of Early Warning System Tools on the Functionality of Municipal Service Delivery Process', at the Graduate School of Public and Development Management at the University of the Witwatersrand. He earned his Master of Management degree at the same school. He completed his undergraduate degree in philosophy shortly before he had to leave Burma in 2002. His research interest includes public sector reform, the role of the state in the economy, new institutional economics (NIE), and local government and municipal service delivery.

Anyway Ndapwadza-Chingwete works for IDASA as the Project Manager for Afrobarometer. Prior to that she was the Senior Programmes Officer for IDAZIM's Public Policy Programme. She holds an MSc in Population Studies and a BSc degree in Economics from the University of Zimbabwe. Ndapwadza-Chingwete has more than six years experience in research and research methodology, and data analysis and reporting.

Mary Ndlovu is a educationist, historian and social justice activist. She has degrees in History and Languages, Education and Law from University of Toronto, Columbia University and UNISA. She pursued a career as a secondary school teacher and then as a teacher educator in Zambia and Zimbabwe before leaving the field of formal education to work with an NGO specializing in legal services. Ndlovu is now retired but continues to write and edit and undertake consultancy work. She is currently a member of the National Education Advisory Board.

Lyndon Tuyani Nkomo is currently reading for a PhD degree at the University of the Witwatersrand and holds a BL from the University of Zimbabwe, an LLB from the University of the Witwatersrand, and an MBA from the University of Zimbabwe. He is a registered Legal Practitioner, Notary Public and Conveyancer whose research interests are in human rights, with a special focus on freedom of expression and the right to privacy, telecommunications law, broadcasting law and cyber law.

Owen Nyamwanza holds an MSc in Sociology and Social Anthropology from the University of Zimbabwe. He is currently a water governance researcher at the UZ Centre for Applied Social Sciences. He is also registered for an MPhil in water resource management and his research sites include the Mzingwane Catchment area of the Limpopo Basin.

Jabusile Madyazvimbishi Shumba joined IDAZIM in 2009 and currently works as Public Policy and Governance Programme Manager. He is a PhD candidate at the University of the Witwatersrand in the field of development studies, where he undertook his MMS in public policy. His experience spans programme management, scenario planning, policy analysis, research and advocacy. Previously at IDAZIM, he worked for four years in charge of advocacy and training targeted at enhancing citizen participation in local governance, building structures for popular participation and making use of multi-stakeholder engagement processes to influence decision-making.